Faith in the Great Physician

LIVED RELIGIONS

Series Editors   David D. Hall and Robert A. Orsi

Faith in the Great Physician

Suffering and Divine Healing in American Culture, 1860–1900

HEATHER D. CURTIS

The Johns Hopkins University Press
Baltimore

2 4 6 8 9 7 5 3 1

The Johns Hopkins University Press
2715 North Charles Street
Baltimore, Maryland 21218-4363
www.press.jhu.edu

Library of Congress Cataloging-in-Publication Data

Curtis, Heather D.
Faith in the Great Physician : suffering and divine healing in American culture,
1860–1900 / Heather D. Curtis.
p.   cm. — (Lived Religions)
Includes bibliographical references and index.
ISBN-13: 978-0-8018-8686-7 (hardcover : alk. paper)
ISBN-10: 0-8018-8686-4 (hardcover : alk. paper)
1. Spiritual healing—United States—History—19th century. I. Title.
BT732.5.C88 2007
234′.131097309034—dc22
2007010558

A catalog record for this book is available from the British Library.

Special discounts are available for bulk purchases of this book. For more information,
please contact Special Sales at 410-516-6936 or specialsales@press.jhu.edu.

For Clark, Jonathan, and David

CONTENTS

ACKNOWLEDGMENTS

This scripture verse from the New Testament letter to the Hebrews was a favorite among the people whose story I endeavor to narrate in the pages that follow:

> Wherefore seeing we also are compassed about with so great a cloud of witnesses, let us lay aside every weight, and the sin which doth so easily beset us, and let us run with patience the race that is set before us. (Hebrews 12:1, King James Version)

They were individuals who believed that unlikely, even ostensibly impossible feats could be accomplished through faith in the power of God. They were equally convinced that the example, encouragement, and fellowship of others would help to motivate, support, and sustain them in their ongoing efforts to act out their convictions, especially when the inevitable trials that ensued threatened to hinder their progress or bring them to a halt altogether.

Although writing a book cannot be compared to the kinds of remarkable projects undertaken by many of the women and men who participated in the divine healing movement of the late nineteenth century, the process has been something like running a race—one that I never would have finished (or even started) without my own "cloud of witnesses" to inspire and assist me along the way. From the beginning, David Hall has offered unflagging encouragement, wisdom, and friendship. His insights regarding the study of religion as lived practice will, I hope, be evident throughout this work. What will be less apparent to the reader, but always foremost in my mind, is his gracious and generous manner as he helped me pursue my scholarly aims while remaining true to the commitments and priorities I hold most dear. Ann Braude has also provided steadfast support and judicious advice. Her expertise in women's history and gender studies has enriched my own thinking in ways that I hope will be apparent here as well. Sarah Coakley's constant affirmation, combined with incisive comments at critical junctures, have challenged me to consider how this study might address issues of broader theological and pastoral concern. Robert Orsi graciously agreed to participate in this project when it was already well underway. His own work on pain, illness, and healing helped to inspire the study in the first place, and his thoughtful criticisms have proved invaluable at several key moments in its progression.

Colleagues in the North American Religions Colloquium at Harvard University, both past and present, have offered valuable recommendations throughout the project's development. I am especially grateful to Emma Anderson, David Bains, Candy Gunther Brown, the late Virginia Brereton, David Hempton, the late William Hutchison, Mark Massa, Alexis McCrossen, James Reed, Jon Roberts, and Chris White for commenting on various chapter drafts or providing wise counsel on broader conceptual issues. Adrian Weimer read the entire manuscript, offering both instructive critique and steady encouragement for which I am deeply appreciative. Others who have furnished helpful suggestions and guidance include Peggy Bendroth, Bret Carroll, John Corrigan, Carolyn DeSwarte Gifford, Marie Griffith, Mark Noll, Charles Rosenberg, Ann Taves, and Laurel Ulrich.

Early on in my research, I had the good fortune to encounter a group of scholars who share an interest in divine healing and who value the constructive possibilities of open academic exchange. Chris Armstrong, Jonathan Baer, Pamela Klassen, Bruce Mullin, James Opp, Amanda Porterfield, and Grant Wacker have all served as lively and enthusiastic conversation partners. Grant's encouragement as well as his thoughtful and incisive comments on the manuscript have been invaluable. I am grateful for his friendship. I owe special thanks to Bruce Mullin for supplying several rare primary sources. I am also deeply indebted to Jon Baer, who shared not only the fruits of his own research, but also his time and his home. He and his wife Carolyn are models of warm and generous hospitality.

Participants in the History of American Christian Practice Project, directed by Laurie Maffly-Kipp, Leigh Schmidt, and Mark Valeri, and funded by the Lilly Endowment, also helped bring clarity to my thinking through spirited exchanges about the meanings and workings of healing as a devotional discipline. Catherine Brekus, Anthea Butler, Kathryn Lofton, Michael McNally, Rick Ostrander, Sally Promey, Roberto Lint Sagarena, Tisa Wenger, and David Yoo, along with the three project directors, taught me the joys and challenges of collaborative scholarly enterprise. It was a privilege to work with them. I also benefited from the perceptive observations of senior advisors Dorothy Bass, Richard Fox, and Charles Hambrick-Stowe; practical theologians Kathleen Cahalan, Rob Langworthy, and Craig Townsend; and participants in the HACPP final conference at the University of North Carolina, Chapel Hill, especially Christopher Coble and David Hackett.

The Center for the Study of World Religions at Harvard University also provided a forum for insightful discussions of the relationships between religious practices and experiences of illness, pain, and healing. Through the Religion, Health and Healing Initiative, directed by Susan Sered, I profited from opportunities to present my work at the Religious Healing in Urban America conference and other gatherings. In addition, I obtained research support in the form of a Religion, Health and Healing Initiative Summer Research Grant and Center for the Study of World Religions Dissertation Fellowship. The Harvard Divinity School also provided funding for this project through a Dean's Dissertation Fellowship. I am particularly grateful for the generous financial assistance I received from a Woodrow Wilson Foundation Charlotte W. Newcombe Dissertation Fellowship, a Mary Baker Eddy Library for the Betterment of Humanity Fellowship, and a Postdoctoral Fellowship at Harvard University funded by the John Templeton Foundation.

For support of another kind, I am indebted to the archivists and librarians at numerous institutions. Without the aid of Michelle Gauthier, Gloria Korsman, and other members of the Andover Harvard Theological Library staff, Cambridge, Massachusetts, this project could not have been written. I benefited from the expertise of archivist Ginny Hunt, first at the Congregational Library, Boston, where I was also assisted by Hal Worthley and Jessica Steytler, and later at the Countway Library of Medicine, Harvard University. At the Christian and Missionary Alliance Archives, Colorado Springs, Colorado, Patty McGarvey, Jenn Whiteman, Joseph Wenninger, and Brian Wiggins offered enthusiastic and assiduous research support; as did Meredith Kline and Freeman Barton at Goddard Library, Gordon-Conwell Theological Seminary, South Hamilton, Massachusetts; and John Beauregard and Kevin Belmonte at the Jenks Library and Learning Research Center, Gordon College, Wenham, Massachusetts. Glenn Gohr and Joyce Lee of the Flower Pentecostal Heritage Center, Assemblies of God, Springfield, Missouri, helped me to navigate their excellent archival Web site. Martha Sachs of the Alice Marshall Women's History Collection, Penn State Harrisburg Library, Middletown, Pennsylvania, responded to a research inquiry with impressive alacrity. My appreciation also extends to the research staffs at the Mary Baker Eddy Library for the Betterment of Humanity, Boston; Simmons College Archives, Boston; Wheaton College Special Collections, Wheaton, Illinois; Boston University School of Theology Library; Boston Public Library; New York Public Library; Olin College Library, Needham, Massachusetts; and Schlesinger and Widener Libraries, Harvard University.

For permission to reprint portions of this work that originally appeared as "'Acting Faith': Practices of Religious Healing in Late-Nineteenth-Century Protestantism," in *Practicing Protestants: Histories of Christian Life in America, 1630–1965*, edited by Laurie F. Maffly-Kipp, Leigh E. Schmidt, and Mark Valeri (Johns Hopkins

University Press, 2006), 137–58, I am grateful. I also acknowledge the American Society of Church History for giving me permission to reprint some material from "Houses of Healing: Sacred Space, Spiritual Practice, and the Transformation of Female Suffering in the Faith Cure Movement, 1870–1890," *Church History* (September 2006): 598–611.

Henry Tom, Claire McCabe Tamberino, Juliana McCarthy, and other members of the Johns Hopkins University Press, as well as copy editor Elizabeth Yoder, have provided critical assistance and excellent advice as I have prepared this manuscript for publication. I wish to thank them for their patience and professionalism. I am also grateful to David Hall and Robert Orsi for conceiving and editing the Lived Religions series in which this book appears.

For their persevering and patient love, encouragement, and care, I offer thanks to the many friends and family members who have surrounded me with their support. When I have stumbled or lost heart, it is this group of "witnesses" who have picked me up and cheered me on to the finish. My parents, grandparents, and siblings (Clark and Lynne Curtis, Ian and Michele Maw, and Barbara and Hamlin Pakradooni; Robert and Lois Hofstetter, Doris Maw, the late Deborah Miller, and Rose Marzullo; Suzanne and Bob Casey, Jennifer and Michael Curtis, Marsha Curtis, Geoff and Kristine Maw, Tyler Pakradooni, and Jay and Terri Petrullo) have nourished me with their unwavering confidence and unconditional devotion. Friends such as Naomi Brooks, Sarah and Gates Bryant, Kristen Cloonan, Dawn and Daniel Harrell, Karen Hurley, Emily and Ross Jones, Karen and Gordon Jones, Rochelle and Gustavo Karakey, Laura and Kurt Leafstrand, Kelli and Derek Lewis, Stephanie Lowell, Jen and Paul Oakley, Mari and Gary Ruzich, Michelle and David Swaim, Gretchen and John Tenbrook, Susan and Ted Touloukian, and Deb and George Veth have helped me to stay focused on the things that matter most. Don and Eunice Schatz have provided wise counsel. Violeta Vargas and Anita Waite have offered ongoing support for my family. No one has witnessed my scholarly endeavors in closer proximity than my husband, Clark, whose abiding love and faithful support have made it all possible. I have been blessed to have such a constant partner running the race at my side. To him, and to our sons, Jonathan and David, who continuously remind us of the grace that sustains us, this work is dedicated.

Faith in the Great Physician

Introduction

Late in the evening on April 23, 1878, Jennie Smith stood on her feet for the first time in more than sixteen years. From the age of fifteen, when she wrenched her back while pitching a load of hay into her father's dry-goods storeroom, to the age of thirty-five, when she was finally healed, Smith endured countless ailments, including typhoid and bilious fever, spinal disease, inflammation of the stomach and bowels, paralysis, paroxysms in her limb, a withered arm, blindness, and nervous prostration that kept her bedridden. Over the course of these years of invalidism, Smith consulted many physicians who "subjected" her "to nearly every species of torture." She was salivated with calomel and shocked with a galvanic battery for a period of several months. By 1870, the spasms in her right leg were so severe that she had to keep a "fifty-pound weight of marble on the limb" to keep it still.[1]

Smith recorded her tribulations in *The Valley of Baca: A Record of Suffering and Triumph,* published in 1876, two years before her healing. This popular work, consisting of extracts from Smith's journal interspersed with narrative accounts of her experiences, highlighted her struggle to see her "afflictions in the right light": as "blessings" sent or permitted by God for her benefit and for the good of others. The "triumph" Smith alluded to in the title of her autobiography did not refer to a defeat of disease, but to a spiritual victory couched in terms of "submission to the divine will." "Perfect submission," Smith maintained, meant "passively to endure pain," "becoming more patient and resigned to my lot," and being "willing to suffer any thing that would be to the glory of God." Although Smith desired health and actively sought it, she was determined to make the most of her afflictions, accepting them as opportunities to minister to others through her own example of "cheerful" obedience.[2]

The assumption that physical pain opened up opportunities for spiritual blessing was widespread among Protestants in the mid-nineteenth century. Drawing on scriptural images of the suffering servant and centuries of Christian ascetic tradition, many of Smith's contemporaries interpreted sickness as a means of grace

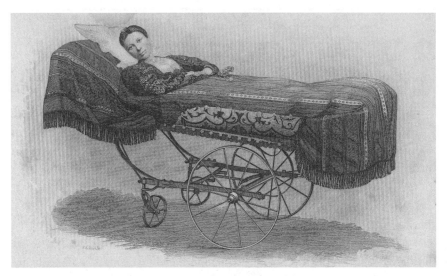

Jennie Smith reclining on her invalid cot. Frontispiece to *The Valley of Baca: A Record of Suffering and Triumph* (1876). Courtesy of Andover-Harvard Theological Library, Harvard Divinity School, Harvard University.

and valorized resignation as the appropriate response to affliction. Popular authors such as Susan Warner, Harriet Beecher Stowe, and Elizabeth Prentiss were promoting a devotional ethic of patient endurance in their best-selling works of fiction and trumpeting the pious invalid as the epitome of Christian sainthood. Autobiographies such as Smith's also helped to elevate the frail and sickly person who practiced self-renunciation and serenity in the face of physical distress to the status of spiritual virtuoso. Ministers affirmed this devotional model in sermons on suffering as well as in their writings. In the introduction to *The Valley of Baca*, for example, the pastor of the Methodist Episcopal Church in Dayton, Ohio, to which Smith belonged, praised her example of long-suffering and "submission to the divine will, which has led thousands of Christians who have known her to a loftier trust in God."[3]

For some of Smith's acquaintances, however, her acquiescence to affliction signified a lack of adequate faith rather than proper Christian practice. In the spring of 1873, Smith noted, "I received several letters from friends who were so exercised about the healing of my body, that they feared I was limiting the power of God by unbelief." According to these correspondents, Christ the "Great Physician" provided both forgiveness of sins and triumph over sickness for the believer who claimed these gifts through faithful prayer. Basing their argument on the promises of spiritual and physical healing put forth in scriptural passages such as Exodus 15:26, "I

Jennie Smith after her healing. Frontispiece to *From Baca to Beulah: Sequel to 'Valley of Baca'* (1880). Courtesy of Clarke Historical Library, Central Michigan University.

am the Lord that healeth thee," and James 5:15, "The prayer of faith shall save the sick, and the Lord shall raise him up," proponents of "faith-healing" insisted that ongoing invalidism was not an appropriate posture for believers. If Christians like Smith remained confined to their cots, how were they to take the gospel to the ends of the earth? God, these individuals insisted, desired active service, not passive endurance.[4]

How believers should comprehend and cope with pain is a perpetual question in the history of Christianity, one that was increasingly contested among American Protestants in the latter half of the nineteenth century. Smith's struggles to harmo-

Jennie Smith at an advanced age. Frontispiece to *Incidents and Experiences of a Railroad Evangelist* (1920). Courtesy of Ira J. Taylor Library, Iliff School of Theology, Denver.

nize her friends' convictions regarding bodily healing with the model of patient resignation that had long provided her with a framework for interpreting and responding to her illness reveal the mounting tensions over the meaning and practice of suffering that surfaced in this period. In *From Baca to Beulah*, the sequel to her first book, Smith noted her ongoing ambivalence about the possibility of physical healing through prayer. By resigning herself to illness and invalidism, was she failing to claim a blessing from God? How was she to reconcile rejoicing in her afflictions with praying for recovery? Caught between competing devotional ethics, Smith continued to wrestle with these questions for a number of years. In a journal entry dated August 4, 1877, Smith poured out her heart to God, confessing her confusion, declaring her commitment to remain content with her circumstances, and praying for guidance: "Am I limiting thy power? Am I robbing thee of glory, and this suffering body of the blessed boon of health, by *unbelief?* . . . Is there relief for me? . . . I am willing to endure and to suffer all the will of God if *there is still a need-be.* Oh, what wilt thou have me do? Only let thy will be done!"[5]

Several months later, Smith entered the homeopathic hospital in Philadelphia, where she underwent surgery that relieved her "spasmodic limb" but left it "utterly helpless." Despite some improvement, Smith remained discouraged about her lack of progress and felt her "helplessness more than ever." Finally, on March 26, 1878, Smith recorded, "I found the first glimmer of hope to dawn, that God might in answer to prayer, restore me." For the first time, Smith grasped the central insight of the nascent divine healing or faith cure movement that had begun to capture the imaginations of increasing numbers of Protestants in this period: that protracted suffering was not God's will for anyone, and therefore that it must be God's will to heal her. On the 19th of April, Smith wrote to five of her friends, asking them to unite in prayer for her restoration the following Tuesday evening, when a prayer-meeting was to be held in her behalf in Philadelphia.[6]

When Tuesday arrived, Smith "suffered more and was weaker than usual all day." In the evening, Smith's physician and her sister Fannie, along with ministers from the local Methodist and Presbyterian churches and at least eight others, gathered around her and began to pray. Smith "lay in quiet expectancy, still suffering, but with a remarkable sense of the divine presence." The prayer continued for two hours, until Smith finally prayed aloud herself, offering God her "body anew" and asking, one final time, that God's will be done. "After a brief silence," she recalled, "I was conscious of a baptism of strength, as sensible and as positively as if an electric shock had passed through my system. I felt definitely the strength come into my back, and into my helpless limb. Laying my hands on the chair arms, I raised myself to a sitting posture." Then, for the first time since she had taken to bed at the age of nineteen, Smith stood up. Overwhelmed with thankfulness, she fell down upon her knees, then arose again and walked around the room. "My limb and body seemed as if new," Smith reminisced. "I realized fully how great a change had taken place. I had no pain. My back was strong and the soreness gone. . . . From this time I was on my feet more or less every day. I never had any trouble since that night with my lame limb, nor any symptoms of my old malady."[7]

The story of Jennie Smith's remarkable transformation from a bedridden invalid to an indefatigable evangelist who traveled the nation preaching temperance and salvation to America's "railroad men"—a ministry she took up soon after her healing and pursued until her death in 1924, at the age of eighty-two—offers an arresting example of how the divine healing movement that flourished among evan-

gelical Protestants in the latter decades of the nineteenth century worked to transform the ways Christians interpreted and responded to illness and pain as well as
how they defined and pursued bodily health. This study is about Jennie Smith and
the many women and men like her who embraced divine healing in an attempt to
break free from the ideal of sanctified suffering that demanded passive forbearance
in the face of sickness and somatic distress. By emphasizing victory over affliction
and active service beyond the confines of the sickroom, advocates of faith healing
endeavored to articulate and embody an alternative devotional ethic that uncou-
pled the longstanding link between corporeal suffering and spiritual holiness.[8]

The Emergence of Divine Healing in the Nineteenth Century

When Jennie Smith first encountered emissaries of divine healing, the movement was in its infancy. Although accounts of miraculous healing had always been a
part of Christian tradition, most mid-nineteenth-century Protestants viewed these
events as exceptional, believing that the "age of miracles" had ceased at the conclusion of the biblical era. In the 1850s, however, reports of "marvellous cures" taking
place at various locations in Europe began to circulate among British evangelicals.
The news of these ongoing healing ministries reached North American shores in
the late 1860s, when Boston physician Charles Cullis (1833–92) came across a copy
of *Dorothea Trudel; or, The Prayer of Faith*. This work recounted "the remarkable
manner in which large numbers of sick persons were healed in answer to prayer" at
Trudel's home in Mannedorf, Switzerland.[9]

By the time he encountered Trudel's text, Cullis had grown weary of watching
the hundreds of patients under his care endure the agonies of illness with little,
if any, hope of relief or recovery. For more than ten years, Cullis had been working to alleviate "the miseries of the afflicted" as a homeopathic doctor with a busy
downtown practice and as the founder and superintendent of several institutions
where indigent and "incurable" patients suffering from tuberculosis, cancer, and
spinal disease could receive free room, board, child care, medical treatment, and
spiritual consolation. Although he joyfully reported that most, if not all, of the
"homeless and hopeless" sufferers who died while residing in one of the homes had
"been converted" during their stay and "died in the faith of Jesus," Cullis had begun to wonder if his ministry to the sick ought to encompass more than soothing
bodily pain and offering spiritual counsel. After ruminating on "the instructions
and promises contained in the fourteenth and fifteenth verses of the fifth chapter
of the Epistle of James" and reading the story of Trudel's life and work, Cullis felt
emboldened to ask Miss Lucy Reed Drake, a young woman suffering from a brain

tumor that kept her bedridden, if she would be willing to "trust the Lord" to remove the malignancy and restore her to health. Drake agreed, and Cullis proceeded to pray. Soon after, Drake rose from her sick bed and returned to her work as a city missionary. The tumor had disappeared.[10]

Drake's cure in January 1870 marked the commencement of Cullis's faith healing ministry. Although Cullis was not solely responsible for the rise of divine healing in North America, he was a central figure in the movement's growth and development. Through his many contacts among influential members of the Methodist Holiness and Reformed Higher Life movements, Cullis helped propagate the notion that Christians ought to trust God's promises "as to the healing of the body." Participants in these interdenominational and transatlantic networks were especially receptive to faith cure because the message of physical and spiritual rejuvenation through the indwelling power of the Holy Spirit complemented their own conception of the Christian life. Like all nineteenth-century evangelicals, Holiness and Higher Life teachers emphasized the authority of the Bible in matters of faith and practice, the centrality of Jesus' atoning work on the cross for the salvation of sinners, the importance of conversion or "new birth" followed by sanctification or "growth in holiness," and the imperative of evangelism through fervent preaching and social reform. From the mid-1850s on, however, evangelicals from a variety of theological traditions and denominational backgrounds increasingly stressed the necessity of "entire sanctification" through a "second blessing," or "baptism with the Holy Spirit," following conversion that endued believers with the power to conquer sin and the energy to engage in effective Christian service.[11]

Drawing upon John Wesley's teaching that believers could obtain "Christian perfection"—defined as freedom from sinful acts and inclinations—this side of heaven, mid-nineteenth-century Methodist leaders such as Phoebe Palmer (1807–74) encouraged Christians to claim the blessing of holiness through an act of personal consecration that would result in an immediate experience of entire sanctification and an ongoing life of "self-sacrificing service of God." Although many within Reformed circles found this understanding of sanctification inimical to Calvinist ideas about human nature and eschatology, some Reformed leaders were intrigued by the possibility of perfection and endeavored to modify Wesleyan notions of holiness to better fit their own theological framework. Charles Finney (1792–1875) and Asa Mahan (1799–1889) had begun to articulate a Reformed version of Christian perfectionism while at Oberlin in the 1840s. In 1858, Presbyterian minister William E. Boardman (1810–86) published *The Higher Christian Life*, an exceedingly popular work that extolled the possibility of victory over sin through a "second experience" distinct from conversion. According to Boardman and colleagues such as Hannah Whitall Smith (1832–1911), this "deeper work of grace" was the source of a believer's "power for service" and "the Christian's secret of a happy life."[12]

By the time Charles Cullis embraced divine healing in 1870, Holiness and Higher Life teachings had spread throughout many evangelical denominations in North America and Great Britain. While the pursuit of Christian perfection prompted some to abandon churches they deemed hopelessly corrupt, most early proponents endeavored to reform their denominations through the development of new extra-ecclesial organizations and publications founded for the express purpose of disseminating the message of salvation and entire sanctification to the whole Christian community. From 1837 until her death in 1874, for example, Phoebe Palmer presided over the Tuesday Meeting for the Promotion of Holiness at her home in New York City, a gathering that attracted Methodists, Baptists, Congregationalists, Presbyterians, Episcopalians, and others who sought a more intense spiritual experience. In 1867, a group of Methodist pastors who had been influenced by Palmer's teaching organized the National Camp Meeting Association for the Promotion of Holiness. Although Methodist in origin, the Association was ecumenical in character and aimed to include "all, irrespective of denominational ties, interested in the subject of the higher Christian life." The annual Keswick Conventions, held in England from 1875, served a similar purpose, as did D. L. Moody's American revivals and yearly Northfield Conferences. While participants in these ventures often disagreed about the precise theological meaning of the "second blessing" of entire sanctification, they were all "friends of holiness" who worked together toward a common goal of reviving the church and realizing the "blessed hope" of personal purity and spiritual power.[13]

The pervasive preoccupation with the pursuit of holiness among mid-nineteenth-century evangelicals on both sides of the Atlantic prepared the way for the rise of faith cure in the 1870s and 80s. The overlapping organizational alliances and relational networks that arose in association with the Holiness and Higher Life movements provided a ready platform for promulgating the doctrines of divine healing to a broad-based and largely sympathetic audience. During the decades following Lucy Drake's miraculous cure, faith cure rapidly gained popularity among lay people and clergy from a wide range of denominations across North America, Great Britain, and Europe. In the winter of 1871, Cullis convinced the Reverend John S. Inskip (1816–84), a prominent Methodist leader and the first president of the National Camp Meeting Association, of the propriety of praying for healing according to the directives given in James 5. Previously skeptical regarding "certain views of the question of healing" that some of his acquaintances had begun to endorse, Inskip allowed Cullis to pray with him for relief from a disabling headache caused by the lingering effects of severe sunstroke. When Cullis laid hands upon his head, Inskip experienced instantaneous release from his pain. The following Sunday, Inskip "spoke of the matter in the public congregation" and then "narrated the occurrence in the Boston Preachers' Meeting on Monday."[14]

Inskip's embrace of faith healing lent legitimacy to Cullis's teaching and practice, and helped spread the word among members of the Holiness movement. Meanwhile, Cullis continued to share his convictions with his many acquaintances in the wider evangelical community. When William Boardman visited Cullis soon after Drake's healing, Cullis enthusiastically recounted how God had fulfilled the promises offered in James 5 and persuaded Boardman to put his "faith in the Lord as Healer." In December 1875, Boardman and his wife Mary carried the tidings of Cullis's activities to London, where they shared their new-found faith with friends such as Elizabeth Baxter (1837–1926), an evangelist and active participant in the Keswick conventions whose husband, Michael, edited the influential *Christian Herald* magazine. Several years later, Mrs. Baxter and the Boardmans, along with Baxter's evangelistic co-worker Charlotte C. Murray, opened Bethshan, a "house for the healing of the sick" that quickly become the epicenter of the divine healing movement in England.[15]

By the mid-1870s, leading figures from many evangelical denominations had espoused divine healing after learning of Cullis's ministry. In addition to earning endorsements from Inskip and Boardman, Cullis also received the approval of fellow Bostonians Daniel Steele (1824–1914), a theology professor at Boston University and a prominent Methodist spokesperson, and Adoniram Judson Gordon (1836–95), minister of Boston's Clarendon Street Baptist Church and an important figure in evangelical movements of the late nineteenth century such as temperance, foreign missions, and Moody's revivals. Captain Russell Kelso Carter (1849–1928), a professor of chemistry, civil engineering, and mathematics at the Pennsylvania Military Academy and an active participant in Holiness endeavors, also became an avid supporter after Cullis prayed for his healing from an acute heart condition in the summer of 1879. Two years later, Albert Benjamin Simpson (1843–1919), a Presbyterian pastor who would eventually become the minister of the nondenominational Gospel Tabernacle church in New York City and the founder of the Christian and Missionary Alliance, accepted the truth of divine healing after hearing Cullis preach at a faith convention at Old Orchard Beach, Maine.[16]

While many apologists for faith cure were male ministers, women played vital roles in shaping the movement's theology and practice. Women who served in important leadership positions included Episcopalian Carrie Judd Montgomery

(1858–1946), author of one of the pivotal texts on divine healing and editor of a popular periodical promoting healing and holiness; Mary Mossman (c.1826–after 1909), who established and operated a healing home at the popular Holiness seaside retreat in Ocean Grove, New Jersey; and Sarah Mix (1832–84), an African American Adventist who ministered to the sick throughout New England.[17]

As African American leaders, Mix and her husband, Edward, were somewhat exceptional. Although many African Americans participated in divine healing (evangelist Amanda Berry Smith was a sometime devotee), individuals of Northern European descent dominated the movement's leadership ranks. Similarly, while faith cure appealed to a diverse constituency, making disciples of both wealthy citizens and the working poor, leaders tended to be well-educated members of the middle and upper classes. Finally, while divine healing flourished in rural areas as well as in cities, urban centers such as London, New York, Boston, and Philadelphia became hubs of the movement's organizational activity.[18]

Throughout the 1870s, faith cure spread primarily through the endeavors of proponents like Cullis as well as through the ministries of itinerant evangelists such as Sarah Mix and her mentor, Ethan O. Allen (1813–1902), a Methodist layman who traversed the northeastern United States laying hands on the sick and praying for their recovery. Individuals like Jennie Smith also contributed to the movement's growth and development by publishing personal narratives describing their experiences of physical and spiritual restoration. Thousands of these testimonies appeared in popular religious newspapers such as the Methodist *Guide to Holiness,* in periodicals established for the express purpose of promoting divine healing, and in widely circulated anthologies like Mix's *Faith Cures, and Answers to Prayer.* By the time Smith composed her own account of her cure in 1880, divine healing had begun to take institutional shape with the regular inclusion of healing services at camp meetings and faith conventions, the founding of faith homes for invalids who desired to seek healing in a nurturing environment, and the publication of treatises defending faith cure theology.[19]

In the absence of any official governing body, texts such these, alongside the articles and narratives published in religious periodicals, served as the primary vehicles for developing, defining, and propagating the doctrines and practices of divine healing—a process that reflected the movement's vibrancy, its vernacular base, and its ambiguous boundaries. Although some leaders attempted to regulate the theology and practice of faith cure, establishing and enforcing consistency was a challenging prospect, given the lack of a formal authority structure and the importance of lay testimonials in shaping and sustaining the movement's progress. While this heterogeneity may have proved frustrating for some practitioners, faith cure's multiformity contributed to its ability to attract participants from a wide range of theological and social backgrounds and helped to preserve its vitality throughout the latter decades of the nineteenth century. The movement's widespread popularity became apparent in June of 1885, when more than fifteen hundred representatives from at least nine countries gathered in London for an "International Conference on Divine Healing and True Holiness."[20]

Divine Healing as a Devotional Movement

As a transatlantic and interdenominational phenomenon, divine healing influenced a broad and diverse segment of Protestant Christianity in the late nineteenth century. During the 1870s and 1880s, faith cure was a frequent topic of discussion among Methodists, Baptists, Presbyterians, Episcopalians, Adventists, and other evangelicals throughout the United States, Great Britain, and Europe. Both the religious and secular presses devoted attention to divine healing, as medical professionals, clerical leaders, and lay persons contributed to an increasingly vigorous debate over the validity of faith cure as a form of Christian healing. As the movement expanded, converts to divine healing faced escalating criticism from detractors who accused them of misinterpreting the meaning of suffering and of kindling false hope in God's ability and willingness to perform miraculous cures in the modern era. Some opponents equated divine healing with quackery and complained that faith cure threatened the health of individuals who abandoned their doctors in favor of the Great Physician. Divine healing also aroused the ire of theologians and ministers who protested that the movement undermined attempts to defend the reasonableness of Christianity against the attacks of its cultured despisers. Even some evangelicals worried that proponents of faith cure went too far in their efforts to revise the doctrine of God's afflictive providence and the corresponding ethic of passive resignation. A number of prominent Holiness and Higher Life figures, including Methodist Bishop William Taylor and evangelist D. L. Moody, always maintained their distance from divine healing and sometimes even chided their colleagues for propagating "extreme" views on the subject. Although both of these leaders affirmed their belief in God's power to heal, they resisted the notion that Christ's atonement guaranteed a miraculous recovery for every invalid who offered the prayer of faith.[21]

In response to their critics, apologists for faith cure insisted that the doctrines and rituals of healing they promoted represented a return to the basic teachings and practices of Jesus and the apostles, not a form of fanaticism. Reclaiming the reality of biblical healing in the modern era was a reasonable enterprise, they argued—an effective alternative to medical materialism, a convincing rejoinder to scientific naturalism, and a powerful antidote to philosophical skepticism. Employing the "primitivist" rhetoric so common among religious reformers, partisans of faith cure portrayed themselves as champions of "true" Christianity who endeavored to recover the lost legacy of miraculous healing as a means for revitalizing the church, transforming the culture, and evangelizing the world.

Like most "restorationist" movements, divine healing involved both doctrinal and devotional reform. Changing what Christians thought about corporeal affliction entailed altering the spiritual disciplines believers employed in their efforts to cope with sickness and pain. Looking to the Bible for inspiration, advocates of faith cure strung together a series of ritual practices that provided participants with an alternative to the devotional ethic of patient endurance. Rather than remaining resigned to suffering, they insisted, sick persons ought to seek relief through scriptural "means" such as prayer, laying on of hands, and anointing. Overcoming illness required acting to translate belief into behavior. Indeed, leaders of the faith cure movement constantly reminded their constituents that theology and practice were reciprocally related in the therapeutic process. Healing, they maintained, meant believing that God had banished sickness from the body, despite any sensory evidence to the contrary, and acting accordingly. Trusting the Great Physician, therefore, involved training the senses to ignore lingering pain or symptoms of sickness and disciplining the body to "act faith" by getting out of bed and serving God through energetic engagement with others. For the ailing women and men who espoused this perspective, participating in devotional exercises like meditation and prayer, confession of sin and fasting, laying on of hands and anointing with oil, helped foster the requisite mental habits, corporal behaviors, and spiritual dispositions that faith in divine healing demanded.

Despite the emphasis proponents of faith cure placed on religious practices as means for modifying the meaning and experience of pain in the Christian life, the story of divine healing as a devotional movement remains largely untold. Although historians have analyzed the theological debates and cultural shifts that fueled the emergence and flowering of faith healing in the late nineteenth century, we know comparatively little about the particular rituals and observances through which participants in this movement contended with illness and pursued health. This book stresses the centrality of spiritual practice, or what I have sometimes chosen to call devotional ethics, to the enterprise of divine healing. By employing the term "devotional ethics," I aim to accentuate how patterns of piety could serve both as effective channels for sustaining customary norms governing the relationship between sanctity and suffering, and as resources for reimagining conventional modes of belief and behavior. Religious practices, as theorists such as Catherine Bell have argued, are "able to *reproduce or reconfigure* a vision of the order of power in the world." Habits of devotion, from this perspective, can promote both social discipline and cultural transformation, perhaps even simultaneously. "Practice," explains David Hall, "always bears the marks of both regulation and what, for want of a better word, we might term resistance. It is not wholly one or the other."[22]

Examining how devotional patterns served as media for transmitting and transposing cultural expectations about suffering also sheds light on illness and healing as lived experiences. Attending to the specific ways in which practitioners of faith cure sought physical and spiritual wholeness illumines the "everyday thinking and doing" of individuals as they confronted the challenges of disease, infirmity, and pain. What did individuals like Jennie Smith, Charles Cullis, Lucy Drake, and the many other women and men who were drawn to the faith cure movement do when they or their loved ones got sick? Why did they find the ethic of passive resignation unsatisfying, and how did they go about devising an alternative? Which theological idioms and cultural resources did they draw upon in their efforts to reinterpret the significance of bodily affliction? What, exactly, did participating in the practice of divine healing accomplish? And perhaps most importantly, what was at stake in this effort?[23]

Focusing on the devotional aspects of divine healing elucidates how Christians in a particular time and place worked through the problem of pain within the context of their daily lives. In so doing, this approach exposes the ambiguities, inconsistencies, and ironies that accompanied their attempts to make sense of sickness and to recover health. Sick persons turned to faith cure because the movement provided them with a framework for interpreting their suffering and specific directives for alleviating it. But everyone did not understand these instructions in the same manner, and individuals sometimes appropriated ideas and practices in creative and inventive ways that took the movement in diverse, unforeseen, and occasionally controversial directions. Even those who emerged as leaders did not always agree about the meanings and modes of faith cure. Divine healing, in other words, was a polysemous practice open to multiple and sometimes competing interpretations, and subject to ongoing and often contentious revisions.

In part, this hybridity was due to the fact that the faith cure movement, like the Holiness and Higher Life networks out of which it arose, had no formal hierarchy and no authoritative method for imposing "orthodoxy" in theology or practice. But the equivocal character of divine healing stemmed from other sources as well. In their effort to reclaim what they characterized as an archetypal Christian practice, late-nineteenth-century proponents of faith cure evoked a whole series of recurring doctrinal and devotional dilemmas. What was the relationship between divine sovereignty and human agency in the curative process? Was bodily restoration a matter of grace or faith? Or both? Did ritual practices play a causal role in healing? What happened when a person prayed for a cure and nothing seemed to happen? How was an individual to discern the workings of God in body and soul? As they wrestled with these perennial issues, participants in faith cure recycled some classic strategies for coping with Christianity's most puzzling problems. Like many of their forbears in the faith, proponents of divine healing appealed to paradox as a way of working through the perplexing mysteries they encountered as they endeavored to live out the Christian life. Rather than resolving the apparent contradictions and conundrums that arose when they put their faith into practice, participants in divine healing embraced these enigmas as essential features of authentic Christianity. Faith cure was, therefore, a fundamentally ambiguous experience, freighted with inherent antinomies and tensions.

To outsiders, the incongruities that characterized divine healing suggested that the practice was patently illogical, probably foolish, and possibly perilous. But for insiders, the tensile theology and devotional disciplines associated with faith cure served as means for marking out and maintaining what they saw as a scripturally sound, personally beneficial, and culturally savvy method of dealing with fleshly infirmities. Paradoxes and polarities, from this perspective, endowed divine healing with an intrinsic elasticity that enabled participants to adapt an "age-old" strategy for surmounting suffering to diverse personal circumstances as well as to variable cultural, social, and theological conditions. Although proponents of faith cure liked to point out the parallels between the apostolic epoch and the modern period, individuals who turned to the Great Physician during the latter decades of the nineteenth century were living in a vastly different world than the one recorded in the New Testament. While some of the challenges they faced may have been analogous to the trials that Jesus and his disciples confronted, practitioners of faith healing also had to contend with the long legacy of Christian healing that developed in the centuries following the biblical era as well as with the unique predicaments of modernity. Within this contemporary context, the multivalent practices of divine healing were supple enough to operate both as tools for spiritual formation of the self and as tactics for coping with the various gender norms, medical theories, and theological discourses that shaped the experiences of pain, illness, and health in this period.

Divine Healing in Historical Perspective

By focusing on the devotional ethics of divine healing, then, this study also underscores the connections between faith cure and broader aspects of cultural and religious change. As many historians have observed, shifting theological and social currents prompted a widespread rethinking of the relationship between physical illness and spiritual health in the mid- to late nineteenth century. An extensive and ongoing effort to emend the doctrinal heritage of the Calvinist tradition, for example, encouraged many Protestants to question the notion that God had ceased to work miracles after the apostolic age—a key tenet of Reformed theology—and to challenge the corollary belief that sickness was a godsend that ought to be accepted and endured with thanksgiving. Similarly, the growing tendency among eighteenth- and early-nineteenth-century moral philosophers, ministers, and social reformers to emphasize God's benevolence and mercy made belief in afflictive providence less palatable for Protestants of both liberal and evangelical leanings. Widespread conviction among believers of all sorts that the Second Coming was fast approaching fueled missionary fervor and mobilized both pre- and postmillennialists to elevate energetic pragmatism over resigned passivity as an urgent necessity of the end times.[24]

Mounting dissatisfaction with the kind of "heroic" medical therapeutics that Jennie Smith underwent, alongside the development and proliferation of new technologies for the alleviation of pain, such as the use of anesthesia during surgery and childbirth, also enabled Protestants from midcentury on to envision an alternative to a pattern of piety that promoted long-suffering acquiescence in the face of physical distress. Although physicians continued to debate the benefits of using anesthetics such as ether, chloroform, and nitrous oxide for decades after the initial discovery of these analgesic agents, the very possibility of rendering a person impervious to pain undercut the notion that bodily suffering was an inescapable reality of human existence that ought to be endured with resignation. By the 1870s, the use of anesthesia was widespread among American and European physicians of every class, and patients facing surgical operations as well as chronic conditions clamored for palliative remedies of all kinds. The pervasive popularity of pain-killers made passive acceptance of suffering seem not only needless, but sometimes even pathological. Anyone who "chose to hurt," as Ariel Glucklich has put it in his study of the relationship between sanctity and suffering, "had to be, in some sense, abnormal." Because pain had become "naturalized and medicalized," he explains, it lost much of its currency as a "spiritual and religious" phenomenon.[25]

Transformations in the economic realm also affected the way individuals of Jennie Smith's generation interpreted and responded to suffering. Middle- and up-per-class concerns about the rising demands of consumer capitalism in the latter decades of the nineteenth century contributed to a growing unease with the ideal of the passive sufferer as the paragon of Christian virtue. During these years, many began to see the attitude of self-restraint that had helped middle-class entrepre-neurs to succeed in the smaller-scale capitalism of the antebellum period as a hin-drance to personal advancement and broader economic growth. Related worries over the perceived threats of over-civilization and neurasthenic paralysis engen-dered increasing suspicion of spiritual frameworks that associated sanctity with sickliness, weakness, and inactivity. In the view of certain cultural critics, passivity and physical frailty were symptoms of a disease that needed to be cured if modern civilization were to succeed, not characteristics of Christian holiness that ought to be cultivated.[26]

Finally, debates over the meaning and performance of "manly" and "womanly" virtue in this period helped to unsettle assumptions about the relationship be-tween physical suffering and spiritual blessing. Although gender norms are never stable, uncontested concepts, the late nineteenth century was a period in which be-liefs about the essential nature and proper enactment of masculinity and feminin-ity were subject to particularly intense scrutiny and vigorous contestation. As Gail Bederman has observed, for example, ideals of manliness based on self-denial that had helped to create and shore up middle-class consciousness in the antebellum period became increasingly problematic within the overlapping contexts of eco-nomic instability, rising consumerism, challenges to the political authority of An-glo-American men from both women and foreign immigrants, and a growing fixa-tion with the virility of the male body. The emergence of "muscular Christianity" in these years represented, in part, an attempt to elevate vitality and strength over serenity and submission as the quintessential traits of the spiritual exemplar.[27]

If models of Christian manhood were in flux during the latter decades of the nineteenth century, notions of Protestant female sanctity were also becoming markedly unstable. For women who came of age in the antebellum era, a devo-tional ethic that promoted passive resignation as the appropriate Christian re-sponse to pain resonated with prevailing gender norms that associated true wom-anhood with self-sacrifice and submission. According to influential interpretations of the "domestic ideology" that shaped so many discussions of women's nature and role in society during the first half of the nineteenth century, the ideal woman was a devoted wife and mother who delighted in denying herself for the sake of oth-ers and who achieved sanctification precisely through the physical, emotional, and spiritual suffering that self-abnegation and submission engendered.[28]

By the time Jennie Smith reached maturity, however, both the gender ideals and the devotional norms that had provided her female forebears with a framework for understanding and dealing with suffering were becoming less authoritative as the material conditions of women's lives eroded several key assumptions of the domestic ideology. Greater participation in higher education, urban life, and certain sectors of the growing economy, for example, helped stretch the boundaries of women's sphere beyond the home. Legal reforms that gave women expanded property rights and easier access to divorce diminished the hegemony of male authority and offered alternatives to submission as the proper posture of women in relation to their male kin and social contacts. The physical education movement advanced a view of the female body as "naturally healthy, not feeble, and saw suffering as an aberration not as an inevitable consequence of being female." By the 1870s, historian Nancy Theriot has persuasively argued, these developments, among others, called into question the "feminine script" that emphasized self-denying motherhood, innate feminine frailty, and the consequent necessity of female suffering and submission. For women like Smith and her younger contemporaries, then, the attainment of physical and spiritual health might involve "self-control" rather than self-sacrifice, "purposeful action," rather than passive resignation.[29]

These social, cultural, and theological factors, among others, helped create an environment congenial to the emergence and expansion of faith cure in the 1870s and 1880s. But advocates of divine healing were not the only ones to challenge deeply rooted associations between suffering and sanctification in this period. For decades, in fact, a panoply of health reform and healing movements such as Grahamism, Thomsonianism, hydropathy, homeopathy, Adventism, and Spiritualism had been working, each in its own distinctive way, to present alternatives to the regimens of "regular" or "orthodox" medicine and also to the devotional ethics of "orthodox" or "Reformed" Protestantism, both of which disciplined their subjects to embrace patient endurance of affliction as the pathway to somatic health and spiritual holiness. In the 1870s and 1880s, Christian Science and New Thought joined the ranks of earlier reform movements in the attempt to re-map the road to spiritual and physical wholeness.[30]

Historians of American religion and culture have long been attuned to the revisionist efforts of health reform and healing movements like Adventism, Spiritualism, Christian Science and New Thought—groups that are often classified as "radical" or "alternative" religions in relation to evangelical Protestantism. In this study, I argue that advocates of faith cure also contested inherited ideas about the role of sanctified suffering in the Christian life, even as they claimed to uphold and defend classic Protestant theology and spirituality. By exploring how proponents of divine healing constructed and enacted a model of spiritual experience that entailed active service to God rather than passive acceptance of pain, this book draws attention to the common objectives, curious resemblances, and complicated interactions among healing movements of the late nineteenth century. Highlighting these similarities and exchanges, I suggest, calls into question a long-standing and extremely influential tendency to segregate "mainstream" from "unorthodox," "insider" from "outsider," and "evangelical" from "liberal" forms of American religion.[31]

In addition to exposing the inadequacy of conventional historical categories for capturing the complexities of the late-nineteenth-century religious landscape, juxtaposing faith cure with rival healing movements shows that the pursuit of health in this period occasioned both explosive creativity and sharp contestation in the realms of Christian doctrine and practice. Proponents of divine healing, like their counterparts in Spiritualism, Christian Science, and New Thought, asserted that remaking the meaning and experience of affliction required a reappraisal of inherited philosophical, theological, and devotional idioms. All of these movements, in fact, indicated that healing involved rejecting a materialistic view of the body, challenging a chastening understanding of God's providence, and resisting the devotional ethic of passive resignation. But common concerns rarely made for common cause. Although they often proposed strikingly similar strategies for solving the problems of physical illness and pain, for example, advocates of faith cure and Christian Science never joined forces. Instead, they engaged in fierce and often bitter battles over the proper interpretation and practice of Christian healing. Within this highly charged context, apologists for faith cure struggled to present their movement as the only authentic incarnation of Jesus' teaching. Because they based their beliefs and behavior on the Bible, these evangelicals insisted, they avoided both the "errors" of modern rationalism and the "heresies" of rival healing movements like Spiritualism and Christian Science. Recovering a scriptural ministry of healing, advocates implied, meant marking out a middle path between a series of extreme positions that distorted the heritage of "true" Christianity.

Examining the ways proponents of faith cure sought to situate themselves in relation to their competitors reveals the range of theological meanings and the repertoire of spiritual practices available to those who sought relief from suffering in the latter decades of nineteenth century. That so many of these seekers were women also merits comparative analysis. One of the most noteworthy parallels between divine healing and other contemporary religious healing movements is the prominent role that women played as leaders and adherents. Although women formed the majority in most Protestant denominations during the late nineteenth century, they rarely attained the level of leadership in traditional church settings that they often achieved through their participation in health reform and healing movements such as hydropathy, Adventism, Spiritualism, Christian Science, New Thought, and divine healing. Curiously, recent work on faith cure largely ignores the issue of gender in interpreting the movement's appeal. Those studies that do consider the gendered dynamics of divine healing characterize the movement primarily as a means for contesting male authority (religious, medical, and scientific) over the female body. My own analysis nuances this scholarship by considering faith cure's attraction for men and by offering a more cautious assessment of the movement's status as an unequivocal strategy of cultural resistance. Focusing on divine healing as a form of devotional practice, I argue, provides a distinctive perspective on the movement's interaction with the increasingly complex gender politics that characterized late-nineteenth-century culture. Elucidating the complicated ways in which participants in faith cure described and performed the enigmatic relationship between divine power and personal passivity in the healing process reveals how certain ritual practices and religious beliefs provided these evangelicals with a means for working against and through, but also within, the cultural norms and ideals that shaped their experiences of embodiment.[32]

Additionally, although historians of divine healing have discussed the criticism that the movement received from other Protestants, few have analyzed the gender politics that shaped these reactions. Attempts to regulate movements of religious healing by dismissing them as marginal at best or fanatical and dangerous at worst, I contend, were explicitly linked to normative and deeply gendered conceptions of both religion and health. At stake in the effort to recast the place of pain in the Christian life, then, were larger debates about the character of "true" religion, and related arguments over the nature of true womanhood, virile masculinity, muscular Christianity, race perfection, and even the advancement of Western civilization.

Having articulated the agenda for this study, let me now indicate what I do not accomplish in the following pages. First, although I interpret divine healing as one manifestation of a wide-ranging and multifaceted effort to reconfigure the relationship between suffering and sanctification that included disciples of Sylvester Graham and Samuel Thomson, Seventh-Day Adventists, Spiritualist Mediums, Christian Scientists, and practitioners of New Thought, among others, I have not attempted a comparative analysis of the health reform and healing movements of the late nineteenth century. While I do evoke Christian Science, Spiritualism, and other healing movements at various points throughout this work, my aim in doing so is to illumine the rich and variegated history of evangelical faith cure. I do not seek, in other words, to provide equally detailed treatments of divine healing and its better-known contemporaries.[33]

Instead, my goal in this book is to offer a "retrospective ethnography"—a finely grained, richly textured account—of the spiritual practices that evangelicals who participated in faith cure employed as they struggled to make sense of sickness and to pursue spiritual and physical health, and to ask what was at stake, culturally, socially, and theologically, in the devotional ethics of divine healing. As a result, I have not endeavored to provide a comprehensive rendering of the emergence and development of the faith cure movement. Since several studies now exist that chart the chronology of divine healing, narrate the biographies of the movement's many founders and leaders, and trace its diffuse and diverse dispersal among the many denominational branches of American Protestantism, I have felt free to concentrate on specific facets of faith cure without addressing every aspect of the movement's multifarious history. The result is a study that is more limited in scope on several fronts.[34]

First, I focus principally on divine healing as it flourished among middle- and upper-middle-class urban Protestants of Great Britain and the northeastern United States. While I argue that faith cure spread well beyond these geographic regions and included devotees and some leaders from more diverse socioeconomic and racial backgrounds, I also submit that the movement's most influential members hailed mainly from prosperous families and resided chiefly in cities such as Boston and London. Upper-middle-class Protestants such as Charles Cullis, A. J. Gordon, Carrie Judd, and A. B. Simpson, I contend, were primarily responsible for shaping the devotional ethics of divine healing, and it is for this reason that they are the main protagonists in my story. These leaders, along with a handful of others like Elizabeth Baxter, William Boardman, and Sarah Mix, wrote the texts, established the institutions, edited the periodicals, and headed the ministries that constituted the faith cure movement during the latter decades of the nineteenth century. Despite the crucial roles these figures played in propagating the "gospel of healing," the movement would not have prospered had not so many people put their faith in the promise of miraculous restoration. As much as possible, therefore, I have endeavored to broaden my cast of characters to incorporate the women and men who read the faith healing literature, visited the faith homes, participated in the reform efforts, and prayed to the Great Physician for relief in this period. Because so many recipients of divine healing recorded their experiences in written testimonials, I have been able to recover the stories of adherents from a variety of places, social classes, ethnic communities, and religious traditions. These narratives have yielded especially rich insights about how individuals who took part in faith cure appropriated, transformed, resisted, and conformed to the various theological and cultural norms that structured the meaning of suffering and practice of healing in the late nineteenth century.

Second, whereas many studies of divine healing encompass more than six decades, stretching from approximately 1870 into the 1920s, this book covers a much tighter time frame. Because I am concerned predominantly with teasing out how evangelicals who engaged in faith cure employed devotional exercises and ritual gestures in order to alter their experiences of pain and to contend with the broader cultural and religious conventions that shaped these experiences, I concentrate on a narrower historical period. Chapter one, which opens in the late 1850s, examines the devotional ethic of passive resignation to suffering that influenced how many mid-nineteenth-century Protestants interpreted and responded to bodily illness and distress. Highlighting the theological, cultural, and gendered discourses that helped create and sustain the connection between physical pain and personal holiness, this chapter sets the stage for the emergence of divine healing in the early 1870s. Chapter two charts the rise of faith cure amidst a host of theological and cultural transformations. Challenges to several key doctrinal positions, I argue, encouraged a variety of health reform and religious healing movements to question associations between somatic affliction and spiritual blessing. Within this context, Spiritualism, Christian Science, and divine healing, among other movements, proposed alternative devotional ethics that required neither long-suffering of sickness nor passive withdrawal from the world in order to gain spiritual or physical well-being. Focusing on faith cure, chapter three explores the hermeneutics of divine healing. Trusting the Great Physician, I maintain, meant embracing distinctive definitions of illness, health, and recovery that invoked a classic and thoroughly paradoxical understanding of the relationship between divine power and human activity in the curative process. Insisting that healing involved both receptivity and exertion, I contend, represented a strategy for negotiating various late-nineteenth-century cultural conundrums, including an increasingly contentious set of gender ideals.

Chapters four, five, and six depart from a chronological narrative in order to examine the particular ritual behaviors, institutional settings, and social agendas that advocates of divine healing espoused over the course of the 1870s and 1880s—the decades during which the movement formed and flourished. In chapter four, I argue that faith cure entailed not only physical restoration and spiritual transformation but also a reformation of the mental faculties. Practices such as contemplative prayer, laying on of hands, and anointing, I contend, provided a ritual framework that helped to facilitate the process of epistemological reorientation. "Faith homes" are the primary topic of chapter five, which investigates how proponents of divine healing created sacred spaces in which suffering individuals could enact a separation from the skepticism and sensuality of the surrounding culture in order to embrace the teachings and practice of faith cure. As criticism of the movement intensified in the 1880s, "houses of healing" became increasingly important sites for defining the doctrines and defending the methods of faith cure as well as for differentiating divine healing from competing forms of therapy. Finally, chapter six traces the links between individual bodily healing and evangelical efforts to reform society and evangelize the nations. The devotional ethic that encouraged the sick and weary to get out of bed also required them to engage in some form of active service of God. For many individuals, divine healing served as an apt analogy for envisioning and attempting to achieve a reformation that would spread outward from the individual to church, city, society, and ultimately, to the world.

As many historians of divine healing have suggested, the emergence of separatist Holiness groups in the 1890s and the birth of Pentecostalism at the turn of the twentieth century, among other factors, such as the increasingly widespread acceptance of biblical criticism and the passage of stricter public health and medical licensing legislation, fundamentally reshaped faith cure's theology, practice, and demographics. For this reason, the early 1890s provide a logical end point for my study. Although I briefly consider the ways in which divine healing changed as the result of its encounter with Pentecostalism in the conclusion, a fuller historical account of this transformation is ultimately beyond the scope of this study, which is more concerned with exploring divine healing as devotional practice than with charting change over time.[35]

Throughout the course of my research, many people have asked my views on the reality of divine healing. Do I believe that God miraculously cured individuals like Lucy Drake? Can I quantify how many of the petitioners who sought relief from the Great Physician were "actually" restored to health? Did persons such as Jennie Smith suffer from real—meaning organic rather than psychogenic—diseases, and were the recoveries they claimed to experience "genuine"? These inquiries reflect a range of assumptions, concerns, motivations, and anxieties that have been shaped by the contemporary political, social, and religious context. In recent decades, debate about the relationship between faith and healing has intensified as both medical researchers and religious believers from a variety of traditions have posited that "spirituality" is positively correlated with physical, mental, and emotional well-being. Studies intended to assess the value of contemplative practices for coping with pain or to test efficacy of petitionary prayer for curing bodily illness have fostered vigorous and often contentious deliberations among scientists, theologians, ethicists, medical professionals, and lay persons. While some have welcomed these efforts to enumerate the connections between religion and health, others have viewed such experiments with unease or even alarm. Some detractors complain that both the questions posed and the techniques employed in these studies are insufficiently scientific. Others worry that applying empirical methods to matters of faith violates the ineffable character of religion. Still others protest that the definitions of "spirituality" employed in most research efforts mask significant theological distinctions among religious traditions and in so doing fail to take into account the particular ways in which people of different faiths interpret illness and respond to bodily discomfort.[36]

In any case, the passion and consternation that characterize current discussions about the intersections among religious belief, medical science, and the therapeutic process suggest that the experiences of sickness and suffering continue to vex contemporary believers and nonbelievers alike. Despite, or perhaps because of, the fact that numerous technological advances have helped assuage some kinds of corporeal affliction, the question of how to comprehend and cope with pain remains an extremely controversial subject in contemporary North America. Contests over issues such as elder care, euthanasia, abortion, and stem cell research reveal how deeply Americans care about these matters and how divided they are about the meaning of suffering and the proper manner of dealing with disease, infirmity, and physical distress.

By scrutinizing the politics of sickness, health, and healing during an earlier period of American history, I aim to place current conversations about the relationship between religious faith and physical well-being in broader perspective and to provide a wider frame for thinking about the ethical and spiritual implications of bodily suffering. Although I understand the concerns that have prompted so many individuals to ask questions about the authenticity of faith cures, I do not believe that I am competent to judge these matters. As a historian, I am acutely sensitive to the dangers of retrospectively diagnosing a person's physical condition or spiritual state. If doctors who employ the latest tools of medical technology admit the difficulties of evaluating their patients' pathologies, how could I, or anyone, for that matter, possibly deduce the nature of Jennie Smith's maladies or the legitimacy of Lucy Drake's cure? Drawing conclusions about the explanation for these recoveries—whether or not they were supernatural acts of God—seems an equally dubious venture. Such determinations are, in my view, matters of faith upon which the historian should not presume to opine.[37]

While I refrain from speculating about the miraculous character of divine healing, I do marvel at the extraordinary transformations that many women and men underwent when they put their faith in the Great Physician. Clearly, something happened the night that Jennie Smith asked the Lord to heal her: a woman who had been bedridden for almost two decades arose and walked. For the next half-century, she traversed the country, tirelessly sharing the "good news" of the gospel and avidly working to reform the conditions that tempted "sinners" to stray. As a Christian believer myself, I am open to the possibility that God heard and answered Smith's prayer. I am aware, however, that many readers will not share my sympathies, and I hope that I have presented Smith's story and those of others who claimed to have received divine healing in a way that allows for multiple, even competing interpretations.

I also hope that my analysis of how people in the past dealt with the dilemmas of pain and illness will encourage readers to reflect upon the kind of issues—theological, cultural, and social—that come into play when questions about the purpose of suffering and the possibility of healing are being contested. Who stands to gain as the result of efforts to resolve these conundrums? What might others lose? As I perused hundreds of testimonials proclaiming the faithfulness of the Great Physician, I could not help feeling inspired when I came across accounts like Jennie Smith's or Lucy Drake's—narratives that recounted remarkable rejuvenations of bodies and souls; tales of men and women (but especially women) who had resigned themselves to life-long invalidism suddenly able to abandon their sickbeds and to engage actively in the recreation of their worlds. But faith cure was not always so unambiguously empowering. Sometimes sick persons who prayed for healing were left waiting, wondering why relief did not come. Although some of these individuals continued to exercise faith in the midst of uncertainty, others felt abandoned by the Great Physician or disheartened that the "failure" was somehow their fault. Because so many apologists for divine healing suggested that health was an integral part of the gospel, they too struggled to make sense of prayers that seemed to go unanswered. Within this context, chronic illness or infirmity became increasingly problematic. Once able-bodied activity replaced passive resignation as the norm for Christian life, intractable invalidism was either a bewildering puzzle that cast doubt on God's promises or an embarrassing indictment of a person's faith and character. So divine healing had a dark side too: in addition to enabling many individuals to overcome debilitating diseases, faith cure suggested that sick persons were somehow responsible for their condition and therefore suspect. Rather than risking God's reputation or their own, many chose to suffer their pain silently or to hide it all together.

Certainly, proponents of divine healing never intended to stigmatize suffering,

and they often worked hard to undo the inadvertent repercussions of their theology and practice. Even so, it seems fair to suggest that faith cure helped foster
disparaging attitudes toward the body in pain that have persisted throughout the
twentieth and twenty-first centuries. Invalids often occupy a precarious position
in the moral imagination and social reality of Anglo-American Protestant culture;
and while I do not mean to imply that divine healing is entirely or even chiefly to
blame for this fact, I do believe that it is important to recognize both the positive
and negative ways in which the devotional ethics of faith cure have influenced the
perception and treatment of infirmity and illness. Promoting a greater consciousness of how religious beliefs and practices have shaped contemporary perspectives
on sickness and health will, I hope, encourage honest and constructive conversations about the politics of pain, the history of medical ethics, and the significance
of suffering and healing in American history and culture.[38]

CHAPTER ONE

A Thorn in the Flesh

Pain, Illness, and Religion in Mid-Nineteenth-Century America

On the night of October 18, 1842, twenty-one-year-old Mary Rankin was lying in bed, surrounded by a small group of physicians and friends. After binding a tourniquet around her leg, Rankin's surgeon, Dr. J. Christy, commanded her to "brace every nerve" as he was prepared to amputate. Having refused any kind of analgesics to dull the pain, including the opiates and wine that her doctors had offered, Rankin felt the initial incision with acute clarity. "My first impulse after the introduction of the knife," she later recalled, "was, '*I cannot endure it; I* will tell them to desist.'" But Rankin did not speak; in fact, she was told afterward that she moaned only once in the twelve minutes it took the surgeon to sever her limb from the rest of her body. Fully conscious for every cut, Rankin retained her composure even as she heard the sawing of the bone.[1]

Reflecting on the ordeal, Rankin refrained from describing the pain she experienced during the surgery—"To be known," she remarked, "it must be felt!" Instead, she explained how it was that she found herself able to tolerate the experience. When tempted to cry out in agony or beg the surgeon to stop, Rankin instead "felt a sweet sinking into the will of Providence. Never did I realize more powerfully the fulfillment of that blessed promise, 'My grace shall be sufficient for thee.' His arms of love were underneath me, and by them I was upheld in this trying moment." Refusing to accept any credit for the manner in which she bore the operation, Rankin averred that she had remained utterly passive in the process, relying entirely on

God's grace to sustain her. "'Not unto me, not unto me,'" she insisted, "but unto God be all the praise for enabling me to endure it."[2]

Like many Protestants of her generation, Rankin believed that patient resignation represented the proper Christian response to physical pain. In her aptly titled autobiography, *The Daughter of Affliction: A Memoir of the Protracted Sufferings and Religious Experience of Miss Mary Rankin,* first published in 1858, Rankin recounted her unflagging efforts to conform to the ideal of passive forbearance as she suffered a wide assortment of bodily ailments and endured an eclectic array of remedial yet frequently painful therapies. This chapter explores how mid-nineteenth-century Protestants like Rankin drew upon various theological, scientific, and cultural discourses in their efforts to understand the significance of suffering in the Christian life. Rankin's meditations on the theological meaning of pain, for example, reflect her indebtedness to a particular version of the Reformed tradition, and especially to a theodicy that interpreted corporeal affliction as a blessing permitted, even ordained, by divine providence. Since bodily suffering was good for the soul, Rankin surmised, then pain and illness ought to be accepted with thanksgiving and endured with equanimity. Rankin's encounter with the medical therapeutics of the mid-nineteenth century reinforced her perception of pain as a salutary force. Within the province of medical practice, pain was often construed as a positive indicator of therapeutic progress. To suffer discomfort at the hands of a physician or as the result of his prescriptions was to be confident that one was actively moving toward the goal of physical health. Finally, Rankin's experience as a woman who came of age during the heyday of the "domestic ideology" undoubtedly encouraged her to interpret pain as spiritually fruitful and to embrace a devotional ethic that demanded silence and submission in the face of affliction. An exploration of the relationship between gender norms and Protestant responses to pain in this period also helps to explain why women like Rankin served as the primary exemplars of passive resignation and to elucidate the distinctive ways that the ideal of sanctified suffering worked in the spiritual practice of both women and men.

Bodily Illness, Heroic Therapy, and Afflictive Providence

Rankin was no stranger to suffering when she submitted to the surgeon's knife in the autumn of her twenty-first year. Born in Huntington County, Pennsylvania, to "humble but respectable parents," Rankin's early childhood was marked by sickness and loss. Her father died when she was very young, leaving her mother to support a family of seven children. When she was eight years old, Rankin was sent away from home to board with another family, in whose household she remained for six years. Around the age of fourteen, Rankin stepped on a white thorn that penetrated the joint of her small toe. Despite "all the efforts of surgery and medical skill" applied to her case, the thorn festered in Rankin's flesh, eventually causing her foot and limb to contract painfully. The injury also irritated her nervous system, which was "of the most sensitive character," resulting in debilitating spasms. Gradually at first, but then more rapidly, Rankin's health declined until she had to be sent home to be cared for by her mother. Soon she became "permanently confined" to her bed with multiple ailments.[3]

From the onset of her illness, Rankin sought help from a number of physicians, some of whom called her case "hopeless" and admitted that they could do nothing for her. Other, more enterprising doctors hoped that by healing such a "singular" case, they might make reputations for themselves and achieve the eminence that was so difficult to obtain in the crowded, competitive, and often unprofitable medical marketplace of the antebellum era. One such practitioner, a Dr. Greene, pronounced Rankin's disease "nothing more nor less than inflammation of the spine," and prescribed a series of treatments premised on a set of widely held assumptions about bodily illness and health. "For more than a year," Rankin recalled, "I had to endure the excruciating process of blistering, cupping, scarifying, cauterizing, and setons, of which he introduced no less than ten along the region of the spine."[4]

As medical historian Charles Rosenberg has explained, early-nineteenth-century physicians and lay persons shared certain common understandings of the body and its functions that helped to promote and sustain a system of aggressive or "heroic" therapeutics characterized by the prescription of painful remedies such as those Dr. Greene ordered. First, the body was viewed holistically, as a system in which "every part . . . was related inevitably and inextricably with every other." The thorn embedded in the flesh of Rankin's little toe could thus agitate her nervous system, irritate her spine, and inflame her liver. Such a local injury was presumed to promote systemic derangement, so that Rankin's whole body was thought to be diseased. Second, the body was believed to be a closed system with only a finite amount of energy. As Rosenberg put it, "The body was seen as a system of intake and outgo—a system which had, necessarily, to remain in balance if the individual were to remain healthy. . . . Equilibrium was synonymous with health, disequilibrium with illness."[5]

Prior to the nineteenth century, most medical theorists had argued that "disease could result from either an excess or a deficiency of some bodily elements." In this view, "the physician's most potent weapon was his ability to 'regulate the secretions'—to extract blood, to promote the perspiration, or the urination, or defeca-

Mary Rankin, c. 1858. Frontispiece to *The Daughter of Affliction: A Memoir of the Protracted Sufferings and Religious Experience of Miss Mary Rankin* (1871). Reproduced by permission of the United Brethren Historical Center, Huntington University, Huntington, Indiana.

tion which attested to his having helped the body to regain its customary equilibrium." Accordingly, remedies were designed either to stimulate a debilitated system or, more commonly, to deplete a body suffering from some sort of overabundance. This second approach was actively promoted by the influential Philadelphian physician Benjamin Rush around the beginning of the nineteenth century. Rejecting the theories of his predecessors, Rush maintained that the imbalances that led to illness were always the result of excess nervous energy. Based on this understanding of disease, Rush believed that equilibrium was restored exclusively through the application of "depletive" therapies such as bleeding, purging, sweating, and salivating. Rush was also of the mind that, as historian Martin Pernick has put it, "the efficacy of a remedy was proportional to its impact on the body. . . Rush therefore prescribed the depletive remedies until they produced 'heroic' results: repeated massive bloodlettings, to or beyond a state of collapse; calomel till the gums hemorrhaged."[6]

Although Rush's system was strenuously challenged in the 1830s by both "regular," or "orthodox" physicians—those who relied primarily on observational techniques and invasive or chemical therapies to diagnose and treat disease—and by various health reform movements, Mary Rankin's experience at the hands of Dr.

Greene, among other evidence, reveals that many physicians continued to employ heroic methods well into the latter half of the nineteenth century. Excruciating treatments like those Rankin underwent remained popular among physicians and acceptable to patients in this period in part because, as Rosenberg and others have argued, they appeared to work. Since doctors relied almost solely on their senses in diagnosing disease and charting a patient's prognosis, they were attracted to therapies that produced "visible and predictable physiological effects." When Dr. Greene broke the surface of Rankin's skin with his scarificator or lancet and applied his "doctor's sucking glass"—a glass cup that had been heated over a hot torch—to her lacerated flesh in order to siphon her blood more effectively, he was taking action that generated obvious and consistent results that he could see. He also would have assumed that the external effects of his treatments—the bruise and burn marks left from the incisions and the cups, as well as the amounts of blood drawn—provided ample evidence of corresponding internal changes that would bring Rankin's system back into balance.[7]

In addition to assuring physicians that their prescriptions were effective, the drastic effects produced by heroic therapies also served to demonstrate to patients and their families that the doctor was actively striving to combat the patient's disease. Since patients and physicians shared an understanding of how the body worked, Rankin would have viewed Dr. Greene's attempts to regulate her secretions as an appropriate means for restoring her body's equilibrium and therefore her health. Pain, in this context, offered proof that the physician was doing his job and confirmation that the body was responding as it should. Because "insensibility" was so frequently thought to herald impending death, many individuals—doctors and patients alike—assumed that pain was a vital sign of life. According to this logic, the experience of acute physical discomfort signaled that a person was on the road to recovery. Similarly, painful remedies were thought to aid in the process of healing by stimulating the patient's system. Patients assented to heroic therapeutics because the pain these procedures produced inspired confidence that the flesh was being affected for the better.[8]

Unfortunately for Rankin, Dr. Greene's treatments did not generate the desired results. After fifteen months, all the blood-letting and burning "appeared of no avail." Despite the obvious sensory and painful effects of these therapies, Rankin's overall condition did not seem to improve. Lacking any lasting evidence of recuperation, Greene gave up the case, leaving Rankin with multiple scars but without any real relief. About two years later, in June of 1842, Rankin resorted to another round of heroic therapy, this time turning to "mercurial medicines." The widespread popularity of toxic drugs such as antimony, arsenic, and especially calomel (mercurous chloride), a powerful purgative that, if taken in substantial or frequent doses, caused violent diarrhea followed by involuntary salivation, has been well documented by medical historians, one of whom has dubbed this period "the poisoning century." Like blistering and bleeding, drugs were thought "to modify the body's ongoing efforts to maintain or restore a health-defining equilibrium." And, like other kinds of heroic remedies, the administration of emetics, cathartics, and diuretics produced obvious physiological results that confirmed their efficacy for practitioners and patients alike. After quaffing a large draught of one such medicine, for example, Rankin's throat and tongue became so swollen that she could scarcely swallow. Since the mercury did seem to help her paralysis, however, her physician "thought it was of some benefit" and continued to administer the medication along with "opiates" to quiet her nerves. But rather than calming her, these drugs only caused Ranking greater irritation. Looking back on this experience, Rankin thanked God for the "peculiar providence" that enabled her body to reject these narcotic medicines. "I trust I fully appreciate the motives of my physician," she remarked, "but had these opiates produced their desired effect, they would more than likely have been administered to such an extent as to render my mind imbecile and unfit for future mental effort."[9]

Trust her physician's intentions though she might, Rankin's comments suggest that she harbored some doubts about his prescriptions. Throughout her memoir, in fact, Rankin recalls her reluctance to undergo the treatments her various doctors ordered. When she initially heard the course of therapy Dr. Greene recommended, Rankin resisted, consenting only "after a great deal of persuasion." After she began to suffer spasms, another "strange physician," a Dr. Burnet, proposed to cauterize her injured toe. Again, Rankin "objected" until her family physician convinced her that allowing acid to eat away at her diseased flesh might bring her some relief. Finally, when this and all other remedies seemed to have failed, Rankin's physicians concluded that amputation of her leg was the only remaining option. When they informed her of their opinion, she flatly refused to consider the operation. "*No! no! rather let me die. You shall never amputate my limb!*" she cried. No amount of argument from physicians, friends, or family could sway her. Even when the surgeon insisted that amputation was her "only hope" and threatened to leave without helping her in any other way, Rankin refused to be budged. "*I can not submit,*" she replied.[10]

But eventually Rankin did acquiesce to the amputation, just as she had agreed to try all of the other torturous therapies her physicians prescribed. For in Rankin's view, something more than physical suffering was at stake in her struggle to reconcile herself to her physicians' recommendations. Submission to the doctors' orders was not just a means for pursuing bodily health, it was also a matter of spiritual scruples. As a member of the United Brethren in Christ, a Reformed church influenced by pietistic revivalism and Methodism, which she had joined soon after her injury, Rankin learned to interpret her sufferings as afflictions sent by God for her own advantage as well as for the good of others. "Often when reflecting on the providence of God in afflicting his people," Rankin wrote, "I have thought of how very necessary these afflictions are, which at times we are so unwilling to bear; for they serve to remind us that here is not our home." Placing her own injury in this perspective, Rankin described the thorn in her flesh as "the external means of separating my heart fully from the world, and uniting it to Christ." Without it, she insisted, "I might have become vain and forgetful of God."[11]

When an apparently well-meaning friend challenged Rankin's theological views, suggesting that her suffering was the result of "an accidental *injury*," Rankin responded with incredulity. "Can it be that you are not a believer in the *afflicting providence of God?*" she queried her friend. "There is no doctrine I think more clearly taught in the Bible than this." Rankin went on to explain why this conviction was so compelling for her. "Could I believe that all which I have been made to suffer was merely in consequence of having violated a physical or organic law, (and not as directed by an unerring Providence for some wise purpose)," she wrote, "I would then also believe God had dealt unjustly with me." Believing that God ordained her afflictions enabled Rankin to trust that her suffering was meaningful. Without that hope, she explained to her friend, she would lose her faith in God's goodness. And losing the faith that provided her with an explanatory framework for her experiences was a theological crisis that she was simply unwilling to endure.[12]

Instead, Rankin embraced the doctrine of God's providence with passionate and persistent fervor, disciplining herself to accept afflictions with equanimity. "Although his providence has often appeared mysterious to me, and his ways past finding out," she stated, "I have endeavored to submit to the severe stroke of his unseen hand with Christian resignation and patience." At times, she admitted, acquiescing to God's designs proved difficult. Once, when a physician "proposed to introduce a seton," Rankin confessed that she "felt almost unwilling to submit" and could scarcely suppress her tears. "For a moment it seemed as if I were called not only to suffer in every possible way from disease, but also from the means resorted to for my relief," she remarked. Troubled by these circumstances, Rankin began to question: "Why have *I* to suffer more than appears to fall to the common lot of mankind? Is it because I am a more rebellious child than others, that it requires such means to keep me humble?" But to continue along this line of inquiry threatened to undermine her faith, so Rankin quickly pulled herself back by focusing her thoughts, not on her doubts, but on the promises of scripture. As she meditated on Jesus' words—"What thou knowest not now thou shalt know hereafter"—Rankin was "filled with an unusual comfort" and "felt calmly to sink into His will."[13]

To lose her own will in God's was Rankin's greatest solace in suffering and the highest goal of her spiritual life. Rather than rebelling against doctors who proposed painful remedies or railing against circumstances that seemed unfair, Rankin strove to adopt an obedient pose. After twenty years of practicing patient resignation, Rankin wrote in her journal, "I feel to say, come life, come death, come what may, *I can bow in humble submission, and gently kiss the rod that smites me,* knowing full well that it is directed by a Father's hand, and trusting in Him who said that 'all things work together for good to them that love the Lord.'" Afflictions, Rankin affirmed, were not only to be accepted but to be cherished, for they brought blessing both to the sufferer and to others. Throughout her testimony, in fact, Rankin linked "excruciating pain" with "exquisite" religious enjoyments. "During my severest pain and suffering I frequently realized the greatest joys and richest blessings," she declared. Once, when enduring an attack of "inflammatory disease," Rankin experienced "hights [*sic*] and depths in the love of God, to which I had hitherto been a stranger." Recounting the rapture, she wrote: "I lay for several hours in an unconscious state, at least so far as all around me was concerned. But to my spiritual vision was disclosed heaven with its weight of glory. I have no suitable language with which to describe the glories of that place which mortal eye hath not seen nor ear heard, and which have never entered into the heart of man to conceive." Such ecstatic, visionary spiritual experiences, Rankin believed, were the fruits of affliction—gifts of God available through patient endurance of intense physical pain.[14]

Many of Rankin's physicians, ministers, and friends affirmed her interpretations of her experiences and held her up as a kind of spiritual virtuoso. Mrs. M. V. Snyder, a friend of Rankin's and the wife of a missionary to Kansas, commended Rankin for enduring all her afflictions with "submission and patience." Snyder was especially impressed with Rankin's attitude toward physical suffering. "She . . . has so long experienced the spiritual benefit resulting from sanctified pain," Snyder noted, "that she seems rather to enjoy it, and turn it into occasions of thanksgiving and praise, than otherwise." The six physicians and fourteen ministers representing four different denominations who signed the "testimonial" endorsing Rankin's book also praised her fortitude in the face of affliction and suggested a close causal connection between her "almost unparalleled sufferings" and "the remarkable communications of divine grace" she had experienced over the course of her invalidism.[15]

Rankin's admirers also corroborated her efforts to make herself "useful"—a desire that she expressed frequently in her journal entries and correspondence, and one that echoed a broader evangelical discourse that stressed the responsibility of each Christian to exercise all of her available energies, faculties, and resources to exert a sanctifying influence on other individuals, on the culture, and even on the world. In a letter to a friend dated April 1859, Rankin articulated her belief in the priesthood of all believers and the corollary conviction that "in the economy of grace all have a purpose to fill; and there is no situation in life in which we can be placed in which we can not glorify God if we strive to do so." Bedridden though she might be, Rankin believed that she could serve God acceptably by demonstrating her faith in Christ to others through her attitude toward suffering. Capitalizing on the abiding tradition of Christian hagiography and auto-hagiography, a textual form that became increasingly abundant with the expansion of evangelical publishing in the nineteenth century, Rankin agreed to publish her memoirs in order to reach the widest possible audience with her message. "I had a great desire to be useful in some way," she explained, "and this appeared to be the only way in which I could likely accomplish that laudable end." Supporting Rankin in her endeavor, the twenty testimonial-signers called her book both "interesting"—a term that nineteenth-century evangelicals used to indicate a text's ability to rouse pious emotions and inspire holy actions—and "useful," recommending it "to all Christians, as a monument of God's faithfulness and as a solace in the hour of affliction."[16]

Sanctified Suffering in Historical Perspective

The link between bodily suffering and spiritual blessing that Rankin embodied and her admirers endorsed has deep roots in the Christian scriptures and tradition. Although the Bible itself is ambivalent about the meaning and nature of pain (contrary to popular perception, for example, the book of Job treats suffering as an enemy sent by the devil rather than as a gift of God), Christians throughout the centuries have often exalted physical affliction as a means for imitating Jesus—the suffering servant, who through his pain brought healing and reconciliation between God and humanity. The martyrs of the early church have frequently been commended for enduring horrible tortures at the hands of their imperial persecutors and thereby emulating the passion of Christ. In the hands of medieval hagiographers, such identification with Jesus' sufferings signified a person's sanctity and often secured her candidacy for sainthood. Many medieval mystics believed that meditating on Christ's wounds, or experiencing these torments in one's own flesh—whether through feats of asceticism and self-flagellation or through receiving the stigmata—offered means for entering into closer communion with God.[17]

Although sixteenth-century reformers like Martin Luther and John Calvin contested models of sanctity that stressed corporeal mortification as a strategy for achieving mystical contemplation, insisting instead that union with God was a gift of grace offered through Christ's death on the cross rather than a prize to be won as the result of human endeavor, their emphasis on God's sovereignty and the corollary doctrine of divine providence assured that physical illness and bodily injury retained a crucial role within Protestant spirituality. According to the theological framework articulated in the works of Calvin and his followers, especially, all manner of suffering, including somatic pain, represented God-given occasions for weaning the affections from the snares of earthly existence, for purifying the sinful impulses of the flesh, and for learning the lessons of self-denial and submission to the divine will that led to personal holiness. Additionally, because Protestant reformers rejected the monastic ideal of withdrawal from the world and relocated the spiritual life from the cloister to the household, they broadened the types of experiences that could contribute to an individual's sanctification. The ordinary trials of everyday life, including the disappointments and sufferings associated with sickness and disease, offered opportunities for imitating Christ through the practice of patient acquiescence to the fiats of divine providence.[18]

As part of their continuing efforts to reform Christian theology and spiritual practice, Protestants began to develop their own hagiographical canon. Texts like John Foxe's *Book of Martyrs* (1563), which memorialized the English Protestants executed during the reign of Catholic Mary Tudor as well as the martyrs of the early church, emphasized the ability of all individuals—not just cloistered or clerical saints—to imitate Christ through the faithful endurance of trial and affliction. For the Protestant who sought instruction on how to cope with ongoing earthly tribulations of various types, John Bunyan composed his spiritual autobiography, *Grace Abounding to the Chief of Sinners* (1666), and later his classic allegory of the Christian life, *The Pilgrim's Progress from This World to That Which is to Come* (1678). Throughout the seventeenth and eighteenth centuries, authors such as Richard Baxter, Cotton Mather, Jonathan Edwards, and John Wesley, to name just a few, added to the growing body of hagiographies, memoirs, and autobiographies intended to provide believers with appropriate models for sanctity, and particularly for perseverance in the face of divinely sanctioned hardships and distress.[19]

Encounters with native Americans fueled the production of missionary memoirs such as Jonathan Edwards' *Life of David Brainerd* (1749), a specialized genre of Protestant hagiography that became increasingly popular in the nineteenth century as the passion for foreign missions spread among American and British evangelicals. The "labors, suffering, and death" of Adoniram Judson and of his

wife, Ann Hasseltine Judson, who were among the first American foreign missionaries, were memorialized in numerous biographies, beginning with the *Memoir of
Mrs. Ann H. Judson* (1829), a book that went through ten editions in nine years
and was "universally known," according to Lydia Maria Child, within four years of
its initial publication. The popularity of this work demonstrates the growing tendency among nineteenth-century evangelicals to lionize pious women, in addition
to male ministers like Bunyan and Brainerd. While Protestants had always included
women among the "saints" that they honored in funeral sermons, memoirs, and
martyr stories, accounts of the holy lives, arduous ordeals, and triumphant deaths
of female "worthies" like Ann Judson became increasingly common in the early
decades of the nineteenth century.[20]

Drawing upon the longer tradition of Protestant hagiography and the more recent focus on female sanctity, Mary Rankin's text was both a classic expression of
Protestant piety that shared some aims and attributes of abiding works such as *The
Life of David Brainerd* and a distinctive product of nineteenth-century sensibilities. Like most Protestant hagiographies, *The Daughter of Affliction* emphasized the
importance of suffering as a means provided by God for personal sanctification.
The particular kinds of trial that Rankin encountered and the manner in which
she bore her tribulations, however, distinguish her story from both standard tales
of Protestant martyrdom and popular biographies of evangelical missionaries. Although David Brainerd was commended for "his humility, his self-denial, his perseverance," especially in the face of disappointments in his work, bouts of physical
sickness, and periods of mental depression, for example, he did not suffer from the
kind of protracted invalidism that marked Mary Rankin's life. When Brainerd did
fall ill, he struggled against his sickness, lamenting the fact that physical prostration
kept him from his evangelistic tasks and deprived his Indian converts of his pastoral ministrations. While he thoroughly accepted the doctrine of divine providence
and acknowledged that contentment was a proper response to bodily affliction,
Brainerd's zeal for missionary endeavor complicated this ideal. Sickness, in other
words, was not the hallmark of Brainerd's sanctity.[21]

Similarly, although Ann Judson suffered from various illnesses and ultimately
succumbed to death as the result of "the weakness of her constitution, occasioned
by the severe privations and long protracted sufferings which she endured" during
her missionary career in Burma, she was revered by her contemporaries not only
for the "meekness, patience, magnanimity and Christian fortitude" with which she
bore her physical ailments, but also for the "genius and heroism and piety" she dis-
played as she negotiated with Burmese authorities for her husband's release from
prison, for her courageous work among and on behalf of Burmese women, and for

her bravery and self-sacrifice in leaving the comforts of home to labor in a foreign land. While Judson's endurance of bodily affliction was a estimable practice worthy of emulation, forbearance of physical illness and discomfort represented only one of the many occasions for the development of holiness and the display of Christian character that she encountered.[22]

For Mary Rankin, on the other hand, pain was the primary reality and the principal means of her sanctification. In this way, the model of sanctified suffering that Rankin promoted in her book and strove to embody in her life was not altogether unlike the somatic piety of certain medieval saints. In particular, Rankin's tendency to link the endurance of severe physical pain with the enjoyment of ecstatic visionary states is evocative of the experiences described in hagiographies of late-medieval mystics such as the *vita* of Beatrice of Nazareth (1200–1268), James of Vitry's life of Mary of Oignes (1176–1213), or Raymond of Capua's biography of Catherine of Siena (1347–138), *Legenda Major*. Sanctity, in these works, is explicitly connected with the experience of intense bodily suffering, which was understood to be a sign of an individual's identification with Christ.[23]

By the fourteenth century, a specific type of physical suffering—corporeal illness—marked the lives of an increasing number of mystics. In one of the major auto-hagiographies of this period, for example, the Dominican nun Margaret Ebner (1291–1351) suggested that sickness served as the stimulus for deeper mystical experience and interpreted invalidism as a sign of God's favor. The connection between somatic infirmity and sanctity was especially compelling in cases of female mysticism, for the long-standing tendency to associate "woman" with body, flesh, and physicality fueled a corollary assumption about women's distinctive ability to imitate Christ through corporal suffering. While experiences of sickness and pain often featured in the lives of late-medieval men, "there is no question," historian Caroline Walker Bynum has argued, that physical suffering was "more prominent" in hagiographical depictions of women's religiosity. As late-medieval theology grew increasingly concerned with the centrality of Christ's humanity, and particularly with his physical nature and his material body, women gained the opportunity to serve as spiritual virtuosi who bore the burden of imitating Christ through a literal identification with his bodily sufferings. Within this context, Bynum has written, "patient suffering of disease or injury was a major way of gaining sanctity for females but not for males." Through their endurance of illness and other forms of somatic pain, late-medieval women attained sanctification and achieved more intense experiences of mystical union with God. By suffering in the flesh, as Christ himself had suffered, female invalids also incarnated the divine presence for their contemporaries. The "sensibly marked" bodies of female saints, as historian Amy

Hollywood has put it, served as signs of "Christ's presence on earth"; a woman's wounded flesh made the "divine presence" visible.[24]

While vast temporal, theological, and cultural chasms separate Mary Rankin's experiences from those of her late-medieval forerunners, highlighting the gendered assumptions that influenced ideals of sanctity and shaped cultural norms regarding the place of pain in the spiritual life during the late Middle Ages helps shed light on an analogous process of cultural prescription, also driven by gendered notions of selfhood, at work in the mid-nineteenth century. During the early decades of the 1800s, a potent complex of ideas about the fundamental nature of "manhood" and "womanhood," and a related collection of regulations regarding the social and spiritual roles of women and men began to hold sway among increasing numbers of Anglo-American Protestants (and others). By parsing human nature into constituent categories, posing fundamental dualisms between these separate parts of the self—head/heart, intellect/affections, reason/emotions, mind/body—for example, and associating men and women with opposite sides of these dyads, many Protestants in this period, like their medieval predecessors, contributed to the development of a deeply gendered somatic piety that linked female sanctity with passive forbearance of physical suffering.

Female Invalidism and the Gendering of Somatic Piety in Nineteenth-Century America

Mary Rankin's status as a spiritual virtuoso whose patient resignation to the afflictive providence of God resulted in religious raptures and marked her as a kind of Protestant saint worthy of esteem and emulation drew support from several prominent assumptions about women and their relationship to society that were extremely influential in the early nineteenth century. Driven in part by the shift from an agricultural to an industrial economy in which men increasingly worked outside the home and women were charged with the education of children, the "doctrine of separate spheres" insisted that the public domain was the province of men, while the domestic sphere was woman's place.

This division between the public world of affairs and the private realm of the home contained within it another important supposition: that a properly ordered household served as the model for the good society. The "cult of domesticity" upheld the home as the seat of religion, virtue, and morality. Within this private domestic arena, women were called upon to exercise their moral influence upon family members, servants, and guests. Through their influence within the home, promoters of this ideology asserted, women had the power to transform individual character and even public culture. This conception of women's mission rested on a third assumption about woman's nature. According to the "cult of true woman-hood," woman's "natural" dependence and weakness were signs of her moral purity and spiritual superiority. Women, in this view, were inherently more attuned to the emotions, to the sentiments of the heart, and especially to religion. Because of their heightened sensitivity to affections and to spiritual realities, women were more ca-pable of redeeming individuals and society through their virtuous examples.[25]

While these ideas were not entirely new in the early nineteenth century, they took on a particular force in this period as they were combined into a "domestic ideology" that established a prevailing set of norms and expectations for and about women's nature and roles within society. The domestic ideology also stipulated a corresponding collection of assumptions and prescriptions about manhood and proper male behavior. Whereas women were thought to be inherently dependent, submissive, passive, and self-sacrificing, men were supposed to be essentially au-tonomous, assertive, active, and self-interested. Because of male participation in the public domain, white middle-class masculinity, in particular, was associated with ambition, competition, and production, qualities a man needed to possess and exercise in order to succeed in the ruthless arenas of republican politics and entrepreneurial capitalism. Although early-nineteenth-century Protestants recog-nized the importance of "manly passions" for economic advancement and political achievement, they simultaneously condemned these characteristics as signs of a corrupt and sinful nature. Unless male aggression and avarice were appropriately channeled through the discipline of self-mastery, they might wreak havoc with the social order. In order to contain the potentially destructive possibilities of mas-culine passions, the domestic ideology dictated that men's selfish impulses were subject to the chastening influence of female virtue within the home, and, as histo-rian Anthony Rotundo has put it, "symbolically quarantined by the separation of spheres." By segregating the public realm from the private, aspiring middle-class Protestants found a way to assuage the ambivalences associated with male passions and to achieve productivity without sacrificing social stability or pious morality.[26]

Like all dominant cultural dogmas, the domestic ideology provoked several competing interpretations among its contemporaries. Opponents such as aboli-tionists and early women's rights advocates Sarah and Angelina Grimke argued vehemently against the grounding assumptions that delineated male and female nature and isolated the public realm from the private sphere. In their view, the domestic ideology was a fiercely repressive social philosophy that created a false, unbiblical distinction between women and men, and undermined women's po-litical agency by circumscribing them within the home. Others insisted that the tenets of the domestic ideology—and particularly its claims about woman's superior moral nature—provided a platform for asserting that the future of American society was dependent upon the influence of women. The greatest spokesperson for this interpretation of the domestic ideology was Catharine Beecher, the eldest of Lyman and Roxanna Beecher's thirteen children and Harriet Beecher Stowe's older sister.[27]

In 1837, Beecher and the Grimke sisters engaged in a public, printed debate over woman's proper role in American society that continued for the better part of two years. In this dispute, Beecher challenged the Grimkes' interpretation of the domestic ideology as a philosophy that devalued women and denied them moral agency and political power by restricting their domain of influence to the home. In Beecher's view, the doctrine of separate spheres, the idea that the home is the ideal model for society, and the belief in the moral superiority of female nature offered women powerfully influential roles as agents of social and political change. She argued that it was precisely *because* women were restricted to the domestic arena that they could exercise a reforming influence on society. Against the corruption of the male-dominated political sphere, Beecher lifted up the home as a pure, moral realm—a place set apart that sheltered its inhabitants from the temptations of the world. Since women who remained in the private, domestic arena avoided the pollutions of the public domain—the vices of democratic politics and the materialism of capitalist economic culture—they were "uniquely qualified" to serve as mirrors to corrupt society and as stabilizing forces for the young nation. By cultivating their unique and superior moral sensibility within the domestic sphere, Beecher proclaimed, women would have a far-ranging influence beyond that arena.[28]

For Mary Rankin, the notion that the private realm could become a place of power offered a satisfying strategy for asserting agency and exercising influence, not despite, but precisely because of, her circumstances. Drawing upon the rhetoric of separate spheres but changing the language slightly to suit her situation, Rankin proposed a distinction between the arena of health, in which an individual was called to actively pursue God's will in the world, and the state of sickness, in which she was constrained to submit to the afflictions of divine providence within the confines of the sickroom. "Let our whole business in life to be to serve him acceptably, each in our different sphere," Rankin wrote to a friend in 1859. "If I bear patiently the afflictions he sees fit to lay on me, I may be said to suffer *passively* the will of my Father in heaven," she wrote to her healthy friend, "whilst you, in your more favored sphere, must do *actively* his will: and thus, by letting our lights shine others may be attracted to Christ, and we be made the happy instruments of bringing them to him."[29]

Rankin's admirers took her argument one step further, claiming both that her separation from everyday affairs heightened her purity and that her endurance of affliction increased her sanctity. As a woman who patiently bore excruciating pain within the cloistered arena of the home, Rankin embodied both the principles of the domestic ideology and the Christian ideal of suffering servanthood. Her influence, her devotees insisted, was potent and essential. "In an active sphere of life you might be ready to conclude she was made in vain, that her physical inability to act and the seclusion from duties would entirely cut off her influence for good," wrote Dr. Samuel M. Ross. "Not so, she has a circle of friends who feel that they can not properly estimate her worth; and that they cannot dispense with her counsels."[30]

As the years passed and Rankin's experiences became increasingly well known, people began to seek out her advice on spiritual matters. When Rankin had been bedridden for about twenty years, an "old gentleman" called to see her. "He had been for some time anxious to obtain that grace which (to adopt the language of Paul) would enable him to overcome 'those roots of bitterness which are continually springing up in the heart (such as anger, etc.),'" Rankin recalled, "and for this reason he had called to converse with me on the subject, believing that I had experienced those things for myself." By the 1850s, Rankin's former physician Dr. Hoffman was regularly requesting Rankin's prayers and asking for guidance about how to cope with his own difficulties. On account of her experiences with affliction and her secluded status, Rankin became a living saint from whom seekers garnered insight and understanding.[31]

If prevailing gender norms such as the cult of true womanhood and the doctrine of separate spheres promoted the perception that cloistered women like Rankin possessed extraordinary spiritual wisdom, medical discourse regarding women's health also helped to foster the notion that female bodies were especially suited to endure sanctified suffering because of their inherent weakness and sensitivity. While medical theories maintaining the comparative frailty of women were rooted in longstanding assumptions about the innate differences between female and male nature and physical strength, certain influential nineteenth-century physicians associated women's health primarily with the proper functioning of their reproductive systems and thus encouraged a growing tendency to see women as fundamentally prone to illness as the result of menstrual irregularity, or even of menstruation itself. A woman's "whole organism," wrote E. H. Dixon in his text *Woman and Her Diseases* (1847/55), is ruled by her uterus and will "respond to its slightest affectations." Positing an "intimate" relation between the reproductive organs and the nervous system, physicians like Dixon could attribute virtually any bodily or emotional ailment to some sort of uterine or ovarian malfunction. "Woman's reproductive organs are pre-eminent," wrote one physician in 1854. "They exercise a controlling influence upon her entire system, and entail upon her many painful and dangerous diseases. They are the source of her peculiarities, the centre of her sympathies, and the seat of her diseases. Everything that is peculiar to her, springs from her sexual organization." Hysteria, in particular, was linked both etiologically and diagnostically with women's anatomy, so that physicians increasingly came to understand the ever-more-endemic disease in gendered terms, as "'the natural state' in a female, a 'morbid state' in the male."[32]

While a woman's intrinsic physical frailty increased her vulnerability to disease, her essential weakness also heightened her capacity for feeling pain. Because women's nerves "are smaller" and "of a more delicate structure," one doctor explained, "they are endowed with greater sensibility." Another physician maintained that "a blow of equal force produces a more serious effect" on a woman than on a man "in consequence of her greater sensitiveness to external impressions." According to this logic, sensitivity to physical pain, like bodily weakness, was a feminine trait. "The female sex," wrote one physician in 1827, "is far more sensitive and susceptible than the male." Men, as members of the stronger sex, were less likely to feel corporal discomfort. The more robust a man was, the more impervious to pain he was thought to be. In this formulation, physical strength and sensitivity to pain were inversely related.[33]

Because female delicacy and sensitivity were imaginatively linked with moral authority and spiritual preeminence in this period, medical theories that stressed women's natural (and, indeed, inevitable) physical infirmity and sensibility encouraged the tendency to associate bodily suffering with female sanctity. Female invalids who, like Mary Rankin, passively endured painful corporal afflictions, were, in this view, particularly qualified to serve as exemplars of somatic piety. Male invalids, on the other hand, were rarely exalted as models of Protestant sainthood. Since sickness, submission, and sensitivity to suffering were culturally connected with femininity, patient forbearance of protracted illness (as opposed to stoic fortitude in the face of acute pain such as a battle injury or the "heroic" ministrations of a physician) was an emasculating behavior for men. The doctrine of separate spheres, which conferred upon men sole responsibility for providing for their families, also made invalidism impractical, especially for male members of the lower and middle classes who aspired to upward mobility. When men did fall ill, they could rarely afford long periods of convalescence. In accordance with the economic realities of men's status as heads of households, and also with ideals of manhood in the early nineteenth century that associated white middle-class men with vitality, reason, and self-mastery, physicians often encouraged sick men to take action in order to overcome their illnesses. Through energetic physical activity that required them to exercise will-power and self-control, men weakened by disease would replenish their "natural" strength and be refitted for their social roles. In some cases, of course, men were too sick to engage in vigorous forms of therapy and required rest in order to recuperate. But because such passivity contradicted cultural prescriptions for male behavior, men who were forced to adopt a recumbent posture for anything but a brief interlude seldom, if ever, received accolades for bearing their afflictions with patience. While memoirs of men who endured illness and persevered under trial certainly existed, works of this genre devoted to recounting the long-sufferings of invalid women were much more prevalent and well-known.[34]

The predominance of the saintly female invalid in works of popular fiction also reflected and abetted the propensity to uphold women as paragons of Christian piety who passively resigned themselves to the divine will (not to mention exemplary patients who always acquiesced to their doctors' prescriptions). Although male invalids are not absent from the cast of such nineteenth-century literary characters, women played the pious but sickly protagonist far more frequently than men. As numerous literary historians have observed, the creation of "a new aesthetic type—the delicate, sickly heroine" whose saintliness increased in proportion to her physical weakness—both expressed and endorsed the notion that ill-health was a marker of genteel femininity, moral superiority, and spiritual sanctity. Characters such as Nathaniel Hawthorne's Priscilla, the fragile heroine of *The Blithedale Romance* (1852), and perhaps most famously, Harriet Beecher Stowe's Evangeline St. Clare—Little Eva—of *Uncle Tom's Cabin* (1852), helped give rise to the literary "cult of female invalidism" and furthered the increasingly widespread perception that middle- and upper-class white women were inherently frail and, by virtue of this vulnerability, angelically pious. In evangelical works of sentimental fiction like Susan Warner's *The Wide, Wide World* (1850), invalid women such as the physically delicate yet spiritually robust Alice Humphreys personified the lessons of self-renunciation and serenity in the face of suffering that the novels were designed to teach. Alice's death, like that of Little Eva in *Uncle Tom's Cabin*, highlighted the beauty of her character as she preached a sermon advocating patient resignation to divine providence and encouraged those around her sick-bed to set their sights on heaven. When "little Ellen Montgomery," the main character of the novel, expressed dismay at her mentor's impending death, Alice chided her spiritual apprentice by restating the devotional ethic that she herself lived by and that she hoped Ellen would espouse: "We *must* say 'the Lord's will be done;'—we must not forget he does all things well."[35]

Similarly, in her best-selling novel, *Stepping Heavenward* (1869), popular evangelical author Elizabeth Prentiss linked medical theories about women's health with

Alice Humphreys, the fictional heroine of Susan Warner's *The Wide, Wide World* (1850), proclaiming the message of patient resignation to her pupil Ellen Montgomery. Line drawing from the 1892 edition. Courtesy of Portland Public Library, Portland, Maine.

devotional norms that esteemed passive endurance as the proper response to suffering. As a sixteen-year-old young woman, Katy, the female protagonist of Prentiss's story, fell sick after hurrying off to school in the snow without overshoes and then staying up that night to write in her journal in a cold room. Katy's frequent bouts with illness continued throughout her young adulthood, often occasioned, Prentiss suggests, by immoderate work or even by her very active social life. Soon after making his acquaintance, Katy's future husband, Dr. Ernest Elliott, warned her that unless she learned to subdue her emotions, her "passionate nature" would put her health at serious risk. When Katy's health began to falter, Ernest suggested that too much "feverish activity" had irritated her peculiar "nervous organization" and recommended that she refrain from undertaking any work that she could not "carry on calmly." When Katy did become ill, Ernest insisted that she desist from her activities in order to rest and regain her strength. Katy objected that she feared becoming a "mere useless sufferer," but Ernest replied that "God's children please Him just as well when they sit patiently with folded hands, if that is His will, as when they are hard at work." Although Katy felt "like an old piece of furniture no longer of any service," she consented to Ernest's prescription, and what she perceived to be God's chastening will.[36]

Like the many other "trials" she experienced as she struggled to subdue herself in order to fulfill her roles as wife and mother, Katy interpreted sickness as a blessing sent by God for her edification. After a particularly long bout of infirmity, she wrote, "All these weary days so full of languor, these nights so full of unrest, have had their appointed mission to my soul." Although she longed for health, Katy submitted to sickness as a necessary affliction. Illness, in this view, afforded opportunities for suffering through which God transformed the willful and selfish sinner into a rejoicing and restful saint whose only purpose was to worship. Katy writes: "Not till I was shut up to prayer and to the study of God's word by the loss of earthly joys, sickness destroying the flavor of them all, did I begin to penetrate the mystery that is learned under the cross. . . . To love Christ, and to know that I love Him— this is all!"[37]

Prentiss's novel was a great success in part because it provided women with a devotional framework that helped to make sense of both physical suffering and social situation. By encouraging women to see both illness and the seclusion of the sickroom as opportunities for the pursuit of holiness, Prentiss offered her readers a strategy for interpreting even the most painful of circumstances as spiritually fruitful. An invalid herself for most of her life, Prentiss sought solace in the notion that God sent physical affliction as a means for her own spiritual improvement. Sickness, Prentiss believed, was a disciplinary experience that enabled her to accept with patience not only the "helplessness" that physical debility occasioned but also the particular domestic obligations that came with marriage and motherhood. "I do thank my dear Master that He has let me suffer so much," she wrote in her journal in May of 1857; "it has been a rich experience, this long illness, and I do trust He will so sanctify it that I shall have cause to rejoice over it all the rest of my life. Now may I return patiently to all the duties that lie in my sphere."[38]

As literary historian Jane Tompkins has so persuasively argued, female audiences in this period were hungry for the kind of message that works like Prentiss's conveyed—a message that gave women who were politically, economically, and often physically dispossessed access to a more potent kind of authority: the power to transform their inner lives and, through this endeavor, the opportunity to influence others and even to reshape society and culture. Although the ethic of submission promoted in sentimental fiction did not directly challenge the conditions of oppression that structured women's lives, Tompkins has maintained, this model of behavior did provide women who could not, in her view, openly rebel against their culture's value system with a strategy for transcending some implications of their position. As Tompkins put it, "These novels teach the reader how to live without power while waging a protracted struggle in which the strategies of the weak will finally inherit the earth." In other words, by changing the stakes involved, authors such as Prentiss, Warner, and Stowe redefined the struggle for power so that woman's weakness became a sign of strength, her death the ultimate victory rather than the decisive defeat.[39]

The overwhelming popularity of works like *Stepping Heavenward, The Wide, Wide World,* and *Uncle Tom's Cabin* helped to make the pious female invalid a stock figure in mid-nineteenth-century American culture. By the time Mary Rankin published the first edition of her autobiography in 1858, the frail and sickly woman who patiently endured physical distress and therefore served as an exemplar of Christian virtue and even as a mediator of spiritual power would have been familiar to many readers. Modeling her own life story according to an analogous interpretive framework, Rankin imbued her experiences with purpose and subtly claimed for herself the sort of spiritual authority that self-renunciation and patient submission to God bestowed.[40]

Rankin's autobiography also provided her female readers with something that most works of sentimental fiction failed to offer. By and large, the invalid heroines of popular novels like *Uncle Tom's Cabin* did not endure the agonizing therapies that Rankin underwent. The sickroom of Victorian literature was usually a soothing space filled with flowers, not a torture chamber spattered with blood or marked by the scent of blistered flesh. Nor did the female protagonists of most nineteenth-century novels have to tolerate a lifetime of bodily affliction or social oppression. Usually, after a relatively brief period of unspecified bodily suffering in which they demonstrated perfect submission to divine providence, fictional characters died in what would have been the prime years of their youth. Mary Rankin was not so blessed. When *The Daughter of Affliction* first appeared in print, Rankin had been confined to her bed for more than twenty years. At the age of thirty-seven, she was certainly no longer a young maiden. In the final chapter of the second edition of her memoir, the fifty-year-old Rankin wrote, "As this volume closes September 1870, I am still an invalid, confined to my couch of pain." Unlike the fictional heroines who populated the pages of so many mid-nineteenth-century novels, Rankin was a real person afflicted by very specific symptoms for an extremely long time, and these facts gave her memoir a different kind of force than readers would have gleaned from the romanticized accounts they encountered in sentimental fiction. Whereas Little Eva sickened of a broken heart and died because she was "too good for this world," as one literary historian has put it, Mary Rankin had to find a way to continue to live out her invalid life this side of heaven. Rankin's life story, while undoubtedly idealized, did seek to present a strategy for enduring affliction over the long haul. Although she often wished for the release that death would bring, Rankin had to learn to live with the fact that, as she put it, "an all-wise God, for reasons beyond the scan of mortals, ordered my destiny otherwise." In Rankin's case, submitting to a painful life, rather than accepting a victorious death, was the ultimate challenge.[41]

The enduring popularity of Mary Rankin's autobiography alongside other works of this genre reveals that the question of how to interpret and endure physical suffering remained a matter of urgency for Protestants throughout the middle and latter decades of the nineteenth century. Just one year after the first edition of *The Daughter of Affliction* appeared, for example, the American Sunday School Union published *Chloe Lankton; or, Light Beyond the Clouds. A Story of Real Life* (1859). This text purported to be "neither myth nor fiction, but a true, unvarnished tale without comment or colouring." Like Rankin's work, this book sought to speak to those struggling to reconcile themselves to chronic illness and pain by presenting a living example of a woman who had learned to accept her sufferings with "sweet patience and resignation." After twenty-five years of confinement to her bed, Lankton insisted that she continued to find meaning in her afflictions by placing them in a theological frame. Indeed, she commented, "I am so thankful that I can see the providence of God in all his dealings with me, and that I can see it all for my good; for, if I did not see it so, how could I have borne it at all?"[42]

While accounts of long-suffering endurance of bodily affliction such as Lankton's and Rankin's provided Protestant women in this period with exemplars for emulation that helped explain and sanctify their own experiences of pain and protracted illness, these narratives offered a different kind of spiritual encouragement for men. Indeed, although female invalids like Rankin served as the principal paragons of passive resignation, their stories were intended for and read by both women and men. In the testimonial endorsing *The Daughter of Affliction*, a cadre of Rankin's male devotees revealed the appeal that her autobiography held for them. Rankin's life story, this group of men affirmed, offered "a monument of God's faithfulness and solace in the hour of affliction." One of the signers, Dr. Samuel M. Ross, described Rankin herself as "a victim of suffering, but a monument of amazing grace." In other words, these men implied, Rankin served as a sort of shrine bearing witness in her body to God's afflictive yet sustaining power. Whereas her patient forbearance of intense and ongoing somatic suffering presented women readers with a model for imitation, Rankin's afflicted flesh itself appeared to these male admirers as a physical symbol of divine providence.[43]

Of course, Rankin's tormented body may have served a similarly representative function for her female disciples, just as it is likely that not all men would have looked upon her corporal suffering as a means of incarnating God's sovereign power. Nor did the penchant for venerating Rankin's flesh as material evidence of divine prerogative necessarily preclude Rankin's male votaries from also upholding her as a spiritual exemplar for all Christians. Dr. D. R. Good, Rankin's physician for a number of years and the scribe to whom she dictated her experiences, proclaimed in the preface to her memoirs: "Mary still lives to teach us lessons of patience in long-suffering and submission to the will of 'God.'" Rankin's purpose, Good declared, was to provide an "example of Christian resignation" from whom others should "learn . . . a lesson of gratitude for the blessings of health, and many temporal privileges and enjoyments bestowed upon us, of which she is deprived." Even in Good's estimation, however, Rankin's passive endurance of prolonged physical affliction served primarily as a foil for the reader's own presumed experience of bodily wholeness, rather than as an ideal for imitation. By reflecting on Rankin's deprivations and the laudable manner in which she bore them, Good suggested, readers would be inspired to give thanks that they had been spared such sufferings and to praise God for the boon of physical health, with all of its attendant advantages and benefits.[44]

The ideal of sanctified suffering that Rankin embodied seems to have served several purposes for Protestants in the mid- to late nineteenth century struggling to comprehend and cope with the problem of pain. For her fellow female invalids, and even for healthy women who were nevertheless obliged to conform to the norms of self-sacrificing domesticity, Rankin's example of patient resignation offered a model of sanctity worth emulating. For Protestant men striving to measure up to the cultural prescriptions of mid-nineteenth-century manhood, Rankin's passive forbearance provided an inverted reflection of their own call to active achievement outside the domestic realm. Finally, Rankin's somatic piety furnished her contemporaries with assurance that physical pain was a spiritual blessing ordained by God for the sufferer's sanctification and for the good of others. Rankin's afflicted body itself thus took on spiritual significance as a material sign of God's providential care for his children.

Texts like *The Daughter of Affliction* reveal the ways in which cultural norms, medical theories, and theological doctrines worked together to advance and sustain a potent and closely entangled set of assumptions about the nature of female and male bodies, the proper roles of women and men in society, and the correct Christian interpretation of and response to physical suffering. The ideal of patient en-

durance promoted in this and similar works of nineteenth-century Christian hagiography powerfully shaped the way many Protestants in this period understood
and contended with corporal pain and illness. Like Mary Rankin, numerous Protestant women saw bodily sickness as an opportunity for spiritual sanctification and
service to others, and strove to submit to what they believed was God's sovereign
will. During the four years that she was confined to her bed and "never free from
pain," Mary Lamb of Rochester, New York, thought her illness was sent "as a cross
from God and tried to bear it with cheerfulness and patience." When she was completely prostrated from "a combination of diseases" that brought "suffering beyond
description," Mrs. L. W. Bush of Brookline, Vermont, "felt that God had mercifully
afflicted" her and prayed, as she put it, that "He would perfect His own work in me,
whatever I might suffer, and teach me His will." "O, the weary days and sleepless
nights, none but God can ever know," Bush proclaimed, "but He gave me that calm,
sweet peace . . . and I could lie passive in the arms of my blessed Saviour, waiting his
teaching and guiding."[45]

In keeping with mid-nineteenth-century gender norms, fewer Protestant men
indicated that passive resignation represented a significant feature of their own responses to bodily infirmity or physical pain. While many men testified to their belief in God's afflictive providence, most suggested that long-suffering endurance
of protracted invalidism simply was not an option for them, given their economic
and social circumstances. When the Reverend A. P. Moore was taken sick, he noted
that he was "so situated" that he could not stop work. Similarly, after spending
several months convalescing from what his doctor described as "congestion of the
brain and partial paralysis of the vocal organs," Methodist minister John Haugh
"felt obliged to resume work," against his physician's better judgment, because he
had "a large family dependent upon" his labor. When men did discuss the ideal of
sanctified suffering, they usually linked passive forbearance with female piety, suggesting that women were uniquely qualified to bear physical affliction, and in so
doing, to serve as representatives and reminders of God's sovereign power.[46]

Despite the enduring power of patient resignation as a normative model and as
a spiritual practice, not all Protestants endorsed this particular way of construing
the relationship between providence and pain. Rankin's own story, in fact, offers
evidence of dissent on multiple levels. At one point during her illness, as we have
observed, Rankin felt threatened by a friend's suggestion that her suffering was the
consequence of an accident, rather than the result of divine decree. This alternative explanation of her experiences provoked from Rankin a strong affirmation
of God's sovereignty and of the purposeful nature of physical affliction over and
against the interpretive schemes of what she identified as a particular, falsely con-

ceived version of "science." In a related manner, one of Rankin's male sponsors, Dr. S. M. Ross, felt compelled to defend her practice of resigned endurance over and against those pragmatists who might view her "physical inability to act" as an impediment to more effective Christian influence.[47]

These two incidences of discord suggest that the meaning and practice of suffering were matters of significant dispute among Protestants in the late nineteenth century. Competing frameworks of interpretation were raising challenges to the doctrine of afflictive providence. Rival models of Christian service that stressed active evangelical engagement, such as those celebrated in missionary biographies like *The Life of David Brainerd* and the *Memoir of Mrs. Ann H. Judson* (1829), contested the association between passivity and sanctity that Rankin's text so adamantly promoted. Within this context, the carefully constructed (and profoundly gendered) link between physical suffering and spiritual blessing was beginning to unravel.

CHAPTER TWO

Resisting Resignation

The Rise of Religious Healing in the Late Nineteenth Century

Jennie Smith heard Lucy Drake narrate her "experience in being healed" at a gathering held near Smith's home in Ohio in May of 1872. Drake, who was traveling across the country with William and Mary Boardman helping to promote "The Higher Christian Life," had shared her testimony in numerous settings since her cure in January 1870 and had encouraged many individuals to trust the Lord for healing. Although another six years would pass before Smith would write to Charles Cullis and ask him to join in the prayer meeting that led to her own dramatic restoration, hearing Drake's story piqued Smith's curiosity and strengthened her "hopes of recovery," despite the fact that her physicians were increasingly pessimistic about her prospects. If Drake, who "was at one time a great sufferer" and whose case, Smith concluded, had been "more hopeless" than her own, was now a healthy and active missionary, perhaps patient endurance of protracted pain was not the only possible option for invalids like herself.[1]

Over the course of the late nineteenth century, thousands of ailing women and men came to doubt that the devotional ethic of passive resignation was the requisite way for Christians to cope with bodily suffering. In their narratives of illness and recovery, countless numbers of these individuals described how their encounter with the teachings and practices of divine healing led them to question many of the doctrinal tenets that linked resigned acceptance of physical affliction with spiritual holiness. Focusing on these testimonials as well as on several of faith cure's foundational texts written by leaders such as Charles Cullis, A. J. Gordon, R. K. Carter and A. B. Simpson, this chapter explores the theological and cultural transitions that helped set the stage for the emergence of divine healing in the 1870s. Examining the development of faith cure within the broader context of religious and social change in the late nineteenth century reveals that divine healing was part of a much more extensive effort to revise the ways Christians interpreted and dealt with illness and somatic distress. Participants in evangelical faith cure, like many other Protestants in this period, were rethinking the ideal of sanctified suffering in light of changing views about the causes of disease, growing discontent with "orthodox" medicine and heroic forms of therapy, and, perhaps most importantly, increasing dissatisfaction with certain features of Reformed theology. Although anti-Calvinism is often associated primarily with the emergence of Protestant liberalism in the late eighteenth and early nineteenth centuries, the history of divine healing shows that challenges to "orthodox" conceptions of God's character, human nature, and sacred history also provided many evangelicals with resources for remaking the meaning and practice of pain.

"The Lord That Healeth Thee": Resisting the Doctrine of Afflictive Providence

In the winter of 1872, one of Charles Cullis's patients came to him seeking relief from a chronic knee ailment. Numerous physicians had examined the leg, and one had even performed surgery, but none had been able to effect a cure. Rather than prescribing medical treatment for what appeared to be a hopeless case, Cullis asked his patient, who was also a "minister of the Gospel," whether he could trust God to restore his handicapped limb. The man replied that although he did not doubt God's ability to heal him, he wondered whether it was God's will to do so. "I was not sure," the minister later recalled, "that it would be for my good or His glory to have it done."[2]

The conviction that ongoing illness brought glory to God and benefit to the afflicted was an obstacle that Cullis encountered frequently when he encouraged sick persons to pray for healing. "Many persons, followers of the Lord Jesus, think and say that their sickness has been sent for some good—that they ought to be willing to bear it, and say, 'Thy will be done,'" Cullis observed in his 1879 text, *Faith Cures; or Answers to Prayer in the Healing of the Sick.* Indeed, many of the testimonies included in this anthology and its two sequels—*More Faith Cures* (1881) and *Other Faith Cures* (1885)—indicate that belief in God's afflictive providence presented a major stumbling block to faith in divine healing. "My wife believed God could cure her, if it was His will . . . but she was under the impression that it was the Lord's will for her to suffer," one narrator wrote. Another author concluded that his chronic headache was his "thorn in the flesh," and that it was not God's will that he "should be cured of it." S. A. Hanscome, who suffered from spinal disease, rheumatism, and a painful tumor on her breast, wrote that she tried to bear her affliction "as cheerfully as possible." Although she did not "doubt the Lord's power to heal diseases," she believed that "to expect healing in this way was simply presumptuous."[3]

Cullis rebutted these protests with the observation that "while these persons think they are patiently bearing the Lord's will, they are using all the means in their power to be rid of their diseases, and do not hesitate to employ physician after physician, and to spend 'their all,' if need be, to recover their health." If Christians really believed that God sent sickness as a blessing that ought to be accepted and endured with thanksgiving, Cullis reasoned, they would and should not seek relief from their suffering. By pursuing health through all sorts of medical therapies, individuals like S. A. Hanscome, Jennie Smith, and even Mary Rankin—that paragon of passive resignation—were, in practice, working against the divine sovereignty that they claimed to acknowledge. This discrepancy between behavior and belief, in Cullis's view, revealed that the devotional ethic of patient endurance and the doctrine of God's afflictive providence that sustained this ideal were deeply problematic for the many people who professed to affirm them.[4]

In order to address this inconsistency, Cullis struck at what he took to be the root of the problem: an erroneous understanding of God's will regarding bodily illness and health. To those who hesitated to pray for healing because they believed God had ordained their affliction, Cullis replied, in no uncertain terms, that "it was *not* the Lord's will" that they should suffer. On the contrary, God's will was "to fulfill His promise, 'the prayer of faith shall save the sick,'" and the appropriate response to illness, therefore, was not acquiescent submission but believing prayer. "If we are truly desirous that His will shall be done in us," Cullis proclaimed, "let us claim *all* He promises, and look with confidence to Him 'who healeth all our diseases.'"[5]

As Cullis and his growing cadre of compatriots continued to preach against afflictive providence and passive endurance, they encouraged many individuals to revise their understandings of sickness and to question their previous means of coping with it. Looking back on years of chronic illness, countless visits to doctors, several hospital stays, a surgical operation, and the many "stimulants" and "tonics" she imbibed, Katherine Brodie marveled at the incongruity between her theology and her conduct. "Sickness I always thought God's will, to which I must submit, little thinking how those medicine bottles mocked my ideas of submission," she wrote. Mrs. Belle Lewis told a similar story about her battle with pneumonia. "I thought I was resigned to be sick, if it was His will," she remarked. "Still I did not give up trying to be well." Through their encounters with emissaries of faith healing, invalids like these two women concluded that God ordained rejoicing rather than suffering, health instead of sickness. To submit to God's sovereignty, from this perspective, was "to believe and trust the Lord" to make them well.[6]

The conviction that "God willeth the health of his people and not their hurt," as the Reverend A. J. Gordon put it, became a foundational principle of evangelical divine healing. In his pivotal text, *The Ministry of Healing, or, Miracles of Cure in All Ages,* which represented one of the earliest attempts to systematize the theology of the fledgling faith cure movement, Gordon noted that "while very few enjoy being sick, very many are afraid seriously to claim healing, lest it should seem like rebellion against a sacred ordinance, or a revolt from a hallowed medicine which God is mercifully putting to their lips for their spiritual recovery." Like Cullis, Gordon challenged the notion that "God often allows his servants to be sick for their good" and suggested that Christians ought not to "willingly accept sickness . . . as their portion, instead of seeking for health" by offering the prayer of faith.[7]

R. K. Carter, another of Cullis's converts, also argued against the doctrine of afflictive providence and the corresponding ethic of passive endurance. "To know God's will, read His word," he proclaimed. "Now God gives just one specific direction in His word to the sick, and that is a direction to get well." In this view, invalids who remained resigned to their afflictions were actually rebelling against God. Such "supposed humility," Carter asserted, was really "evidence of obstinacy." "Truly the only real way to glorify God in sickness is to give Him a chance to manifest his power in destroying it, as one of the works of the devil," he insisted. "He who is thanking God for the equanimity with which he bears his sufferings, had better ask for grace to open his eyes wide enough to see the finger of Jesus beckoning him on to a more complete self-surrender and simple faith."[8]

A. B. Simpson, who also became one of faith cure's most forceful apologists, made a similar point in his many works on divine healing. Writing in *Word, Work and World,* the journal he founded shortly after his own recovery from heart trouble and nervous prostration, Simpson countered several common objections to "the gospel of healing." Chief among these protests, he contended, was the belief that "glory . . . redounds to God from our submission to His will in sickness and the happy results of sanctified affection." Repeating Cullis's charge that few who claimed to espouse this position "really accept their sickness and lie passive under it," Simpson went on to argue that the ideal of patient forbearance rested on a mistaken reading of scripture regarding "God's dealings with his dear children."

A. J. Gordon. Frontispiece to *Adoniram Judson Gordon: A Biography* (1896). Courtesy of Harvard College Library.

According to his interpretation of biblical passages such as 1 Thessalonians 5, a Christian's "normal state" was one of "soundness both of body, soul, and spirit." Furthermore, God's "own prayer for [His children] is, that they may be in health and prosper." Given this theological framework, Simpson wrote elsewhere, "it becomes an impertinence and a presumption to doubt His gracious will to redeem and re-store our bodies as well as our souls. And the presumption grows into a wonderful mockery when we cover our unbelief under the name of a virtuous resignation."[9]

Passive endurance, in this view, was really a veiled form of cowardly skepticism rather than a saintly standard. Although Simpson was careful to qualify this judg-ment, stating that he did not "question the deep and fervent piety, and spiritual ad-vancement of many an invalid," he did imply that the inability of these long-suffer-ing individuals to "trust God for healing" represented a shortcoming on their part. This lack of faith, Simpson suggested, resulted from a misguided view of God's character that emphasized judgment, discipline, and punishment. Instead of cow-

A. B. Simpson. Courtesy of the Christian and Missionary Alliance National Archives.

ering in doubt and fear before a stern, chastening sovereign, sick persons needed to appeal to God's tenderness and "to claim His gracious deliverance." To restore his ailing children to health, Simpson argued, was "ever 'the good pleasure *of his goodness,*'"—the "good perfect and acceptable will" of a gentle, compassionate Father.[10]

As Simpson's comments suggest, an effort to reform the way Protestants conceived of God's nature was central to the enterprise of challenging belief in afflictive providence and revising the devotional ethic of passive resignation. In their testimonies of healing, numerous individuals recounted how they found the faith to pray for healing only after they came to see God more as a loving parent than as an austere judge. For more than seventeen years, one woman recalled, "I did not ask Him to restore my health, but for grace to sustain, for patience to endure, desiring to lie passive in His hands, willing to bear whatever He saw fit to lay upon me, not realizing that the loving, sympathizing Father longed to take away the burden of pain, and all that He required of me was simple trust in Him." Another invalid described her experience in similar terms: "I felt, or thought I did, entirely resigned,

and only prayed for patience to endure all that the dear Lord had for me of suffering. I felt that God was doing all things right, but I wanted to feel that He was
personally near me, and to realize, as I did not, that He sympathized with me in
my pain." For both of these women, relief came once they gained "a clearer sense
of God's presence and love"—a sense that gave them the confidence to ask "to be
restored to health."[11]

Participants in the divine healing movement were neither the first nor the only
Protestants to question whether a merciful, compassionate Father would send or
sanction bodily affliction in order to reprove, regulate, or even sanctify his beloved
children. Throughout the nineteenth century, a growing tendency to emphasize
God's benevolence made it easier for individuals from both liberal and evangelical
backgrounds to abandon the notion that physical pain was a providential blessing
to be accepted with gratitude and endured with equanimity. Challenges to Calvinist orthodoxy during the early nineteenth century, for example, prompted "Christian physiologists" such as Sylvester Graham, a Presbyterian minister with many
connections within the evangelical community, and William Alcott, the cousin of
Transcendentalist Bronson Alcott and the leader of the "Physical Education" movement, to reject explicitly the belief that illness was "the result of God's punishment
or a test by God to sanctify the virtuous still further." In his study of Grahamism,
Physical Education, and a host of other forms of what he has called "hygienic religion," historian James Whorton has observed that "as God came to be regarded
more as a loving father than a wrathful sovereign," fewer Protestants could countenance the tendency to attribute disease to "an unpredictable act of Providence."
Within this context, reformers like Alcott "repeatedly stigmatized resignation as . . .
a state of mind unworthy of a Christian." The widespread appeal of health reform
among antebellum Protestants of all sorts suggests that many individuals were
eager to cast off "orthodox" interpretations of suffering and to adopt alternative
strategies for coping with sickness that assumed the primacy of God's goodness,
mercy, and love.[12]

Belief in a benevolent deity, and particularly in God's parental character, also inspired a large cohort of Protestants to participate in Spiritualism, a movement that
assailed orthodox Calvinist assumptions about the relationship between spiritual
health and somatic distress with strident ardor. Spiritualists viewed God as a sympathizing parent who permeated nature with divinity. Such a "loving Father," as
clairvoyant physician Julia Crafts Smith put it in her autobiography, could never be
accused of sending suffering to which "we must submit without a murmur." Illness,
in this view, was by no means the active will of an all-merciful God, who "is more
loving than an earthly parent." Like their contemporaries in various health reform

movements, Spiritualists argued that health was "the natural condition of human beings," and they consequently refused to see disease either as a deserved punishment or as a God-given blessing.[13]

By the 1870s, a host of health reform movements, including Adventism, Grahamism, hydropathy, physical education, and Spiritualism, alongside several others, had directly challenged the doctrine of God's afflictive providence. During this decade, Mary Baker Eddy added her voice to the growing chorus of Protestant reformers who objected to the notion that God ordained bodily suffering in order to promote personal holiness. After years of wrestling with what she called the "relentless theology" of her strict Calvinist upbringing in the Congregational Church, Eddy eventually rejected the "merciless" God of her fathers in favor of a deity who was "altogether lovely." Through her discovery of Christian Science, Eddy came to understand God as a "Father-Mother"—an appellation that indicated "His tender relationship to His spiritual creation." Because she believed the deity to be "wholly good," historian Stephen Gottschalk has maintained, Eddy deemed God "incapable of causing or countenancing suffering" and finally abandoned her own attempts to cope with chronic illness by treading "the orthodox Christian path of resignation."[14]

From the 1870s on, many Protestants followed in Eddy's footsteps. Numerous accounts of healing published in the *Christian Science Journal,* the official organ of Eddy's nascent organization in the latter decades of the nineteenth century, expressed dissatisfaction with "orthodox" Protestant theology and echoed her teachings about the character of God, the nature of sickness, and the futility of passive endurance. Laura Nourse, a Methodist-raised convert to Adventism, attributed her eventual embrace of Christian Science to her aversion to the doctrine of afflictive providence. When one of her attendants tried to comfort the invalid Nourse with the "assurance that God had sent this suffering upon me to make me better," she retorted: "I don't believe it! He never did it! I have a better opinion of God that that." Through her discovery of Christian Science, Nourse found a theology that better suited her faith in an all-loving, thoroughly munificent God.[15]

In an article entitled "From Trinitarianism to Christian Science," another recent convert described orthodoxy as "a fruitless faith and a doubtful theology." Having been taught that sickness was "a dispensation of Providence; death the gateway of Life, through which all must pass to gain a heaven," this sufferer tried to believe that God "was chastening for a purpose; that He was compelling His children to 'pass under the rod'; that some day when all these salutary lessons were learned, I would win a home beyond this world of chance and change." This interpretation proved so unsatisfactory that eventually, "in the extremity of my despair," the author recalled, "I determined to drink from the fountain of Christian Science, whose waters could not be more bitter than those already drunk from the ancestral well." Finding refreshment in this faith, the new disciple wrote, "I left forever the old paths, to walk in the new, wherein was the solution of life's mystery."[16]

Christian Scientists, Spiritualists, and health reformers agreed that the orthodox road of passive resignation was a dead-end. Drawing on the logic of liberal theology, the many Protestants who participated in these movements resisted the notion that patient endurance of pain and illness characterized the route to holiness marked out by a chastising Providence. When Cullis and his cohort began to proclaim the gospel of healing through faith, they joined this ongoing and widespread attempt to revise the theological framework and devotional model inherited from Calvinist orthodoxy. Like their fellow reformers (who were often also their competitors or even their adversaries, as we shall see), proponents of faith cure worshipped a God who was more a sympathetic parent than a strict disciplinarian. And just as their counterparts reasoned that a benevolent deity would neither afflict his children with sickness nor require them to endure it indefinitely, divine healing advocates assumed that a loving Father would not prescribe long-suffering as a means of sanctification. As Cullis put it, "We rejoice to see our children well, how much more does He?"[17]

Physical Arminianism: Revising the Ethic of Passive Resignation

The questions that Cullis and his contemporaries raised regarding God's character and the nature of human suffering opened up a host of other theological dilemmas. If a compassionate and sovereign God was not the author of affliction, what (or who) was the source of sickness? And if acquiescence was not the appropriate course for a suffering Christian to follow, what path was she to take? The answers that leaders of the divine healing movement posed to these queries reveal the extent to which they were indebted to other anti-Calvinist currents in nineteenth-century theology, not least of which was the increasingly ubiquitous Arminianism that was steadily transforming the character of both American and British Protestantism. Just as liberalism bequeathed to these evangelicals a gentler view of the deity that prompted them to reconsider the doctrine of afflictive providence, it also offered a more optimistic perspective on human nature that enabled them to propose alternative explanations for disease and to recommend different strategies for coping with physical suffering.

Cullis's biography, and especially his background in homeopathic medicine and his connections with the Holiness movement, illumines the ways Arminian sensibilities about human nature could help to recast ideas about health and affliction. As a young man, Cullis was frail and sickly. His only "recollections of childhood," he recalled, were "of being carried up and down stairs, in the arms of one and another, and doctored and cared for as a sick child." During his school days, Cullis was "too miserable in health to enjoy play, much less study," and eventually "broke down completely." At the age of sixteen, he became a merchant in a dry goods store in Boston, a position he held for three years, until his health "gave way again." When rest failed to revive him, a physician suggested that he consider the study of medicine and offered to fund his education. Cullis received his degree from the University of Vermont at the age of twenty-four, and returned to Boston to practice homeopathic medicine.[18]

By the early 1860s, homeopathy had become a popular alternative among American physicians and patients who had grown disillusioned with the painful and expensive therapies offered by the allopaths—a term originally invented by Samuel Hahnemann, the founder of the nineteenth-century homeopathy movement, to distinguish his system from that of "regular," or "orthodox" medicine. Despite persistent and often vehement persecution by the American Medical Association, organized by "regular" doctors in 1847 in an attempt to establish their professional authority over and against "irregular" practitioners, homeopaths like Cullis built up "large and profitable" practices in major cities such as Boston, New York, and Philadelphia. Their success was grounded, in part, on the appeal of homeopathy's two major principles: the law of similars (the notion that a substance that produced symptoms of a particular ailment in a healthy individual could cure a person suffering from that same disease), and the law of infinitesimals (the conviction that the smaller the dosage, the more potent a drug's effect). Both of these tenets, in practice, greatly reduced reliance on heroic remedies such as blood-letting and blistering as well as the prescription of toxic medicines like calomel and arsenic in deleterious, if not deadly, quantities.[19]

In their critique of allopathy, and especially the heavy use of noxious drugs to treat illness, homeopaths joined proponents of Grahamism, Thomsonianism, and hydropathy in promoting bodily purity as a key factor in the prevention and cure of disease. While each of these movements offered a slightly different method of purification (Grahamism, for example, urged vegetarianism and sexual restraint; whereas Thomsonians recommended herbal remedies, and hydropaths extolled the cleansing properties of water), all shared the conviction that regular physicians contradicted the healing powers of nature by polluting the body with large quantities of poison. The best way to maintain or restore health, in this view, was to keep oneself uncontaminated by drugs and other debilitating substances such as alco-

Charles Cullis. Frontispiece to W. H. Daniels, *Dr. Cullis and His Work: Twenty Years of Blessing in Answer to Prayer* (1885). Courtesy of Andover-Harvard Theological Library, Harvard Divinity School, Harvard University.

hol, tobacco, and fatty foods, and thereby to live in accordance with the God-given laws of nature. Evincing a confidence in the inherent goodness of the natural order typical of Enlightenment science and philosophy, these alternative systems attributed illness and infirmity to the flouting of immutable physiological laws. "Pain is but the result of violated Nature," one homeopathic physician intoned, "hence it is of vast importance that we should all understand those laws which govern our own constitutions, and how to obey them in order to enjoy all the blessings designed by nature to flow from their obedience, as well as to escape the penalties attached to their infraction."[20]

Implicit in this understanding of how to avoid illness and achieve health was a crucial assumption about human nature that set homeopaths and health reformers apart from those who taught that disease was an affliction of divine providence to which one must remain meekly resigned. If pain and sickness were the products of human error, and purity and health were the results of human effort, then invalids were both responsible for their own infirmity and capable of overcoming it. This "physical Arminianism," as James Whorton first called it, resonated with several key trends in mid-nineteenth-century American culture. First, the spirit of optimism that characterized the Jacksonian era encouraged Americans to engage in all sorts of reform campaigns premised on the supposition that the betterment of both individual and society could be achieved through personal endeavor. A corresponding emphasis on the importance of self-determination as the hallmark of a healthy democratic society fueled the anti-elitism that marked the early national period and led many people to reject the authority of medical experts in favor of sectarian reformers like Samuel Thomson, who declared that every man ought to act as his own physician. Enlightenment faith in reason, particularly as it was translated to the American public through the Scottish Common Sense philosophy, suggested that all persons were capable of apprehending the laws of morality and nature, including the physiological ordinances that were built into the order of creation. Finally, the more sanguine anthropology that characterized the humanistic theology of nineteenth-century Unitarians and Universalists as well as the revivalist preachers who advocated "new measures" during the Second Great Awakening undermined the Calvinist doctrine of total depravity and the consequent assumption that human beings were powerless to affect their spiritual destinies, let alone their physical health. In Whorton's view, it was this "liberalized theology," more than any other factor, that fostered "physical Arminianism, a belief that bodily salvation might be open to all who struggled to win it, and that disease and death were not an ineradicable part of the earthly passage." Just as human beings could and should work actively toward spiritual regeneration, so too, they possessed both the ability and the duty to seek physiological renewal. Passive submission to pain and illness, from this perspective, represented a failure to fulfill one's religious obligations rather than the appropriate posture of a true Christian.[21]

As a homeopathic practitioner and an active participant in the Holiness movement that grew out of antebellum revivalism, Cullis was familiar with Arminianism of both the physical and spiritual sorts. Although born and raised an Episcopalian, Cullis came into close contact with Holiness leaders through his "faith work" among Boston's indigent consumptives. In the summer of 1862, Cullis himself prayed for entire sanctification through the "keeping power of Christ," to which he attributed both his experience of "full assurance" of salvation and his ongoing ability to remain pure in his inner life and his actions. Although he maintained his membership in the Episcopal Church until 1873, Cullis opened a chapel in connection with the Consumptives Home in the spring of 1868 and began to hold Tuesday afternoon prayer and "consecration" meetings "for the advancement of believers in the knowledge and experience of holiness" in his own parlor in 1869. Like Phoebe Palmer's famous "Tuesday Meetings for the Promotion of Holiness," after which his gatherings presumably were patterned, Cullis's meetings quickly drew packed audiences. By March 1872, the meetings had become so crowded that Cullis and his colleagues determined to build a chapel for the express purpose of accommodating the Tuesday afternoon congregation. The Beacon-Hill Church, which could seat between six and seven hundred attendees, opened in April of 1875 and began holding regular Sunday services in addition to the Tuesday afternoon meetings in the fall of the same year. Cullis himself took charge of these services intermittently, while also preaching from time to time at the Consumptives' Home chapel. In addition to overseeing these two independent Holiness churches, Cullis began conducting annual faith conventions "for consecration and the advancement of the spiritual life of believers" in the summer of 1874, first at Framingham, Massachusetts; then at the Methodist National Holiness campgrounds in Old Orchard, Maine; and finally, at Intervale Park, New Hampshire. He also published a monthly paper, *Times of Refreshing*, designed "to present Jesus as a full and perfect savior," and founded a tract repository that printed cheap editions of works by Holiness and Higher Life authors such as William Boardman, Hannah Whitall Smith, Theodore Monad, Asa Mahan, and Thomas Upham. Through all of these activities, Cullis cemented his status as a key leader of the late-nineteenth-century Holiness revival and an influential advocate of sanctified living through the act of personal consecration.[22]

Cullis's confidence in the "second blessing" of entire sanctification represented neither a belief in absolute perfection nor an utter rejection of divine sovereignty in favor of human free agency. This theology did, however, promote a more positive attitude toward human nature, and especially toward the capacity of human beings to overcome sin. Combined with his background in homeopathic medicine, Cullis's embrace of perfectionist theology helps explain why he found the devotional ethic of passive resignation increasingly problematic, and it puts his espousal of faith healing in broader cultural and theological perspective.[23]

The overlapping contexts of the nineteenth-century Holiness and health reform movements provide crucial background for excavating the origins and development of divine healing because so many of the movement's seminal figures were influenced by these two powerful cultural currents. Many of the ministers who supported faith healing, including John Inskip, William Boardman, and Asa Mahan, were also prominent leaders of various Holiness endeavors and activities. In addition to these renowned clergymen, lesser-known pastors, such as John E. Cookman, minister of the Twenty-Street Methodist Church in New York City, and Smith H. Platt, author of numerous works on Christian holiness and minister of the DeKalb Street Methodist Church in Brooklyn, New York, applied the more optimistic anthropology associated with perfectionist teachings to the problem of somatic suffering. If human beings could hope to attain sanctity of heart and freedom from sin this side of heaven, Holiness advocates reasoned, surely they could also expect to experience physical purity and bodily health in this life. As A. J. Gordon maintained in *The Ministry of Healing*, corporeal fitness represented "the first fruits of redemption" promised to the believer in Christ. Rather than regarding the body as a "house of clay" that "was never intended to be repaired or beautified by the renewing Spirit," Gordon argued, Christians ought to claim the scriptural promises of deliverance "from sickness as well as from sin; from pain, the penalty of transgression, as well as from transgression itself." R. K. Carter drew similar conclusions about the relationship between spiritual holiness and physical heartiness. "Is it going too far to imagine that a perfect body presented perfectly to God, and able to run His errands of mercy in all directions, is more 'acceptable' to Him than a poor, dilapidated, sickly weakling, whose every moment is necessarily absorbed with health?" he asked. [24]

While leaders like Carter and Gordon employed apologetic treatises and essays to articulate the implications of perfectionist theology for physical existence, lay persons within the Holiness movement who embraced "the gospel of healing" relied on word-of-mouth and personal testimonials in order to spread the good news. Holiness prayer meetings, summer conventions, and periodicals were key forums for the propagation of this message. After encountering Lucy Drake in the spring of 1872, for example, Jennie Smith attended several Holiness camp meetings where she met individuals who were deeply "exercised about the healing of [her] body." In August of 1877, Smith traveled to the Methodist campgrounds at Ocean Grove, where she renewed her acquaintance with Drake, attended services led by John Inskip, and most likely met Mary Mossman, a fervent advocate of divine healing who led a prayer meeting for Smith's recovery the following March. After her healing, Smith continued to frequent Ocean Grove and other Holiness conventions, where she gave public testimony of her experience to a widening circle of prominent acquaintances, including Daniel Steele, Robert Pearsall Smith, Hannah Whitall Smith, and Walter and Sarah Lankford Palmer.[25]

Although faith healing never became the principal focus of the New York Tuesday Meeting held at the Palmers' home, this gathering did become an important venue for sharing testimonies of healing and for informal conversations about the scriptural promises of physical restoration. During her first visit to the meeting at the Palmer residence in the summer of 1883, for example, invalid Katherine Brodie was approached by "seven strangers" who expressed their sympathy for her condition and asked if she "had ever heard of 'Faith Healing.'" The Palmers also helped promulgate the message of divine healing by publishing accounts of miraculous cures in *The Guide to Holiness*, one of the Holiness movement's leading periodicals once Phoebe and Walter Palmer acquired it in 1864. As belief in faith cure proliferated, healing testimonials appeared in other popular Holiness newspapers and magazines as well as in more recently established journals such as A. B. Simpson's *Word, Work and World.* Some stories, like Jennie Smith's, made their way into secular publications (her testimony first appeared in the Dayton *Democrat*) or edited anthologies of healing narratives compiled by leaders such as Mix, Cullis, and Simpson.[26]

Many of these accounts reveal how deeply the growth and development of the divine healing movement was indebted to various health reform teachings and establishments. First, these testimonies show that many invalids turned to "irregular" physicians, including homeopathic doctors and health reform practitioners of sundry sorts in their quests for relief from physical suffering. Visits to sanitariums such as the famous "Our Home on the Hillside," a hydropathic establishment at Dansville, New York, were often part of a sick person's search for health. Jennie Smith, to take just one example, traveled to a water-cure near Columbus, Ohio, consulted several eclectic physicians who employed alternative therapies such as electricity, and finally checked in to the Women's Homeopathic Hospital in Philadelphia, where she remained until she experienced divine healing through prayer. Through their contacts with a diverse range of health reformers and alternative physicians, invalids like Smith encountered and often absorbed the views of illness and health that these sectarian practitioners imparted. Not only did their more hopeful assumptions about human nature and the physical body help to unsettle the old ethic of passive resignation that kept invalids confined to their cots, but these more sanguine suppositions also shaped the doctrines and practices of the emerging faith healing movement in significant ways.[27]

Like their health reform predecessors, for example, many advocates of divine healing believed that maintaining bodily purity through conformity to the God-given laws of nature was crucial to preserving and regaining health. Sickness, in this view, was the consequence of sin and could be avoided or overcome through faithful obedience to divine decree. At a faith-healing meeting held at the Beacon Hill Church in February of 1883, for example, Lucretia Cullis, Charles's second wife, "spoke earnestly about our duty with regard to the laws of health, and especially in the manner of diet," one attendee reported. "We cannot expect God to heal us, and keep us well," she avowed, "if we live in a manner contrary to the laws of our being." Other devotees of divine healing agreed. "Many a chronic disease has been brought on by persistent, careless violations of a known law," R. K. Carter asserted. "It is almost incredible how many 'good Christians' are persistent, habitual gluttons, stuffing their stomachs with unhealthy foods at all sorts of hours." In his written testimony of healing, Thomas Whitehall of Philadelphia also encouraged his readers to attend to the treatment of their bodies. "As we are taught that sickness is the result of sin," he averred, "let us prayerfully set to work to find out what are the *divine* laws which govern these wonderful bodies of ours, and let us be *fervent* about it." Expanding on this exhortation in an article published in the faith-healing journal *Triumphs of Faith,* Edward Ryder asserted that "a true faith will honor God in the keeping of His laws," including those that pertained to "the by no means unimportant matters of diet, rest, physical protection." Ryder went on to report that he had "much improved the tone of [his] health by resolutely abstaining from certain articles . . . such as coffee, cake, and rich desserts . . . which tend either unduly to stimulate or to clog the 'river-courses of life' which ought to remain pure and open."[28]

Just as proponents of divine healing like Ryder echoed the physical Arminianism of Sylvester Graham and other advocates of temperance and dietary restraint by insisting on the importance of undertaking "a succession of faithful efforts to keep all God's laws" in order to "build up health and strength," they also mirrored their health reform counterparts in eschewing toxic drugs and other allopathic remedies. Sounding strikingly similar to both hydropathic physicians such as W. T. Vail, who equated the therapeutic practices of regular doctors with "Satan's system of poisoning," and to homeopathic practitioners who complained that "the filthy touch of Allopathy" contaminated people through the prescription of "deleterious poisons" like calomel and opium, many advocates of faith cure also decried the dangerous effects of chemical therapeutics and encouraged their followers to forgo these supposed remedies. "You don't need the physics nor powders, nor plasters, nor the other dreadful things to which the physicians are subjecting this beautiful body," one leader proclaimed. "Let us beware of these things, and take God for our doctor."[29]

Although this message seemed shocking and fanatical to some members of the medical and clerical establishments, as we will see, the notion that drugs such as mercury and antimony defiled the body and ought to be avoided was certainly not a novel idea within the cultural context of the late nineteenth century. Indeed, in their testimonies of healing, some individuals indicated that they had renounced such remedies prior to embracing the teachings of faith cure, finding that the drugs and therapies their doctors had prescribed were ineffective at best and often exacerbated their discomfort without alleviating their ailments. "Medicine usually aggravated my disease," Helen Dawlly wrote in her narrative of healing, "till I finally abandoned it altogether." For those who had experimented with various health reform regimens or spent time at a water-cure, the practice of relinquishing chemical therapies was a routine part of the pursuit of both physical and spiritual whole-ness. During her thirteen-month sojourn at the Home on the Hillside, for exam-ple, a city missionary from Chicago who was later cured through Cullis's prayers abstained from the homeopathic remedies prescribed by her physician, "rest, not medicine, being the 'cure' method" at the sanitarium.[30]

In addition to habituating invalids to the custom of giving up medicine, health reform establishments also became important sites for circulating the news of di-vine healing. While staying at the Dansville Home during the summer of 1882, the Reverend Spencer R. Wells, on furlough from his post as an American Board mis-sionary in India, "heard much" about "persons being restored to health in answer to the prayer of faith" and decided to give divine healing a try. "A day was set aside for prayer," and Wells was restored to health. The next day, he shared his testimony of "entire cure" at the regular prayer meeting. As a result, another patient put her faith in Jesus to "restore both body and soul." Libbie Osborn had a similar experi-ence at the water-cure near the Delaware Water Gap in Pennsylvania. "I had only been at the 'cure' a few months," she recalled, "before the subject of 'divine healing' was brought before my mind by some tracts and books which a lady lent me." Al-though she "was at once filled with a great longing for healing directly from Christ," Osborn worried that she ought to "go on bearing sickness" in order to remain "sub-missive to God's will." She continued to agonize until another woman at the hy-gienic institute gave her "new light on the subject of 'Divine Healing'" that eventu-ally helped her to overcome her doubts. After returning home to Delaware County, Ohio, Osborn wrote a letter "containing an account of her wonderful healing" to Agnes Ormsbee of Montepelier, Vermont, a friend she had made while residing at the water-cure. "That this dear girl with whom I had parted in Pennsylvania was restored to health," Orsmsbee wrote, "led me also to seek strength from Christ."[31]

Rather than opposing the spread of divine healing among their inmates, physi-cians at hygienic establishments often encouraged their patients to pray for physical restoration. Osborn's doctor at the water-cure, for example, "had encouraged [her] getting well on the grounds that God answers prayer." When an invalid suffering from repeated bouts of spinal fever sought advice from Dr. Henry Foster, who ran the Clifton Springs Water Cure in Oneida County, New York, Foster replied: "You are far beyond the reach of human aid; but there is the Great Physician. Have you ever thought of going directly to Him for healing?" As Foster's comments suggest, medical professionals sometimes turned to divine healing as a last resort. When they could do nothing more to restore their patients to health or even to ease their suffering, physicians such as Foster and Cullis evoked the healing power of God.[32]

By advocating faith cure, these practitioners acknowledged the limitations of

their own therapeutic systems. Despite their confidence in the curative properties of pure water or the remedial benefit of infinitesimal doses, or perhaps most
significantly, the ability of individuals to overcome illness by obeying the divinely
ordained laws of health, experts like Cullis and Foster ultimately conceded that
in certain cases neither the healing power of nature nor the exertions of the human will were adequate to alleviate illness and pain. For some invalids, physical
Arminianism proved both insufficiently effective and too strenuous a strategy for
contending with suffering. Before she espoused faith healing, for example, Libbie
Osborn grew increasingly frustrated that her dogged efforts were failing to produce
the promised salubrious results. "I was taking treatment and faithfully endeavoring
to carry out all the doctor's directions," Osborn recounted, but after nearly seven
months at the hydropathic Home, "I was secretly almost in despair . . . I knew I
could only stay a few months longer, and that it would be impossible to continue
that line of living in my home, and up to this time I could see very little if any
change in my old stubborn diseases." Osborne's friend Agnes Orsmsbee also noted
that her condition "continued to grow worse" despite her firm adherence to "hygienic measures" and "all the care of the skilled physicians" at the water-cure. After
a few months she returned home "very much reduced in strength, and with disease
little, if any, abated."[33]

Instead of abandoning these seemingly "incurable" invalids to their fate, as
many doctors were wont to do, physicians like Cullis and Foster prescribed prayer
as the one remaining remedy. As Cullis put it in the preface to *Faith Cures: Or, Answers to Prayer in the Healing of the Sick,* "'Man's extremity is God's opportunity'. . . .
When the 'profession' pronounces a case hopeless, the promise of God remains as
a testimony to the truth of His Word." Or, as another proponent of divine healing
proclaimed, "Where only a miracle can save, then are we to expect a miracle."[34]

"The Present Exercise of God's Power": Miracles, Millennialism, and Missions

While many invalids eagerly abandoned their earthly remedies and applied to
the Great Physician for healing without hesitation, others found the notion that
God would restore them to health in response to faithful prayer harder to accept.
For individuals raised within the Calvinist tradition, in particular, the idea that
God actively intervened in the everyday events of individual lives jarred discor-
dantly with one of the key teachings of Reformed theology: that Jesus had performed miracles such as healing the sick in order to demonstrate his divinity, and
that once the Christian church had been established, miraculous signs were no lon-

ger necessary. The age of miracles had ceased with the apostles, in this view, and although it was still permissible to pray for relief from suffering, Christians should expect God to heal them through natural agencies, or "secondary causes," rather than through a supernatural act of divine power.[35]

In their testimonies of healing, numerous individuals indicated that the cessationist view of miracles proved a major hindrance to their embrace of faith cure. "When I first heard of the prayer of faith," F. P. Church wrote to Cullis, "I was like many others; I thought the day of miracles was over, and at first gave it very little attention." S. H. Wasgatt became "interested in the 'Prayer Cure'" after more than thirteen years of invalidism, but struggled to "accept Jesus as [her] Physician" because she "had been taught from childhood that the days of miracles were past, and that Christ only healed the sick when He was here upon earth to attest His divine mission." George F. Donaldson of Long Pine, Nebraska, reported a similar experience. "I had read occasionally of 'faith cures,' but had no confidence in them as the direct manifestation of Divine power, not because I doubted God's ability," he declared, "but my whole education had led me to believe that 'the age of miracles is past.'" For Alford H. McClellan, a shopkeeper in Reed City, Michigan, stories of miraculous healing were "so different" from what his "'Scotch Presbyterian' training" led him "to think possible" that he did not believe he "could receive a similar blessing."[36]

When sufferers like these did begin to wonder whether the teachings of their youth were misguided, their friends, families, ministers, and even their own consciences often reproved them for their apostasy. While a student at Auburn Theological Seminary, a Presbyterian institution in New York City, Lansing Van Shoonhoven "was led to consider the possibility of a Faith Cure" for chronic synovitis of the knee, but his friends, he reported, "ridiculed the idea of throwing away my medicines and trusting the Lord to cure me without natural means." After one woman, who described herself as "a conservative in many things, timid about ventures in religious and moral movements; not readily yielding to innovations," dared to question why she should not say, "Jesus . . . *heals* me *now*," she immediately wrote to her rector seeking his opinion of miraculous healing. When he failed to address her question directly, she began to worry that she was "not sound in doctrine" and resigned herself to "her couch of suffering." Other pastors were more aggressive in their efforts to stifle heterodox ideas among members of their flock. When Mrs. Thomas H. Davy told her minister that she had asked God to heal her "*just now*" in a moment of intense agony, he replied: "The days of miracles are past, Mrs. D., and I think, after your sufferings, there can be no possible hope of your recovery."[37]

Comments like these incensed advocates of faith cure such as Cullis, who "could not see why, with such explicit and unmistakable promises" of bodily healing put forth in scripture, he or anyone else "should limit the present exercise of God's power." Like many other evangelicals in the late nineteenth century, and particularly those who took part in the Holiness and Higher Life movements, Cullis was convinced that the Holy Spirit worked in the souls and bodies of believers to influence the course of events in dynamic and supernatural ways. Recovering "the theology and presence of the Holy Spirit," historian Grant Wacker has asserted, was a prominent preoccupation among nineteenth-century Protestants of both Wesleyan and Reformed persuasions, and arguably the "central impulse of the higher life movement" that inspired so many exponents of divine healing. From this theological perspective, the idea that history was divided into two separate phases—the apostolic epoch and the post-biblical era—and that God worked miracles only during the previous period was patently unscriptural and dangerously impudent. "'Why should it be thought a thing incredible with you,'" Cullis wondered, "that the Lord should bestow upon His church in this day the same 'spirit of faith with power,' with which the first communities of Christians were endowed?" Other proponents of faith cure raised similar questions. "Those who oppose the healing of the sick in answer to 'the prayer of faith,' do so on the assumption that 'the age of miracles is past,' and was confined to the Apostolic age," observed the Reverend A. P. Moore, a minister from Alexander, New York, who had been healed of consumption through Cullis's ministry. "But where in the Bible are we taught this?" In an article titled "For Us, or For the Apostles?" another writer put the question this way: "Who may presume to limit to Apostles the things promised to follow 'them that believe,' or doubt the working of Him who declared, 'Lo, I am with you always, even to the end of the world?'"[38]

According to these authors, the pledge of the Holy Spirit's continuous presence with believers implied that the promises of healing found in the epistle of James and other passages of scripture remained valid for Christians in all ages. Indeed, a brief survey of sacred history, suggested apologists such as A. J. Gordon, revealed that miraculous healings had not ceased once the church had been established, but have "appeared more less numerously in every period." Although he admitted that "the apostolic age . . . was a particularly favored one" for the demonstration of the Holy Spirit's operations, Gordon cited numerous examples of supernatural healing drawn from the annals of the post-biblical era. Church Fathers such as Justin Martyr, Irenaeus, Tertullian, Origen, and Clement all testified to the ongoing occurrence of miraculous healings during the second and third centuries. While "the simpler and purer forms of supernatural manifestation" waned during the Middle Ages as a result of the Church's growing worldliness and corruption, an upsurge of miracles, including experiences of healing, always accompanied movements of spiritual renewal. Ironically, then, the period following the Protestant Reformation witnessed an outpouring of divine power in response to faithful prayer for physical restoration. Culling testimonies from the chronicles of numerous movements, including the confessions of the Waldensians; the writings of the Moravian leader Count Zinzendorf; "that book of religious adventure and heroic faith, '*The Scots Worthies*'" which recounts the experiences of the Scotch Covenanters; the stories of the French Huguenots; the journal of George Fox; and various Baptist and Methodist texts, Gordon concluded that "modern times" were no less full of "miraculous interventions" for bodily healing than any previous epoch, including the biblical era.[39]

At the same time, however, Gordon acknowledged that the contemporary period posed a greater challenge to faith in divine healing than any other historical moment. Like the medieval church, nineteenth-century Protestantism was plagued by a spirit of "adaptation" to the surrounding culture. The twin currents of "rationalism and worldliness," Gordon argued, had contributed to "the swelling unbelief of our age," and had caused the church to drift "into an unseemly cautiousness toward the miraculous." Even "true hearted and sincere" Christians, he lamented, were "in danger of being frightened out of their faith in the supernatural" as the result of a growing skepticism regarding the reality of biblical miracles and the stubborn tendency of "traditionalist" theologians to inveigh against modern instances of divine intervention. "How deeply we need the demonstration of the Spirit in these days!" Gordon proclaimed.[40]

While he implied that conformity to current ideologies and acquiescence to worldly comforts hindered the ability of his fellow Christians to recognize and accept the present activities of the Holy Spirit, Gordon also suggested that miraculous healings stood as a bulwark against the corrosive tides of contemporary culture. The "gracious deliverance" of a consumptive from the "edge of the grave" or the instantaneous cure of an opium addict whose habit had "baffled for years every device of the physician"—these kinds of exhibitions of divine power proved that the Holy Spirit was ever at work in the world, and thus helped to shore up the faltering faith of wavering Christians against the "indignant clamor of skeptics" and the "stern frowning of theologians."[41]

Many proponents of faith cure shared Gordon's confidence that modern displays of supernatural healing could help contemporary Christians defend against the pernicious influences of "this present evil age." First, recent reports of physical restoration offered evidence of God's existence in contrast to the pervasive naturalism that characterized much of scientific inquiry in the late nineteenth century. "Who can tell but God may have chosen these very manifestations of His power upon human bodies, in this material age," one writer queried, "to answer the un-belief of science, and speak more loudly than all our learned lectures for His eter-nal power and Godhead?" Against the growing sway of Darwinian determinism, miraculous cures testified to the reality of a personal, transcendent, yet ever-pres-ent deity, who overrode the seemingly inviolable laws of evolutionary progress in response to petitionary prayer. And they did so, their defenders argued, in keeping with the "scientific method" of "rigid induction." In this view, accounts of divine healing represented verifiable data of the kind demanded by the most rigorous em-piricist. Whereas spiritual experiences such as conversion or sanctification could be "deceptive and difficult to interpret," A. J. Gordon maintained, physical cures provided tangible, observable proof of the Holy Spirit's ongoing and supernatural activity. "This is a kind of testimony," Gordon asserted, "which is not easily ruled out of court."[42]

Drawing upon this "evidentialist apologetic," as historian Rick Ostrander has named it, proponents of faith cure also contended that contemporary demon-strations of divine healing undermined the claims of rationalists who denied the authenticity of scriptural miracles. As the onslaught of higher criticism made the healing ministry of Jesus seem increasingly incredible, leaders of the faith cure movement countered that modern manifestations of supernatural power bolstered the authority of the Bible. Reversing the cessationist argument, which eighteenth-century theologians had employed to repel skeptical assaults on biblical miracles from Enlightenment philosophers like Hume, advocates of divine healing asserted that if God exhibited his ability to override the natural order in the present, it was certainly reasonable to conclude that Jesus had done so in the past. In this view, current miracles of healing refuted the unbelief of the philosophes, the barbs of biblical criticism, and what A. B. Simpson dubbed the "spirit of . . . cold traditional theological rationalism" that characterized liberal Unitarians, Calvinist Presbyteri-ans, and other Protestants who maintained that God ceased to work in a supernat-ural manner after the apostolic era. Theologians who insisted that God healed only through "causes, effects, means, second causes, and the order of nature," Simpson contended, constructed "a little fence" around God and refused to allow God "to step out of the enclosure for a moment, or the poor sufferer even to reach Him through the bars." According to this framework, God became "a prisoner in His own world," and "His poor children" could not "get at Him except through the of-ficial red tape of the old economy of nature and law." Recent instances of miracu-lous healing shattered this stifling system, Simpson asserted, by proving that God's Holy Spirit could not be confined by the rules of cause and effect or the dictates of human logic. "Blessed be His Holy Name," Simpson exclaimed, "the resurrection of

Jesus Christ from the dead has burst the iron bars of mere natural law, and given us a living Lord."[43]

Simpson's comments about the risen Christ reveal the importance that advocates of divine healing attached to the figure of Jesus. Just as they worked tirelessly to reclaim the centrality of the Holy Spirit for the modern world, champions of faith cure insisted that the doctrine of the resurrection offered contemporary believers assurance of Christ's authority over disease and death, a power that he promised to impart to all who sought it. "Jesus is Victor" became a rallying cry for early European proponents of faith healing through the work of German pastor Johann Blumhardt, whose healing ministry became well known in the United States after R. K. Carter published his biography in 1883. By focusing on Jesus' triumph over the grave, rather than on "a crucifix" or "a dying Christ merely," apologists like Blumhardt and Simpson proclaimed, Christians could gain access to "the power of His resurrection"—the greatest miracle of all—in their own souls and bodies.[44]

"The Resurrection of Christ," Simpson preached on Easter Sunday of 1883, "is the ground of physical healing, and the spring of our true bodily life. . . . a pledge to us of all the resources of Infinite power and love." This living Christ, Simpson suggested, continued to intervene in the world in a supernatural manner, making his presence manifest in the spiritual lives and "mortal flesh" of faithful believers. "Jesus Christ is the Same, Yesterday, To-day, and Forever," Simpson reminded readers of his journal in an article defending modern miracles of healing. If this historical Jesus had performed supernatural acts, Simpson reasoned, surely the resurrected Christ continued to make himself known in this manner. Countering the notion that miracles served only to testify to Jesus' divinity, Simpson insisted that Christ had healed the sick in order to reveal "His boundless love." To argue that Jesus' sympathy for the afflicted had ceased at the end of the apostolic era, Simpson implied, was to deny that Christ's "heart is still the same"—a claim that no true Christian ought to countenance. Simpson closed his article with a hymn stanza that depicted Jesus as the "Kinsman, Friend and Elder Brother" who had wept for the sufferings of his disciples, and as the "Living One" who had the power to make their pains cease.[45]

Although Simpson, Gordon, and other leaders of the divine healing movement were perhaps the most strident champions of modern miracles against their scientific and theological detractors, they were not the only ones to invoke supernatural manifestations of God's power as a means of countering the related threats of naturalism, rationalism, and traditionalism. Many of their arguments in favor of the present exercise of divine power, in fact, were reiterations of those put forward by Horace Bushnell, the Congregationalist pastor whom many later claimed as the father of American theological liberalism, in his 1858 study *Nature and the Supernatural*. Bushnell, like many other mid-nineteenth-century Americans, was deeply worried about the effects of modern life on the vitality of the Christian faith. Both the skepticism of philosophers who refuted the reality of biblical miracles and the materialism of contemporary scientific, economic, and political culture concerned Bushnell, and led him to challenge the Calvinist tendency to limit the purpose of miracles to attesting Jesus' divinity and therefore to confine supernatural interventions to the apostolic age. Christ's character, Bushnell contended, offered more than enough evidence of his divine nature and authority; his miracles, in this view, merely confirmed what had already been made apparent through his superior morality and virtue.[46]

Rather than relegating the miraculous to the margins, however, Bushnell suggested that the stories of supernatural happenings recorded in scripture provided incontrovertible proof of God's vital and transcendent, yet personal and benevolent omnipotence. Jesus worked miracles of healing to show that he had the ability to overrule the natural order but also (and, in Bushnell's view, more importantly) because he felt compassion for the sufferings of humanity. From this perspective, the notion that God ceased to relieve human misery and distress through supernatural means after the biblical era was morally and theologically offensive. Instead, Bushnell argued, God had continued to perform miracles throughout church history, and especially in those periods when faith in the supernatural had ebbed to a low point. According to this schema, the present age was particularly ripe for the demonstration of God's miraculous power. Through "his supernatural communication," Bushnell maintained, God offered empirical evidence of his existence and concrete confirmation of his compassion to the nineteenth-century believer who was beset by the faith-dulling forces of contemporary culture. Modern miracles provided a "an experimental knowledge of God" that was, as Bushnell put it, "strictly Baconian": an experiential encounter with supernatural reality that would "lift the church out of the abysses of a mere second-hand religion, keeping it alive and open to the realities of God's immediate visitation."[47]

Despite the controversy that *Nature and the Supernatural* provoked among members of the orthodox establishment as well as among liberal theologians, Bushnell's conviction that a dose of direct divine intervention would revive Christians from their spiritual torpor and restore the nineteenth-century church to a condition of vitality struck a chord among many of his contemporaries who shared his qualms about the influence of modern culture on the state of Christian faith. In the decades following the publication of Bushnell's treatise, American Protestants of both evangelical and liberal persuasions became increasingly anxious about the debilitating effects of philosophical skepticism, positivist materialism, and bureaucratic capitalism. All of these forces seemed to sap Christianity of its doctrinal and spiritual vigor by undermining belief in a transcendent realm and a supernatural God. While this perceived crisis of faith was certainly not unique—indeed, Romantics, Transcendentalists, and antebellum revivalists all lamented the decline of true religion and called for its renewal through direct spiritual experience—the doubts that late-nineteenth-century Protestants expressed prompted a particularly intense craving for positive assurances of God's personal, active power. According to one scholar, "The renewed quest for spiritual experience of an intimate deity" was the driving force that "fueled much of late-nineteenth-century religion."[48]

Although Protestants in this period adopted various strategies for reinvigorating the church—some, for example, turned back to the Middle Ages in an attempt to recapture what they perceived to be a more organic, authentic expression of the Christian faith—few tactics proved as compelling as the promotion of miraculous healings. Drawing on the primitivist impulse that characterized so much of nineteenth-century Protestantism, numerous reform movements, including Mormonism, Adventism, Spiritualism, and Christian Science claimed experiences of physical restoration as part of their repertoire. While each of these movements explained instances of healing in distinct ways—Spiritualists, for example, often attributed miraculous cures to the ministrations of angels, whereas Mary Baker Eddy and her followers insisted that physical healings demonstrated the truth of "divine power" over the illusion of material reality—all suggested that these experiences of bodily transformation represented signs of a return to a purer form of religion unmarred by the accretions of dogma and creed or the corruptions of institutional politics and cultural conformity. The purpose of Christian Science, argued Eddy and her first disciples, was an effort "to reinstate primitive Christianity and its lost element of healing." By reviving the healing practices of Jesus and the apostles, Christian Scientists provided demonstrable "proof that Christian promises were to be fulfilled in the present," as historian Stephen Gottschalk has put it, and "claimed to offer new and vital truths to a spiritually unsettled age." Although Spiritualists were less intent on rebuilding the apostolic church in the present, many of the movement's leaders insisted that healing mediums established a direct connection with spirit guides that not only supplied empirical verification of the spiritual realm but also dispensed with what one clairvoyant physician called "this monster, 'The Established Church.'" Instances of physical cure through spirit communication confirmed that individuals had direct access to spiritual power, without institutional interference from a corrupt and vitiated Christianity.[49]

The widespread tendency to appeal to bodily healings as a means for legitimating claims to spiritual purity or Christian primitivism provoked acute consternation among evangelical Protestant advocates of faith cure, who saw themselves as the rightful heirs and only true representatives of biblical Christianity. Like those they condemned as imposters, advocates of divine healing such as A. B. Simpson asserted that experiences of physical restoration verified the reality of the supernatural realm over and against "a growing spirit of rationalism among professing Christians." Quoting directly from *Nature and the Supernatural*, A. J. Gordon argued that modern miracles of healing offered believers a "way out of the dullness of second-hand faith, and the dryness of merely reasoned gospel" and a means for fulfilling their "longing for a kind of faith that shows God in living commerce with men such as he vouchsafed them in former times." Not only did physical healings prove that an omnipotent God still intervened in the natural world in order to alleviate the sufferings of human beings, Gordon suggested, but these supernatural events also represented the reinvesting of the church with "her apostolic powers."[50]

Critics of modern miracles—both Reformed theologians who continued to defend the cessationist position and liberal rationalists who insisted on the inviolability of natural law—were quick to point out the parallels between the arguments that advocates of faith cure advanced in favor of divine healing and those put forth by Spiritualists, Christian Scientists, and even Roman Catholic apologists for healings at Lourdes, France, or Knock Chapel in Ireland. Many, if not all of the cures claimed by these groups, argued detractors such as Presbyterian minister Marvin R. Vincent, pastor of the Church of the Covenant in New York City, could be attributed to the healing power of nature, "stimulated into curative efficiency by external influences, either another's exertion of will, a plausible delusion, or causes awakening faith and hope in divine power." In an influential essay published in the July 1883 edition of *The Presbyterian Review*, Vincent compared purported cases of divine healing with "the curative miracles, so called, of the Romish Church," as well as with assorted incidences of "humbug" and "quackery," including accounts of remarkable recoveries resulting from "the word of a skillful charlatan" and cures wrought through "the virtues of tar-water." While these diverse panaceas might have succeeded in curing certain ailments, Vincent suggested, they did so primarily through the "operation of ordinary physical laws" without the intervention of any miraculous power.[51]

Methodist minister and Boston University Professor Luther T. Townsend advanced a similar argument in his 1885 treatise *"Faith-Work," "Christian Science," and Other Cures*. Drawing on "modern" theories of "disease and cure," including experiments in "mental therapeutics," Townsend highlighted the "striking similarity" between the supposedly "miraculous" cures associated with the divine healing movement and those "effected by saints' relics, mesmerism, holy wells, touching for 'king's evil,' by 'metallic tractors,' by blue glass, by Prince Hohnlohe, by Jacob the Zouave," as well as by the "the so-called allopath, the homeopath, the isopath, the physiopath, the eclectic, the botanic, the cold-water curer, the electrician, the so termed Christian scientist." Finding "no essential difference" among the remarkable healings ascribed to these various agents, Townsend concluded that most could be explained on purely "natural" grounds.[52]

Although detractors like Townsend and Vincent conceded that God was capable of performing miraculous cures, they insisted that such supernatural events were the exception rather than the rule. Reversing the schema of sacred history set out by Bushnell, Gordon, and other champions of modern miracles, Vincent argued that "the whole drift of Christian history is away from these special, evidential demonstrations." Miracles, in his view, represented "a kind of object-teaching for a rudimentary stage of faith" that mature Christians should no longer require. Those who called for "a miraculous economy for the Church of the present," he contended, were encouraging Christians to return to "the conditions of spiritual childhood." From this perspective, proponents of divine healing were guilty of promoting an ignorant, superstitious and fanatical brand of religion, not a pure, primitive, and apostolic Christianity.[53]

Loath to have their movement regarded as spiritually regressive, let alone conflated with quackery—or, worse, with what they considered to be the erroneous, dangerous, and un-Christian teachings of Spiritualists and Christian Scientists—supporters of divine healing such as A. J. Gordon maintained that demonstrations of God's miraculous power in the present age were necessary in order to combat the "alleged miracles of the Romish Church," the cures purportedly wrought "through the agency of spirits," and the healings ascribed to Christian Science—all of which derived from the agency of the devil. Although some proponents of divine healing were willing to entertain the possibility that "the wonders at Lourdes and elsewhere" were "true" miracles performed in accordance with the "devout and simple faith" of the Catholic petitioner, most evangelicals followed the example of Bushnell, who argued that a distinction should be made between Jesus' miracles and the counterfeit claims of pagan wonder-workers and Roman Catholics. Apologists like Gordon and Simpson, for example, asserted that "the gifts of divine healing" were being revived in the contemporary church in order to reprove the "miracles of the Antichrist," who was capable of performing "wonders of a superhuman character, only demoniacal instead of divine, wrought through the agency of evil spirits to simulate the works of the Spirit of God." According to these authors, "lying wonders" were on the rise. "In our own time," Gordon wrote, "we have witnessed an extraordinary forth-putting of satanic energy in the works of modern spiritualism." Lamenting especially the "pretensions of spiritualism . . . to effect miraculous healing," Gordon surmised that the church ought to confront this "outbreak of satanic empiricism" with "sweet and gracious and humble displays of the Spirit's saving health."[54]

Simpson offered a similar diagnosis of and prescription for the modern period, linking the upsurge in false miracles to an eschatological vision of church history. "The Age of Miracles is not past. The Word of God never indicated a hint of such a fact," Simpson declared. "On the contrary, they are to be among the signs of the last day; and the very Adversary himself is to counterfeit them and send forth at last the spirits of devils working miracles, unto the kings of the earth." Experiences of divine healing were not only valid in these end times, Simpson insisted, but they were necessary for combating the works of Satan. "The only defense against the false miracles," he remarked, "will be the true."[55]

Simpson's conviction that signs and wonders—both demonic and divine—offered evidence that his generation was living in the last days sprang from his premillennial eschatology. According to this perspective, which was steadily replacing the postmillenialism that marked most of antebellum evangelicalism, Christ's return to earth was imminent. Unlike their more optimistic forbears, premillennialists did not believe that the world was progressing toward a period of peace and righteousness that would culminate in Christ's second coming. Instead, they argued that "the personal return of Christ is the only hope of the world and the church." As one proponent put it: "Morally, the world to-day is wabbling in its orbit, madly plunging towards despair and destruction. Religiously, the professing church is rapidly approaching a state of petrifaction and putrefaction . . . . According to the Scriptures, this dispensation will end in dissolution and destruction." Although many interpreters have stressed the otherworldly emphasis of premillennialist eschatology, most of its early proponents insisted that this doctrine was "a motive to Christian work." Before Christ could come again, the church had to fulfill its mission to preach the gospel "in all the world for a witness unto all nations." Only when this task had been accomplished would "the Lord himself appear, take up His part of the programme and carry it out to the glorious consummation." The "speedy evangelization of the world," therefore, became an urgent imperative.[56]

While not all participants in the divine healing movement embraced premillennialism, Christ's imminent and cataclysmic return became a major theme for several key proponents, including Gordon and Simpson. For these leaders, and for the many other late-nineteenth-century evangelicals who adopted this increasingly popular perspective on the end times, miracles of healing provided a vital tool for undertaking the task of evangelism both at home and abroad. "The blessed gospel of physical healing in the name of Jesus," Simpson proclaimed "will prove an invaluable handmaid to the cause of missions." Just as cures accomplished through the miraculous manifestation of God's supernatural power refuted the rationalism of modern culture and contested the counterfeit wonders of demonic forces, so they would also reveal the "living power and presence of God" to the "Confucians and the Brahmans" who touted their own sophisticated yet skeptical philosophies, and to the "heathens" who remained captivated by the machinations of "evil priests." If the "civilized world" was a battleground in which the conflict between God and Satan was being fought out, the "pagan nations" represented the front lines of the war. In either arena, divine healing offered a formidable weapon for the Christian soldiers who sought to prepare the earth for the final apocalyptic confrontation.[57]

The zeal that premillennialists brought to their missionary endeavor also influenced their attitude toward sickness. Given the urgency of the enterprise, premillennialists stressed the pressing need for a host of healthy, energetic individuals who would spread the good news to all nations prior to Christ's second coming. Time was short, false "miracle-mongers" were multiplying, skepticism was gaining ground, and the devil was on the prowl, seeking to "convert people to the creed of the prince of darkness" through "the most signal displays of superhuman power." How then, could Christians—even those afflicted by pain and laid low by suffering—sit passively by and resign themselves to a life of ongoing invalidism? "We are in the Age of miracles, the Age of Christ, the Age which lies between two Advents, and underneath the eye of a ceaseless Divine Presence; the Age of Power, the Age which above all other ages of time should be intensely alive," Simpson proclaimed. Surely Christians ought to claim the promises put forth in scripture, trust the Great Physician for healing, and rise up from their sickbeds to go forth and serve the Lord! "We believe there are hundreds of the children of God who to-day are prevented from taking an active part in work for the salvation of souls by sickness, which may be taken away if they would but take God at his word," one proponent of divine healing intoned. Taking direct aim at the ideal of sanctified affliction, another supporter put it this way: "Oh, if those of His dear children who believe that they are glorifying God by their sickness and suffering, could be led to see how much *more* they might glorify Him, even in one year of active service for Him, than in a lifetime of suffering I believe many would reach out and accept this free and full salvation. He does so use even His humblest servants."[58]

The urgency of the end times, the appeal of the primitivist apologetic, the revival of modern miracles—all of these factors suggested to evangelicals in the late nineteenth century that passive resignation was not an appropriate posture for Christians to adopt when confronted with the problem of sickness or pain. The present age called for a different devotional ethic—a model of spiritual experience that emphasized God's beneficent power rather than the doctrine of afflictive providence, that required human beings to act their faith rather than accept their suffering, that led all of God's children—even the "humblest servants"—out of the confines of the sickroom into the active sphere of the world.

CHAPTER THREE

Acting Faith

The Devotional Ethics and Gendered Dynamics of Divine Healing

Carrie Judd became an invalid at the age of eighteen. One morning in the early winter of 1876–1877, Judd slipped on an icy sidewalk on her way to the Buffalo Normal School where she was studying to become a teacher. Her arms loaded with heavy books, Judd hit the stone walkway hard. Although she managed to make it to class that day, the "severe fall" led to "a gradual decline in health." Within several months, Judd was confined to her bed, suffering from what she described as "spinal difficulty," "a most distressing hyper-acuteness, called hyperaesthesia," and "blood consumption." For most of the following two years, she "was obliged to lie in a darkened room," powerless to move without assistance and unable to endure "the tiniest jar or noise" without "dreadful" repercussions. By February of 1879, Judd could no longer eat solid food. She grew "emaciated to a shadow" and "was not expected to live from one day to the next." About this time, Judd's father came across a newspaper article describing "the wonderful cures performed in answer to the prayers of Mrs. Edward Mix, a colored lady, of Wolcottville, Conn." Although she had read of faith cures before, Judd was particularly impressed by the account of Sarah Mix's ministry. At the prompting of her parents, Judd asked her sister Eva to write to Mix, requesting prayers for her recovery. In her reply, Mix assured Judd that "God has promised to raise up the sick ones." Directing her to the passage in James 5, Mix wrote, "Now if you can claim that promise, I have not the least doubt but what [*sic*] you will be healed."[1]

But what did it mean to claim the promise of faith cure? Mix went on to explain that in order to be healed, Judd must not only pray and believe but also act. First, she was to demonstrate her trust in "God and His promises" by laying aside "all medicine of every description" and by refusing to call upon physicians. Second, she was to begin praying for faith. Finally, on Wednesday, February 26, between three and four in the afternoon, Judd was to "pray for herself" while the female prayer meeting at Mix's house in Connecticut also made her "a subject of prayer." "I want you to pray believing and then *act faith*," Mix wrote. "It makes no difference how you feel, but get right out of bed and begin to walk by faith."[2]

Despite her initial skepticism that she would be able to arise and walk after so many months of "confirmed helplessness," at the appointed hour Judd prayed for "an increase of faith"; then she "turned over and raised up alone, for the first time in over two years." Through active obedience to Mix's directives (which echoed Jesus' own commands in the Gospels), Judd overcame her doubt not only in word but in deed. Healing was a matter of belief put into practice. Over the next few weeks, Judd continued to perform acts of faith that had been impossible for her prior to February 26: she walked around her room and up and down the stairs, she visited neighbors, and she began to study and write without suffering the headaches that had so troubled her during her illness. By mid-March, the rector of the local Episcopal church to which Judd and her family belonged testified that the former invalid appeared to be "in perfect health."[3]

Several months later, Judd composed a brief narrative of her healing that was published in the local paper. The article "attracted so much attention," Judd later recounted, "that it was copied into many other papers, and finally reached England, where it was published in the Christian Herald." Encouraged by the "hundreds of letters" from inquirers who wanted to know if her story was true and also from "sufferers who saw the account and took courage," Judd wrote *The Prayer of Faith*, which contained not only several accounts of healing (including her own) but also "Bible teaching on the subject." Published in 1880, this book rapidly became one of the foundational texts of the divine healing movement in North America and abroad. Soon Judd sensed a call not only to write her story but to offer public testimony, first at prayer meetings, then as a "woman preacher" in churches, and eventually at national camp meetings and world-wide conventions sponsored by healing advocates such as Cullis, Boardman, and Simpson. "After my marvelous healing," Judd wrote, "I felt that God had raised me up for His special service, and while I was glad to fulfill the little duties which lay nearest at hand, in the home and neighborhood, yet I had a great desire to engage in some definite work for the Master, who had done so much for me." In years to come, Judd's work included

Carrie Judd after her healing. Courtesy of the Flower Pentecostal Heritage Center.

founding, financing, editing, and publishing a monthly journal; establishing and operating a "faith home" for invalids seeking instruction on divine healing; leading a WCTU Gospel Mission to "fallen men"; serving as a founding member and officer of the Christian Alliance; migrating to California with her husband, George Montgomery, and building a second faith home in Oakland that she later expanded to include a Bible Training School, a chapel, and an orphanage; and finally, authoring numerous tracts, editorials, and articles on faith healing and other religious subjects.[4]

By acting her faith, Judd was transformed from a feeble invalid who "lay gasping faintly for breath" on her cot to an energetic worker who was able to undertake the active ministries to which she felt ordained by God. Throughout her long confinement, Judd had struggled with the notion that she could best serve God by passively resigning herself to ongoing invalidism or even imminent death. When she first became incapacitated, Judd felt "a deep regret that I had been obliged to give up all my plans for a fine education, and my ambitions for the future." Even when her physicians despaired of her recovery, Judd refused to believe that her work on earth was done. "I feel that I have a mission yet," she told her mother, Emily. Drawing on the devotional ethic that had shaped her own experiences of pain and affliction, Emily Judd gently suggested to her daughter that her mission might be to "lie here and suffer and be an example of patience to others." This was a message that Carrie could not accept. "No, Mother," she replied, "I mean an *active mission.*"[5]

This exchange between mother and daughter reveals that the image of the suffering servant as the epitome of Christian sainthood was less compelling for young persons of Carrie Judd's generation than it had been for their parents. By the 1870s, as we have observed, many of the theological and cultural conditions that had lent authority to this ideal of Christian sanctity in the earlier decades of the nineteenth century had begun to shift. Focusing on the practice of "acting faith," this chapter considers how the divine healing movement presented invalids like Carrie Judd with a strategy for surmounting the afflictions that beleaguered their bodies as well as a means for rewriting the deeply gendered script that linked the pursuit of health and holiness with passive endurance of corporal pain. By instructing sick persons to rise up and walk regardless of their feelings or physical symptoms, ministers of faith cure were promoting a hermeneutics of healing that elevated the spiritual over the material, the miraculous over the natural, the ineffable over the empirical. The capacity to trust in and act according to the authority of scripture, in this view, trumped the diagnoses of the doctors as well as the skepticism of the doubters in determining an individual's ability to overcome illness and engage in energetic service.

Although proponents often suggested that acting faith entailed a considerable expenditure of human effort, they always insisted that this healing practice required absolute dependence on God. Only through an infusion of the Holy Spirit could invalids adopt a devotional ethic that promoted active resistance rather than patient resignation as the appropriate response to bodily affliction. For these evangelicals, accentuating the paradoxical relationship between human agency and divine sovereignty in the curative process served as a tactic for recasting the meaning and experience of physical suffering amidst a host of complex religious, cultural, and social circumstances. First, embracing such an enigmatic understanding of healing, leaders such as Charles Cullis and Carrie Judd indicated, allowed ailing individuals to affirm God's power and willingness to perform miracles in the modern era even when prayers for physical recovery seemed to go unanswered. By stressing God's sovereignty and questioning the sufficiency of the senses to apprehend spiritual realities, faith cure advocates sought to resist the growing sway of medical material-ism while simultaneously circumventing the perplexing predicament of apparent failure. Second, the practice of acting faith helped distinguish divine healing from mental therapeutics. Since healing involved a mysterious amalgamation of divine priority and human action, advocates like A. J. Gordon argued, faith cures could not be attributed to will power and should not be conflated with Christian Science or other forms of mind cure. Finally, maintaining that the devotional ethics of di-vine healing were rooted in an inscrutable mixture of personal volition and divine intervention enabled exponents of faith cure to navigate the intense and often bit-ter gender politics that marked debates about the relationship between religion and health in the late nineteenth century. According to adherents such as A. B. Simpson, the paradox embedded in the practice of acting faith made it possible for both women and men to engage in active service to God without transgressing conven-tional norms of female submissiveness and male vigor. By acting their faith while "resting in God," invalids like Simpson and Judd embodied a model of spiritual experience that stretched, but did not violate, prevailing medical theories, cultural conceptions, and religious ideals of true womanhood and virile masculinity.

The Hermeneutics of Healing and the Problem of Unanswered Prayer

By the time Carrie Judd received Sarah Mix's letter containing instructions for claiming healing from the Great Physician, she had already sought relief from a succession of irregular practitioners and orthodox doctors, none of whom had been able to help her. Even prior to her fall on the ice, Judd had spent a season at the "Home on the Hillside" in Dansville, New York, at the urging of her eldest brother Charlie, who served as private secretary to the hygienic institute's director, Dr. James Caleb Jackson. Concerned about his fifteen-year-old sister's fragile ap-pearance, Charlie suggested that the benefits of fresh air, exercise, and a "healthful diet" of "Graham gems" and "simple sanitarium foods" would fortify her feeble health. Unfortunately, Carrie fell seriously ill during her stay at the water-cure and left Dansville in an even more frail condition. After her accident, Judd tried a myr-iad of home remedies and physician's tonics, all to no avail. Although she obtained treatment from a number of prominent doctors, "no medicine seemed to help," and she grew progressively worse. Eventually, her condition became so bleak that her friends and neighbors gave up hope of her improvement. Judd, however, re-fused to despair. Despite her pain and regardless of her physicians' grim prognoses, she continued to believe that God had something more in store for her. When she read Mix's message indicating that physical healing was not only a possibility but a sure promise, she was eager to make one last effort toward regaining her health and fulfilling her desire to engage in a life of active Christian service.[6]

Like Judd, many of the other invalids who visited or wrote to Mix seeking prayers for healing sought her out after months or years of medical treatment failed to produce any permanent or perceptible recovery. Charles G. Hart, who resided in Mix's home town, "had tried all kinds of medicine . . . and employed a good physician" in an attempt to redress his inflammatory rheumatism, "yet all to no effect." Finally, he was "suffering so intensely" that he sent for Mix. Elizabeth Baptist of Springfield, Massachusetts, consulted four different doctors over a six-month period "until, like the woman in the gospel," she wrote, "I had spent all my living on physicians, and made nothing better but grew worse." Convinced that "no medicine could ever cure" her prostrated nerves, Baptist asked Mix to pay her a visit. Mrs. Herbert Hall sought Mix's prayers after "powerful remedies" offered no relief from "enlargement of the spleen, inflammation of the bowels and falling of the uterus," and her doctors "gave [her] up to die."[7]

Notwithstanding the apparent hopelessness of their situations, none of these individuals resigned themselves to their doctor's dire predictions of incurable invalidism or imminent death. Turning in desperation to what seemed like "a last resort," as Charles Hart put it, they hoped that Mix's prayers might prompt a miracle, and they were not disappointed. Less than half an hour after Mix began to pray for Hart's recovery, he recalled, "I could walk all about the room, and I rested well the rest of the night." Five months later, he remained "well and free from rheumatism, and serving the Lord." Elizabeth Baptist described her cure in even more immediate and sensory terms. When Mix "offered the prayer of faith, and, anointing me with oil, laid her hand upon me in the name of the Lord," Baptist wrote, "I felt the power of God passing all through my body, and through faith in the name of Jesus, the nerves quieted down, and I arose from my bed as if filled with new life." For Mrs. Hall, healing was an equally palpable and instantaneous experience. At five minutes before seven o'clock, Mix knelt at Hall's bedside, began to recite a "very simple prayer," and laid her hands upon Hall's bowels and heart, beseeching God to heal both body and soul. "As she drew her hand over my bloated body," Hall recalled, "I felt the swelling going down." Finally, Mix bade the sick woman to "rise up and walk." At that moment, Hall got out of bed, dressed herself, and went down to the kitchen, startling her family so much that one of her sisters fainted in surprise.[8]

For these three sufferers and for many others who appealed to the Great Physician, divine healing was a decidedly dramatic and thoroughly tangible event. Where remedies and doctors disappointed, faith in God's healing power produced prompt, discernible results. Pain ceased at a precise moment. Bodies that lay prostrate suddenly arose. Pallid complexions quickly gained color, and paralyzed limbs became animated. Indeed, some of the most celebrated cases of faith cure, such as Jennie Smith's remarkable restoration after sixteen years of "utter helplessness," emphasized the rapid and markedly sensate manner in which God imparted strength and health. In her testimony of healing, Smith compared the vivid sensations that she experienced on the night of her recovery to "an electric shock." Within moments of feeling this "baptism of strength" pass through her system, Smith was up and walking. As she rose to her feet, Smith dramatized the change that had taken place: at that instant, she was no longer a bedridden invalid but a "new creature."[9]

Such spectacular "instances of God's power," one advocate of faith cure remarked, "may lead even this faithless generation to acknowledge that 'All things are possible to him that believeth.'" Healed bodies, in this view, were epiphanies: proof of God's immediate, intimate, incarnational presence in the lives of faithful Christian believers. While accounts of extraordinary recovery inspired faith in God's miraculous intervention in the modern age, however, stories like these also caused confusion and doubt among the many individuals who prayed for healing but failed to experience instantaneous or perceptible answers to their petitions. When Helen Dawlly asked God for health, for example, she expected "to be healed with accompanying manifestations. For this I waited," she wrote, "and wondered that they did not come." If lack of sensation posed problems, so did delay. In September of 1882, L. A. Baldwin acknowledged that eight months had elapsed since she had followed the command to be anointed as given in James 5, without much in the way of "immediate help." "I have never had the startling and sudden revelations mentioned by some," she conceded, "but the ministry of waiting has been mine."[10]

Explaining situations such as these became a pressing problem for advocates of divine healing like Sarah Mix and Charles Cullis. Why did some experience such tangible feelings while others were insensible of any change? What could account for the fact that certain prayers seemed to remain unanswered while others received dramatic and immediate results? And perhaps most troubling of all, why did some seem to be kept waiting for restoration indefinitely? If healing was God's will, as proponents of faith cure insisted that it was, then whose fault was "failure"?

Early leaders of the movement offered several different answers to these questions. Some, like Cullis, suggested that although Christians ought to trust God's promises "as to the healing of the body," God's will remained mysterious. Reflecting on some cases in which healing did not follow the prayer of faith, Cullis wrote, "I offer no explanation upon this point. He who 'directs our paths,' and whose 'grace is sufficient,' has also said, 'What I do thou knowest not now; but thou shalt know hereafter' (John xiii.7)." In the *Ministry of Healing*, A. J. Gordon echoed Cullis's response: "It is as true here as in any other field that God acts sovereignly and according to his own determinate counsel. He sees it best to recover one person at the instance of his people's prayers, and he may see it best to withhold such recovery for a time from another." Indeed, throughout his treatise, Gordon tried to chart a middle way that would preserve some ambiguity about the relationship between divine sovereignty and human agency in the calculus of physical healing. For example, he insisted on maintaining a measure of uncertainty in his interpretation of scriptural passages such as Matthew 8:16–17 that alluded to Jesus' ministry of healing. "In the atonement of Christ," he wrote, "there seems to be a foundation laid for faith in bodily healing. Seems—we say, for the passage to which we refer is so profound and unsearchable in its meaning that one would be very careful not to speak dogmatically in regard to it." While Gordon consistently sounded a note of caution and moderation in his attempts to articulate the tenets of divine healing, his hesitation did not preclude him from pursuing the idea that Christ's death on the cross atoned for both sin and its consequences, including illness. "It is at least a deep and suggestive truth," he surmised, "that we have Christ set before us as the sickness-bearer as well as the sin-bearer of his people. In the gospel it is written, 'And he cast out devils and healed all that were sick, that it might be fulfilled which was spoken by Esaias the prophet, saying, 'Himself took our infirmities and *bare our sicknesses.*'"[11]

Despite Gordon's judicious approach, the idea that the biblical message included both spiritual salvation and bodily healing quickly became a fundamental supposition of faith cure theology. Few were as tentative as Gordon in their efforts to explain this principle. In a series of articles entitled "Gospel Parallelisms: Illustrated in the Healing of Body and Soul," published in a popular magazine in 1883 and 1884, the Reverend Robert Livingston Stanton of Washington, D.C., former moderator of the Presbyterian General Assembly and past president of Miami University of Ohio, endeavored "to show that the atonement of Christ lays a foundation equally for deliverance from sin and for deliverance from disease." Unlike Gordon, who emphasized the inscrutability of biblical passages that to him only seemed to *suggest* that healing was included in the atonement, Stanton insisted that "the teaching of the Scriptures on which this twofold redemption is based is very plain," citing as evidence the very same verses that Gordon characterized as enigmatic: Matthew 8:16–17 and Isaiah 53:3–5. R. K. Carter offered a similarly strong reading of these texts in his book *The Atonement for Sin and Sickness: or, A Full Salvation for*

Soul and Body, published in 1884. "The clear meaning is, that Jesus did take upon Himself our diseases and our mental troubles, in precisely the same way that he 'bore our sins in his own body on the tree,'" Carter wrote in reference to Isaiah 53:4. "Surely nothing but the blindest prejudice can close the eyes, in the light of these facts, to the great truth that sickness is included in the vicarious Atonement, every whit as emphatically as sin, in this great proof chapter of Isaiah."[12]

Neither Carter nor Stanton shrank from pushing the consequences of the "healing in the atonement" doctrine to their logical extreme. "Assuming that Christ's atonement was made for the deliverance of the body from disease and the soul from sin," Stanton reasoned, "we may conclude that God's gracious purpose will be accomplished in all who accept the Gospel offer in its fullness. If the divine provision fail in any case, whether relating to the body or the soul, this failure must be charged upon man and not upon God." Unanswered prayers for physical healing, Stanton argued, could not be explained by resorting to the mystery of divine sovereignty. God's will had been made perfectly clear through the ministry of Jesus as recorded in the Bible. In cases of failure, it was human agency that had somehow missed the mark. In response to the question, "Why are not all healed immediately, who are healed at all?" Stanton wrote: "The responsibility for the failure of an immediate cure lies somewhere with the sick, or with some of the persons or instrumentalities employed in seeking a cure." For illness and suffering, human beings, not God, were to blame.[13]

Although Carter was willing to grant that the sovereign God might withhold an answer to prayer for healing "until the time best adapted to glorify His Son," he too suggested that in most cases "apparent failures" were the fault of petitioners. "We must not be discouraged if the answer appears to be delayed," Carter counseled, "but diligently seek for possible hindrances in ourselves." Deferred or gradual healings, he explained, were more common than instantaneous cures because of "the imperfect consecration and faith in so many patients." Deficient devotion was also the most likely explanation for intractable invalidism. "It may seem a hard thing to say, but it is plain that the saintly reputation of so many lingering invalids, can not be built upon their years of suffering, for these are rather the evidence either of some great sin in the past, or of a persistent lack of conformity to the will of God in one way or another," Carter asserted. "A long continued affliction *may* indicate an obstinate refusal to follow Jesus entirely."[14]

Stanton and Carter were not alone in proposing lack of faith as the solution to the problem of unanswered prayer. Many of the leading advocates of divine healing asserted that failure to receive healing was in some measure a result of insufficient trust in God's promises. Nor was this solely a theological argument, rehearsed by prominent spokespersons for the faith cure movement. Lay participants also charged unanswered prayer to the sick person's own account. One woman, who suffered for years from excruciating headaches, recalled a conversation with an elderly stranger, who told her, "'It is your own fault if you have headaches. *God* does not want you to have them.'" Even those faith cure proponents like Cullis who tried to maintain a place for mystery within divine healing sometimes implied that unbelief might, in certain cases, be to blame for failure. Early on in his ministry of healing, Cullis noticed that while some cures were instantaneous, others were gradual or perhaps not forthcoming at all. "My explanation is . . . that there has been oftentimes a question or lack of faith on the part of the patient, for some seem to come, not in faith, but as a matter of experiment."[15]

Although he always lamented the tendency of petitioners to "experiment" with prayer for healing, Cullis eventually found an alternate way to accommodate the theology of faith cure to those who experienced gradual, rather than dramatic and immediate answers to prayer. "As to healing, it is always according to our faith," Cullis preached at one of his weekly faith cure meetings in 1883. "But we must not expect new lungs or a new head in a moment or that a tumor is to jump out of us. It may in some cases be days or weeks before the cure is complete. The position we are to take is this: 'Lord, I *am* healed.' Don't pray any more to *be* healed, but rest upon his word." In other words, Cullis suggested, while unbelief might sometimes be the reason prayers went unanswered, *assumptions* might also be to blame. Rather than looking for instantaneous results and then despairing when suffering failed to cease immediately, supplicants needed to revise their expectations about the experience of healing altogether. To have true faith was to trust that God heard and answered prayers for healing despite physical evidence to the contrary. "A man who had been prayed with said to me yesterday, 'I have the pains yet, what am I to do?'" Cullis reported. "I told him to take this stand—*I am healed.* You may have the symptoms of your disease, but count the work as done and leave the symptoms with God." According to this interpretation, tangible results—or their absence—became irrelevant. What mattered, in Cullis's view, was a person's ability to believe: "Let me remind you again that the blessing God gives is always according to your faith, not your doubts, or feelings, or symptoms, but according to your faith."[16]

By emphasizing belief rather than experience, Cullis dealt with failure by redefining it. Faith, not feeling, was the measure of success. Divine healing, in this view, operated according to a unique hermeneutics that valued personal conviction over sensory perception, spiritual commitment over empirical evidence. If an invalid trusted God's promises and believed she was healed, the persistence of pain was immaterial. She could still date her cure to a specific instant—the moment she prayed and believed. In a testimony published in September 1883, for example, H. A. Steinhauer insisted that although "I am again consigned to room and bed, the measure of strength and freedom from pain which is the world's test of cure not yet having been given . . . I shall still say I was healed July 12, 1883." Citing a number of scripture passages in her defense, Steinhauer argued that the continued presence of symptoms should not invalidate her claim to have been cured. "I am healed," she wrote, "for my heavenly Father is a prayer-hearing and promise-keeping God. . . . But this all-mighty Lord is also a God 'who calleth those things which be not, as though they were' (Rom. iv:17), and this is a *faith*-cure. 'Now faith is the substance of things *hoped* for, the evidence of things *not seen*' (Heb. xi:1)." In fact, Steinhauer suggested, the tendency to look for "immediate results, that instant and perfect cure," could actually hinder the work of healing. By looking for "physical evidence," petitioners revealed a failure to trust fully in God's promises. For this reason, Steinhauer asserted, God sometimes allowed symptoms to remain until a supplicant learned to "'walk by faith and not by sight'" (2 Cor. v:7).[17]

Trusting God's promises, however, meant something more than simply believing them. Walking by faith implied action. "If I say I have faith that I am healed in the name of the Lord, and yet do not show forth my faith by acting as if I were healed it is apparent to myself and to others that my faith is without works and dead," wrote Carrie Judd several years after her own restoration to health. "If I say that I believe a certain thing, my actions must testify to that belief." Following in the footsteps of her mentor Sarah Mix, Judd became a major emissary for the idea that human agency played an integral role in the healing process. Just as Mix encouraged Judd to arise and walk, regardless of how she felt physically, so Judd urged the many invalids who sought her counsel to act according to their convictions rather than their senses or circumstances. In her own testimony of healing, for example, Judd stressed the lack of tangible sensations accompanying her prayers. While she did note that "a decided change was perceptible" in her "color, circulation and pulse" within the hour, Judd emphasized the gradual rather than immediate restoration of her physical strength. Her healing was a process that took several weeks, during which she continued "simply to look to the Lord for improvement," trusting that "as He had begun the work, He would carry it on."[18]

The message Judd conveyed through her narrative, then, was that petitioners need not expect instantaneous and sensate answers to their prayers for healing. That "extraordinary . . . sensations are often experienced in connection with faith-healing we admit," Judd wrote, "but many times they are not, and we are required to believe God's word before we see 'signs and wonders.'" In *The Prayer of Faith*, Judd explained that "belief or faith is the *evidence* in our mind of things as yet un-

seen. Before we have the evidence of our senses in regard to the matter, we accept
the evidence of faith." And accepting this evidence, in Judd's view, meant acting on
it. "There is a simple test which, in many cases, we may apply to our conduct, which
will speedily convince us whether or not we are really believing that our prayers are
answered, and that is, to *act* out our faith," Judd wrote. "Whatever we really believe,
we are ready to act in accordance with."[19]

Over the course of the next several years, Judd printed dozens of articles encouraging sufferers to trust God for healing by acting faith in *Triumphs of Faith: A
Monthly Journal Devoted to Faith-Healing, and to the Promotion of Christian Holiness.* This publication, which Judd founded in January of 1881, became a primary
vehicle for spreading the doctrines of divine healing. In addition to editing the
journal, Judd authored many of the articles herself, including the lead editorial in
the very first issue, entitled, "Faith's Reckonings." In this piece, Judd defined many
of the key terms and expressions that would come to populate the vocabulary of the
faith cure movement. Employing rhetoric reminiscent of the Holiness movement,
and particularly of Phoebe Palmer's "altar phraseology," Judd opposed faith (defined in terms of profession put into practice) to feelings or emotions as well as to
sensory manifestations or appearances. In her own work, Palmer had insisted that
the experience of "holiness" or "entire sanctification" did not necessarily involve
"ecstatic emotions" or other "*sensible* forms of acceptance." The only "evidence"
required was trust in God's promises, demonstrated by an act of faith. By "laying all
upon the altar," Palmer insisted, a person confirmed her trust in the atonement of
Christ and thus received the blessings of holiness that Christ had achieved. "It matters not what my feelings may be," Palmer wrote, "I am called to *live* a life of *faith*."
In "Faith's Reckonings," Judd echoed Palmer's teachings regarding spiritual blessing, stating that "it is not necessary to *feel* some particular emotion in our hearts,
but to *act* as though we believe what we *profess* to believe." To obtain "holiness of
heart," Judd insisted, "we are to believe that the blessing prayed for is ours solely on
the assurance of God's word, without any reference to the apparent state of things
. . . and then in God's own time . . . we shall have that possession made manifest to
our human sense as well as to our faith."[20]

Taking these ideas a step further, Judd claimed that the pathway to bodily health
followed the same route as the road to spiritual sanctification. "If, after prayer for
physical healing, we reckon the work as already accomplished in our bodies," she
reasoned, "we shall not fear to *act out* that faith, and to make physical exertions
which will justify our professed belief in the healing." Following such a course, Judd
assured her "dear invalid readers," would ultimately result in manifest blessing. "After each venture of faith look steadfastly at Jesus, without regard to your apparent

weakness," she advised, "and you will surely receive according to your *faith* and not according to your *feelings*."[21]

For Judd, Palmer's Holiness theology provided a helpful means for dealing with the problem of prayers for healing that seemed to go unanswered. Just as Palmer's "altar terminology" overturned the expectation so prevalent among some proponents of revivalism that ecstatic emotions always accompanied the experience of sanctification, so Judd's explanation of acting faith unsettled the assumption that tangible physical sensations necessarily attended the experience of healing. Both women found a way to uncouple the quest for assurance from sensible experience by shifting the emphasis onto faith in action.

Despite the continued presence of testimonies like Jennie Smith's that described healing as a dramatic and palpable event, the alternative Judd offered proved much more prevalent both as a theological strategy and as a narrative framework. Many invalids highlighted the importance of acting on conviction rather than according to their senses or emotions in their own experiences of healing. "I accepted Jesus as my Physician, and when I arose I *believed* my cancer was gone," proclaimed Sara Burdge of Buffalo, New York, in the testimony she submitted to *Triumphs of Faith.* "I did not feel any different, but we walk by *faith* and not by sight. When we trust to *feelings,* we are walking by sight. I began to *act* faith at once. . . . I was not out of pain for four months, but I knew I was healed." Anna Prosser, a close associate of Carrie Judd's who partnered with her more famous friend in a variety of ministries, described her healing from a lingering illness in a similar fashion in her autobiography *From Death to Life:* "Believing steadily that I am eternally redeemed both from sickness and 'all iniquity,' I shall continually praise God that such is the case, and it will be unto me according to my faith." Although "circumstances, symptoms and feelings may seem contradictory and perplexing," Prosser declared, "we have authority from the Scriptures to declare ourselves healed of all our diseases, once for all, through the finished work of our Lord Jesus Christ. . . . Accept the truth of your healing accomplished long ago on Calvary's cross, and in God's own time (perhaps very quickly) the evidence of your senses will be added to that of your faith." Like Judd, Prosser adopted Phoebe Palmer's syntax of salvation and sanctification in order to explain the grammar of divine healing. Once "you have offered yourself a living sacrifice upon His altar," she advised her audience at a convention for the promotion of "Christian Life and Work and Divine Healing" held at Buffalo in December 1887, "then you are to believe that you receive Christ as all your strength; receive Him by faith, as your Healer, just as you received Him as the Savior from your sins."[22]

Through spokespersons such as Prosser and Judd, acting faith became a principal idiom in the devotional ethics of divine healing. Other prominent proponents of faith cure commended this practice as well. During one of her weekly addresses at Bethshan, the faith home she founded along with Charlotte Murray and William and Mary Boardman in London, Elizabeth Baxter exhorted attendees to "tread out upon God's word, like Peter upon the water." Reminding her audience that "we must believe that everything we have trusted to His hands is a thing already begun," she preached this message: "Now let us, this afternoon, just have real faith in our God; let us be able to trust Him out of our sight and out of the circle of our feelings, too, so that when we do not feel or see, or have the evidence of our senses that God is doing His work, yet we have a distinct word, *I AM*, that He has spoken to act upon."[23]

A. B. Simpson reiterated this message in numerous sermons, essays, and treatises outlining the tenets of divine healing. After they met in the early 1880s, Simpson and Judd became life-long associates and worked together on various endeavors for the promotion of divine healing and holiness. Simpson regularly contributed articles to *Triumphs of Faith*, many of which expounded on the theology and practice of acting faith. In a piece entitled "'The Gospel of Healing,'" for example, Simpson counseled his readers to "begin to act as one that is healed. Treat Christ as if you trusted Him, by attempting in His name and strength what would be impossible in your own; and He will not fail you if you really trust him."[24]

Human Agency, Divine Sovereignty, and the Problem of Will Power

The solution that Cullis, Judd, and other proponents of faith cure posed to the dilemma of apparent failure provoked another set of predicaments. For many sufferers, the command "Arise, take up thy bed and walk" seemed a rather tall order. How were immobile invalids who were unable even to lift a finger supposed to stand up on their feet? In their attempt to accommodate the theology of divine healing to those who did not receive palpable or instant answers to prayer, had promoters of acting faith lifted one burden only to replace it with a heavier load? What if an individual could not muster up the courage—not to mention the physical energy—to get out of bed? Did the devotional ethics of divine healing put too much emphasis on the role of personal volition in the curative process?

Leaders of the faith cure movement endeavored to address these concerns by complicating the concept of human agency through an appeal to the primacy of divine sovereignty. Reflecting on his own initial encounter with divine healing, for example, A. B. Simpson recalled that his first efforts to step out on God's promises failed miserably because, as he put it, "I was trusting in myself, in my own heart, in my own faith." As a result, he found himself sicker than ever and sorely discouraged. Only when he recognized that faith itself was a gift of God rather than a work of the human will, was he able to obey the command to arise and walk without faltering. "Our very faith is but the grace of Christ Himself within us," he explained. "We can exercise it, and thus far our responsibility extends; but He must impart it." Working hard to make faith for healing accessible, Simpson insisted that "lack of faith" need never be a hindrance. "If I need faith for anything," he declared, "I don't agonize in prayer until I get a certain degree of faith; I just say: 'It is Thy faith, not mine' . . . and I take His faith, and depend upon it to be mine, I go forward and act as if I had it, and I find that He meets me and gives me the blessing and confidence in His healing and His power."[25]

Carrie Judd also emphasized the necessity of depending solely on God when acting faith. "It was especially noticeable, during my healing," she remarked, "that whenever I made any extra exertion on my own, suddenly, and without the least apparent cause, my strength would fail me." When she relied solely upon her own agency, Judd implied, she was liable to sink, but "the more fully I cast myself upon Him, the more I was supported, and often I felt borne up as if by some buoyancy in the air, while there was little or no effort of my own." Elizabeth Baxter made the same point in a sermon she preached at Bethshan. Rather than looking to them-selves—for faith or for the strength to act it out—Baxter urged her audience members to allow their bodies to become "a theatre for God's acting." This was possible, she explained, because God, "the source of all strength," was alive within them. "I am crucified with Christ," she proclaimed, citing Galatians 2:20, "nevertheless I live; yet not I, but Christ liveth in me."[26]

Acting faith, then, meant trusting God for the ability to believe and the strength to do. Sufferers who were intimidated by the command to rise and walk needed only to recognize the power they possessed—or the power that possessed them—in order to carry out this directive. "The body of Christ is the living fountain of all our vital strength," Simpson wrote. "The healing which Christ gives us is nothing less than His own new physical life infused into our body. . . . It is the very life of Jesus manifested in our mortal flesh." If an individual could grasp this incarnational no-tion, acting faith would become effortless: "This principle is of immense impor-tance in the practical experience of healing. . . . When we cease to put confidence in the flesh, and look only to Christ and His supernatural life in us for our strength of body as well as spirit, we shall find that we can do all things through Christ that strengtheneth us."[27]

According to these evangelical Protestants, acting faith was a performance inspired, not by individual agency, but by an influx of divine energy. Turning once again to the Holiness movement for insight, spokespersons like Judd maintained that both spiritual salvation and bodily redemption involved "yielding" to God and ceasing "all self-effort, as a new and wonderful life-power takes possession of us, thinking, speaking, moving through us." In surrendering the self to God, Judd explained, an individual entered into "complete harmony with His blessed will" and became one with Christ: "We are no longer separate beings, with different wills and designs, but His life in me, I have 'the mind of Christ,' . . . and, moreover, I am 'flesh of His flesh and bone of His bones.'"[28]

Within this theological framework, acting faith involved, not an exertion of the will in order to bring behavior into conformity with belief, but rather a setting aside of the self in order to make way for the transforming influence of the Holy Spirit, who stood ready to invigorate both body and soul. "Real faith," Judd wrote, "is letting go, dropping down, down into the blissful rest of the Everlasting Arms." Accordingly, the weaker a person was, the more likely a candidate she became to attain the spiritual and physical wholeness she lacked. Judd therefore counseled her readers to see their "helplessness . . . as giving God opportunity to manifest his own power." "In the meek reception of your own utter powerlessness, at the same time recognizing God's strength," she advised, "you may nestle down like a weary child, into the strong rest of the 'everlasting arms' and be forevermore *'kept by the power of God.'*"[29]

This rather complicated understanding of the relationship between personal volition, divine power, and healing served several purposes for the people who espoused it. On the one hand, instructing invalids to act faith but not in their own strength was a way of lowering the bar, a means for making a daunting command to arise seem feasible. And for many, this strategy proved effective. Numerous narratives testify to the power that "resting" in God supplied, enabling the bedridden to walk and the mute to speak. When Mrs. Violet Edmunds was first encouraged to "step out on the foundation of the faith of God" by claiming a healing and acting accordingly, for example, she admitted that the advice startled her. Edmunds, an elderly African American woman who had migrated north to Pittsburgh, Pennsylvania, from her native West Virginia during the Civil War, was plagued with numerous ailments, including "tumors or abscesses" in her mouth "which destroyed the power of speech to a great extent." After years of domestic service during which she struggled with inveterate illness, Edmunds eventually became "a confirmed invalid" and retired to "The Aged Colored Woman's Home." In the fall of 1885, A. B. Simpson and Elizabeth Baxter held a convention in Pittsburgh, which Edmunds attended. Through their teaching she first heard of divine healing and also discovered the prayer meeting at Bethany Home, a "house of healing" operated by Mary Morehead. When Morehead encouraged Edmunds to "say you *are* healed from this time forth, on the Word 'calling those things which be not as though they were,'" Edmunds balked. "The idea of my saying, with all my tumors, aches, pains and loss of speech, that I was healed, seemed unreasonable, to say the least," she recalled. Despite her incredulity, Edmunds decided to try. "I went home and wrestled with God for hours," Edmunds remembered, "not having then learned that it is not wrestling but believing that avails with the Father." It was not until she was "entirely exhausted" and "stopped trying" that she experienced "the healing power of God." Instantly overcoming her inability to speak, Edmunds woke her roommate with the cry, "I'm healed! I'm healed!"[30]

Insisting that healing involved acting faith without expending effort also enabled advocates of divine healing to counter the allegation that cures such as Violet Edmunds' were the product of will power. Throughout the nineteenth century, a growing recognition of the "intimate relation between the mind and body" lent credence to the notion that "marvelous effects" could be "produced upon disease by various kinds of mental excitement." During this period, various forms of "mind cure" made headway on both sides of the Atlantic, as popular audiences and eventually even some medical professionals embraced the idea that mental suggestion represented a potent means for bringing about bodily healing. According to proponents of what ultimately came to be known as mental therapeutics, a physician's role was to prescribe not only treatments designed to call forth a response from the patient's body, such as the "drastic purge," but also, or even instead, to enjoin "cheerfulness, hope, pleasant occupation of the mind," and "kindly dispositions of heart," upon the patient, in order to "call forth the energies of his will on the side of recovery."[31]

Some supporters of divine healing, such as the persistently diplomatic A. J. Gordon, were initially willing to entertain the possibility that will power and supernatural intervention might not be mutually exclusive. Responding to those who attributed Jennie Smith's recovery to "a sudden and powerful reassertion of the will," Gordon suggested that, even if this were the only explanation for her cure, her restoration could still be considered a miracle performed by the Great Physician. "Is it not a great thing," he asked, "even to find a physician who can discover that nothing ails us when all the doctors have pronounced it a desperate case? If this were all, which we do not for a moment admit, it would certainly be a vast triumph of faith-healing over medication." While Gordon clearly did not want to concede that Smith's illnesses were "nervous and largely imaginary," he did not directly contradict the idea that her will was a factor in her cure. Nor did he reject the notion that faith healing often dealt successfully with cases of nervous disorders. In instances such as these, he insisted, invalids ought to be thankful to have "the insight of the Great Physician," whose "penetrating glance goes to the root of disease when ours can only understand the symptoms."[32]

Despite Gordon's openness to the notion that personal volition might somehow play a part in the healing process without undermining the divine element, most advocates of faith cure saw this kind of concession to critics as dangerous. "Is it not fearful sin to ascribe the direct power of the Lord Jesus in healing to any other sources, as so many presume to do, such as the will, imagination, or nervous excitement?" asked Annie Van Ness Blanchet, a missionary to Japan who was healed of foot trouble through the ministry of the Reverend Arthur T. Sloan and his wife Kitty, Episcopalians who established a faith healing home in Stratford, Connecticut. Elizabeth Baxter also lamented the widespread tendency to explain healings solely in terms of will power. "When a blind person . . . comes boldly forward to trust his case avowedly into the hands of Jesus, the majority of those who know him think he is fanatical or excited, tell him he is acting in self-will, and thus throw every hindrance in the way of his faith," she complained. Interpreting miraculous healings as "natural" events, these evangelicals warned, was insulting both to bed-ridden invalids who "had willed again and again, and fallen back fainting in weariness an despair," as well as to the God who finally enabled them to get up.[33]

Over time, even Gordon seems to have felt the need to clarify his stance on the issue of mind cure and will power. No one who believes in the scriptural promise that the prayer of faith will save the sick, Gordon wrote in 1885, "has ever, so far as we know, considered that its fulfillment depends on the action of mind upon mind. All who credit 'faith cures' as they are sometimes called, hold that they are the result of God's direct and supernatural action upon the body of the sufferer." Gordon made this statement in an article entitled "'Christian Science' Tested by Scripture," a piece he wrote in an effort to distinguish divine healing from the "bad religious teaching" of Mary Baker Eddy. Although Gordon argued that the "antagonism" between these two systems of healing ought to be obvious to any attentive observer, many outsiders failed to perceive the difference. About a year after Gordon's article first appeared, Methodist minister James Monroe Buckley, editor of the influential denominational newspaper *The Christian Advocate* from 1880 to 1912, published an essay in which he highlighted the similarities between "faith-healing" and various forms of what he called "mind cure," including animal magnetism, mesmerism, Spiritualism, Mormonism, Roman Catholicism (particularly the miracles reported at Knock Chapel in Ireland and Lourdes in France), and—last but not least—Christian Science. Without disputing the reality of the healing claims made by these various systems, Buckley drew upon theories of mental therapeutics in order to explain how these cures were effected. All of these movements, Buckley asserted, succeeded in healing certain nervous ailments and sometimes even acute diseases, but they did so, not through any religious or supernatural force, but through the purely natural power of suggestion. Faith cures, he argued, were "a natural result of mental or emotional states."[34]

The tendency of critics like Buckley to conflate Mary Baker Eddy's movement with divine healing, coupled with the growing popularity of Christian Science in the 1880s, only served to exacerbate the tensions over the role of human will in faith cure. Gordon was one of the first to address this issue, but others quickly rallied to the defense of their movement, insisting that the doctrines and practices associated with divine healing were distinct from what they considered to be the false and dangerous teaching of Mary Baker Eddy and her disciples. A. B. Simpson called Christian Science "fatally antagonistic to the Gospel of Jesus Christ." Eddy's system, he wrote, relied on a "dim" metaphysics that denied "the existence of matter or disease as a fact" and promoted a pantheistic view of God. Like other forms of "mind cure," Christian Science placed too much confidence in will power: "It is an attempt to make a man a self-constituted and independent being, able to do without God," Simpson argued. And on this point hinged the real difference between mind cure and divine healing. "Faith is a kind of will power, but it is not human will," Simpson explained. "It is God and His Spirit working in us, and, best of all, it has back of it a real, substantial God, without which it were only as a fulcrum floating in the air. And it is His will, His power, His spirit that supplies its force and works through its channel."[35]

In articles such as "Christian Science (not Christian and not Science)," "'Christian Science' Unmasked," and "So-Called 'Christian Science,'" other advocates of divine healing made similar complaints about Eddy's emphasis on the powers of "mind." Many authors also objected to her apparent dismissal of the reality of evil, sin, sickness, and death, cautioning readers that denying the existence of matter led to antinomianism in practice. As Gordon put it, "If the body is only a phantom and the flesh only a shadow, it is logically certain that by and by some very practical sinners will take refuge under this system, and insist that the sins of the body and the transgressions of the flesh are harmless, since they are only the phantom of a phantom and the shadow of a shadow." Evangelicals like Gordon and Simpson also warned that Christian Science smacked of "theosophy, esoteric Buddhism, Kabalism, and pantheism," citing passages from Eddy's *Science and Health* in which she refuted the existence of a personal devil and a personal God, insisting instead that "man is co-eternal and co-existent with God."[36]

Evidence of escalating evangelical anxiety about Christian Science also appears in healing testimonials published during this period. Elizabeth V. Baker, who was cured of a throat ailment in 1882, finally composed a written account of her healing in 1891. Like so many individuals who participated in divine healing in these years, Baker described her cure in terms that echoed the teachings of Carrie Judd, A. B. Simpson, and other authors who advocated acting faith. After asking God for "perfect deliverance," Baker determined to rise and go about her work "like a well woman," despite feeling herself "possessed of an indescribable weakness." "To sight and sense this seemed utterly impossible," she wrote, "yet I thought, God has not asked me to furnish any strength, but to count upon Him to furnish what I lack as I need it, hence I can at least 'yield my members' to Him in obedience, leaving all the results with Him." For an entire week, Baker engaged in her regular household work, remaining "conscious of weakness," but accomplishing tasks that seemed physically impossible by drawing upon a strength not her own, which she claimed moment by moment. "It was a wonderful week of blessed experimental teaching of the reality of 'calling those things that are not as though they were,'" she recalled. "It was not will power. It was not so-called Christian Science, that subtle *counterfeit* of truth which denies the reality of sickness, but it was the constant appropriation of the fullness there is in Jesus Christ for our life physically as well as spiritually."[37]

Despite vigilant efforts to erect and police the boundary between divine healing and Christian Science, many seekers after physical health seemed to have difficulty appreciating the differences between the two movements. "Although a great deal has been written explaining the errors of Christian Science, and many of our pulpits, also, are earnestly warning their people to beware of its dangerous teachings, yet . . . many are still being drawn into this net," complained Anna Prosser. A. J. Gordon also worried that many were being lured into Christian Science "without suspicion" because it appeared to represent "some finer quality of Christianity."[38]

Subtle (if real) doctrinal differences aside, the fact was that at some level, faith cure and Christian Science did seem to propose a similar hermeneutics of healing. Both movements counseled sick persons to question the reliability of sensory evidence in order to overcome illness and its effects. "Dismiss the first mental admission that you are sick; dispute sense with science. . . . Not to admit disease, is to conquer it," Mary Baker Eddy (then Glover) instructed her readers in the first edition of *Science and Health*. "When symptoms of sickness are present, meet them with the resistance of mind against matter, and you will control them. . . . Silently or audibly, according to the circumstances, you should dispute the reality of disease." Although proponents of faith cure insisted that they never meant to deny the actual existence of sickness or bodily suffering, they did encourage ailing individuals to think of illness as "the Devil's lie" and to disregard the "testimony of the senses" once they had put their trust in the Great Physician. "Saying by faith we are healed *now* though this great sacrifice," one author wrote, "we are not to look at our bodies and feelings to prove God's truth, but only to Christ, willing to wait His time to give us the evidence that will show to the world His power over disease, and bring glory to His name." A. B. Simpson advised his audiences to "ignore all symptoms, and see only Him there before you. . . . Do not look always for the immediate removal of the symptoms. Do not think of them. Simply ignore them and press forward, claiming the reality, back of and below all symptoms." For both practitioners of Christian Science and participants in faith cure, healing required an ability to act on a belief grounded in a divine truth that lay beyond the body. The flesh, with all its feelings, was not to be the arbiter of experience.[39]

Acting Faith: Paradox and the Politics of Gender

As troubling as the increasing confusion about Christian Science was for proponents of faith cure, there were other issues at stake in the debates about the role of human volition in healing. In the late nineteenth century, conversations concerning the relationship among will, mind, and body were inextricably bound up with contests over the proper interpretation and enactment of healthy womanhood and manhood, especially amid mounting anxieties over the future of the Anglo-Saxon race. This broader context provides an essential framework for understanding the idiom of acting faith, and particularly the emphasis its proponents placed on the complicated relationship between divine power and personal agency in the curative process.

Although an array of economic, political, and cultural forces worked to destabilize associations between true womanhood and self-sacrifice during the latter half of the nineteenth century, certain aspects of the domestic ideology remained remarkably influential during this period. While many health and physical education reformers challenged the notion that women were inherently frail and delicate, prominent medical theorists continued to champion the idea that the vagaries of the female reproductive system wreaked havoc on women's physical, mental, and emotional well-being. Specialists in the nascent fields of neurology, psychology, and gynecology contributed to a burgeoning corpus of "scientific" literature that associated a woman's health primarily with the maintenance of menstrual regularity, a feat that required careful and vigilant conservation of energy, especially during the critical phase of puberty. In order to navigate safely and successfully the passage from adolescence to womanhood, certain leading physicians argued, a young girl approaching puberty ought to avoid rigorous mental activity or emotional excitement and engage only in domestic tasks that would facilitate the proper development of her maternal organs. Moderate exercise, a bland diet, and especially a sufficient amount of rest were also thought to be crucial for the attainment of fully functioning reproductive systems. In his controversial text, *Sex in Education: or, A Fair Chance for the Girls* (1873), Harvard physician Edward Clarke insisted that young women ought to dress sensibly, eat moderately, and refrain from both "muscular and brain labor" during adolescence in order to "yield enough force for the work" of establishing regular menstrual periods. Translating the domestic ideology into the discourse of medical science, Clarke argued that a woman who transgressed the boundaries of her appropriate sphere by pursuing educational or other so-called unwomanly activities drew her limited vital energies away from the crucial task of regulating her monthly cycle. Women who pursued such a course at any age ran the risk of ruining their reproductive systems and therefore of failing to fulfill their proper roles as moral guardians of their households and progenitors of healthy children who would carry forward the advancement of civilization.[40]

The remedies physicians prescribed when women did fall ill closely resembled the therapies they recommended for developing adolescents. Treatments were often premised on the supposition that the patient's ailment must be related to the malfunction of her menstrual rhythm or to some sort of inappropriate exertion that had overtaxed her innately delicate physical and emotional constitution. Either way, doctors frequently suggested that a sick woman needed to assume a retiring posture, avoid all endeavors that might excite her nervous system, and undertake only those activities that reinforced her maternal role in order to replenish her vital energy and regain her health. As the century progressed, orthodox physicians, in particular, increasingly emphasized the importance of rest as a treatment for women's diseases. S. Weir Mitchell, a renowned Philadelphia neurologist, first recommended the "rest cure" in 1872. Initially developed as a therapy for battle-weary Civil War soldiers, the rest cure became an extremely popular prescription for women suffering from nervous disorders and from organic diseases such as cardiac and kidney ailments in the latter decades of the nineteenth century.[41]

Under the rest cure, potentially stimulating behavior of any kind, often including reading, writing, and visiting with family or friends, was strictly prohibited in order to assure that the patient's mental and emotional energies could remain dormant. When L. Etta Avery, who suffered from neurasthenia and spinal trouble, was admitted to the Adams Nervine Asylum just outside of Boston, she underwent "the perfect rest treatment, not being allowed to raise my hand to my head, or do anything for myself." As Avery's comment suggests, the rest cure also compelled an individual to cede control of her treatment to her physician, submitting to his instructions without comment, question, or complaint. After straining the nerves of her spinal cord while practicing gymnastics in a ladies seminary, Almena J. Cowles of Amherst, Massachusetts, struggled to regain her health for several years until her nervous system became so taxed that, as she put it, "my brain was nearly worn out." Her physicians told her that her "indomitable courage and will-power" alone had been keeping her up, but that she would never recover her strength if she continued to pursue this active course. Instead, "she must have rest." Accordingly, on January 1, 1881, Cowles was admitted to the Adams Nervine Asylum, where she was "confined to bed" for eight months and placed "under the care of the most skillful physicians in New England," who did everything "in their power" to help her. In August, after reading Judd's *The Prayer of Faith,* Cowles wrote to Sarah Mix, expressing some concern about her ability to carry out the directives she found there: "About *acting faith,*" she wrote, "I would not be allowed to do more than at present, unless I say my pain is gone or greatly relieved."[42]

For Avery, Cowles, and countless other women, submission remained an integral element of the experience of illness and recovery, despite efforts by reformers to link the achievement of physical health with personal agency and voluntary activity. Obedience to an authority other than "self-will" was required, it seemed, in order to overcome, or at least to endure, troubling physical ailments. With the growing popularity of mind cure in the 1880s, submitting one's own will to that of a more powerful other took on added resonance as respected physicians like Mitchell and George Beard began to experiment with this increasingly acceptable form of treatment. The theory of mind cure was especially applicable, its adherents argued, in cases that involved "nervous conditions" such as hysteria—complaints that were peculiarly, if not exclusively, associated with women. In situations such as these, "the stimulus of sudden command from a stronger will" provided the necessary catalyst that enabled bedridden invalids to arise. "By the direct influence of a strong will over a weaker one," an author explained, "an invalid may be controlled and raised from his debilitated and diseased condition to soundness of mind and body."[43]

Given this context, the reasons for Cowles' anxiety about acting faith become more comprehensible. If she were to "get right out of bed and begin to walk," as Mix had instructed, she would be disobeying doctors' orders by exercising both her body and will in ways that they had prohibited, and thus, she feared, potentially undermining her bid for health. When Cowles failed to respond to prescribed treatments, however, her physicians eventually discharged her from the Nervine Asylum and made arrangements for her transfer to the Home for Incurables in Brooklyn, New York. At that point, Cowles decided to give divine healing a try. She sent for "some faith people" to come pray with her. After she had been anointed according to the command in James 5, Cowles finally found herself able to act faith. "God gave me the strength to rise," she recalled, "and I walked the length of the room without pain, then knelt and praised the Lord for His wonderful goodness, rose and dressed and walked downstairs wholly healed of my diseases." Over the next six months, Cowles returned to her home in Amherst and took on many duties, "by simply trusting in the healing power and sustaining grace of Him who said, 'My strength is made perfect in weakness.'" Her new-found potency was not, Cowles adamantly insisted, the product of self-assertion. "I am not allowed to use any will-power," she wrote, "but rest in God's love and receive strength from Him moment by moment." Healing, for Cowles, still involved obedience to a will other than her own. But by submitting to God, paradoxically, she received the power to perform actions that disproved her doctor's diagnoses. Cowles was not incurable—she merely needed the right prescription. Where the rest cure had failed, resting in God succeeded, empowering Cowles to arise and walk without overstepping the medical theories and gender norms that required her to remain passive in the curative process.[44]

If acting faith without effort offered women like Cowles a way of consenting to the rhetoric of passivity while at the same time enabling them to transcend some of its implications, this strategy posed distinctive problems for men. In the late nineteenth century, submissiveness and weakness were not male virtues. Even the Victorian ideal of manly self-restraint was becoming suspect in a climate of cultural and economic change. Mounting anxieties over an apparent epidemic of nervous exhaustion among white upper- and middle-class businessmen, in particular, contributed to the reevaluation of self-denial as a characteristic of true manhood. According to neurologists such as George Beard, who coined the term "neurasthenia" in his 1869 text *American Nervousness,* overexposure to books, "brain work," and other pressures of modern civilization had depleted many men of their vital energy. Within this context, virility, strength, and forcefulness became increasingly important markers of healthy Anglo-Saxon masculinity. Consequently, when men did suffer from "nerve weakness" or other sorts of illness, doctors rarely ordered them to adopt a recumbent pose and remain utterly immobile for weeks in order to regain their equilibrium. Although physicians did sometimes recommend the remedy of rest for men, especially for those suffering from neurasthenia, they usually combined this prescription with other forms of treatment such as vigorous physical activity designed to help replenish their "natural" strength and nerve-force.[45]

Given the close association between masculinity and virility, any therapy that required men to admit their weakness and assume a submissive posture in order to receive healing was bound to arouse the ire of critics, and faith cure did. Opponents like the vociferous and tireless detractor James Buckley were quick to point out the threats that the divine healing movement posed to prevailing gender norms. "Faith-cure . . . is a pitiable superstition, dangerous in its final effects," Buckley charged. "Its tendency is to produce an effeminate type of character. . . . It destroys the ascendancy of reason in the soul." Theologian George H. Hepworth made an analogous argument in an article on "The Faith Cure" published in the New York *Independent*. "The whole theory," Hepworth charged, "is the embodiment of a sickly sentimentalism, rather than of sturdy scholarship, and if its expounder could be furnished with a lisp, the eternal fitness of things would be attained." Framed in this manner, acting faith might restore a man to health, but it would emasculate him in the process.[46]

Defenders of divine healing countered that Buckley and other naysayers misunderstood the complex relationship between the divine will and human agency in the therapeutic process. Submission to God, they argued, did not result in quietism or "mere passivity," nor did it turn a willing individual into "an enervated, mindless being" or a "weak creature, without backbone." According to the Reverend A. P. Moore, who frequently published articles in Judd's journal after his healing through Cullis's ministry, "the rest of faith" was not inconsistent with "those accounts of Christian living which describe it as a race, as a warfare, as involving toil, and earnestness and exertion." Indeed, it was only by resting in faith, by yielding to God, that an individual had any chance of vanquishing disease and living a truly victorious Christian life, for only by submission could a person receive what Moore called "the nerve-power of the soul." Through this indwelling force, Moore wrote, "the mighty life of our Risen Glorified Head flows through our every fibre, and with God in us, through faith, we attempt and achieve a life and service beyond our utmost dreams before." As A. B. Simpson put it, human beings in their natural state "wanted a positive fountain of vital energy" that Jesus supplied. By acting faith, individuals gained access to this essential force. "His bodily energy vitalizes your body, and you can take it, you have a right to take it to-day," Simpson proclaimed. "I take it afresh to-day from the living Christ—His nerves, and heart, and brain, and bodily strength for my own life." Furthermore, Simpson suggested, sick people were not the only ones who needed this infusion of divine strength. Everyone (including, presumably, healthy men) would be better off if they learned to partake of this power "every morning," as Simpson himself was in the habit of doing. In this view, the indwelling power of God trumped all individual efforts. "It is a better kind of health," Simpson insisted, "and it has given me many times the strength of my own natural energy."[47]

By focusing on the vitality, power, and energy that infused a person once he submitted his own will to God, men like Simpson and Moore attempted to accommodate the idiom of acting faith to their culture's notion of true masculinity. Rather than emphasizing the need for passivity in the healing process, they shifted attention to the empowering outcome, even going so far as to suggest that men who drew strength from the "Christ-life within" were, in fact, more vigorous and manly than those who relied on their own will power. For the many clerical and lay men who participated in divine healing, this argument seems to have been convincing. When the Reverend T. C. Easton, pastor of a Reformed church in New Brunswick, New Jersey, recognized that healing involved not only "a full and unreserved surrender of my entire being to God" but also "the risen life of Jesus as my life," he was able to overcome his conviction that "faith-cure may be all well enough for weak, nervous women, and hysterics," and trust the Great Physician rather than the surgeon's knife to mend the metatarsal bones in his lame foot. Similarly, in his testimony of healing, George P. Pardington insisted that the "power of the Lord" in his body enabled him "always to conquer in his strength." Through this incarnational energy, Pardington wrote, "I am no more the helpless boy, but the strong, firm, vigorous young man." The Reverend Henry Wilson, assistant minister of St. George's Episcopal Church in New York City, reported that he experienced "a vigor and freshness never known before" through Jesus' healing presence. "I am a younger man, in every faculty of my being, than I was twenty years ago," Wilson proclaimed. "More than twice the work . . . is now done with an ease and pleasure never mine before. The body that for years hardly knew what one day's freedom from pain was, now rejoices in robust health."[48]

Accounts such as these demonstrate that the rhetoric of vigor and power helped make divine healing appealing to men of both ministerial and lay status. Indeed, many of the apologists for divine healing were male theologians, and lay men actively participated in all aspects of the movement. The fact remains, however, that women far outnumbered men in ranks and also achieved remarkable status as leaders. Despite their efforts to mask passivity, or at least to make it palatable to the male population, proponents of faith cure found a more willing audience among women, who could acquire the blessings of health by acting faith without losing too much of their cultural capital.[49]

Testimonies of healing published in journals like Judd's *Triumphs of Faith*, as well as in collected volumes put together by prominent leaders like Cullis and Mix, proclaimed that remarkable things happened when sick people acted faith. After earthly remedies had been tried and found wanting, when physicians and family members had given up hope, invalids who had been bedridden for years rose up and walked. The deaf heard and the blind received their sight. Even modest endeavors resulted in a great deal of awe. For Mrs. R. W. Fuller, standing on her feet long enough to dress and wash herself was "as wonderful . . . as a trip to Europe would be to some."[50]

While testimonies like Fuller's highlight the astonishing, if everyday, feats accomplished through acting faith, they also show that empowerment often came at a price. If acting faith enabled individuals to perform astounding deeds through an incursion of divine power, it did not always relieve the pain from which they longed to be released. Although some declared that their bodies were immediately and completely restored as soon as they stepped out upon their beliefs, others acknowledged that their symptoms failed to disappear and confessed that acting faith caused them considerable discomfort. Ironically, performing acts of faith often increased a person's suffering, at least at first. When Mrs. Mattie Littell, who had lain prostrate for almost three years obeyed the command to "arise and walk," she admitted that the exertion caused her "great pain." One young woman whom Sarah Mix visited tried to get out of bed on a number of occasions, but "each attempt made had resulted in paroxysms of distress." Upon reading the biblical command "Be careful for nothing," Urwin Sterry, who suffered from sciatica, headaches, back pain, and lameness, worried that he had been too cautious in his actions, and so, he wrote, "I . . . pushed right ahead *in the name of Jesus,* pain or no pain, and I suffered for two weeks terribly." Ruth Whitney, who served as the matron at Carrie Judd's Faith-Rest Cottage for a number of years used the same scriptural injunction as inspiration for walking around on an injured ankle. "Without carefulness," she recalled, "[I] went about my duties. Day after day I limped along, often suffering considerable pain, but accomplishing what had been given me to do."[51]

By pushing through the pain, many of these individuals eventually found relief. Interpreting their sufferings as "trials" allowed by the Lord to "test their faith," they claimed that enduring these afflictions taught them "beautiful lessons" as they learned not only to act faith but to walk by it. If the symptoms of their diseases resurfaced—as they so often did—believers went on acting faith, praising God for the afflictions through which they learned "trust, faith and patience." As A. B. Simpson put it, "trials," in the form of chronic or recurrent symptoms, "come to show you your need of Christ and to throw you back upon Him. And to know this and so to put on His strength in our weakness and live in it, moment by moment, is perfect healing."[52]

The tendency to treat the ongoing endurance of pain as an integral part of "perfect healing" suggests that rather than truly challenging the notion that corporal sufferings ought to be accepted as blessings sent or allowed by God for an individual's spiritual benefit, the hermeneutics of divine healing often worked to reinscribe the longstanding association between bodily pain and sanctification. Although proponents of faith cure maintained that God was the Great Physician, not the author of affliction, suffering still played an important role in their understanding of the devotional life. While they instructed invalids not to remain resigned to their illnesses, which were not God's will, they also insisted that the experience of healing frequently involved the persistence, or recurrence, of painful symptoms, which provided opportunities for spiritual transformation. "All allow that sickness is a discipline," wrote R. K. Carter. "Many a Christian comes for bodily healing to-day with a very imperfect idea of the depth and breadth of spiritual renunciation and consecration required by the *law of perfect love*. Hence the healing is gradual, that the soul may learn, and learning may be purified through faith by the blood."[53]

If advocates of divine healing ultimately failed in their efforts to break free from a devotional model that linked physical suffering with spiritual sanctity, they did succeed in revising this older ethic in at least one significant way. In their view, enduring pain no longer required the kind of passive resignation that was so key to Jennie Smith's early spiritual practice. Rather than remaining confined to their invalid couches or darkened bedrooms, individuals like Carrie Judd, A. B. Simpson, and countless others claimed health in spite of their sufferings. By acting faith, many women and a good number of men who were weighed down by debilitating illnesses reengaged in social and familial life, went back to work, and pursued all sorts of ambitious projects that had previously seemed unimaginable. For these evangelicals, healing by faith called for inspired action.

CHAPTER FOUR

The Use of Means

Divine Healing as Devotional Practice

One Sunday afternoon in January 1884, Emma Whittemore made her way from her stately Park Avenue home through the streets of New York City. Prompted "purely by curiosity," Whittemore had accepted a friend's invitation to hear Carrie Judd give an account of her healing at one of A. B. Simpson's religious services. Sitting in the audience, Whittemore listened incredulously as Judd related how the "power of Christ" had healed her of a severe spinal injury. Having suffered from chronic back pain herself for the past twelve years after a tumble down a flight of steps, the thirty-four-year-old Whittemore was highly skeptical of Judd's story. "I felt assured," Whittemore later wrote, that such ideas "were decidedly fanatical." Her disapproval growing, Whittemore rose to leave before the meeting ended, "rather pitying the deluded people who remained to hear such an incredible narration."[1]

Although Whittemore had been a Christian for several years, it had never occurred to her to trust God "in the hour of sickness." Over the next several months, her aversion to "faith healing" intensified. Whittemore regarded anyone who mentioned divine healing "scornfully, and ridiculed their ideas." Nevertheless, in early May she agreed to attend another of Simpson's meetings at the 23rd Street Gospel Tabernacle. "After being present at three or four Bible Readings there and constantly hearing statements of marvelous cures, and even witnessing some truly wonderful manifestations of God's willingness and power to heal," she recalled, "my former conceptions of His love were seriously put to confusion, and my own heart began to question if *something* could not be accomplished for myself."[2]

Despite her growing openness to the possibility that God might be able and willing to heal her body, a major stumbling block remained in Whittemore's way. While she felt compelled "to admit that those who professed to have been healed in answer to prayer, appeared to know the Lord in a more intimate way than had ever been my privilege," as she later put it, Whittemore could not "even then perceive how any one was justified in stating that he or she was healed by faith before it could be experienced by sight or feeling." How could individuals who continued to suffer from symptoms visible to the eye assert that God had healed them of their diseases?[3]

Leaders of the divine healing movement acknowledged that claiming healing and acting faith, regardless of the ongoing occurrence of painful physical symptoms, was a difficult assignment, especially in a culture that increasingly valued empirical evidence as the proper measure of reality. To accept as credible the testimonies she heard at Simpson's meetings, let alone to claim healing for herself, these evangelicals counseled, Whittemore would need to undergo a profound epistemological reorientation. Rather than relying on the observations of her physical senses to interpret her experiences, she would have to learn to view the world through the "eyes of faith." "Christ has provided for the redemption and restoration of the human mind," wrote S. A. Lindenberger during her tenure as overseer at Berachah, the house of healing A. B. Simpson had founded in New York City in 1883. "He will deliver from all evil thoughts, and then He will come in His indwelling presence and hold captive our thinking." Divine healing, in other words, involved not only the restoration of physical health but also a reformation of the mental faculties.[4]

Although they insisted that only an influx of the Holy Spirit could, as one practitioner put it, "bring us to abstain from the sight of our eyes, and the hearing of our ears, and to see God over against the odds, whatever they be," proponents of divine healing also asserted that human beings could engage in religious exercises and ritual ceremonies that would facilitate the interdependent processes of mental, spiritual, and corporeal transformation. Searching the scriptures for insight, advocates of faith cure identified three practices that were "given of the Lord" as "means" of healing: *prayer* (sometimes called "believing or prevailing prayer"), as commended in Matthew 18:19; *laying on of hands,* as described in Mark 16:18; and *anointing with oil,* as commanded in James 5:14–15. Bolstered by biblical authority, these three devotional disciplines, along with a constellation of connected practices such as fasting, partaking of communion, and confession, became the principal ritual framework through which evangelicals encouraged skeptical sufferers like

Emma Whittemore to "be transformed by the renewal of [their minds]" (Romans 12:2) so that they might "look not to the things that are seen but to the things that are unseen" (2 Corinthians 4:18) and so learn to "walk by faith and not by sight" (2 Corinthians 5:7).[5]

Surveying the repertoire of practices that these evangelicals recommended as means of healing reveals the pivotal role that devotional disciplines played in their efforts to alter the experiences of illness, pain, and recovery. While acting faith served as the primary strategy through which proponents of divine healing endeavored to challenge the notion that passive resignation signified the apposite Christian response to physical affliction, the particular spiritual and ritual practices they employed represented tactics for cultivating the patterns of mental perception, the rhythms of bodily comportment, and the qualities of spiritual conviction that claiming healing and acting faith required.

Even as advocates of faith cure readily embraced a set of religious exercises as tools for making the mind and body receptive to the redemptive influence of the Holy Spirit, they also worried that participating in some practices exposed petitioners to the perils of spiritual pollution or physical exploitation. Efforts to police the proper conduct of healing rituals as well as debates over whether certain ecstatic forms of practice represented valid means of healing elucidate how anxious apologists for faith cure were to preserve personal agency as a indispensable part of the curative process. Although they constantly encouraged sufferers to submit to Jesus as healer, they warned ailing individuals—especially invalid women—not to entrust their bodies, minds, or souls to the ministrations of "unsanctified" persons who might subject them to corporeal molestation, mental abuse, or even demonic possession. The concerns that these evangelicals expressed about the potential dangers of self-surrender illumine, once again, the complicated gender politics that shaped the practice of healing among Protestants in the late nineteenth century.

Arguments over the propriety of rituals such as laying on of hands, anointing, and "trance evangelism" also show how difficult it was for champions of divine healing such as Charles Cullis, A. J. Gordon, and William Boardman to enforce any kind of "orthodoxy" within the movement they helped to establish. For leaders who sought to defend faith cure against skeptical detractors, this internal dissent was particularly disconcerting. By rigorously regulating the practice of divine healing, spokespersons such as Carrie Judd and A. B. Simpson hoped to distinguish "legitimate" forms of faith cure from "fanatical" systems of healing that, in their view, promoted bodily well-being at the expense of spiritual health. From this perspective, devotional disciplines provided means for constructing and maintaining boundaries that sheltered sick persons from the dangers of defilement while simultaneously opening them up to the purifying and rejuvenating power of the Great Physician.

"Pray for One Another, That Ye May Be Healed": Practice as Personal Transformation

By the time Emma Whittemore heard Carrie Judd offer her testimony of healing in the winter of 1884, faith cure was an established, if heterogeneous, movement. Through the evangelistic efforts of apostles such as Judd, Cullis, Gordon, Simpson, Baxter, and others, invalids across North America, Great Britain, and beyond had embraced the "gospel of healing." Following the lead of converts like Judd, and often at the prompting of leaders such as Mix and Cullis, many beneficiaries of faith cure composed narratives describing remarkable recoveries from all sorts of distressing ailments and disabling diseases. During the early 1880s, testimonials became a stock feature in many religious newspapers and magazines as well as at Holiness faith conventions, camp meetings, and church services. By the thousands, people of all ages, socioeconomic classes, and denominational backgrounds professed to have been cured of boils and blindness, of catarrh and cancer, of dyspepsia and drug addiction, of fevers and "female complaints," of headaches and heart disease—in short, of all manner of illnesses, ranging from seemingly minor maladies to life-threatening afflictions, and from ostensibly "nervous" disorders to infirmities that were obviously organic in nature.

Much to the chagrin of apologists for faith cure, however, accounts of divine healing failed to convince many skeptics that God had anything to do with restoring sick persons to health. Reactions like Whittemore's plagued the faith cure movement from its inception and continued to trouble leaders who sought to establish divine healing as a bona fide expression of true Christianity. Cynics raised several criticisms of faith cure testimonials and, by extension, of the divine healing movement as a whole. Some detractors highlighted the conspicuous parallels between narratives that attributed remarkable recoveries to the Great Physician and those that credited some other cause for the purported cure. Reports of divine healing sounded notably similar to Christian Science testimonials as well as to patent medicine advertisements. All such statements were, according to some critics, empirically unverifiable and therefore exceedingly dubious. In the view of opponents like British folklorist T. F. Thistleton Dyer, such unsubstantiated accounts swayed only "low and rudimentary minds." Faith cure, from this perspective, represented a residual manifestation of "primitive culture" that had been passed down amongst "rural and unlettered communities" and appealed mostly to "the vulgar," the "peasantry," and "unsophisticated folk." Adopting an evolutionary perspective on the development of religion, Dyer associated divine healing with the "superstitious credulity" that marked the "folklore of most savage and uncultured tribes" and the "spasmodic outbursts of exaggerated faith which characterize popular religious movements."[6]

While some detractors were willing to acknowledge that faith in God's miraculous power—even if misguided—frequently produced positive physical effects, other observers were less sanguine about the ostensible benefits of divine healing. According to opponents such as Boston University professor Luther Townsend, advocates of faith cure vastly overstated their rates of success. "The fact is," Townsend declared, "that many sick people who apply to our faith cure establishments are not in the least benefited." Presbyterian A. F. Schauffler made a similar observation: "Let it be well noted, hundreds are not healed at all, who yet want to be healed." For every testimonial that faith cure leaders presented as proof of God's power to vanquish sickness in the modern era, observers like Townsend and Schauffler argued, numerous incidents of failure went unreported. Furthermore, these authors insisted, the evidence that advocates of faith cure did offer on behalf of their theory and practice of healing was inconclusive if not utterly specious. Many of those "reported as 'cured,'" Schauffler contended, "are not at all 'cured.'" Some, he maintained, were merely "benefited," while others experienced relapses. The most troubling cases, in his view, were those who professed healing even when signs of disease remained evident. "Faith-cure folk . . . are taught by their leaders to claim that they are healed as soon as they have been anointed and prayed over, and that in spite of any subsequent symptoms that may remain," Schauffler reported. "We are left in doubt as to the reality of the cure by the singular use of language which faith-cure folk employ," he declared. "Such unwonted use of language staggers ordinary mortals, and makes them wary in receiving testimony from those who allow themselves such liberties."[7]

The practice of acting faith provoked equally strong denunciations from skeptical physicians like Walter Moxon, who scoffed at "sham miracles" that could be easily invalidated by empirical observation. Professing to be healed while manifesting sensory evidence of illness or injury was not only inappropriate behavior for educated adults in an age of scientific advancement, Moxon implied, but it was also irresponsible and dangerous. Lambasting the proprietors of the Bethshan healing home in his native London for encouraging sick people to ignore "the pain by which we are warned of danger," Moxon condemned faith healing as a threat to public health, an impediment to the progress of truth and reason, and a retrograde variety of religion that "lowers the tone of the spiritual life."[8]

Proponents of divine healing responded to detractors like Moxon, Schauffler, Townsend, and Dyer by questioning the epistemological assumptions that lay behind their criticisms. Although they did insist that instances of healing offered proof of God's willingness and ability to perform miracles in the modern era, spokespersons for faith cure simultaneously warned against gauging God's healing activity according to empirical standards alone. Those whose purview encompassed only the physical realm, they suggested, were in danger of sliding into skepticism and failing to perceive the supernatural power through which God promised to restore ailing bodies and reform sinful souls. From this perspective, naturalistic empiricism represented a kind of epistemological captivity that ensnared sick persons within a web of sensory stimuli and bound them to believe and to behave according to the physical appearance and sentient experience of their bodies.

In order to break free from the materialistic outlook that fettered both their faith and their flesh, advocates of divine healing argued, individuals like Emma Whittemore needed to develop a spiritual mindset through the practice of prayer. Drawing heavily on the classic works of mystical authors such as Madame Guyon and Fenelon as well as on the devotional writings of contemporaries like Phoebe Palmer and poet John Greenleaf Whittier, proponents of faith cure commended various forms of meditation as methods for training the mental faculties to dismiss sensory evidence and for disciplining the body to act accordingly. In her book on divine healing, S. A. Lindenberger encouraged her readers to prepare themselves to receive the mind of Christ by engaging in contemplative prayer. "You will be helped by holding your mind in stillness and keeping it a blank, waiting for His thoughts, and as you form the habit it will become easier and easier, until you are established in this way," she declared. Mary Mossman, in her autobiography *Steppings in God; or, the Hidden Life Made Manifest,* cited the teachings of numerous spiritual writers who stressed the importance of seeking, as her contemporary Thomas Upham put it, "a perfect coincidence of the finite mind with the Infinite" through the practice of contemplation. In order to "receive the manifestation of healing," Mossman suggested, we must "pass on into deeper spiritual life and affiliate more with the Divine mind concerning us." When our minds are brought into agreement with God's mind, she explained, "we no longer see the old man with its fleshly desires and diseases, but the new man created in Jesus Christ, and in the new life which we by faith receive we press on to apprehend all that for which we are apprehended of Christ Jesus (Phil 3:12). Receiving life and light from this higher plane, we lose sight of material things." Although she often "seemed to be very ill," Mossman insisted that by "seeing *Jesus only*," she was able to disregard the feelings of her flesh, concentrating instead upon "wonderful manifestations of God's loving care."[9]

For those seeking healing of body, mind, and soul, Mossman contended, "looking unto Jesus" was the "watchword." This catchphrase appeared in countless narratives, periodical essays, tracts, and treatises commending faith cure. In a widely circulated article entitled "The 'Look on Jesus,'" pastor Otto Stockmayer (1838–1917), one of the principal advocates of divine healing in Switzerland, exhorted his readers to "obey thy God, and contemplate Jesus." Meditating on Christ as he was revealed in "the Holy Scriptures" was necessary, Stockmayer argued, because of the power of contemplation to shape perception. "When we fix our eyes upon an object, we put ourselves in contact with it, we place ourselves under its influence, we allow it to act upon our hearts," he explained. "Looking around about us, as well as constantly looking at ourselves, cannot but awaken and nourish evil in us," he continued. "The world which man carries within him . . . as well as the world that surrounds him, keeps him always a captive, he feels himself chained to visible things." Only by setting his sights on Christ could a man gain release from the sensory phenomena that imprisoned him. To gaze at Jesus, Stockmayer affirmed, was to look away from one's self and one's surroundings; to focus attention on the eternal, rather than the temporal; to deny the physical in favor of the spiritual. Contemplating Christ, in other words, reoriented a person's perspective so that certain realities suddenly became visible, while other things were obscured from view. As Anna Prosser intoned in her testimony of healing, "Since my eyes were fixed on Jesus, / I've lost sight of all beside, / so enchained my spirit's vision, / looking at the crucified."[10]

Acquiring and maintaining such a singular focus on Jesus was, these writers argued, a difficult endeavor that required practiced vigilance on the part of believers, especially since denying the testimony of the senses ran directly against the grain in a "worldly" culture that appealed to and even cultivated sensory pleasures. In her autobiography, Mossman suggested that while Christians in all ages had recognized the value of devotional disciplines such as meditation and contemplative prayer, the late nineteenth century posed particular challenges for the person who hoped to develop her spiritual perception. The tantalizing array of consumer goods, the world of fashion and display, the ever-expanding selection of stimulating food and drink and drugs—all of these "external pressures" conspired to focus an individual's attention on things material, including the desires and discomforts of the flesh. Tearing ones eyes away from these temptations was no simple task.[11]

Although some might succeed in disengaging their minds from the sensual enticements of the surrounding culture solely by engaging in contemplative prayer, these evangelicals argued, most needed additional aid in order to escape from what Stockmayer called "the covetousness of the senses." To this end, Mossman exhorted her readers to "mortify the affections" through fasting—a discipline that included both refraining from food and reticence in conversation, or what she called "outward silence." By abstaining from eating as well as from speaking, Mossman asserted, an individual subdued her "fleshly appetites" so that "the mind might centre in God." Contemplation, in other words, was closely connected with certain bodily practices that helped prepare the person to focus on Christ. "In order to have the operations of the Holy Ghost realized in the soul," she wrote, "the fleshly activities must be still. . . . For the flesh must be subject to the Spirit, before spiritual things can be discerned." For Mossman, then, corporeal mortification preceded the epistemological reformation that made walking by faith rather than by sight feasible. This rather circular relationship between disciplining the body, meditating on Christ, ignoring sensory evidence, and acting faith suggests that healing, for evangelicals who participated in the faith cure movement, involved a complete reordering and reorienting of the whole self: body, mind, and soul. Physical, mental, and spiritual renewal were inextricably linked.[12]

Many of Mossman's fellow evangelicals shared her sentiment that the late nineteenth century was an increasingly sensual and exceptionally skeptical era, and concurred with her conviction that ascetical disciplines such as fasting helped to inculcate the mental and spiritual habits that divine healing demanded. In her seminal text *The Prayer of Faith*, for example, Carrie Judd suggested that the "humiliation and denying of the body" through fasting enabled Christians to resist "the blind spirit of unbelief" that kept them from apprehending God's promises of healing. Like Mossman, Judd indicated that prayer alone was not always enough to lift suffering individuals out of the morass of skepticism and sensuality that hampered their faith in the Great Physician: "By subduing our fleshly appetites I believe that we become prepared for a higher spirituality; and with the renewing of the Holy Spirit, our requickened faith is powerful enough to grasp the blessings awaiting us."[13]

Subjugating fleshly desires, however, did not necessarily entail ascribing to a "gospel of asceticism." As A. B. Simpson put it in a text entitled *The Lord for the Body*, the "spirit of true restraint" ought to be coupled with the principle of "moderation." In other words, while abstaining from corrupting influences such as "wine and strong drink" was important for maintaining spiritual purity and gaining physical strength, self-regulation required discernment rather than legalistic adherence to a strict behavioral code. The Reverend James P. Ludlow, a missionary who was forced to return from his post in Japan because of physical weakness, lobbied for moderation in even stronger terms. "Asceticism is not sanctity," Ludlow declared. "Robust Christianity requires a robust body. Be wise in your nightly vigils and in your fastings on the mountainsides before the Lord. Take prayerful care of your body, since it is the Temple of God, and be not unwise in its mortification. Take care of your health for the Master's fullest use." The point of engaging in ascetical practices like fasting, Ludlow argued, was not to attain holiness by identifying with Christ's physical sufferings. Instead, these disciplinary exercises were intended to prepare the mind, flesh, and soul to receive the healing power of the Holy Spirit. If fasting promoted purity, a sufferer seeking relief ought to refrain from food, but if it weakened the body to the point that a person could no longer work for God, the practice was pointless or even detrimental. Citing the scriptural text, "Whether therefore ye eat or drink or whatsoever ye do, do all to the glory of God" (1 Cor 10:31), Mossman explained that she "was to care for the body as a sacred trust, in such a manner as would make it most efficient for God. . . . The question for the Christian is, 'Will it make me stronger for God?'"[14]

Although Carrie Judd was more confident that fasting would fortify rather than enfeeble both spirit and flesh, she also rejected the notion that uncompromising asceticism fostered sanctity and reminded ailing sufferers to treat their bodies as temples of God. Like other supporters of divine healing, Judd insisted that fleshly mortification was not an end in itself but a means for both physical and spiritual rejuvenation. In her chapter on prayer and fasting in *The Prayer of Faith*, Judd suggested that Christians who abstained from eating earthly food ought to partake of the "Heavenly Manna" of the Lord's Supper, "that wondrous means of grace and strength" through which God imparted "renewed physical life as well as spiritual." Participating in "the sacred feast," Judd wrote elsewhere, helped Christians to "realize with wondering joy, that mystery which fleshly sense can never perceive, that we are members of His body, of His flesh and of His bones." Communion, in other words, was another practice through which suffering believers could pursue epistemological, physical, and spiritual transformation. "Availing ourselves of this gracious provision, there is no longer any need for our physical natures to drag down and hinder the working of the spiritual," Judd proclaimed. "Let us yield our whole being to God, 'as alive from the dead,' and by the resurrection life of Christ He will cause all the crippled energies of soul, mind and body to spring forth into new and joyful activity in His service."[15]

A. B. Simpson encouraged sick persons seeking healing to think about the sacrament in a similar manner. If "looking only to Christ" rather than focusing on the "signs and evidences" of the flesh proved problematic, ailing individuals could take comfort in the ritual of communion, a ceremony in which humans enacted the oneness with Christ that was theirs to enjoy. In the Lord's Supper, "We eat his flesh and drink His blood, and He dwelleth in us and we in Him," Simpson wrote. "As He lived by the Father, so he that eateth Him shall live by Him." Through participation in this rite, "the great, the vital, the most precious principle of physical healing in the name of Jesus" was made not only apparent, but achieved.[16]

While advocates of divine healing like Simpson and Judd insisted that Christ stood willing and ready to inhabit infirm bodies, imparting strength to act in spite of the circumstances, they also maintained that believers bore the responsibility for preparing themselves to receive "His healing and life-giving power" through the practice of repentance. Invoking scriptural passages such as James 5:16—"Confess your faults to one to another and pray one for another, that ye may be healed"— leaders of the faith cure movement like the Reverend John Salmon, one of the chief promoters of divine healing in Canada, insisted that the confession of sin must always accompany divine healing. "Until your hearts are right with God," Salmon preached at a convention organized by Carrie Judd in 1887, "you have no business with this Divine healing." Elizabeth Baxter made a similar argument in an article entitled "Deliverance from Sickness." Citing several cases in which "no prayer availed for healing" until the sufferer repented of some previously unacknowledged sin, Baxter asserted that "failure to confess" often stood as a "hindrance in the way" of a cure. "As long as we are not standing right with man," she wrote, "the flow of the Holy Spirit's power throughout our being is interrupted." Charles Cullis also insisted that repentance was a prerequisite for receiving divine healing and made prayers of confession a central feature of his ministry. At the weekly meetings for divine healing he held at the Beacon Hill Church, Cullis habitually led attendees through a ritual of repentance prior to offering up prayers for the restoration of the sick. On the morning of January 4, 1883, one participant reported, "Dr. Cullis addressed those present, asking them if they knew of any sin, no matter how great or how small it might be, to confess and put it away, that their prayers be not hindered. 'As we all bow in prayer let God, by his Spirit, sweep through our hearts and cleanse his temples.'"[17]

"They Shall Lay Hands On the Sick": Practice as Access to Divine Power

As Cullis's remarks imply, champions of divine healing believed that various forms of prayer and ascetical discipline helped point the mind toward spiritual realities and purify the flesh from sensual desires, and in so doing, opened the soul and body to the transforming power of the Holy Spirit. In addition to commending classic Christian devotional practices such as contemplation, communion, and confession as means through which sufferers might "be joined to our Lord by the vital energy of the Holy Ghost," ministers of faith cure also advocated less familiar methods for accessing God's healing power. Laying on of hands and anointing, they asserted, represented divinely sanctioned yet often neglected healing rites that ushered ailing individuals into the presence of the Great Physician. "Laying on of hands," one proponent declared, "is like opening the door to let Christ in. Anointing with oil . . . is bringing the patient where Christ can touch him."[18]

Sick persons who participated in these practices indicated that the physical touch of another human being often prompted particularly potent, even sensible experiences of the divine. When the itinerant healer Ethan O. Allen offered prayer and laid his hands on Mrs. W. J. Starr, of Groton, Connecticut, for example, she felt what she later described as "an intense heat and moisture over the surface of my body, until at length my whole being was permeated by this divine healing power." Immediately, Starr declared herself healed and rose from her bed. Sarah Battles, of North Adams, Massachusetts, experienced a similar sensation when she sought out the prayers of Sarah and Edward Mix. "When Mrs. and Mr. Mix laid their hands upon me, anointing me with oil in the name of the Lord, as we are commanded in the fifth chapter of James," she recounted, "I felt a thrill go through my whole being and knew that I was healed of my malady." Ruth L. King related her experience at the hands of Charles Cullis in comparable terms, "When Dr. Cullis prayed with and anointed me, I felt the power of the Holy Spirit like a great wave of peace, from the crown of my head to the soles of my feet. It was indescribable." For the Reverend John Allen of Trinity Church in Hackney, England, anointing occasioned an experience akin to a "flash of lightening." "Down came the power," Allen declared, "and my soul was filled with the Holy Ghost. I have never been able to describe it." Struggling with his inability to capture fully the essence of the experience, Allen turned to another metaphor. "I have thought of the old mythological bath," he mused, "of people going in old, and coming out young, it seemed something like that. It was so sweet, so soft, so full, so glorious."[19]

For each of these individuals, the hands of a faithful believer, whether laid upon the affected parts of the flesh in prayer or upon the forehead for anointing, served as a conduit for the passage of the Holy Spirit into both body and soul. Since not everyone who participated in these practices experienced such intense, palpable sensations, however, proponents of divine healing were careful to insist that laying on of hands and anointing worked symbolically. Drawing on the classic language of Protestant sacramental theology, leaders of the faith cure movement argued that the "ordinances" of laying on of hands and anointing offered "outward" signs of "inward" realities. They were visible symbols that signified an internal, and therefore imperceptible, transformation. "Laying on of hands is a symbol of divine power and the communication of divine gifts," wrote Presbyterian minister R. L.

Stanton. "The 'anointing with oil in the name of the Lord,' for the recovery of the sick, is for the same purpose. It symbolizes the Spirit's power in healing the body." In his well-circulated work *Inquiries and Answers on Divine Healing,* A. B. Simpson affirmed that anointing "signifies His personal coming into the body" and "sustains to the matter of healing a similar relation to that held by baptism and the Lord's Supper in connection with our professions of Christ as a Saviour, and our deeper communion with Him spiritually."[20]

Simpson's comments suggest that, like the sacraments, laying on of hands and anointing served a confessional purpose. Through these practices, individuals enacted their separation from sin and sensuality, and acknowledged their consecration to God. "As in Baptism the disciple confesses his faith in the cleansing power of Christ's atonement, by the use of water; or, as in Communion he declares his dependence on Christ for spiritual sustenance, by the use of bread so here he avows his faith in the saving health of the Spirit by the use of oil," affirmed A. J. Gordon in his influential treatise *The Ministry of Healing.* "In other words," Gordon continued, "this whole ceremony is a kind of sacramental profession of faith in Jesus Christ as the Divine Physician acting through the Holy Ghost." Judd employed similar language in *The Prayer of Faith.* If anointing served as "the outward sign of the inward anointing which is to heal and renew the soul and body," she stated, it also symbolized "the setting apart to holy use of the new life and strength imparted by the Holy Spirit." From this standpoint, anointing was both a rite of passage through which a sickly sinner was transformed into a strong and vigorous servant of God as the result of an influx of divine power, and a public declaration on the part of the individual that she belonged, body and soul, not to herself or to her family or to her culture, but to the community of believers who acknowledged Christ as healer—and indeed, to Christ himself. As the Methodist minister John Cookman put it, being anointed with oil served as "a seal that I had given myself over wholly to the Lord."[21]

Although leaders of the divine healing movement taught that anointing was not necessarily a prerequisite for healing, they also insisted that participation in the ceremony was neither superfluous nor optional. "Such public profession of faith in Christ as the Healer the Lord seems rigidly to require," Gordon noted, "just as he demands baptism as a confession of faith in him as Redeemer. Neither in the forgiveness of sin nor in the remission of sickness will he permit a clandestine blessing." Working against the apparently prevalent notion that anointing was "some unimportant Jewish custom" or an "idle or meaningless ceremony," proponents argued that this healing rite held "deep and peculiarly sacred" significance. Anointing was not an empty form (although it could be, if unaccompanied by belief), but, as Charlotte Murray explained, "a living picture of a very blessed exchange of gifts." Just as God worked through the sacraments of baptism and the Lord's Supper to impart and strengthen faith, and just as a person's participation in these rituals confirmed her status as a child of God, so also, advocates of divine healing claimed, did anointing function as a "means of faith" that was "essential because commanded." Indeed, A. B. Simpson remarked, anointing "IS A COMMAND. It ceases to be a mere privilege. It is the divine prescription for disease; and no obedient Christian can safely dispense with it." According to this interpretation of scripture, anointing was not an obsolete ordinance relevant only to an earlier era but an obligatory injunction that remained binding for believers in every epoch.[22]

Evidently, however, numerous seekers after divine healing were attempting to shirk anointing, preferring to lay claim to the promises of God in private. "There are many who would gladly secure his healing virtue by stealth, laying hold of it secretly, but avoiding the publicity and possible reproach of having applied to such a physician," Gordon observed. While engaging in united prayer and even requesting the laying on of hands seemed acceptable, many apparently felt that anointing—especially if performed in a public ceremony—went too far. Fearing that they would look "foolish" in the eyes of their friends, family members, and communities, individuals like Elizabeth Baker "objected to the anointing" even after they had come to faith in the Lord as healer. "What is the use," one detractor asked R. K. Carter, "of anointing the sick with oil, as directed in James v: 15? It seems to be absurd in our day to do such a thing as that."[23]

The trouble with anointing, this minister implied, was that it smacked of a kind of ritualistic primitivism that was, in his view, decidedly irrational, blatantly regressive, and patently un-Protestant. Among those who fervently embraced the ideals of progress and feared the influence of immigrant Catholicism, such a seemingly "superstitious following of tradition," as one woman called it, occasioned virulent condemnation and even ridicule. Rites of healing, within this context, raised the specter of sacerdotalism—that the tripartite formula of prayer, laying on of hands, and especially anointing, were a new kind of legalism that would encourage sick persons to place false confidence in the potency of ritual ceremonies rather than in God alone. Some worried that anointing "might be no more a believing act than partaking of the mass or being sprinkled with holy water." To participate in such a practice, opponents charged, was not only futile; it was "fanatical" and potentially even "dangerous."[24]

Advocates of anointing countered that rituals of healing offered important "helps to such as need auxiliaries to faith." Requesting prayer, receiving the laying on of hands, or participating in a ceremony of anointing, they insisted, did not guarantee that an individual would be restored to health, but engaging in these practices did provide aid for those who were struggling to embrace and to act upon the promises of healing contained in scripture. From this perspective, fulfilling the instructions contained in James 5 was necessary, not vain or foolish. "It is not fanaticism to take a plainly pointed out means for obtaining the blessing of health. It is the height of folly *not* to take it," wrote the Reverend A. P. Moore.[25]

In fact, evangelicals such as Moore and his colleagues argued, all of the outcry about fanaticism and superstition was misdirected. Skepticism posed a more potent threat. "We should be cautious against fanaticism and superstition, but not too cautious," one writer warned. "Lukewarmness and unbelief are the great perils of the last times." Within this cultural context, these writers maintained, rituals of healing such as laying on of hands and anointing served as rites of separation that gathered Christians out of an increasingly agnostic environment and symbolized their "being set apart for God's service; consecrated to a holy life or purpose." By obeying the directives given in the Bible, believers who participated in these practices could regulate the influence of rationalism and materialism on their minds so that they could resist the effects of illness and pain on their flesh. Through the practice of prayer and sacred touch, suffering individuals opened themselves to receive the "the Divine Spirit of life"—a power that promised to transform their minds, heal their bodies, and redeem their souls.[26]

The Perils of Practice: Pride, Pollution and Possession

Despite their strong advocacy of healing rituals, leaders of the divine healing movement admitted that these practices could, under certain circumstances, carry significant risks. The most serious threat came from "false teachers" who purported to possess "peculiar personal gifts." "Some of them claim special gifts of healing and power, and speak of the people they have healed, and give out that they are 'some great one,'" Simpson complained at a convention held at his Gospel Tabernacle in October of 1885. Decrying this tendency to boast, Simpson insisted that "no man can claim that he is a healer or a power, or anything but a helpless instrument whom God may be pleased to use in a given case."[27]

Simpson's concerns about "false teachers" seem to have stemmed from several sources. On the one hand, he feared that such individuals were a menace to sufferers because they called attention to themselves rather than pointing people toward God. Indeed, as the divine healing movement gained in popularity, leaders observed what they saw as a disturbing tendency among sick persons to attribute some kind of special agency to prominent figures and even to the healing rituals they performed. As early as 1881, for example, Charles Cullis observed that "some have been inclined to rob God of his glory in healing, by attributing some power to my personal presence." Similarly, several years into her ministry of healing, Carrie Judd noticed that many people sought her out because they deemed her "more highly favored than themselves." Instead of relying solely on God, these individuals came "clamoring after something they are expecting from *us*," Judd lamented. Elizabeth Baxter discerned a like attitude among the many people who wrote requesting her prayers on their behalf. "I get the greatest quantity of letters asking me to pray for them. . . . They seem to think I am a barrel full of spiritual power, and all they have to do is to turn the tap and healing comes," Baxter complained.[28]

But by "looking to man instead of to the Lord," these leaders insisted, people were placing their faith in the "means" through which God channeled his healing power rather than trusting in God alone. Instead of fixing their eyes on Jesus, those who trusted in the power of charismatic leaders or in the practices they performed were leaning on "the arm of flesh." Such mislaid faith was utterly futile. "You will never be healed in that way," Baxter insisted. "It is not the prayer that heals, but the answerer of prayer. . . . God is no respecter of persons." To promote oneself as a person possessed of "power to communicate divine blessing and Divine influence and healing," then, was to "lead men away from . . . the Lord Himself, to look at the instrument," and ultimately to undermine a sufferer's bid for health.[29]

In addition to leading sick persons astray, "false teachers" also jeopardized the status of divine healing movement as a whole. By exalting themselves, Simpson warned, these "counterfeits . . . led many, on their account, to look with suspicion upon the doctrine of Divine Healing." In late-nineteenth-century England and North America, claims to extraordinary personal power in the realm of healing were nothing unique. Often these assertions were associated with a class of practitioners whose standing within the orthodox medical community and the ranks of the respectable was anything but reputable.[30]

During this period, physicians striving to consolidate their professional authority in a competitive medical environment leveled accusations of quackery against any individual who failed to conform to the increasingly stringent educational standards and licensing procedures that the "regulars" proposed. While practitioners from competing schools of medicine such as homeopathy and eclecticism received the bulk of the criticism, orthodox physicians, along with members of the educated elite, aimed especially virulent condemnations against those who claimed to possess the power to heal the sick in and of themselves. In an article published in London's *The Gentleman's Magazine* in 1885, for example, T. F. Thiselton Dyer decried the "local quack" and "false healers of the sick" who, "under the pretence of exercising extraordinary medical skill . . . extort exorbitant sums from those who seek their aid." "Pitch doctors" who promoted their healing powers and peddled their wares at traveling medicine shows were especially easy targets for detractors, who denounced such self-appointed performers as mountebanks, charlatans, and frauds. Although the traveling showmen logged their greatest successes in rural areas of the southern and western United States, where professional medical services were scarce, they frequently tried their luck in the urban areas of the Northeast as well, often putting on extravagant acts featuring music, costumes, various entertainments, and even parades.[31]

It is no wonder, then, that Simpson expressed alarm when outside observers began to associate divine healing with quackery and with the charade of the traveling medicine show. "The subject of Healing by Faith in God is receiving a great deal of earnest attention," Simpson wrote in the editorial section of his magazine in February of 1883, "but it is also in great danger of being paraded and imperiled or perverted by its friends. It is very solemn ground, and never can be made a professional business or public parade." Struggling to distinguish divine healing from the sham doctors who proclaimed their miraculous powers in extravagant performances, Simpson insisted that healing by faith "must not be used to exalt man, but for the glory of Jesus Christ alone. Its mightiest victories will always be silent and out of sight, and its power will keep pace with our humility and holiness. We solemnly warn the people of God against the caricatures and counterfeits of this solemn truth, which they may expect on every side."[32]

While Simpson never suggested that proponents of divine healing desist from encouraging the sick to participate in a public anointing ceremony, he did advise leaders of the movement to exercise caution in conducting these rituals, insisting that the services should be characterized by proper decorum and appropriate modesty. At meetings "of those who believe in Divine Healing," Simpson averred, "There is no man or woman who claims to possess any personal powers." Instead, "there is a simple lesson from His Word, a season of testimony and prayer, and then all bow together at His feet, and ask Him to touch the sick and suffering ones before Him. There is a simple ordinance, the anointing oil, the touch of a holy and loving hand upon the head, and a prayer of faith and consecration."[33]

Other prominent spokespersons for divine healing echoed Simpson's call for sincerity, solemnity, and simplicity in the conduct of healing services. At the first International Conference on Divine Healing and True Holiness, held June 1–5, 1885, in London, William Boardman prefaced the Wednesday afternoon anointing service with these remarks: "Our custom is simply to touch the hair with oil and lay on our hands." While he was careful to clarify that the efficacy of anointing was not dependent on "some special form," Boardman also wanted his audience to understand that he and his colleagues strove "to follow, as nearly as possible the lines laid down in the Word of God, in the manner, as well as in the matter." Conforming their practices to biblical guidelines, Boardman implied, would help to guard against the pitfalls associated with pride and public display.[34]

With the proliferation of conferences for divine healing and holiness following the first international meeting, leaders seem to have felt compelled to emphasize the decorum that characterized anointing ceremonies. George W. McCalla, an author, publisher, and Holiness advocate who was heavily involved with the divine healing movement in Philadelphia, described the anointing service held during a December 1885 conference in his home city as "especially solemn and impressive, silent as the grave, save when broken by the notes of the consecration hymn." Accounts of regular weekly meetings for healing also highlighted the sober nature of these events. In his description of the Thursday meetings devoted to "the prayer of faith" for healing held at Cullis's Beacon Hill Church, for example, an observer stressed the "perfect silence" that marked the service. "It seemed like holy ground," he wrote.[35]

For defenders of divine healing like McCalla, Boardman, and Cullis, maintaining an appropriate atmosphere at anointing services helped to deflect the charges of critics who tried to equate these events with the theatrical performances of patent medicine peddlers and traveling impresarios. Even more troubling for these apologists, however, was the allegation that divine healing services were similar to demonstrations of animal magnetism, mesmerism, and Spiritualism, a charge that surfaced early on in the history of the faith cure movement. Dorothea Trudel, one of the pioneers of divine healing in Europe, was accused of employing mesmerism in her prayers with the sick soon after she began receiving invalids into her home at Mannedorf, Switzerland in the mid-1850s. As news of the "extraordinary cures" that took place through her ministry spread, some mistook Mannedorf for a "Mesmeric Institution," and assumed that Trudel possessed clairvoyant or magical powers.[36]

Although Trudel struggled to clear herself and her home from these allegations, evidence suggests that many individuals continued to associate divine healing with some form of animal magnetism or mesmerism. In 1876, for example, Mary Mossman prayed for and laid hands on a young child suffering from "cholera infantum." When the child promptly recovered, some observers attributed the cure to "animal magnetism"—an interpretation Mossman flatly denied. Unlike magnetic healers, Mossman argued, she did not claim to possess any power to cure the sick child in and of herself. In fact, she was struggling with infirmity during this period and often lacked the strength even to sit up, let alone perform the repeated magnetic "passes" necessary to manipulate the child's vital fluid and restore it to health. For this reason, Mossman asserted, the child's remarkable cure could only be attributed to God's power acting through her prayers. "Those who claim that this work was wrought through animal magnetism," she wrote, "must remember that my physical power was at a low ebb. Because of this the Spirit had more full control of me."[37]

Despite the early efforts of leaders like Mossman and Trudel to distinguish faith cure from animal magnetism or mesmerism, seeming similarities between the methods of these two healing movements made disassociating them an ongoing struggle. The practice of laying on of hands, in particular, highlighted the resemblances between divine healing and magnetism, prompting many persons—seekers and critics alike—to assume that the two modalities of healing operated according to the same logic. During the 1885 International Conference, for example, several articles in *The Christian,* a London periodical that expressed only qualified support of the divine healing movement, voiced concern over the apparent affinities between the practices of faith healing and those of mesmeric healers. "We are old enough to know how mesmerism developed into clairvoyance, electro-biology, medical instinct, and at last into full-blown spiritualism," the editor of the periodical noted. "And we are suspicious and afraid of all laying on of hands which has the least semblance of mesmeric passes." Accordingly, the editors warned the International Conference organizers to exercise extreme care in determining who would be allowed to lay hands on and anoint the sick during the public healing ceremonies. "Those who have the control of Faith Healing or other platforms incur a grave responsibility as to those whom they receive and put forward as teachers," the editors cautioned. "Touching the forehead with oil is one thing, passing the hand, mesmerically or otherwise, over the parts affected, is another."[38]

Participants in the International Conference were quick to assure detractors that they recognized the potential perils involved with the practices of laying on of hands and anointing. Throughout the conference, in fact, speakers cautioned attendees and leaders alike to be aware of the hazards that partaking in these ceremonies presented and to guard against improper conduct. "We should be very careful, dear friends, as to whom we choose to lay on hands, and let us be as careful how we do it ourselves," Boardman insisted. "Let each ask the Lord, 'Am I sanctified, am *I* the person who is the fit instrument in Thy hands? Am I a channel through whom the Holy Ghost can convey a real, lasting, eternal blessing to others, so that those whom I anoint with oil, and upon whom I lay hands in Thy name, may receive the Holy Ghost?" In Boardman's view, only those who could claim to have experienced sanctification were qualified to anoint and lay hands on sick persons seeking healing, for personal holiness alone provided assurance that an individual was fit to serve as a conduit for conveying God's healing power.[39]

Without the safeguard of sanctification on the part of those leading the services of prayer and anointing, Boardman warned, healing rituals were susceptible to corruption that opened the individual to infiltration by unholy influences. A person who was not a vessel for communicating the power of the Holy Spirit might instead serve as a medium of demonic forces. "There is such a thing as the transmission of carnal spirits," Boardman asserted. "I have seen and heard of cases in which the evil spirits, instead of being cast out, have come into the persons on whom hands were laid, and subjected them to their influence." Submitting one's self to an individual who might be morally suspect, or perhaps even a force for evil, made a petitioner vulnerable to both bodily abuse and spiritual pollution.[40]

Laying on of hands and anointing, in this view, were not neutral practices, but rituals that opened an individual to receive either great spiritual and bodily blessing or tremendous personal harm. Since the stakes were so high, Boardman urged petitioners to take heed when seeking healing, admonishing them to discriminate among those who offered to perform these ceremonies on their behalf. "I do not hesitate to warn every Christian to beware, and not to receive anointing from every man or woman whom you may meet with, but only from those who are really sanctified," Boardman intoned. At another International Conference meeting, Pastor Schrenk of Bern, Switzerland, "begged his audience not to yield their bodies to any and every one who anointed, without being sure they were holy in life."[41]

Despite cautions and qualifications such as these, however, the specters of animal magnetism, mesmerism, and especially Spiritualism continued to loom large for defenders of divine healing. Just one year after the International Conference, in fact, James M. Buckley published his controversial essay, "Faith Healing and Kindred Phenomena," in which he argued that evangelical divine healing had much more in common with these various forms of what he called "mind cure" than the movement's champions were willing to admit. Buckley's article occasioned vigorous response from the evangelical community. A. B. Simpson wrote one of the most forceful rejoinders, "Divine Healing and Demonism Not Identical: A Protest and Reply to Dr. Buckley in the Century Magazine." This editorial, which appeared in two installments in the July and August 1886 editions of Simpson's periodical *Word, Work and World,* sought to dismantle systematically the connections between divine healing and mind cure that Buckley had attempted to establish.[42]

To make his case, Simpson accentuated what he saw as a key distinction between animal magnetists, mesmerists, and Spiritualists, on the one hand, and "those who exercise the ministry of healing in the name of Jesus," on the other. Rather than attempting "to influence the mind of the sufferer," Simpson insisted, proponents of divine healing encouraged the sick "to act independently on personal conviction. . . . We do not require such persons, as the Mesmerist does, to yield themselves up passively to our influence, or any influence, but bid them, on the very contrary, to exercise a clear, intelligent judgment and faith for themselves, and be most active and earnest in the exercise of their own will." When they anointed and laid hands on the sick, in other words, ministers of divine healing did so without compromising the sufferer's personal agency.[43]

In fact, Simpson argued, divine healing advocates took issue with the premise that informed all modes of mind cure, including the more respectable methods of mental therapeutics that neurologists such as George Beard and S. Weir Mitchell were beginning to employ in this period. All of these approaches assumed that a cure could be effected when a sick person yielded to the dominant will of the healer. But for Simpson and his colleagues, such submission violated the integrity of the individual in a way that was inappropriate and immoral. "We more than doubt if any human being has a right to abandon himself wholly to the will of another or to any influence which may come over them in such a state of passive surrender. We are sure that no man has a right to ask another human being to do so," he wrote.[44]

By contesting the authority of healers who made uncompromising compliance a critical feature of their therapeutic approach, leaders of the divine healing movement like Simpson worked against prevailing gender norms and medical theories that linked female submissiveness, in particular, with the pursuit and maintenance of physical, moral, and spiritual health. Echoing the complaints of critics who highlighted the potential improprieties involved in any form of therapy in which women were required to yield their bodies, minds, and wills to a male physician—whether he hailed from the mesmeric, clairvoyant, or orthodox school of practice—proponents of faith cure implied that both women and men who placed themselves in the hands of potentially unsanctified others were vulnerable to corporal insult, psychological abuse, and even demonic possession. "We should not wonder if, in such a defenceless state of the will a power should come over the soul which is far more than psychological. What better opportunity does the prince of the powers of the air want to pour his legions into the human soul?" Simpson remarked. "We believe the Devil will surely possess every heart that is not constantly yielded to God." Only by submitting to the Great Physician rather than to human healers (male or female), these evangelicals argued, could ailing sufferers seek healing without running the risk of physical, mental, and spiritual contamination.[45]

Carrie Judd's reply to Buckley sounded a similar note of caution. In an article entitled "Ancient and Modern Spiritualism Considered in the Light of God's

Word," published in the October 1886 edition of *Triumphs of Faith,* Judd argued that those who consulted Spiritualist healers for medical advice ran the risk of "the terrible *defilement* which comes to soul, mind and body through contact with the powers of evil." While she conceded that some clairvoyant physicians might accomplish their seemingly marvelous demonstrations through "mere tricks and feats of sleight of hand," Judd maintained "that the majority of wonder-working mediums are controlled by the direct power of a personal devil." Especially dangerous, Judd averred, was the practice of "submitting" to the counsel that Spiritualist healers received "while in a 'trance.'" Clairvoyants who entered into trance, Judd suggested, became "mediums" for demonic spirits. The prescriptions they dispensed while in this state represented the "doctrines of devils" rather than the healing power of God. By taking their advice, Judd warned, sick persons were "dishonouring their bodies (the temples of the Holy Ghost)," and, even worse, opening themselves to the possibility of being "taken possession of by the evil spirits."[46]

As Judd's comments suggest, the stress that proponents of divine healing placed on personal agency as a bulwark against both physical and spiritual pollution made them keenly suspicious of healing practices that, from their point of view, seemed to jeopardize an individual's ability to act independently or to exercise clear judgment. Both Judd and Simpson attempted to distinguish divine healing from mind-cure movements, and especially from Spiritualism, by insisting that the rituals of prayer, laying on of hands, and anointing promoted an individual's dependence on God while preserving her autonomy from the contaminating manipulations of false healers or the defiling influence of demonic powers. Practices employed by animal magnetists, mesmerists, and mediums, they suggested, did just the opposite. In his rejoinder to "Faith Healing and Kindred Phenomena," for example, Simpson reprimanded Buckley for "mixing up" the "lying wonders" of Spiritualism with the miraculous cures wrought by the Great Physician and for eliding the practices of these two healing movements. At the Spiritualist séance, Simpson maintained, "you will find the mysterious circle, the silence, the darkness, the joined hands, the air of mystery, the trance of the medium, the strange manifestations, the claim of personal power by the person who heals, or deep and strange secrets of your life unveiled, and much more, and in the healing medium full consciousness of the potency of his touch and his powers." Divine healing meetings, by contrast, encouraged humility, transparency, and the exercise of free agency. "Those who believe in Divine Healing . . . gather in the light of heaven, and the face of all men. There is no mystery and no secrecy about the service," Simpson avowed. "Is there anything in this that ought to be named in the same breath as a Spiritualist séance? Is it not a strange and horrible incongruity to confound them together?" he demanded. Singling out the experience of automatic writing—in which individuals under the influence of Spiritualist mediums delivered written messages from the dead—as well as the "brutal and course" behavior of individuals who claimed to see visions of heaven while in a medium-induced trance, Simpson highlighted what he saw as the perilous effects of participating in practices that compelled a loss of self-control. "We so thank the Lord," Simpson wrote, "that Divine Healing is wholly free from all these things, without trances, visions, emotions."[47]

Policing Practice: The Cases of "Trance Evangelism" and "Indiscriminate Public Anointing"

Simpson's confidence that the lack of more ecstatic forms of religious practice set faith cure apart from Spiritualism and other rival healing movements would soon be sorely tested, however. As early as the spring of 1885, in fact, Maria B. Underwood Woodworth, an itinerant evangelist who had commenced preaching under the auspices of the United Brethren in her native Ohio around in 1880, began to incorporate "laying on of hands for the recovery of the sick" in her revival services—events that often drew thousands of participants, many of whom experienced visions, trances, and baptisms of the Holy Spirit that caused them to fall prostrate to the ground, scream for mercy, shout for joy, and jump up from sickbeds praising God. News of Woodworth's revivals spread primarily through accounts published in both religious and secular newspapers, many of which highlighted the "ecstatic," "emotional," and "extravagant" features of her evangelistic style and associated her healing practices with magnetism, mesmerism, Spiritualism, and sometimes even magic. While some reporters were sympathetic, the majority characterized Woodworth as a curiosity at best, and others accused her of showmanship, "stupendous humbug," speciousness, and even insanity. "The manner of conduct of these revivals smacks too strongly of sensationalism to assure much sincerity. There is too much of the 'biggest show on earth,' about one which seeks converts under the strain of mental excitement," wrote an Indiana journalist in the *Kokomo Dispatch*. Reporting on an outdoor revival meeting where "twenty thousand people gathered in a small grove" to hear Woodworth preach, a correspondent from the Muncie *Daily News* noted the "singular and peculiar" and "noisy demonstrations" that marked the event. "It was similar to a circus crowd with its bustling curious throng of motley curious pleasure seekers," this author declared.[48]

Although the *New York Times* reported on the "strange scenes"—and particularly the trances—that characterized Woodworth's evangelistic services in January of 1885, several months before she began her ministry of healing, East Coast lead-

Maria Woodworth in the 1880s. Courtesy of the Flower Pentecostal Heritage Center.

ers of the faith cure movement either failed to catch wind of her activities or declined to comment directly upon them until January of 1890, when Carrie Judd attended one of Woodworth's "tent-meetings" during a trip to Oakland, California. When Judd first heard about the visionary trances that accompanied Woodworth's gatherings, she was inclined to be "rather prejudiced and critical," but listening to the evangelist preach changed Judd's mind, and she gave Woodworth her endorsement. Elizabeth Sisson, one of Judd's traveling companions, who had served as a house matron at Bethshan and as a missionary to India, was so taken with Woodworth that she published an article defending the evangelist's practice of putting

St. Louis *Post-Dispatch* cartoon drawing of a Woodworth tent meeting, summer 1890.
Courtesy of the Flower Pentecostal Heritage Center.

people "'under the power' of God" and argued that "trances and visions" could be
legitimately incorporated within the framework of divine healing. Just "because
through so-called Christian Science, Spiritualism, and other devilism there have
been healings, visions, and trances," Sisson contended, "we may not say that God
does not work in these ways among his true people today." Instead, Christians were
called to discriminate between states of ecstasy brought about through "the power
and demonstration of the Holy Ghost" and those wrought through "the work of
the devil." Within several weeks of meeting Woodworth, Sisson began assisting
during her revival services and often fell "under the power" herself, trembling un-
controllably from head to toe. Local journalists soon identified Sisson as a member
of Woodworth's inner circle of "ecstatic contortionists," dubbing her the "Shaking

Elizabeth Sisson in 1883. Courtesy of the Flower Pentecostal Heritage Center.

Matron." Indeed, Sisson became so integrally involved with Woodworth's work that she stayed behind in Oakland when Judd returned to the East Coast.[49]

This was a decision that Sisson would eventually come to regret. Just after Judd left California, Woodworth began to prophecy that an earthquake and tidal wave would obliterate the cities of the Bay Area, including Alameda, Oakland, and San Francisco, on April 14, 1890. Woodworth's prediction ignited a wave of excitement among her followers and sparked a panic among local citizens. Some quit their jobs, sold their possessions, and fled to the hills. Woodworth herself left the area for Santa Rosa in mid-February, at which point she began to back away from the doomsday prophecy, attributing it to George Erickson, one of her disciples who had been most zealous in spreading the message of cataclysmic annihilation. When April 14 came and went without a wave or tremor, Woodworth's credibility in California—already under attack from skeptics and naysayers among the local clergy and press—collapsed, despite her efforts to distance herself from Erickson and the group of devotees (including Sisson) who had continued to forecast a flood of destruction. Erickson himself was arrested and committed to an insane asylum even prior to the date of the unfulfilled prophecy, and Woodworth packed up her tents and returned to St. Louis, where she was soon accused of hypnotizing her audiences and charged with insanity. In September of 1890, two physicians took Wood-worth to civil court, where they attempted to have her declared legally insane and incarcerated within an asylum.[50]

Although Woodworth won the case and retained her freedom, she lost respect among advocates of faith cure like Carrie Judd, who felt compelled to sever themselves from any connection with Woodworth's ministry in order to preserve the reputation of the divine healing movement. Only weeks after returning to the East Coast, in fact, Judd had begun to express alarm about the prophecies being issued back in the Bay Area and suggested that they represented a "delusion of the enemy." Lamenting the fact that Sisson had fallen victim to "Satan's deception," Judd published a notice in *Triumphs of Faith* in May of 1890 indicating that "by mutual consent," Sisson would resign her position as associate editor of the journal. Upon her return to California as a newlywed several months later, Judd authored another editorial in which she stated that she felt "obliged to alter" her previous opinions of Woodworth's ministry after realizing "more than ever what sad havoc the devil has wrought here as a result of the Oakland prophecies." Although she refrained from criticizing Woodworth in detail, Judd concluded that "there must have been something radically wrong with Mrs. Woodworth's teachings and methods of work" and expressed her conviction that the problem lay in Woodworth's practice of employing trance as a means of evangelism and healing. "The great mistake in her work," Judd wrote, "lies in the exaltation of 'the power' as an abstract thing, instead of seeking Jesus Himself as the power for service."[51]

Carrie Judd was not the only apologist for faith cure to condemn Woodworth's use of trance in her revival meetings and healing services. Prior to both the prophecy scandal and the insanity trial, in fact, the Reverend John Alexander Dowie, a Congregationalist minister who emigrated from Sydney, Australia, to San Francisco in 1888, clashed publicly with Woodworth over the issue of trance. Dowie, who would himself become a divisive figure within the divine healing movement in the late 1890s, was an extremely charismatic preacher who began praying for the recovery of the sick in 1876 when a severe outbreak of illness struck down forty members of his congregation. The following year he resigned from the Congregational ministry and became an independent evangelist, eventually founding his own church and establishing the International Divine Healing Association. Dowie remained relatively disconnected from the transatlantic divine healing movement until he migrated to the United States and began preaching and conducting healing services up and down the West Coast. When he initially encountered Woodworth in Oakland, Dowie was supportive of her revival work, but he soon changed his mind and began to denounce her publicly. Although he condemned a number of

Woodworth's theological positions and practices, he was particularly critical of the role that putting people "under the power" played in her healing ministry. In January of 1890, Dowie published an article entitled "Trance Evangelism" in his newly founded periodical *Leaves of Healing* that warned readers to "beware of this false prophetess, who, in the name of Jesus is . . . seducing God's servants." Attributing the "alleged divine trances" that Woodworth promoted to the "power of the devil," Dowie accused Woodworth of "leading many into paths where they will drink the cup of devils, and find themselves at last to be in company with others who also speak lies in the name of Jesus, such as Christian Scientists, Spiritualists, Free Lovers, Papalists and others 'led captive by Satan at his will.'"[52]

For Dowie, Judd, and other spokespersons for divine healing, trances fell outside the bounds of appropriate Christian practice. The apparent resemblance between Woodworth's trance evangelism and the hypnotic or trance-like states induced by mesmeric, magnetic, and Spiritualist healers caused apologists for divine healing considerable discomfort for several reasons, prompting them to conclude that this practice represented a danger both to persons who participated in it and to the reputation of the divine healing movement as a whole. On one level, champions of faith cure like Dowie worried that Woodworth's trances blurred the distinctions between divine healing and other rival healing movements that they so desperately wanted to maintain and defend. Simpson expressed this sentiment clearly in a sermon he preached at a "Christian Convention" held in his New York City Gospel Tabernacle several months after the 1885 International Conference. "There is a great need to draw the line of careful discrimination between the Scriptural doctrine of Divine Healing, and the counterfeits which the enemy is always ready to palm off upon the unwary," Simpson declared. Although he did not mention Woodworth's name in his address, Simpson did criticize individuals who "make startling claims of special revelations and visions" and "claim that the laying on of their hands produces the most wonderful physical manifestations, prostrations and other evidences of power." Such "extravagances," Simpson argued, led detractors to associate divine healing with "counterfeit" healing movements like Spiritualism, or to regard faith cure as a "dangerous" form of fanaticism that promoted "rash and unscriptural views."[53]

Evangelical promoters of divine healing also feared that Woodworth's practice of putting people "under the power" represented an unseemly form of religious behavior that traded on emotion rather than the exercise of reason, judgment, and free will. For once, at least, proponents of faith cure concurred with critics like James Buckley, who contended that Woodworth's trances represented a kind of "emotional contagion" rather than an experience of divine possession. After attending one of Woodworth's revival meetings in St. Louis in 1891, Buckley concluded that trances were a "survival of a state to which increasing knowledge and self-control must put an end." This kind of spiritual regression was entirely unacceptable for mature, intelligent Christians, Buckley implied. "The Bible teaches that we should never lose our self-control under the influence of any religious emotion whatsoever."[54]

Buckley's critique resonated with the rhetoric of divine healing leaders such as Dowie, Judd, and Simpson, all of whom maintained that acting faith required the conscious exercise of the mental faculties. Working hard to mark out a middle way between the rationalism that they wanted to resist and the fanaticism that critics accused them of promoting, advocates of faith cure emphasized the importance of intellectual conviction in the healing process and censured individuals like Woodworth whose ecstatic practices seemed to bypass or even preclude critical engagement altogether. Dowie, for example, contrasted the behavior of one of Woodworth's entranced followers who, "in a state of apparent unconsciousness," was "struggling, writhing, and screaming," with the "calm and composed" comportment of this same individual after he laid hands upon her and prayed that she would find "rest in the Lord." In his view, stillness, quiet, and consciousness were the marks of a person possessed by God's power and ready to receive divine healing, whereas manifestations of unregulated emotion, excitement, and "tension" while "under the power" proved that an individual was subject to an "evil spirit" that needed to be cast out before the Divine Physician could rejuvenate body, mind and soul.[55]

Indeed, safeguarding the sick from the defilement of demon possession was a central preoccupation for proponents of divine healing. In addition to warning sufferers not to engage in ecstatic practices that prevented them from exercising critical judgment or free will and thereby exposed them to infiltration by demonic forces, advocates of faith cure also urged leaders of the movement to ensure that those who sought physical restoration through more acceptable means such as prayer, laying on of hands, and anointing were Christians who were willing to profess their faith in the healing power of God. At the International Conference, Boardman explained that "it was usual for the elders, before anointing, to satisfy themselves that the recipients were believers in Christ" by asking a series of "direct questions." First, he inquired about the state of their souls. "Are you saved? " Boardman queried. "Is Jesus Christ your Saviour?" After explaining that anointing "signified the gift of the Holy Spirit" and that "their bodies were not their own, but the temples of the Holy Ghost," Boardman asked whether "all present [could] accept the Holy Ghost as taking full and entire possession of His own temple, their bodies." Finally, he requested those who desired anointing to affirm their trust in the Great Physician by indicating with a show of hands that they believed that the Lord Jesus would supply their physical needs.[56]

By leading sufferers through a process of catechesis prior to anointing them, Boardman treated petitioners as free agents who were called upon to make up their own minds about the efficacy of divine healing. Rather than requiring the sick to submit their wills to the influence of the human beings who would lay hands on them, Boardman reminded these individuals that God alone had the power to heal, exhorting them to yield their bodies only, but completely, to the Holy Spirit. Cullis adopted a similar practice at his weekly meetings for divine healing, asking whether all present were Christians and if they had "faith in the Lord" to heal them. If someone could not answer in the affirmative, Cullis would converse with the agnostic on the subject until the individual "took Christ as their Saviour from sin, as well as sickness." Simpson was even more cautious, often advising the sick to refrain from receiving anointing unless they were "fully persuaded" of God's power and willingness to heal them. When Emma Whittemore questioned Simpson about divine healing, for example, he cautioned her not to permit herself "to be over-influenced or persuaded by remarks or suggestions into believing as he or others did." Instead, he encouraged her to "commend the entire matter to God, and prayerfully consider His Word on the subject, and then, if prompted by the Holy Spirit, to *freely* accept of that promise: 'The prayer of faith shall save the sick,' and others as plainly given in the Scriptures, if I could with a clear conscience claim them for myself."[57]

Simpson's emphasis on freedom of conscience and personal agency also led him to condemn supposed friends of divine healing who held large services at which they engaged in "the indiscriminate public anointing of all who come forward." Although he avoided naming names, Simpson's admonition was likely directed at the Reverend George O. Barnes, a former Presbyterian minister and missionary who began an itinerant evangelistic and healing ministry in the southern states in the late 1870s. By 1882, five years into his ministry, about 25,000 persons were reported to have made confessions of faith at Barnes's services, earning him the title of "Mountain evangelist." In addition to issuing altar calls to "back-sliders" and "the unconverted," Barnes invited those who had "faith to believe God will heal them to come forward" at the conclusion of his meetings. According to contemporary accounts, "He then unites with them in prayer, and anoints their foreheads with oil, telling them to disregard feelings or symptoms, but to trust God and He will cure them."[58]

At some point in the early 1880s, however, Barnes seems to have dropped the requirement that those coming forward for anointing demonstrate faith in the

Great Physician. Instead, he "came out in open declaration that God called him to anoint any and all who came to receive Jesus as their Healer, stopping to ask no questions as to their spiritual state." While Simpson refrained from censuring Barnes directly, he did imply that Barnes's practice smacked of a "wonder-seeking spirit." Such demonstrations, Simpson worried, were precisely the kind of spectacles that led skeptics like Buckley to associate divine healing with "knavery and unbridled fanaticism," and Boston University Professor Luther T. Townsend to perceive "a striking similarity between ordinary quacks and these professional faithworkers." Indiscriminate anointing also threatened to undermine the efficacy of divine healing for those who participated in the ceremony before being fully convinced that God could and would restore them to health. "We have no doubt, in some cases great numbers are hastily anointed who are quite unprepared both in knowledge and faith for such a step," Simpson remarked.[59]

Simpson's reaction to hasty or indiscriminate anointing underscores both the political import and the spiritual significance that he and his colleagues attributed to ritual and devotional healing practices. Properly conducted, Simpson believed, rites such as anointing served as boundary markers that delineated faith cure from the fraudulent performances of medical impresarios as well as from the dangerous exhibitions of demonic power on display at Spiritualist séances, mesmeric demonstrations, and even purportedly evangelical revival and healing services like those conducted by Maria Woodworth.

If practices helped to distinguish divine healing from its rivals, spiritual exercises also provided methods for cultivating the "knowledge and faith" that enabled suffering individuals to trust the Great Physician for healing and to act out their convictions regardless of their circumstances. Engaging in contemplation and prayers of confession, adopting ascetical disciplines, participating in the sacrament of the Lord's Supper or ceremonies of anointing, receiving the laying on of hands—all of these practices were part of the healing process. Through these "means" skeptical sufferers such as Emma Whittemore trained their minds to focus on spiritual realities while ignoring empirical evidences of illness, opened their souls to the renewing power of the Holy Spirit while guarding against infiltration by evil spirits, and disciplined their bodies to engage in active service to God whether or not they experienced ongoing pain.

CHAPTER FIVE

Houses of Healing

Sacred Space, Social Geography and Gender in Divine Healing

In the autumn of 1876, while attending the nation's centennial celebration, Miss H. M. Barker contracted a case of typhoid fever that left her crippled. While she managed to get about on crutches for several years, Barker's health was gradually failing. By the spring of 1881, she was "completely prostrated." For the next four years, Barker remained a "helpless invalid" whose case "seemed to baffle even the best medical skill." Although she tried various treatments, "all remedies were of but little avail," and her physicians eventually deemed her incurable, predicting that she had only a few months to live, at most. "During all these years of suffering," Barker later recounted, "I prayed so earnestly for patience and resignation to God's will, and for the most part rested quietly, and, as I believed, submissively, under what I felt was His needed teaching of me." But as "the weary years dragged on," Barker recalled, "I began to think of the subject of Divine Healing." At first, she reported, the possibility of healing by faith "seemed a great way off—something for only a chosen few." Although she became "more convinced of the reality of this belief" through discussions with friends who were "deeply interested" in the possibility of faith cure, Barker "was still much in the dark about the matter," reporting that she could not "see it clearly enough to grasp it for myself."[1]

On Monday, December 22, 1885, Barker left her home in Guilford, Connecticut, to travel to A. B. Simpson's Berachah house of healing in New York City, anxious to "receive the teachings given there" and to continue her quest to "see clearly if this blessing were indeed for me." Three days after reaching the home, Barker finally felt strong enough to leave her room. "On Friday evening," she reminisced, "I was carried down to the parlors to attend the services . . . which were especially devoted to the subject of Divine Healing. I was laid upon the sofa with pillows and rugs, being then too weak to sit up for any length of time." During the meeting, Barker heard "many clear and touching testimonies as to Christ's power to heal." After the service concluded, a group congregated around Barker to pray specifically for her recovery. "As the earnest, simple words of prayer went up from the hearts of the friends gathered there," she remembered, "I then and there accepted my healing. It was as though the dear Lord Jesus stood close beside me, laying His tender loving hands upon me and bidding me 'arise and walk,' which I did at once in *His strength,* feeling that my hand was clasped in His, and He was leading and upholding me every step of the way." In the months following her sojourn at Berachah, Barker continued to walk in the strength of Jesus. "Since my healing," she wrote two years later, "I have been engaged in mission work in New York City, a work which requires a great amount of physical strength and endurance. I have sometimes walked five miles in my work, besides climbing many long flights of tenement house stairs, something which I could never have done in my life before, as my powers of endurance were always decidedly limited. But my strength, coming from Him, has never failed."[2]

Barker's narrative suggests that her visit to Berachah profoundly reshaped her attitude toward affliction as well as her actual experience of embodied selfhood. Prior to her sojourn at this healing home, Barker believed that quiet submission was the pathway to both physical health and spiritual holiness. Convinced that she could glorify God by resigning herself to her role as a suffering servant, Barker accepted her sickness as God's will and viewed her body as a broken vessel incapable of accomplishing any service beyond the confines of the sickroom. From this perspective, embracing the notion that Christ, the Great Physician, desired to heal her of her diseases so that she might pursue an active mission for the advancement of his kingdom seemed both medically unsound and spiritually specious. Although she was intrigued by the promises of divine healing, Barker found it difficult dismiss the dominant cultural and theological discourses that sanctified female infirmity and demanded passive forbearance in the face of sickness and somatic distress.

By traveling to Berachah, Barker severed herself from deeply ingrained modes of believing and behaving that she had been unable to relinquish while remaining confined to her sickroom. Within the carefully constructed setting of Simpson's house of healing—a domestic space infused with sacred associations and filled with faithful Christians who proclaimed the healing power of the Great Physician—Barker encountered "the Son of God," the "*complete* Saviour," who enabled her to disavow a devotional ethic of passive resignation, defy her doctor's diagnoses, and act faith "in *His* strength." Berachah's parlor became the portal through which Barker "passed from death (a living death) unto life," the site where she received "new life in Jesus" for body, mind and soul.[3]

Barker's experience at Berachah illumines the vital place that faith homes occupied in the landscape of late-nineteenth-century divine healing. Although leaders like Simpson and Cullis regularly promoted divine healing during church services, and often held special sessions for healing prayer, laying on of hands, and anointing at camp meetings and faith conventions, they realized that these occasions offered only fleeting opportunities to instruct sufferers in the theology and practice of faith cure. While some who encountered the "gospel of healing" in these settings were ready to accept the message on the spot, others required more intensive and sustained training in order to embrace what Barker called "this *true* 'way of life.'" Even those who heard about faith cure through friends or relatives frequently needed additional time and space to consider the claims of divine healing and to observe how people who put their faith in the Great Physician acted out their beliefs on an ongoing basis. Providing invalids like Barker with a supportive atmosphere in which to pursue such total transformation was one of the principal ways in which advocates of faith cure sought to assist the sick in their quest to be made whole. Following in the footsteps of Dorothea Trudel, one of the first teachers of faith healing to open her home to the sick, Elizabeth Baxter, William Boardman, Charles Cullis, Carrie Judd, Mary Mossman, A. B. Simpson, and many other leaders in the transatlantic movement founded "faith homes" or "houses of healing" that offered guests room, board, and an encouraging environment in which to nurture the mental convictions, bodily habits, and spiritual dispositions that made trusting God for healing and acting faith possible.[4]

Even as the establishment, spread, and popularity of these new institutions elucidates the significance of sacred sites for the success of the divine healing movement, controversies over the character, function, and position of healing homes within the social geography of late-nineteenth-century medical practice expose the deepening rift between faith cure and its adversaries. Debates about proper care of the sick, the use of chemical remedies and instrumental therapies, and the definition of disease reveal that competition over the right to treat suffering bodies, to educate uncertain minds, and to minister to sinful souls was intensifying in this period. By distinguishing houses of healing from hospitals, differentiating between "illness" and "injury," and discriminating among "scriptural" and other means of treatment, faith home operators like Cullis, Simpson, and Judd aimed to deflect allegations of medical negligence or malpractice.

In their efforts to demarcate the boundaries between divine healing and clinical medicine, however, founders of faith homes were often forced to contend with the internal fissures that beleaguered the faith cure movement as a whole. Disagreements over what constituted "sickness" and which remedies ought to be employed exacerbated tensions that would eventually fracture the fragile cohesion that leaders like Cullis and Gordon strove to develop and maintain during the formative years of the divine healing movement. Rather than uniting the diverse factions that took part in faith cure, the establishment of common institutions actually aggravated frictions among participants while inciting increasingly vehement hostility from outsiders.

If the proliferation of faith homes provoked indignation among doctors who feared that ministers of divine healing were encroaching on their turf in an irresponsible manner, the appeal of these establishments also inflamed the passions of clergymen who worried about the effects of faith cure on traditional theological and social structures. Opponents of divine healing charged that faith homes and the devotional ethic taught within their walls threatened not only the health of individuals but also the tenor of family life and the integrity of Christianity. By working against the notion that resigned endurance represented the appropriate Christian response to pain and providing invalids like Barker with the time and space to put this teaching into practice, detractors such as James Buckley alleged, faith home proprietors undermined associations between true womanhood, domesticity, and submissiveness that were fundamental to the proper ordering of individual, family, church, and civilization.

Founding Faith Homes

By the time of the International Conference on Divine Healing and True Holiness in 1885, A. B. Simpson reported that approximately thirty faith homes were operating in the United States, including Cullis's Faith Cure Home in Boston, Massachusetts; Mossman's Faith Cottage at Ocean Grove, New Jersey; the Kemuel Home in Philadelphia run by Mrs. Sarah G. Beck; Carrie Judd's Faith-Rest Cottage in Buffalo, New York; the House of Healing, in Brooklyn, New York, overseen by J. C. Young, who formerly served as superintendent of Cullis's work; Simpson's own Berachah Home in Manhattan; and several others in Massachusetts, Ohio, and Kentucky. Elizabeth Baxter identified at least five houses of healing in England in addition to Bethshan, the London institution that she had established along with the Boardmans and Charlotte Murray. In Switzerland, the "Home for Faith Healing" that Trudel had founded in the mid-1850s in Mannedorf continued to operate under the auspices of her successor, Samuel Zeller. Over the years, Mannedorf had produced several offspring, including one home at Hauptweil, run by Pastor Otto Stockmayer and Madame Malherbe, and another at Chardonnes. Representatives from Germany named at least three homes: one near Bonn, another at Cannstadt, and a third at Bad Boll, which Pastor Christoph, another pioneering practitioner of divine healing, had established many years earlier. Finally, missionaries from India reported that there was a movement underway among their colleagues "to have a Home for Divine Healing opened in the city of Bombay."[5]

Although these establishments varied in size and, to a certain extent, in character, leaders of the divine healing movement emphasized their common purpose. "Each of these Homes is a precious centre of Christian influence," Baxter remarked after visiting several of the American homes during her trip to the United States in the latter half of 1885. "From each of them everyone goes out blest in soul, if not in body. From each of them many sick ones go out healed." As Baxter's comments suggest, faith homes were intended to serve as sacred spaces where sufferers could separate themselves from their daily duties and diversions as well as from the prevailing presumptions of the surrounding culture—both of which presented barriers to the mental and spiritual transformation that necessarily accompanied bodily healing. Free from these influences, visitors entered into a liminal space in which they were encouraged to encounter God. "The whole aim of the work at Bethshan is that souls and bodies should be brought into contact with Jesus Himself," declared the advertisement that the founders of that institution circulated soon after the home was established in May of 1882. Bethshan's mission, they explained, was "to afford facilities for those who have been led of God to seek the Lord as their Healer in spirit, soul and body, that they, remaining for a short time, may attend the Meetings of Holiness and Healing, and withdrawn from their ordinary surroundings, may have time and opportunity for communion with God."[6]

A. B. Simpson described Berachah Home, which was first opened on May 1, 1883, in his own home at 331 West 34th Street in Manhattan and later moved to various locations in the city as it grew and expanded, in a similar manner:

> The advantages of such a home are very great. It affords to persons seeking a deeper spiritual life or divine healing, a season of entire rest, seclusion from the distractions of their ordinary life, and often from uncongenial surroundings. It brings them into an atmosphere full of fresh and simple faith and love. It brings them face to face with persons who are constantly receiving the touch of God in their souls and bodies, and whose living testimony is full of inspiration and encouragement. It brings them directly under careful and personal religious teaching from God's word. And, above all,

it is the home of God, where He has chosen to dwell, and manifest Himself to His children, and where He will meet in some way . . each of His waiting children.

Berachah Home, or "the Valley of Blessing," was a place where "the invalid and the seeker after Divine healing" could remove themselves from their everyday circumstances and the demands of their regular routines, both of which might conspire to keep them from trusting the Great Physician, and enter into an environment that offered encouragement on multiple levels: through personal contact with believers who could testify to an experience of healing, through biblical teaching, and, most importantly, through direct encounters with God.[7]

In most cases, the initial impetus for the founding of faith homes came from the pressures that leaders like Cullis, Judd, Baxter, and Boardman experienced to accommodate those who traveled from a distance in order to meet these increasingly well-known teachers in person. Having heard of Cullis's ministry and read the accounts of healing he published in *Faith Cures*, for example, Eliza J. Robertson of Louisville, Kentucky, "resolved . . . to visit Dr. Cullis" in the summer of 1879. "Though very feeble physically," Robertson recalled, "I started on the long journey alone, trusting all the way for strength." Upon her arrival in Boston, Robertson, like the many others who came to consult Cullis or attend his Thursday morning meeting for "those who desired to seek health by prayer," found lodging in a local boardinghouse not far from the Beacon Hill Church. As word of Cullis's meetings and ministry spread, pilgrims like Robertson flocked to Boston in growing numbers. Coping with the influx of invalids became a pressing problem, especially since many of the visitors had difficulty obtaining appropriate accommodations. "People . . . come to the city seeking board (while they receive the prayer of faith), but can find none in the city unless among adverse surroundings, discouraging to faith," Cullis observed. In order to remedy the lack of suitable lodgings, Cullis opened a "Faith-cure House" on May 23, 1882, on his property at Grove Hall, a large estate that also housed his Home for Indigent Consumptives, a Cancer Home, an orphanage, and a church. The purpose of the Faith-cure House, his biographer W. H. Daniels later wrote, was to provide a place where the many who "came from a distance" but "were not in a state of mind to understand and grasp at once the privilege of health as well as grace in Jesus Christ . . . could rest and study and pray for a season."[8]

Across the Atlantic, Elizabeth Baxter and William and Mary Boardman faced a similar dilemma as the weekly meetings held in the Boardman's London home began to attract an increasing number of sufferers seeking healing. "As the Tuesday meetings in Rochester Square grew in numbers and interest," Baxter recalled,

The Berachah Home moved to this location on 44th Street in New York City in 1889.
Courtesy of the Christian and Missionary Alliance National Archives.

"persons from a distance came and took lodgings in the neighborhood. These were often invalids, and again and again the thought occurred to me: 'Why not open a house for their accommodation?'" After discussing her idea with the Boardmans, Baxter and Charlotte Murray opened Bethshan, Hebrew for "House of Rest," in May of 1882. The house "was no sooner opened than filled." The demand was so great, in fact, that "available rooms in other houses near enough to give their occupants the daily benefits of 'Bethshan' were taken," and individuals associated with the work frequently offered to board invalids in their own homes. Eventually Charlotte Murray, who served as the "house-mother" at Bethshan, was able to purchase a larger dwelling at 10 Drayton Park, which could accommodate a greater number of guests.[9]

Offering hospitality within their own homes to sick persons who sought their prayers and counsel was a common practice among leading advocates of divine healing. Soon after her marvelous cure, Carrie Judd and her mother set aside two rooms in their house for the accommodation of invalids who desired to attend Judd's weekly faith meeting and to remain overnight or for a longer time. As news of Judd's healing reached a broader audience, more and more people sent letters

Faith Rest Cottage, Buffalo, New York. Courtesy of the Flower Pentecostal Heritage Center.

requesting permission to visit her in Buffalo. "I remember that people wrote in this way, 'May I come to you for a little time, and see this life of faith lived out?'" Judd later recorded. When housing these travelers in her own residence became too burdensome, Judd founded Faith-Rest Cottage "as a place of temporary refreshing for those who wish to know more of this life of faith." Opened in April of 1882, the original Faith-Rest was a two-story frame cottage in Judd's immediate neighborhood that supplied lodgings for visiting invalids. This home provided weary pilgrims with a place to lay their heads as well as the opportunity to attend the faith-meeting and "meet others of 'like precious faith' for their mutual strengthening in the Lord." Coming into contact with fellow believers and hearing others testify to the healing power of the Great Physician, Judd believed, would help to foster faith that could be difficult to cultivate in everyday environments. At Faith-Rest Cottage, sick persons could answer God's call to "Come ye apart . . . and rest a while," Judd wrote. In this "place of hallowed stillness," invalids could "sit silently at His feet and learn more effectually the lesson of living trust."[10]

Guests at Judd's faith home confirmed that separating themselves from their daily routines and from the company of individuals who greeted their faith in divine healing with skepticism was an essential step in the curative process. Although he tried to trust God for healing from his home in Reed City, Michigan, Alford H. McClellan "lost the blessing" because he was not, as he put it, "rooted and grounded in the faith." It was only when he traveled to Buffalo and spent "several peaceful days at 'Faith-Rest Cottage,' learning more and more of God's wonderful dealings with his believing children," that McClellan was able to claim the blessing of healing for himself. Writing from his home several months later, McClellan encouraged others to seek out the supportive settings and congenial companionship that houses of healing offered. "I think invalids who can should go among God's peculiar children, as it is a step out and away from old notions, beliefs, and *friends,* who ignorantly make it so hard for a trembling invalid to call in the 'Great Physician,'" McClellan counseled. Mrs. S. J. Warner of Friend, Nebraska, also reported that the "sweet fellowship" she enjoyed during her visit to Judd's Faith-Rest Cottage offered a welcome relief from the great "temptations" she faced elsewhere. Only this interlude, Warner suggested, enabled her to overcome the "mental depression" and physical ailments that had plagued her for twelve years.[11]

Creating Sacred Space

For individuals such as McClellan and Warner, physically entering into an encouraging environment where they encountered like-minded believers proved indispensable for experiencing epistemological, physical, and spiritual transformation. Although leaders like Judd insisted that healing was "in no wise restricted to time or place," the emphasis they placed on the salutary benefits that faith homes offered to visitors helped foster a tendency to invest these venues with a special ritual significance. Journeying to a faith home, for many individuals, was akin to making a pilgrimage to a sacred shrine. Several years after Faith-Rest Cottage opened, Judd herself affirmed that "this little Home has been a sort of 'Mecca' for weary feet."[12]

In their testimonies of healing, many former sufferers reported that traveling to healing homes seemed to have brought them into closer proximity to the spiritual realm. Upon his arrival at Mannedorf, for example, Pastor Schrenk felt compelled to remove his footwear. "My first impression, as soon as I got there, weary and sick, was this," he later recalled, "'Put off thy shoes from thy feet; this is holy ground.'" Crossing the threshold of Simpson's Berachah Home in New York evoked a similar experience for Mrs. C. E. Chancey. "A sacred awe came over me as I entered the house," she wrote. Simpson himself described Berachah as "'none other than the house of God' and often 'the gate of heaven.'"[13]

When they passed through the doorways of these houses of healing, sufferers left behind a world of empirical explanation hostile to the doctrines of divine healing and entered a realm where faith reigned. Founders of faith homes intentionally cultivated the "hallowed associations" that many attributed to these venues. The descriptive names that leaders gave their establishments drew attention to the aims of these institutions as well as to their sacred character. Designations such as Bethshan (House of Rest), Berachah (Valley of Blessing), and Kemuel Home (the Risen and Living One), drawn directly from the Bible, lent these locations scriptural legitimacy and also served as heuristic devices that helped to shape a visitor's anticipations of what she would experience within. At Mary E. Morehead's Bethany Home, for example, a person might expect to meet the Jesus of the Bible who raised Lazarus from the dead in this small town outside of Bethlehem. When Dora Dudley Griffin opened her faith home in Grand Rapids, Michigan, in the winter of 1887, she named it "Beulah"—meaning "joined" or "married"—in the hope that the leaders of the home and all who visited there "might be indeed joined to the Lord." Mary Mossman gave scriptural names to each of the rooms in her Faith Cottage at Ocean Grove, New Jersey, a practice that helped to direct guests' attention to the home's biblical foundations.[14]

Rituals of consecration also served to mark off faith homes as sacred spaces. Whenever they established a new house of healing, the founders conducted special ceremonies "for the purpose of uniting in dedicating it to the holy and solemn purpose for which it had been opened . . . and invoking the Divine blessing to rest upon the work." On the day she took possession of Faith-Rest Cottage, for example, Carrie Judd held "informal consecration and thanksgiving services" before receiving the first guests. The ceremony consisted of a scripture reading, followed by a season of "prayer and singing" during which the building was "consecrated to the Lord and rich blessings were asked for all that might enter its doors." After the dedication service, guests were invited to participate in a "cheerful evening meal" and then to attend the Thursday evening meeting for prayer and anointing of "those who were looking to Christ as the healer of disease of the body." Often these consecration rituals were more formal and public in nature, including tours of the new facilities, sermons from well-known guests of honor, and even the commissioning of hymns specially composed for the occasion. In all cases, these events were designed to sanctify the places where invalids would gather to seek divine healing through prayer, laying on of hands, and anointing. Setting apart spaces for this purpose, founders of faith homes believed, helped to model the personal separation from their former pursuits that individuals desiring healing would be called upon to make when they received anointing. As Carrie Judd put it, "The wholehearted consecration of all that we have and are must necessarily precede healing." Through rituals of dedication such as consecration services and anointing, both buildings and bodies became the property and dwelling places of God.[15]

Transforming bricks and mortar into domiciles of the divine also involved decoration. Drawing on longstanding cultural associations between the sacred and the domestic, faith home founders took pains to furnish their establishments, "not in any style of severe solemnity, but with reference to a home-like beauty and graceful simplicity," believing that a comfortable and hospitable ambiance set the proper tone for welcoming guests and encouraging them to encounter Jesus "in the midst." When Judd rented the building that would become Faith-Rest Cottage, for example, she noted that the house was "fresh and attractive with new paint, beautiful wall-paper, decorations, etc., all of which we feel to be of the Lord, that this Faith-Rest for His weary children may be 'pleasant to the sight' (Gen ii: 9) as well as restful in its spiritual atmosphere." Guests at Judd's cottage often commented on the "airy and commodious" rooms, the "neatly kept" furnishings and the "quiet and orderly manner" that characterized the dwelling. "All inmates," Mrs. L. A. Fouke remarked, "are made to feel perfectly at home." When Elizabeth Baxter paid a visit to Buffalo in the fall of 1885, she dubbed the Faith-Rest "a very bird's nest," noting its "small and cosy" rooms. "There is no stiffness or formality about this Home," she wrote, "it is just like its name—a faith rest."[16]

While not all houses of healing were as intimate and informal as Judd's Faith-Rest, even the larger institutions, like Simpson's Berachah Home, which eventually provided accommodation for over one hundred guests, aimed to maintain a home-like atmosphere. By highlighting the decidedly domestic, even familial character of these venues, founders indicated that their establishments were God's abode to which guests were invited for visits, not clinical settings to which patients were admitted for treatment. At Bethshan, for example, residents called William Boardman, one of the institution's principal leaders, "father-kin" and referred to the ever-changing community of workers and guests as an adoptive family.[17]

Staffing practices at faith homes reinforced the notion that these spaces served as spiritual retreats rather than as medical facilities. Proprietors of faith homes like Simpson and Cullis appointed "house-mothers" who welcomed guests and oversaw the daily operations of their facilities. Capitalizing on the cults of domesticity and true womanhood that upheld women as moral exemplars responsible for fostering faith and virtue within the context of the home, founders encouraged these "matrons" to participate in the spiritual nurture of the guests. Ellen Griffin and S. A. Lindenberger, the joint house-mothers at Berachah, were also called deaconesses, as were the various women who supervised Cullis's Faith-cure House. In addition to managing the homes, these women ministered to the spiritual needs of the invalids who visited with what Simpson called "a mother heart."[18]

Most house-mothers had themselves experienced healing through faith in the

Great Physician, and passing on their confidence to ailing guests was part of their job description. When Carrie Judd appointed Helen Dawlly, who had suffered for years as a "helpless invalid" before being "wonderfully healed in answer to believing prayer" as the first matron of Faith-Rest Cottage, she rejoiced that she such would have such "a staunch fellow-helper" to whom she could "confide the domestic arrangements of the Faith-Rest household" while at the same time feeling assured that the depth of Dawlly's "Christian experience and the sunshine of her strong faith and ready sympathy" would "strengthen and cheer the hearts of all around her." Ruth Whitney, who served as the house-mother of Cullis's faith home in 1885, also took the position after having been "healed by the Lord." She and the other deaconesses who worked at the Faith-cure House cultivated a "lovely, joyous, sunshiny" mood. As one visitor to Cullis's establishment observed, "It must not be supposed that this little circle of trusting souls (the workers in these faith homes) are living in the stilted, cloistered atmosphere so often associated with 'the religious life.' On the contrary, there is the heartiest good cheer among them." This liveliness, the author implied, was a deliberate strategy for countering the suffering that guests in the home were experiencing. "The contagion of joy and peace is stronger than the contagion of sickness and pain," he wrote, "so the former and not the latter dominates the atmosphere of the place."[19]

Generous rate policies were another means through which faith home managers and matrons sought to nurture a familial and spiritual tone within their establishments. Following a model established first by George Mueller, an Englishman who founded an orphanage in 1835 without any firm financial resources in place, divine healing proponents who opened faith homes did so according to what they called the "faith principle of financing." Rather than seeking endowments or investors, those who adopted this approach trusted God to provide for all of their monetary and material needs on a daily basis. Critical of what they considered "worldly methods devised by the church to gain money," including "fairs, festivals, donkey shows, grab bags, broom drills, amateur theatricals, etc," faith home proprietors claimed that prayer was the only fund-raising technique they employed. Judd's Faith-Rest Cottage, for example, "was commenced in utter dependence upon the Lord for its means of support." Extending this financing philosophy to the daily operations of their facilities, most faith home managers and matrons refused to establish set rates for room and board. In the majority of cases, guests were invited to stay at houses of healing free of charge, or for a nominal fee of a dollar a day at most. Rather than requiring payment, faith home operators suggested that visitors make voluntary contributions, or "free-will offerings" to the cause as they were able and as led by the Lord.[20]

While some detractors criticized this policy as a not-so-subtle form of extortion, proprietors insisted that this flexible approach preserved important freedoms. Judd explained that these munificent terms enabled her to maintain a welcoming and open environment for all guests, regardless of their ability to pay. "We have not at any time felt at liberty to name a sum for board," she wrote, "as we desired that all who came, poor as well as rich, should feel that they were partaking of the Lord's own hospitality, given 'without grudging.'" Visitors at Judd's Faith-Rest Cottage affirmed that this generosity put them at ease and made them feel at home. As one guest put it, "No one has ever been asked for means to support [Faith-Rest Cottage], but its guests have been welcomed most cordially, to its quiet and peaceful atmosphere, unfettered by the thought of remuneration."[21]

In addition to nurturing a hospitable ambiance, inviting guests to stay at no cost also helped to differentiate divine healing from other forms of treatment in which the sick were asked to render fees for service. Leaders of the divine healing movement insisted that the Great Physician offered healing free of charge. Unlike medical doctors, who often bled their patients dry both physically and financially, God promised healing to all who asked without demanding monetary compensation of any kind. This freedom from financial obligation made divine healing extremely appealing to invalids who had spent many years and vast sums of money seeking relief from their ailments. In their narratives of healing, many individuals compared themselves to the woman mentioned in Mark 5:26, who "had suffered much under many physicians, and had spent all that she had, and was no better but rather grew worse." For those who had depleted their savings in search of health, faith homes offered a kind of last resort where the "balm of Gilead" was available to all who asked at no expense.[22]

Maintaining a financing scheme based on free-will offerings rather than fixed fees also underscored the distinctions between divine healing, on the one hand, and Spiritualism and Christian Science on the other. Whereas clairvoyant physicians and Christian Science practitioners routinely and unapologetically charged for treatments, proponents of divine healing always asserted that receiving remuneration for serving as instruments or channels of God's curative power and hospitality was entirely inappropriate. Praying for the sick was a privilege, leaders like Cullis argued, not a means for making a living. "I never charged a person a dollar in my life for praying for them," Cullis maintained. If anything, Cullis's participation in the divine healing movement had been costly, not lucrative: "I have lost many thousands of dollars by it; never made a cent by it," he observed. Indeed, faith homes were far from profitable ventures. Voluntary contributions rarely covered operating expenses, and many establishments faced ongoing struggles to stay solvent during periods of prolonged financial hardship. Despite these fiscal difficulties, proponents of divine healing defended the "faith principle" of financing as a central feature of their work. Depending on God for their daily bread forced those who managed houses of healing to remain humble and protected them from the temptations of pride and avarice that, in their view, plagued so many of their contemporaries in competing healing movements. Furthermore, they surmised, since God was the source of any and all pecuniary aid, faith homes could be counted as sacred spaces, upheld and maintained by divine mandate and free from the taint of worldliness.[23]

Concerns for cultivating a spiritual atmosphere of freedom in which guests were at liberty to seek a cure without counting the cost and to pursue healing unfettered by the pressures and constraints of their customary obligations also helped to shape the daily rituals and rhythms that characterized the faith home environment. Unlike the rigorous dietary, hygienic, and exercise regimens to which inmates at many health reform institutes were expected to adhere, routines at most healing homes remained fairly flexible. After spending time at Faith-Rest Cottage following a long sojourn at a Pennsylvania hydropathic establishment, Libbie Osborn contrasted the liberty she experienced at Judd's faith home to the highly structured schedule she had encountered at "the Cure." "They were blessed, happy days that followed in your Home, days of growth in grace and in knowledge of God and His ways," Osborn wrote. "It was bliss to go and come, to ride and walk, to read and write, *all I liked.*" Meals at Judd's house of healing also differed from those served at most health reform institutions. Noting that many people who came "to the Home after having been at Sanitariums . . . would bring their little bags of Graham flour . . . or sometimes little gems baked without leaven," Judd encouraged visitors to break their strict diets and "to trust the Lord and eat what we have on the table," including the dessert.[24]

Other than mealtimes, weekly prayer meetings and Bible readings were the only regularly scheduled activities at Faith-Rest Cottage. On Tuesday afternoons, guests were invited to spend an hour examining scripture, and on Thursday evenings, visitors could join with a group of regular attendees to pray for "physical as well as spiritual healing from Christ, the 'Great Physician.'" Judd also encouraged readers of her journal as well as sick persons who wrote to her requesting prayer to participate in the Thursday faith meeting by "remembering the hour with us"—thus incorporating her guests within a wider sacred community that extended beyond the walls of her house to include "believers who are separated from us by distance." By taking part in these gatherings, guests learned that they belonged to a broader fellowship of Christians who supported them in their efforts to claim healing and act faith and who would continue to join with them "around one common Mercy seat" every Thursday evening, long after they left the nurturing environment of Faith-Rest Cottage.[25]

Some houses of healing held more frequent gatherings for prayer and study, infusing every day with activities that helped highlight the homes' spiritual purpose. In addition to conducting "regular meetings" on Wednesdays and Sundays, Bethshan's leaders also led daily services of morning and evening worship. At Simpson's Berachah Home, "religious services" were held every morning at 8:30, and every afternoon at 3:00, except on Friday, Saturday, and Sunday, when guests were invited to participate in larger gatherings at Simpson's church. In addition, Simpson held a reception for "religious conversation" on Mondays and Thursdays from 12 to 2. Sarah Beck and her associates organized meetings for "prayer and scriptural instruction" at Kemuel Home five afternoons a week and encouraged visitors to attend the nightly revival services at the nearby Gospel Tabernacle. On Wednesday afternoons, the Gospel Tabernacle held a meeting for "the deepening of the spiritual life and divine healing" that was followed by an anointing service back at the faith home. At gatherings like these, guests had the opportunity to hear testimonies from "consecrated Christian workers who have experienced for themselves God's energizing, healing power in soul and body" as well as to receive prayer, laying on of hands, and anointing for their own afflictions. For many sufferers, participating in these meetings proved essential for experiencing healing. Within a few hours of entering Judd's Faith-Rest Cottage, the Rev. J. A. Ivison overcame his initial skepticism that he and his wife would derive any benefit by their visit. "My judgment became fully convinced of the glorious possibility of obtaining any blessing that we needed, spiritual or physical in answer to the prayer of faith," he wrote. It was not until Ivison attended the weekly meeting for "the sick and heavy laden," however, that he experienced the blessing he sought. "While enjoying the prayer service in 'Faith Sanctuary' on Thursday evening," Ivison recalled, "the Lord honored the faith of the dear friends present, the faith of others at a distance who were remembering the service in prayer and my own faith, so as to fill my soul gloriously with His Spirit, and to heal my body of heart disease and rheumatism of nine years' standing." For Ivison, as for H. M. Barker, gathering in the presence of believers who could witness to the reality of divine healing within the sacred space of a faith home prompted experiences of God's power that made claiming healing and acting faith possible.[26]

Sacred Sites or Clinical Settings?

By cultivating the sacred associations that marked faith homes as holy spaces, incorporated seekers within spiritual communities, and brought sufferers into the presence of the Great Physician, leaders of the faith cure movement also endeavored to differentiate houses of healing from hospitals. In a period of rising medical regulation, establishing this distinction was crucial to the survival of institutions like Faith-Rest Cottage, Berachah, and Bethshan. Houses of healing occupied a rather precarious position within the context of late-nineteenth-century therapeutic practice, as physicians increasingly asserted their authority as professional healers and the site of medical care shifted from the domestic sphere to the institutional realm. From the movement's earliest days, critics of divine healing had raised grievances against faith homes, charging that these establishments failed to conform to laws governing medical institutions. In 1861 a doctor in Mannedorf entered a complaint against Dorothea Trudel and sought to shut down her home. Although the charges were dismissed on the grounds that Trudel's "institution was carried on quite differently to any other, employing no medicine, and having as a primary object benefit to the souls of the patients," the threat of similar lawsuits continued to plague the divine healing movement.[27]

In order to rebuff such attacks, Trudel and other founders of faith homes insisted that houses of healing were never designed to serve as medical facilities. As Baxter and the Boardmans put it, "Bethshan is no hospital, but rather a nursery for faith." Unlike hospitals, faith homes focused attention on spiritual as well as physical healing. Care for the soul was an indispensable aspect of bodily health. Furthermore, the treatments recommended for guests at houses of healing did not involve medicinal therapies of any sort. With the exception of Charles Cullis, those who established and ran faith homes were not doctors or nurses. They did not dispense drugs or perform surgeries. Although Simpson's Berachah Home did employ Dr. Amelia Barnett of the Women's College of Medicine in New York City as a "consultant" for many years, Barnett herself was a believer in divine healing and encouraged the guests at Berachah, as well as patients in her own private practice, to put their faith in the means prescribed by the Great Physician: prayer, laying on of hands, and anointing.[28]

Ironically, by emphasizing their reliance on spiritual remedies rather than chemical therapeutics or other forms of medical treatment, faith-home operators and proponents of divine healing in general incited the ire of another class of physicians and theologians who interpreted their exclusive use of scriptural means as a dangerous form of fanaticism. Commenting on the 1885 International Conference held at Bethshan, physician Walter Moxon accused divine healing advocates of tres-passing on territory that belonged to the medical profession. "Sickness is too seri-ous to be trifled with by fanatics," he wrote in London's *Contemporary Review*. By meddling in matters best left to physicians, Moxon complained, the proprietors of Bethshan discouraged people from seeking proper medical care. "In this direction the faith-healing movement approaches criminality. It is persuasion to suicide."[29]

Theologian Luther T. Townsend made similar allegations in a series of sermons and addresses he published as a pamphlet in 1885. Lumping together the "ignorant quack, the pretentious mind-curer," and "the fanatical prayer-healer," Townsend as-serted that such practitioners ought to be charged with malpractice and subject to criminal prosecution for treating cases that required surgery or other medical re-mediation. Noting the increasing legal statutes that policed the regular practice of medicine, Townsend asked, "Why should there not be protection by law against the practice of medicine by those who know comparatively nothing of the science and art of medicine. At least, there should be a vigorous prosecution of religious as well as all other fanatics, pretenders, and quacks if criminally careless, or if neglectful of proper remedial agencies."[30]

Townsend was especially critical of parents who refused to seek medical treat-ment for their children because they believed in the power of prayer alone to heal. To entrust a sick or injured child "to some faith-healer whose practice is based upon the theory that all visible agencies, including surgical skill and medicines, should give place entirely to invisible and supernatural agencies," Townsend contended, contradicted "common-sense." Instead, he insisted that parents ought to employ all means available, including "surgical instruments and the prescription of drugs;" "mental influences of the right sort" that would help to cheer, divert, and entertain a child's mind; and "the therapeutics of religion" such as united prayer for heal-ing, to aid their ailing children. Only by taking such a multifaceted approach could parents avoid regret, reproach, and even legal action should a child fail to recover. If a child died as the result of a parent's failure to employ medical aid, Townsend argued, the parent "would be guilty of criminal carelessness and neglect."[31]

Indeed, the issue of parental negligence prompted some of the earliest legal challenges to divine healing in the United States. In June of 1884, the *New York Times* reported that the Society for the Prevention of Cruelty to Children (SPCC) had issued a summons against the Reverend Clement T. Blanchett, an Episcopal minister on furlough from his missionary post in Tokyo, for failing to seek proper medical attention for his six-year-old daughter Annie. Having learned of divine healing from Arthur Sloan, a fellow Episcopal clergyman who had resigned his par-ish ministry in order to establish and operate a faith home in Stratford, Connecticut, Blanchett and his wife "refused to summon a physician" after their daughter fractured her limb while playing with a companion. When the neighbors heard about the accident and the course the parents were pursuing, they tried to persuade the Blanchetts to reconsider, but they refused. Eventually, the local assistant bishop and a representative from the SPCC got wind of the situation and urged Blanchett to call a surgeon for his daughter or suffer disciplinary and legal consequences. Blanchett relented, and the charges that the SPCC had filed against him were dropped. In his treatise, Townsend mentioned a similar case of an Episcopal minister who was arrested in the summer of 1884 "for refusing to call a surgeon to set the arm of his boy, the clergyman believing that faith and prayer alone were sufficient."[32]

Cases such as these proved troublesome for leaders of the divine healing movement like Cullis, who were striving to carve out a territory for themselves and their institutions that did not infringe on the province or privileges of the medical profession but also avoided accusations of fanaticism. After reading Townsend's work when it was first published in the Boston Methodist magazine *Zion's Herald*, Cullis protested that Townsend had misrepresented his position with regard to the treatment of broken limbs. "In no place in God's word is there a promise that we may pray over a broken bone and anoint the sufferer with oil; only the sick," Cullis stated. "A broken bone is not sickness and should be put into the hands of a surgeon." Dr. Daniel Steele, an outspoken Holiness advocate and long-time supporter of Cullis who worked alongside Townsend as a professor of theology at Boston University, also objected to Townsend's characterization of Cullis and his work. "Dr. Cullis has repeatedly and publicly . . . disclaimed all attempts by the prayer of faith to secure from God the restoration of an amputated hand or the setting of a broken limb. It is his theory that these are not included in the directions given in James v. 14, 15: 'The prayer of faith shall heal the sick.' Dr. Cullis does not include broken bones under the term 'sickness' or 'disease.'"[33]

By limiting the definition of "disease" to certain kinds of conditions, Cullis, Steele, and others attempted to navigate the divine healing movement through the treacherous terrain that lay between fanaticism and skepticism. Careful to affirm that the God was able to knit broken bones together, Cullis also insisted that humans had no right to call on God to act in this way without seeking appropriate medical assistance. "I do not believe in any way you can put it that we are to lose our common-sense in this matter," he wrote.[34]

Unfortunately for Cullis and his like-minded colleagues, some individuals failed to discriminate between injuries and illnesses, assuming instead that all ailments ought to be entrusted solely to the care of the Great Physician without recourse to human aid. Critics such as Townsend rightly observed the inconsistencies among participants in the divine healing movement, noting that "'faith-workers' are not agreed as to what are, in case of sickness, the real and possible triumphs of faith and prayer." Even if Cullis held that amputations and broken bones could not be defined as "sickness" and therefore fell outside the scope of God's promises to heal disease, Townsend pointed out that others, like the Episcopal minister who failed to call in a physician to treat his son's broken limb and even prominent leaders like William Boardman, did not exclude these complaints "from the power of faith and prayer." Indeed, Townsend noted, Boardman had included "a remarkable instance of the healing of a fractured arm" in his seminal work, *The Great Physician* (1881), a text that Cullis himself had published through the Willard Tract Repository. Cullis later commented that this case, which involved a young child, was the only one "which I know, personally, of a broken bone being healed" and that it did not represent a norm to which others ought to conform. Despite these qualifications, the inclusion of the story within Boardman's definitional text did inspire some individuals, like the Blanchetts, to assume that fractures and other accidental injuries ought to be treated by God alone.[35]

Disagreements and debates about the boundaries of God's promises of healing and the appropriate method of treatment for various complaints continued to plague the faith cure movement and to stymie the efforts of some leaders to chart what they saw as a moderate course between extremes. In addition to disputing what conditions counted as "sickness," participants in divine healing also failed to reach consensus about the use of remedies for those who suffered from ailments that clearly fell within the category of "disease." Working to offset the claims of detractors who charged them with negligence and malpractice for persuading their followers to forego necessary medical treatments, some members of the divine healing movement maintained that they did not encourage sick persons to give up their remedies or shun their physicians. Cullis, a homeopathic doctor himself, insisted that he "did not ask people to dispense with medicine." In the preface to the first volume of *Faith Cures*, published in 1879, Cullis insisted that "in summing up a report of these cases, I do not in any wise wish to detract from the valuable services of the medical profession, of which I am a member."[36]

To critics who complained that he prevented petitioners from pursuing essential medical interventions, Cullis replied that most who came to him seeking healing from the Great Physician had already consulted countless doctors and experimented with remedies of all sorts to no avail. "The people who are healed are, in ninety cases out of a hundred, the desperate cases that nothing can be done with by the medical men," he reported. Indeed, in the testimonies of healing that Cullis compiled, many explained that their physicians had deemed them "incurable" and had given up their cases. For many sufferers, seeking divine healing at a faith home was a last resort. Only after finding all other options wanting did they turn to God for help. As one observer of Dorothea Trudel's ministry put it, "Most of her patients are such as have already spent all their substance on physicians, and are nothing better, but have rather grown worse; and they often come to her much too late. It is no wonder if, after waiting for years in vain for a cure, the patient at last tries any plan by which he may even hope to be healed." Even in these cases, however, Trudel did not attempt to discourage her guests from taking drugs or following the instructions of their doctors. "If she never used medicinal means herself," her biographer reported, "neither did she forbid anyone to use the prescriptions of a licensed physician." Trudel even allowed guests at Mannedorf to "be attended by their own physicians if they wish."[37]

Defenders of divine healing insisted that Trudel's attitude toward physicians and her practice of neither prescribing nor prohibiting remedies set the standard for the movement. In a response to James Buckley's disparaging critique of faith healing in the *Century Magazine,* R. K. Carter explained that while "faith-healers" always employed "the scriptural means" of laying on of hands, anointing, and prayer, they also believed in "occasional leadings of the Spirit to employ other means." Furthermore, Carter claimed, "No one is advised by any prominent leader or teacher to lay aside all medicines, unless he can do so with perfect spontaneity. Forced abstinence is will-power, not faith."[38]

Although intended to deflect the condemnations of critics who called proponents of divine healing irresponsible fanatics, Carter's comments actually reveal the ambivalence that characterized his stance toward medical therapeutics. While he did not despise doctors or drugs, he did not hold physicians or their remedies in high regard. In Carter's view, the biblical means sanctioned by God occupied a much more honored position than any prescription that a doctor could order. Moreover, while he admitted that "other means" besides the laying on of hands, anointing, and prayer might sometimes be called for, he implied that their efficacy rarely equaled that of the divinely appointed methods laid down in scripture.

Carter was not the only one who established a hierarchy that elevated "scriptural means" over medical remedies. Most prominent leaders of the divine healing movement, in fact, shared Carter's assessment of the relative value and appropriate uses of these two distinct approaches to healing. In his reply to a denunciatory article by the Reverend A. F. Schauffler that condemned leaders of the divine healing movement for teaching that the "use of any means other than that of anointing or prayer is sinful," A. B. Simpson asserted that he and his colleagues understood medicine to be "a natural means of healing"—useful to a certain extent, but not the best or most efficacious approach to curing disease. While tonics and palliatives prescribed by physicians might be somewhat helpful, these were not the ideal. "Jesus," Simpson insisted, "has provided a better way. The one may be 'a good gift,' but the other is 'a perfect gift.'"[39]

Critics of Simpson's position countered that "natural means" were also divinely appointed and should not be devalued in comparison with prayer and anointing. "It is God Himself who has provided all the remedies we now use for the body," wrote British physician Alfred T. Schofield in his work *A Study of Faith-Healing*. Quoting from Aurelius Gliddon's *Faith Cures; Their History and Mystery,* Schofield affirmed that "the Divine Healer is constantly healing through the operation of the forces which He has impressed upon Nature, and in complete harmony with what is know as natural law. Just as He answers our prayers for daily bread through natural channels, so He answers our prayers for bodily healing through the same media." In an address entitled "The Prayer and the Prayer Cure," Presbyterian theologian Archibald Alexander Hodge, who succeeded his father Charles as president of Princeton Seminary in 1878, chastised proponents of divine healing for "praying while refusing to use properly God's appointed means."[40]

Although they agreed that God had provided certain "natural remedies" and admitted that these means "may go a certain length and possess a limited value in relieving and healing the body," leaders like Simpson maintained that medicines were "limited and extremely uncertain." Furthermore, Simpson argued, the vast assortment of competing medical therapies available in this period complicated the question of which treatments God had ordained. How was an individual to determine "just what were the means that God had prescribed, whether the allopathic, or the homeopathic, or the eclectic, or the electric, or a host besides," Simpson wondered, when these various approaches "differ among themselves in the most radical manner, and even declared each other's principles to be essentially false."[41]

Rather than trying to sort through this baffling array of options, Simpson suggested that sufferers turn to the Bible, where God had clearly described the appointed means for healing. "How much more simple is the real prescription of Scripture," Simpson affirmed. Individuals who chose this path could also be assured that they availed themselves of the best possible course of treatment—foregoing the merely "natural" for the "supernatural," opting for "the best God can do" rather than "the best man can do." "He would be a fool," Simpson insisted, "who should take the less instead of the greater." As Carrie Judd put it, "If I rely on medicine, I limit myself to the natural efficacy of medicine; if, however I have faith to cast aside these remedies . . . and obey the instructions in James v: 14, 15, I do not oppose natural laws, but get beyond and above them into the infinite resources of an Almighty Creator."[42]

Eschewing medicine in favor of biblical means, Judd implied, was not only the more certain path to health but also a way for individuals to act out their faith. "If I really have faith to accept the promises of healing in James v: 14, 15," Judd wrote, "I shall consider medicine superfluous (to say the least), and my giving it up will be an evidence of my faith." Doctors and drugs were good and acceptable for those who could not trust in the Great Physician, but for believers there was a better way. "Medicine," Judd wrote, "may be good enough for the world, but not for God's children." Echoing this sentiment, Simpson argued that "natural remedies . . . are not His way for His children." Even Cullis, who took such great pains to affirm his support for the medical profession, claimed that believers who relied on prayer alone chose the best course. "Don't mistake me and say I don't believe in physicians, God bless them, I do," he remarked. "But let the world have doctors and Christians the Great Physician."[43]

Most leaders of the divine healing movement, including Cullis, Carter, and Simpson, encouraged sufferers not to give up their physicians or abstain from medical treatment unless they could do so with full confidence and conviction. "If you haven't got faith in God as a Divine Healer," proclaimed the Reverend Charles Ryder, a minister from Providence, Rhode Island, who worked closely with Judd and Simpson during the 1880s, "it is your religious duty to get a physician, for your body is a very sacred thing." Others, however, were less cautious in their approach to the matter. Some, like Judd's associate Frederick Seely, insisted that because "medicine has no place in the healing economy of Jesus Christ," Christians had an obligation to abstain from all means other than "the power of the Holy Spirit." Drugs and doctors "may be used by unbelievers," Seely reasoned, "but not lawfully or loyally by a person who has passed through the new birth."[44]

Those who adopted more forceful positions like Seely's played right into the hands of detractors who painted proponents of divine healing as dangerous extremists. Not only did these individuals wrongfully distinguish between "divine" and "natural" means, critics charged, they also made refraining from medicine a mark or requirement of true faith. In a *Methodist Review* article written in response to a divine healing conference held in Chicago in December of 1885, George Milton Hammell complained that "the fanatic-spirit exhibits itself throughout the entire procedure in the reiterated insinuation that professing Christians are but sinners and infidels unless they banish physic and physicians from the sick-room, and use only faith internally and oil externally." Rather than liberating sufferers from sickness, this approach threatened both the spiritual and physical health of individuals who adopted it. Those who believed that they had sufficient faith to give up remedies, critics charged, ran the risk of exercising a kind of spiritual pride. Detractors also called attention to the physical dangers that resulted from the practice of presumption. At a meeting of Baptist ministers in New York City, for example, the Reverend H. B. Montgomery of the Willoughby Avenue Church in Brooklyn reported that the "head of the faith cure institution" in that city agreed to "cure" one of Willoughby's former parishioners "if she would give up her physician and all other earthly means." "She did it," Willoughby stated, "and she was dead in three days."[45]

Stories such as these continually challenged advocates of divine healing to defend the orthodoxy of their teachings, the integrity of their institutions, and the credibility of their movement in general. While some leaders attempted to maintain a moderate course that emphasized the inherent, if partial, value of natural remedies, others took a more aggressive approach. Rather than remaining on the defensive, proponents of faith cure like Elizabeth Baxter argued that doctoring and drug-taking often did more harm than good. A person who pursued health through these means was at greater risk of suffering long-term and even deadly consequences than the believer who sought healing through prayer alone. Citing the heroic therapies that caused excruciating pain and "mercurial medicines" that "affected persons and made them ill for life," Baxter maintained that forgoing these prescriptions in favor of "a way of healing" in which "there was nothing hurtful or painful" was a matter of common sense, not fanaticism. Jesus, Baxter asserted, healed "tenderly. . . . He did not take the knife and cut off the cancer; but He spoke the word and that was enough. When healing the foot and ankle, He did not turn and twist the bones in different ways, until He thrilled the poor patient with such pains that he screamed, but He made the lame to walk, O, so wondrously, by His Word." Faced with the prospect of painful therapies that might cause permanent physical damage, what reasonable person would not choose a course of treatment that required no torturous manipulations and threatened no bodily harm?[46]

From this perspective, divine healing provided a healthy alternative to the injurious prescriptions of the regular physicians. Even Simpson sometimes highlighted the harmful effects of "human remedies." Quoting from a number of medical authorities, Simpson underscored the limitations of the medical profession, and especially the dangers of chemical therapeutics. In the view of one Professor Jamison, Simpson noted, "giving drugs to subdue disease, to eradicate it, is simply to *kill vitality.* Such, under all conditions, is the inevitable result of giving medicines— which are drugs, poisons, impurities."[47]

For many individuals, forgoing medicines also represented a bid for freedom from crippling addictions. The literature of the divine healing movement abounds with stories of people whose struggles with illness spiraled into dependencies on narcotic medicines such as opium, laudanum, and morphine, all of which were popular and widely prescribed in this period. Maggie Mitchell, of Chicago, Illinois, recalled that she began taking opium ten years earlier "by the advice of my physician, to quiet pain" and "to keep up my strength." Soon "the habit" grew so strong that Mitchell would ask strangers to get her the drugs without her doctor's knowledge. Finally, in desperation, Mitchell prayed for God to help. Believing that God had heard her prayer, Mitchell vowed, "I will never take the vile stuff any more while I live, with God's help."[48]

In her testimony of healing, Mrs. J. K. Brinkerhoff of Norfolk, New York, confessed that she was "kept alive by morphine" and took "a great deal" of it in order to alleviate the painful symptoms of catarrh of the stomach, nervous prostration, and constriction of the spine. Although her friends and family had conspired to wean her gradually from the morphine, their attempts failed. Only when Brinkerhoff heard about divine healing did she begin to consider giving up the drug on her own. "Upon reflection," she recalled, "I felt that I was not trusting God very much, asking for His aid and as soon as hard pain came to resort to my morphine." Promising God that she would "never touch it again," Brinkerhoff commenced a period of excruciating trial in which she experienced "fluttering and palpitation of the heart," insomnia, loss of appetite, and extreme thirst. Many of her friends expected her to die or that she "would be insane by the sudden disuse of morphine" after thirteen years of steady dependency upon the drug. Writing her testimony a year and a half later, Brinkerhoff related that she had "taken no more morphine or medicine of any kind" since her decision to trust the Great Physician. "I have mentioned particularly my experience with morphine," she recounted, "to help the reader to realize my utter inability to do without it unless aided by Divine strength."[49]

Mrs. J. C. Barrett described herself as "a complete slave to one of the most dreadful forms of opium, viz.: paregoric." Less than a month after a physician in Morristown, New Jersey, prescribed a half-ounce dose of the medication for pain, Barrett was taking "three ounces at a dose, two or three times daily." "At the expiration of two months," she wrote, "I knew I was a slave to its terrible use; and all a human being could do to stop it I did." After several serious efforts to break the habit, all of which were followed by relapses that led to escalating drug use, Barrett, a practicing Catholic, met A. B. Simpson and confessed to her "dreadful opium habit." After Simpson prayed on her behalf, Barrett rose from her knees "perfectly satisfied that God had heard and answered my prayer, and from that moment . . . all desire and bad effect of paregoric gone."[50]

Although some were able to overcome their craving for medicines such as morphine through prayer alone, others found the force of habit too strong to break on their own. For these individuals, faith homes provided supportive spaces in which to conquer their addictions. When Mrs. T. L. Mansfield of Glasgow, Kentucky, heard that there was a "prayer-cure" at Sister Midkiff's "Pink Cottage," a faith home in her own state, she determined to travel there to seek release from her "nervous suffering" and from her longstanding dependency on morphine. Although she had come "to believe that God alone could cure" her from these ailments several months before, she "did not then know how to trust Him" and failed to receive the relief she sought. After spending a short time at the Pink Cottage, however, Mansfield quickly found the confidence to pray for the healing of her soul and body, and "willingly gave up all medicines and earthly physicians." "I even gave up the morphine which I thought I could not live without," Mansfield recounted, "and praise the Lord I haven't wanted any of it."[51]

For women like Mansfield, Barrett, Brinkerhoff, and Mitchell, and for many others who suffered similar addictions to narcotics, eschewing remedies made good medical sense. By relying solely on God for healing, they gained both relief from their diseases and release from the chemical dependencies that had caused them so much added suffering. Ridding their bodies of drugs also represented a kind of spiritual cleansing. For the Christian, proponents of faith cure maintained, protecting the body from insidious substances was not just a matter of maintaining personal health but a religious duty. By giving up chemical remedies, a person engaged in an act of purification that benefited both body and soul. Free from polluting substances, the flesh was now ready to receive the Holy Spirit through the ceremony of anointing and to become the temple of God. In this view, divine healing marked out a path toward greater holiness as well as better health.

Faith Homes and the Transformation of Female Suffering

While individuals such as Mrs. T. L. Mansfield expressed gratitude for the supportive environments and encouraging communities they found at faith homes, opponents of divine healing were troubled by the influence these establishments seemed to exercise over their guests. Detractors like James Buckley worried that "the doctrine taught in some of the leading faith-homes" caused "irreparable damage to religion, individuals, and to the peace of churches and families" by persuading visitors to separate themselves from friends and loved ones whose "disbelief" might dampen their faith in God's healing power. By incorporating inmates within an adoptive family and alternative sacred community, he charged, houses of healing created divisions that threatened existing familial and religious obligations.[52]

Buckley was especially concerned about the effects of these separations on customary gender norms—a set of prescriptions that were crucial, in his view, for maintaining the healthy families that sustained the broader social structure and advanced the progress of civilization. According to the dictates of the domestic ideology, women were obligated to submit to male authority figures in all social arenas, including the spaces of the sickroom. Within the sacred setting of the faith home, by contrast, invalids like Harriet Barker, Libbie Osborn, and many others found themselves relatively free to make their own choices about how they spent their time, what they ate, and who cared for their bodies. Physically separated from their domestic responsibilities as well as from their fathers, husbands, and male physicians, women experienced a level of independence in houses of healing that, in many cases, contrasted sharply with the limits they encountered in other environments. Encouraging such female autonomy, in Buckley's view, produced disastrous results. "Advocates of faith-healing and faith-homes have influenced women to leave their husbands and parents and reside in the homes," Buckley fumed, citing a case of a gentleman whose mother and sister were residing in a faith institution and "neglecting the most obvious duties of life."[53]

Testimonies of healing confirm that some individuals who embraced the teachings and practices they learned while sojourning at a house of healing became estranged from their families as a result. After spending several weeks at the residence of a "Christian woman" who "took the sick into her own home and taught and prayed with them," for example, Anna Prosser returned to her own abode in Buffalo, determined to witness to God's healing power at work in her body and to renounce the "worldly" and "fashionable" lifestyle that her wealthy parents and siblings pursued. Eventually, Prosser's efforts to live out her convictions and to convert her relatives alienated her young stepmother—a practicing Spiritualist medium who, in a fit of anger, commanded Prosser to leave the house. When Prosser's father begged his daughter to moderate her behavior, she replied, "Father I know that my highest earthly duty is to you, but there is one still higher, and if those two duties conflict I must choose the higher." A few days later, Prosser left home. Soon after setting up residence in rented rooms, she quit the "fashionable" Episcopal church in which she had been raised and transferred her membership to the Methodists.[54]

Prosser's story shows that claiming divine healing and acting faith did sometimes disrupt family relationships and provoke changes in church loyalties, just as Buckley feared. For women like Prosser, Barker, and numerous others, visits to faith homes facilitated internal transformations that prompted them to bump up against, stretch, and even contravene the medical and cultural norms that characterized women as naturally and necessarily weak, domestic, submissive, and sick. After taking "the blessing of healing from the Lord" during her stay at Faith-Rest Cottage in March of 1884, for example, Carrie Bates experienced a "buoyancy of health" that enabled her to engage in "mission work in New York City," undertake a three-year course of study at the New York Missionary Training College, and serve as matron at Judd's faith home for a summer. Five and a half years after her first trip to "dear Faith Rest Cottage," Bates parted from her loved ones and journeyed to India, where she worked as a missionary of the Christian Alliance until her death in 1909. No longer convinced that being a model Christian—and especially a model Christian woman—meant passively accepting sickness as a blessing sent by God for her benefit, Bates got out of bed and engaged in activities that would have seemed both improper and impossible prior to her visit to a house of divine healing.[55]

Helen Dawlly pursued a similar course. Following a one-and-a-half-year stint as matron of Judd's Faith-Rest, Dawlly decided to attend a training college for missionaries with the hopes of joining the Faith Mission in Akola, India. "The question came up instantly about my duty to my parents if I went into mission work," Dawlly later recalled. "If they became sick must I leave my work and come back to nurse them?" Turning to Psalm 45:10–11, "Forget thine own people and thy father's house; so shall the king greatly desire thy beauty; for He is thy Lord and worship thou Him," Dawlly determined that proclaiming the good news of the gospel—a message that, in her view, included the redemption of both body and soul—took precedence over maintaining familial bonds or fulfilling domestic duties.[56]

Not all women who visited faith homes attained or even aspired to the levels of leadership and public ministry that Helen Dawlly, Carrie Bates, and Anna Prosser achieved after their stays in these sacred venues. Far more frequently, women reported that being healed enabled them to fulfill the familial, religious, and social duties that they had felt compelled to neglect during their illnesses. The ability to return home and to engage in household work such as cooking, laundry, and caretaking following a period of respite at a house of healing was commonly offered as evidence of a cure. Cases like these suggest that experiencing divine healing did not always lead women to challenge, or even to question, the social and cultural norms that equated true womanhood with maternity and domesticity. For some individuals, visits to faith homes reinforced, rather than unsettled, conventional gender ideologies. Regardless of whether they used their newfound health and strength to pursue projects that satisfied or upset societal expectations, however, women who espoused the devotional ethic they encountered in houses of healing did subvert longstanding and persistently influential associations between female sanctity and passive resignation to physical suffering. Rejecting the role of the retiring female invalid as well as the restrictive prescriptions of the rest cure, women like Dawlly and Bates, as well as their more conventional sisters, sidestepped these sets of expectations by adopting a model of spiritual experience that esteemed active service rather than long-suffering endurance.

For Harriet Barker, and for many other women and men, houses of healing served as important way-stations along the road to mental transformation, physical rejuvenation, spiritual wholeness, and, in some cases, life-changing endeavor. Within the sacred spaces of faith homes like Berachah, Bethshan, and Faith-Rest Cottage, sick persons observed alternative perspectives on the problem of pain and witnessed different methods of coping with affliction. Separated from skeptical critics and pessimistic doctors as well as from the responsibilities and cultural pressures that characterized their everyday worlds, guests at these establishments were surrounded instead with believers who persuaded them to abandon modes of thinking and acting that kept them bedridden, to embrace the promises of healing contained in the Bible, and to embody a manner of living that linked holiness with the energetic pursuit of purity and service.

CHAPTER SIX

The Lord for the Body, the Gospel for the Nations

Divine Healing and Social Reform

Seven and a half years prior to her departure for India as a missionary, Helen Dawlly "was generally regarded as a hopeless invalid." Following the onset of "some disease which baffled medical skill," Dawlly "utterly broke down" and "was compelled to retire from the busy scenes of life and enter upon a dreary season of pain and languishing, which continued, with an occasional abatement of few weeks' duration, for ten years." Lengthy illness was a sore trial for Dawlly, who had long harbored ambitions for her life work. Initially, she "prayed much for health" and held out hope that she might fulfill her "longing for active service for God." After reading of John Wesley's "strong impression that he was some day to begin some special work for God," Dawlly told her mother, "That is just the way I feel. I believe God has a work for me to do, and I shall arise to do it yet." As the years passed and her prayers for physical restoration went unanswered, however, she eventually concluded that "it was the will of God that I should suffer."[1]

But the devotional ethic of passive resignation to afflictive providence did not sit well with Dawlly. Soon after a visitor challenged her to "appropriate the promise" in James 5—"The prayer of faith shall save the sick"—Dawlly became convinced that it was her "solemn duty to be well" and was persuaded that she would be healed. On May 23, 1880, a week before her thirty-third birthday, Dawlly determined to believe God's promises and to act accordingly: "I realized that I was not to wait for any evidence, but by going forward and acting out my faith, I should receive strength. And, praise the Lord! I did." From that moment on, Dawlly endeavored "to fight the fight of faith" despite "many a hard battle," including a relapse of seven months' duration; for God, she declared, had "shown me that it was His blessed will that I should be no longer helpless." Before long, Dawlly was serving as the matron of Carrie Judd's Faith-Rest Cottage and working alongside Judd, Anna Prosser, and other women conducting "gospel meetings" and leading a "class of reformed men in Sunday School" at the Canal Street Mission—an outreach located "in one of the worst parts of the city." After a year and a half in Buffalo, Dawlly concluded that God had other work for her to do and decided to pursue her long-cherished hope of becoming a missionary. Following a twelve-month course of study at a missionary training institute, Dawlly set sail for India, where she spent the five and a half years until her death caring for destitute children, first at the American Faith Mission, an independent organization run by Marcus and Jennie Frow Fuller in Akola, Berar, and later at a "Home" that she established for orphans and other impoverished young people in Poona.[2]

For Dawlly, as for many other leaders and participants in the faith cure movement, personal physical restoration was closely linked with a profound desire to be energetically engaged in serving God and ministering to others. Like Judd, who also believed that God had called her to an "active mission," Dawlly could not resign herself to remaining an invalid, no matter how much others insisted that passive endurance of pain and withdrawal from the world provided plenty of opportunities to serve as a model Christian. By embracing the promises and practices of divine healing, Dawlly, Judd, and numerous others overcame the infirmities that kept them from engaging in the kinds of constructive enterprises that they saw as most useful to God. Indeed, the devotional ethics of divine healing not only enabled, but *required* individuals to employ their bodies in God's service. Those who sought healing for selfish purposes, leaders warned, would either lose the blessing or fail to receive it altogether. As Simpson put it, "Christ is willing to impart to us His wondrous resurrection life, but we may not squander it on the world or ourselves. We keep it only as we use it for Him." Accordingly, many invalids who had previously given little thought to the question of God's calling upon their lives now found themselves confronted with an understanding of Christian ethics that demanded their full, active participation in some form of "godly" work on behalf of others.[3]

The shape this service took in the lives of individuals who participated in the divine healing movement took many different forms. Some were simply grateful for the opportunity to minister to their families by returning to work or re-engaging in domestic duties. For others, personal experiences of physical healing prompted passionate engagement in evangelical endeavors to transform individual bodies and souls as well as to reform the cultural behaviors and social structures that, in their view, contributed to both corporal suffering and spiritual oppression. Many previously incapacitated invalids pioneered or participated in urban ministries, temperance movements, foreign missions, and even dress reform campaigns. Charting the activities of several prominent leaders as well as the efforts of several lesser-known lay people illumines how the divine healing movement served as a channel through which many individuals moved toward greater social engagement. For former invalids such as Helen Dawlly, Carrie Judd, A. B. Simpson, Emma Whittemore, and many other recipients of divine healing, energetic service was a form of acting faith—a kind of spiritual practice through which these individuals embodied the devotional ethic that called them to surmount their infirmities by embracing a life of divinely inspired activity.

Ministering to the Masses: Divine Healing and Social Reform

The story of evangelical participation in late-nineteenth-century social reform ventures, purity crusades, and evangelistic outreach is both a familiar and a complex one. Indeed, the rise of divine healing within the context of the Higher Life movement, which taught that sanctification imparted "power for service" and contributed to the formation and growth of a variety of "gospel welfare" organizations and missions agencies, suggests that the reforming and evangelistic impulses of faith cure recipients were rooted in and nurtured by a broader set of theological prescriptions and motivations. The rising influence of progressive sentiments on both liberal and evangelical Protestant responses to the perceived crises of urbanization, industrialization, and immigration in this period also helped to shape the ambitions and activities of sick persons whose encounter with the Great Physician enabled them to take part in efforts to address the "evils" of poverty, intemperance, and vice. After their healings, many of these individuals joined voluntary associations such as the Women's Christian Temperance Union (WCTU), the Young Men's and Young Women's Christian Associations (YMCA and YWCA), and the Salvation Army—groups whose constituencies extended well beyond the rather indeterminate boundaries of the faith cure movement and even, in some cases, beyond the borders of Higher Life evangelicalism. Within organizations like the YMCA, recipients of divine healing likely encountered the increasingly popular rhetoric of "muscular Christianity," with its emphasis on bodily strength, health, and activity as means for surmounting spiritual and social ills. Similarly, advocates of faith cure like A. J. Gordon, who frequently partnered with Protestant progressives to address problems of "social reconstruction" during the latter decades of the nineteenth century, would have come into contact with the developing discourse of the Social Gospel. Although evangelicals and "liberals" would eventually part ways over certain tenets of progressive ideology and many principles of theology, they continued to hold together "a working alliance," especially on issues of social reform and missions, throughout the 1880s and 1890s.[4]

While the overlapping contexts of Higher Life theology, progressivism, and Protestant voluntarism provide indispensable frameworks for interpreting the various ways in which beneficiaries of divine healing sought to employ their new strength and health for God, the stories of individuals such as A. B. Simpson and several of his associates also suggest that the teachings and practices of faith cure played a crucial role in shaping how some evangelicals conceptualized and carried out their "service to the Master." Focusing on Simpson's experience of bodily restoration and his subsequent efforts to reform the church, transform the city, and evangelize the nations offers an opportunity to examine how the theology and devotional ethics of divine healing, alongside broader theological and cultural currents, enabled and inspired participants to envision and work toward a world set free from both physical suffering and spiritual oppression.

In the summer of 1881, while vacationing with his family, Simpson attended several meetings of Charles Cullis's annual faith convention at Old Orchard Beach, Maine. Earlier that spring, a prominent physician had warned the thirty-six-year-old Simpson that unless he took immediate measures, his constitutional strength would give out within a few months. Not only his usefulness as a minister but his very life was at stake. Obeying doctor's orders, Simpson retired to Saratoga Springs, New York, a popular health resort, to recuperate over the summer. This was not the first time Simpson was obliged to abandon his pulpit in order to convalesce. By his own account, Simpson's "many physical infirmities and disabilities" constantly impeded his vocational aspirations. His first breakdown occurred at the age of fourteen, while he was preparing for college through a course of "hard study." After recovering from his "nervous prostration" and completing his schooling, Simpson became the "ambitious pastor of a large city church" in Hamilton, Ontario, at the age of twenty-one. "Plunging headlong into my work," Simpson later recalled, "I again broke down with heart trouble and had to go away for months of rest." This collapse was followed by two others of long duration, the most recent of which had forced him to step down temporarily from a successful pastorate at the Thirteenth Presbyterian Church in New York City within a year of assuming the post. This latest illness was so severe that it prompted rumors among his friends and former parishioners that he would be "permanently laid aside from all duty."[5]

For Simpson, the prospect of ceasing his pastoral labors was deeply depressing. Ministry was Simpson's passion, so much so that he often had to remind himself to rest from doing "God's work" so that he could sleep. In particular, Simpson was convinced that God had called him not only to preach but also to produce an illustrated missionary magazine designed to promote increased commitment to spreading the gospel around the globe. For this reason, he had uprooted his family from their comfortable home in Louisville, Kentucky, and relocated them to New York—a move that his wife, Margaret, had vehemently opposed. The city, in her view, was no place to raise children. Although Simpson pressed her, and eventually obtained her acquiescence, even he admitted that New York posed "elements of danger" for them all. To quit his pastorate after finally winning Maggie's acceptance of his calling would have been an ordeal. Furthermore, Simpson's brief sojourn in New York had aroused his ardor for urban evangelism. For several months, he had been contemplating how to expand his church's ministry to "the masses."[6]

With such a strong sense of duty to proclaim the gospel to the nations as well as to the "unreached" people of New York, Simpson simply could not accept the physician's recommendations that he curtail his ministerial endeavors indefinitely. In his view, the ideal of the invalid who served Christ best by resigning himself to endure afflictions patiently was both impractical and unappealing. As a husband and a father, Simpson could not afford to retire from the position that provided his family's livelihood. Furthermore, he believed, the strenuous tasks of urban outreach and foreign missions called for active workers who were both spiritually vigorous and physically robust, not passive sufferers confined to their sickrooms. But how was he to avoid the repeated relapses and resulting periods of rest and withdrawal—not to mention the more dire predictions of permanent prostration or even death—that continued to frustrate his endeavors?

Simpson found the answers to these questions at Cullis's convention. "One day," he recounted, "I . . . heard at least two hundred people give an account of their healing." Although he had witnessed a healing in his former pastorate and believed that "cases of healing" did occur, he had not committed himself "in any full sense to the truth or experience of Divine healing." Listening to so many testimonies persuaded Simpson that he had to "settle this matter one way or the other." Turning to his Bible, he became convinced that healing was "part of Christ's glorious Gospel for a sinful and suffering world, for all who would believe and receive His Word." Here was the solution to Simpson's dilemma. If he could take God as his healer, he believed, God would provide "for all the needs of my body until all my life-work is done." Making up his mind, Simpson strolled out "into the silent pine woods" and pledged to accept the truth of divine healing, to trust the Lord Jesus for strength in all circumstances, and "*to use* this blessing for the glory of God and the good of others."[7]

Simpson's healing marked a turning point in both his physical condition and his career path. In early November of 1881, he resigned his position at Thirteenth Presbyterian Church in order to engage in a ministry to the urban masses and in the work of foreign missions to which he felt God was calling him. Although he had attempted to pursue his visionary aspirations of saving the city and the world while shepherding his prosperous and genteel Presbyterian congregation, his efforts had met with little success. While his parishioners were fond of their pastor, few seemed to have been entirely sympathetic with his passion for attracting the "unchurched masses" or evangelizing the nations. As a result, Simpson had shouldered the burden of these ambitions alone and had repeatedly buckled under the strain. Just prior to his trip to Saratoga Springs, for example, he found that the onus of serving as a minister to his congregation prevented him from continuing his work as an editor, and he felt compelled to give up the missionary magazine that he had come to New York to publish.[8]

Simpson's sojourn at Old Orchard Beach and his exposure there to the numerous individuals who had been transformed from sickly invalids to healthy servants of God gave him a new perspective on his previous failures. In order to bring salvation to the lost souls of New York and of the nations, he came to believe, he first needed to overcome his own infirmity. By claiming divine healing for himself, Simpson was suddenly infused with "vitality from a directly supernatural source" that enabled him to keep "pace with the calls and necessities of [his] work." He soon concluded, however, that he could not carry out his mission under the auspices of a church that he saw as crippled by social exclusivity, an apathetic attitude toward evangelism, and an unwholesome concern for respectability. No longer hindered by his own fleshly infirmities, Simpson also desired to be set free from the burdens that he experienced as the minister of a "conventional" congregation.[9]

Simpson articulated his views about the church in the final sermon that he delivered to his Presbyterian flock. Preaching on two texts that expressed his dual sense of vocation—Luke 4:18, "The Spirit of the Lord is upon me to preach the gospel to the poor," and Mark 16:15: "Go ye into all the world, and preach the gospel to every creature"—he argued that caring for and preaching to the poor ought to be the church's priority. Measured against this "standard . . . of a true church and a true Christianity," contemporary congregations were falling far short. "How can I be satisfied," Simpson queried his parishioners, "with the state of things as it is in the Church?"[10]

Rather than following Christ's example of "meeting the poor and lowly in a

commonplace way," New York churches, in particular, had adopted several practices that effectively excluded the poor from their midst. Simpson was especially
critical of pew rents, a pecuniary scheme that made the church exclusive and kept
"many people away." A growing fixation with "social style" and "respectability" further alienated the "poor," the "lowly," and the "working people." Ministers, Simpson charged, were guilty of donning "robes and vestments" and preaching "grand
and eloquent sermons" rather than imitating the "simple" style that Jesus practiced.
Churchgoers spent "fabulous sums" on "personal adorning, style, and equipage,"
and came to services dressed in fancy clothing that accentuated, rather than miti-
gated social distinctions. Congregations were more concerned about architecture
than evangelism: "They have been building up colossal ecclesiastical piles whose
very grandeur walled out the lowly and lost ones, whose weak and weary feet could
not climb the magnificent steps that ascend their portals."[11]

Furthermore, most of these grand edifices were being constructed uptown, "in
the region of Central Park." Denouncing the tendency of New York churches to
desert their downtown locations for the "wealthy and fashionable districts of the
city," Simpson scoffed at the notion that these congregations were merely following the "ascending tide of the population" in the northern section of the city. "The
facts are," he insisted, "that the population is *not* diminishing in the lower part of
the city. There is not a ward in the central and lower portion of the city . . . but has
increased in resident population *very largely* in the last twenty years and has more
need of churches today than ever." The problem was that the people moving into
the downtown areas were not the respectable sort that the "powerful and wealthy
churches" hoped would populate their pews. Instead of inviting the burgeoning
groups of immigrants and working people who were crowding the neighborhoods
below Twenty-third Street to join their ranks, many churches abandoned their
buildings and relocated above the midtown line.[12]

From this safe distance, these congregations founded "mission churches" to
serve the needs of the poor. Although Simpson acknowledged that these efforts
were well-intended and might accomplish some good results, he insisted that segregating the church according to class or social status contradicted the word and
will of God. "This system in New York of having churches exclusively for the rich
and exclusively for the poor is all a mistake," he proclaimed. "It is not well to put
apart the rich and the poor, who God said should everywhere meet together, and
who do meet everywhere but in the church." Not only did this arrangement gain-
say "God's order" by fostering a "divorce" between the wealthiest New Yorkers and
the most destitute, it also left out the "middle classes" altogether. "There are thousands of persons," Simpson maintained, "some of them in reduced circumstances,

others more sensitive to their social surroundings than if they were wealthy, who feel slighted at being consigned to the mission churches, and will not attend them. They are not at home in the exclusive and wealthiest churches, and the result is that they go nowhere." These "working people" constituted the largest, and "most neglected" class in the city.[13]

If the churches of New York were disregarding their duty to minister to the needs of the poor and to provide a spiritual home for "all classes indiscriminately," they were also failing to live up to their calling to carry the gospel to the ends of the earth. Condemning the tendency of his contemporaries to argue "against lay evangelism," Simpson insisted that spreading the "good news" to others "at home and abroad" was "the commission of every Christian" and not just the responsibility of ministers. The church, he believed, ought to serve as a training ground for "an exceedingly great army of living souls and soldiers of the cross" who would work to "save the city—to save the world."[14]

In order to pursue these goals, Simpson severed himself from his congregation as well as from the Presbyterian denomination on November 7, 1881, and embarked on "an evangelistic campaign" among the "non-churchgoers" of New York. The following Sunday, he rented "a cheap hall" on Eighth Avenue and "invited all in sympathy with an aggressive spiritual movement" to attend an "address on the spiritual needs of the city and the masses." A week later, Simpson and a small band of supporters held an evangelistic service and won their first convert. Over the course of the next few months, a growing group of followers gathered around Simpson as he "began to preach the gospel in public halls, theatres, gospel tents, and upon the street corners." In February 1882, this "little flock" of thirty-five individuals formally organized themselves into a church called "The Gospel Tabernacle."[15]

When he first resigned his pastorate in order to "labor among the masses," Simpson had no intention of founding a new church. Indeed, he worried that "organized" churches actually posed an obstacle to evangelism. Determined to avoid the pitfalls that he faced in his former post, Simpson initially conceived of his new endeavor as a "spiritual movement." Within several months, however, he and his comrades concluded that God was calling them "to organize . . . a Christian Church for this special work." Unlike the segregated congregations that Simpson criticized so sharply, the Gospel Tabernacle aimed to "attract all classes indiscriminately." In order to prevent the exclusivity and pretentiousness that plagued so many New York churches, the Tabernacle's founders banned "taxes, assessments, and pew rents." Funding for the new organization was to come solely through voluntary, or "free-will" offerings. This "Free Gospel Church," however, was to be a "self-supporting" institution, not a "mission church" dependent on the contributions of a wealthy uptown congregation for its survival. "Self-reliance," Simpson wrote, "is necessary for a healthy organization." Dependency, on the other hand, rendered an institution "passive and inert."[16]

Within the context of late-nineteenth-century New York, Simpson and his colleagues suggested, apathy was an unacceptable posture for the church. Faced with a growing number of "unreached" souls and social ills, Christians could hardly afford to adopt an attitude of lethargic indifference. The work of the church, Simpson wrote, "should not be passive but aggressive." While Simpson's critique of the contemporary church's sluggishness and superciliousness resonated with the deeply rooted tradition of Protestant lament over perceived declension as well as with the increasingly prevalent complaints of Social Gospelers and other Protestant reformers about the church's moral failures, his rhetoric also recalled certain themes within the theology of divine healing. His insistence on the need for an active response to the wants of the urban poor, the middle-class masses, and the "lost" souls around the world, in particular, echoed the devotional ethic that advocates of divine healing embraced in their efforts to overcome physical infirmity. Rejecting a model of spiritual experience that valorized patient resignation to somatic affliction, participants in the divine healing movement claimed that acting faith represented the appropriate means for dealing with pain and defeating disease. After adopting this perspective in order to conquer his own bodily ailments, Simpson applied a similar logic as he endeavored to address the spiritual and social maladies of the world around him. If energetic resistance was the proper Christian response to personal physical infirmity, he reasoned, the apposite reaction to broader spiritual and social problems was aggressive work. On both the individual and the corporate level, the alleviation of affliction required divinely motivated action.[17]

The particular kinds of actions that Simpson and his cohorts undertook in their efforts to respond to the city also evoked the doctrinal and devotional idioms of divine healing. From the beginning of his new endeavor, Simpson insisted that redeeming the city and its people required Christians to venture out of their church buildings to meet the masses where they lived, worked, and engaged in recreation. "We must go to them, to the streets and lanes of the city, to the highways and lodges," he contended. "Great good might be done by meetings on Sunday nights in theatres and halls. Visitations from house to house should be undertaken more than is now the custom." Saving the city, Simpson implied, entailed a ministry of presence and proximity. Just as the Holy Spirit infused infirm bodies with vital healing power, so Christians ought to permeate secular city spaces with the transforming influence of the gospel.[18]

Simpson and his "band of workers," as they were called, carried out this approach to urban ministry in several ways. Even the name they chose for the church reflected the incarnational lens through which they viewed their work. The tabernacle, according to biblical narrative, was the place where God's presence would dwell. Just as God inhabited and infused individual bodies with divine energy for acts of service, so God would reside among the corporate body of believers, imparting the power to accomplish redeeming works. Rather than holding services in traditional church edifices, the Gospel Tabernacle initially met in music halls, theaters, outdoor tents pitched in vacant lots, and even in Madison Square Garden. New York's poor and working classes were far more likely to respond to an invitation to enter a place of amusement, leaders of the Tabernacle reasoned, than they were to cross the threshold of an established church.[19]

Occupying these locations also suggested that Simpson and his cohorts were literally gaining ground in the battle they were waging against worldly corruption. Because the "gospel of healing" affirmed that finite matter such as human flesh could and should be redeemed through the indwelling of divine power, individuals like Simpson reasoned that the structures of the material world also merited redemption. "There is nothing inherently more evil about matter than spirit," Simpson preached. "Both alike partake of the effects of human depravity, and both alike are redeemed and sanctified by Christ." Drawing upon this logic, Tabernacle members rejoiced when they eventually obtained the lease on a theater that had previously housed a "blasphemous" passion play. By converting the building into a temple of God, they transformed a profane urban place into a sacred space.[20]

If the power of the Holy Spirit could consecrate buildings, the indwelling presence of God could also transform neighborhoods. Unlike the wealthy churches that fled the increasingly congested working-class and destitute districts in the central and lower portions of the city, founders of the Gospel Tabernacle sought meeting sites in close proximity to the people with whom they hoped to share their message of hope and redemption. Venues that were less "well adapted to reach the masses" were abandoned as soon as practical in favor of more opportune locations. In addition to holding regular services in the vicinity of burgeoning immigrant and laboring communities, parishioners of the Gospel Tabernacle regularly walked the streets of these neighborhoods, calling on potential converts in their homes and seeking to make the church a welcoming place for the resident population. Members of the Ladies' Aid Society were especially active in making their presence known among the local people. "Many of the ladies visit regularly the tenement and other houses in the district, distributing cards of invitation and tracts and speaking of Christ to the inmates," Simpson reported.[21]

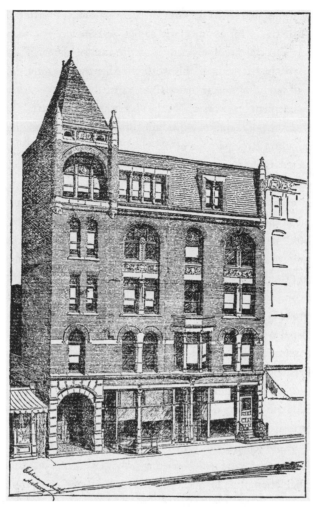

The Gospel Tabernacle moved to this location on the corner of 8th Avenue and 44th Street in Manhattan in 1889. Courtesy of the Christian and Missionary Alliance National Archives.

Redeeming the Flesh: Divine Healing, Poverty Relief, and Purity Crusades

Although Gospel Tabernacle workers primarily characterized their ministry as a labor to lost souls, the material suffering that they encountered in the downtown wards, combined with their commitment to the doctrines of divine healing that emphasized the inclusion of the body in the scheme of salvation, prompted them to conduct their outreach efforts in a manner that incorporated a concern for the physical, economic, and social needs of their constituencies. In addition to doling out evangelistic tracts, for example, the Ladies' Aid Society also formed committees on "charitable relief, employment, and the care of the sick." Emma Whittemore, who participated avidly in this work after her own healing, emphasized the importance of attending to the material wants of the poverty-stricken and often half-starved tenement residents whom she also hoped to convert. "Our equipment for ministry to the poor souls of Slumdom consisted of a tin pail filled with gruel, soup, or tea, and a large package of old clothing done up in newspaper," Whittemore reflected. Only by first helping to alleviate the physical hardships of their intended audience could these workers hope to gain a hearing for their spiritual message. An evangelist who arrived on someone's doorstep with no more than a tract in hand would surely be rebuffed. "The food we carried and the fixing things up a bit would make us at least tolerable visitors," Whittemore wrote. "Often intense gratitude was aroused simply by sweeping out a room, heating a cup of tea, or smoothing over their rumpled and untidy bed. While working thus, the word of cheer or comfort would be spoken as the Lord in answer to prayer prompted." As the Reverend R. Wheatley, one of Simpson's associates, explained in an article entitled "Gospel Work Among the Masses," "The ministration of the Gospel to the multitudes assumes primarily the form of preaching the glad tidings of salvation through Christ. But this is not the exclusive form. The same ministration is manifest in instruction and exhortation imparted from house to house, to individual after individual; in feeding the hungry, clothing the naked, tending the sick, and relieving the distressed. All are parts of the same grand ministry."[22]

While many of the relief efforts that Gospel Tabernacle workers undertook were occasional rather than systematic—seeking only to assuage the symptoms of poverty rather than attempting to ameliorate the root causes—some ministries did try to undertake broader structural reforms of the social order. Whittemore's work with "fallen women," for example, led her to recognize and critique the ways in which laissez-faire capitalism exploited young female workers and often forced them to turn to prostitution out of economic desperation. Many of the women she met on streets of New York had been "willing to work hard, very hard, for an honest livelihood," Whittemore charged, but because of the "greed of wealthy men" their "lifeblood was sweated out to produce the wealth," while they "were allowed to languish in conditions of wretchedness on a wage that would not supply a livelihood." In her view, captains of industry were "oppressors" who had reduced countless women to abject poverty and driven them to sell their bodies in order to keep from starving. Comparing capitalist free enterprise to a "slave market" and employers to "wealthy 'slave drivers,'" Whittemore called on "the women of our land" to "band together and earnestly wait upon God to see what could be done regarding the starvation prices paid for the labors of so many of our dear young girls." Systematic regulation of wages, she implied, was the only way to ensure the physical safety and financial security of working women and to stem the rising tide of female prostitution in North America's industrializing cities.[23]

In addition to entreating other women to agitate for broad-scale economic reform, Whittemore organized efforts to bust organized "vice rings" that duped, drugged, and kidnapped young women—especially unwary immigrant girls—and sold them into prostitution. Rescuing these victims from "entrapping and slavery," providing them with physical protection, safe lodgings, job training, and employment placement services as well as giving them biblical teaching and spiritual nourishment became major foci of Whittemore's New York ministry. In 1890 she opened the Door of Hope under the auspices of the Gospel Tabernacle. This "Home" for "fallen women" promised to shield and train those who wanted to leave prostitution behind in order to "regain their respectability" and "womanhood."[24]

Whittemore's own experience with physical healing convinced her that nobody was beyond redemption. Prior to her encounter with the Great Physician, she confessed, "I had ever felt such a loathing for anything bordering upon impurity that I never could tolerate a wicked woman." Even in her "rescue work" among the poor, Whittemore refused to mingle with anyone whom she considered sexually polluted and shunned close contact with these "desperately vile" street-walkers. In the aftermath of her "own wonderful healing," however, Whittemore was compelled to reconsider her attitude. The doctrine of divine healing had taught her that even the most diseased flesh could be restored to health and holiness. Applying this principle to New York's prostitutes, Whittemore concluded that these women, whose bodies had been defiled, disfigured, and desecrated, could recoup their physical and spiritual purity through the transforming power of the God's indwelling spirit. After working with such "erring" and "wandering" girls for a number of years, she remarked, "I have seen the most degraded re-made by our blessed Lord so that they become charmingly genteel."[25]

Indeed, Whittemore often included "before" and "after" pictures of rehabilitated prostitutes in promotional literature for the Door of Hope. These photographs highlighted the marked physical changes that accompanied a woman's liberation from "a life worse than death." Often the transformation was so dramatic that the reformed woman bore little resemblance to her past self. Whereas the portrait of the "wicked woman" emphasized the havoc that prostitution wreaked upon a person's body—the slumped posture; the weary, worn, and worldly-wise facial expression; the soiled and disorderly apparel—the picture of the newly respectable lady

These before and after photographs of Delia, a rehabilitated prostitute, were included in *Mother Whittemore's Record of Modern Miracles* (1931) to illustrate the transformative power of Christ. Courtesy of the Christian and Missionary Alliance National Archives.

revealed the renewal that was possible through an encounter with Christ the redeemer. Attired in the demure costume of the Door of Hope, her face radiated calm and contentment, and her carriage reflected confidence and optimism.[26]

The notion that an individual's outward physical appearance reflected her inner moral condition led some supporters of divine healing to highlight the importance of bodily presentation as a means of personal and social improvement. In addition to fashioning a uniform for Door of Hope residents, Whittemore and her colleagues also donned special outfits for their visitation work among neighborhood tenement dwellers. Rather than wearing clothing that set them apart from the local population, Gospel Tabernacle workers tried to minimize class distinctions by dressing "as near like" the poor as possible. "Our dress usually consisted of an old calico wrapper, gingham apron, faded shawl and an out-of-date hat," Whittemore observed. Practically, this habit helped visitors to gain entrance into the

These photographs of Emma Whittemore in her Door of Hope uniform and in the costume she wore for visiting slums were included in *Mother Whittemore's Record of Modern Miracles* (1931) and reflect her belief that bodily appearance was a means of evangelism. Courtesy of the Christian and Missionary Alliance National Archives.

homes and hearts of the people they hoped to convert without arousing suspicion or resentment. At a more symbolic level, women like Whittemore used their bodies as a means of enacting the social solidarity that they hoped to achieve in the Gospel Tabernacle. Embracing Simpson's critique of the segregating effects of fashion, these individuals eschewed expensive garments in favor of "simple attire" that suggested neither unapproachable gentility nor intractable penury. Although they hoped to blend in with neighborhood residents, these women were also careful to avoid the appearance of slovenliness or sloth. By donning patched and mended clothing, Whittemore explained, she and her fellow workers presented themselves as object lessons for the downtrodden. Their faded but refurbished outfits were meant to teach observers that "old garments might be made presentable by industry."[27]

The unconsciously condescending tone of some of Whittemore's remarks—and, indeed, of the entire project of upper-class women moving surreptitiously among their less-fortunate "neighbors" cloaked in costumes designed to impart habits of virtue, thrift, and industry—exposes the imaginative limits of the Gospel Tabernacle enterprise. Through their attempts to mitigate class distinctions, Simpson and his associates may actually have reinforced the sense of social distance that wealthy New Yorkers felt toward their economic inferiors. The fact that Whittemore and her compatriots sometimes felt compelled to hide behind veils "for the sake of not too greatly shocking some of our uptown acquaintances that [they] might chance to meet" suggests that they were acutely aware of the pretense that accompanied their efforts to identify with the lower classes. Despite the best of intentions, these Gospel Tabernacle workers found it difficult to live up to the downwardly mobile ideal that Jesus' incarnational ministry demanded.[28]

While the emphasis that divine healing placed on the indwelling presence of the Holy Spirit prompted some adherents to engage in well-meaning but patronizing attempts to minister to the poor, this doctrine also contributed to widespread pre-occupation with bodily purity. Whittemore's work with New York City prostitutes was only one of many ministries associated with the divine healing movement that attested to a pervasive anxiety about the corruption of the flesh. During the 1880s and 1890s, approximately 120 rescue homes for "fallen women" were established in urban areas across the United States. Reports regarding the founding, financing, and volunteer work associated with institutions such as Whittemore's Door of Hope, Margaret Strachen's Catherine Street Mission, the Florence-Crittendon Midnight Mission, and Henry Wilson's Magdalene Home featured prominently in periodicals devoted to the promotion of divine healing such as Simpson's *Word, Work and World* and Carrie Judd's *Triumphs of Faith*.[29]

In addition to contributing to these ongoing and extensive efforts to combat prostitution in American cities, many participants in the divine healing movement also engaged in ministries to "fallen men." Whereas advocates of purity campaigns cast the corruption of the female flesh primarily in terms of sexual adulteration—a "fallen woman" was a sex worker who fell short of society's standards regulating the conduct of the female body—they attributed physical pollution among men chiefly to the debilitating effects of alcohol. When applied to a man, the adjective "fallen" referred, not to his sexual ethics, but rather to his inability to regulate his appetites and his consequent decline into moral decay and financial ruin. Efforts to combat the devastating effects of alcohol on male bodies proliferated rapidly during the latter decades of the nineteenth century through the influence of as-sociations such as the WCTU, the Salvation Army, and other independent Gospel Mission movements. Many members of the faith cure movement found an outlet for their renewed energies in temperance campaigns and rescue work run by these organizations. Soon after her healing, for example, Carrie Judd joined her friend Anna Prosser, who had also been restored to health after a long period of invalidism, in conducting weekly meetings at the WCTU Gospel Mission for "the uplifting" of "poor men who were slaves to drink and other vices." Prosser carried on this ministry for several years and eventually opened a mission of her own in the slums of Buffalo. Prior to establishing the Door of Hope, Whittemore had regularly participated in Jerry McAuley's famous Water Street Mission, where she ministered to "river-thieves, drunkards, gamblers and abandoned women of the streets." Jennie Smith founded a new department of the WCTU designed to serve "railroad men" who often fell victim to the corrupting temptations of alcohol on their long journeys away from families and outside the boundaries of conventional forms of moral restraint.[30]

Bodily purity crusades such as temperance and anti-prostitution attracted the attention of individuals like Smith, Prosser, Judd, Whittemore, and many other adherents of divine healing for several reasons. First, like other late-nineteenth-century reformers, advocates of divine healing believed that sins of the flesh were the source of broader social disorders. The notion that alcoholism both caused and compounded the problems of poverty was widespread among members of the Progressive movement, for example. Likewise, prostitution represented a severe affront to prevailing gender norms that linked female purity to the nurture of upstanding citizens and thereby to the formation of the national character. Women who sold their bodies for profit not only degraded themselves but also undermined the prospects of American civilization. Within this context, to root out vice and impurity from individual bodies was to wage war against the larger ills that plagued the nation.[31]

Furthermore, because divine healing taught that the body was the temple of the Holy Spirit, human flesh became charged with sacred significance. In order to serve as a hallowed inhabitance, however, the body had to be rid of every form of iniquity and corruption. There was no middle ground—the flesh was either the dwelling place of God or the dominion of the devil. Freeing the human body from the bondage of sin thus represented a victory in the cosmic battle between good and evil and helped to make the world a more hospitable place for the presence of Christ.

Eschatological convictions also prompted members of the divine healing movement to engage in vigorous crusades against bodily intemperance and pollution. Although every person who embraced divine healing did not necessarily hold an identical understanding of the "end times," most prominent leaders of the movement, including A. J. Gordon, Carrie Judd, Anna Prosser, and A. B. Simpson and his Gospel Tabernacle colleagues, promoted the doctrine of Christ's premillennial second coming. Unlike their more sanguine postmillennial counterparts, who believed that human efforts to spread the gospel and reform society would ultimately result in the "millennial reign of righteousness and peace" after which Christ would return in person and set up his earthly kingdom, supporters of the premillennialist view tended to hold a more pessimistic outlook regarding the ability of human beings to usher in the kingdom of God. As Simpson put it, "The world was becoming worse and worse," and history was fast moving toward the moment when Jesus would return to destroy the present age prior to initiating his thousand-year reign. While some historians have concluded that premillennialist eschatology fostered an otherworldly and therefore socially indifferent attitude among its adherents, supporters such as Simpson insisted that this doctrine actually inspired a sense of urgency about somatic, social, and spiritual reform. Only purified bodies and souls would survive Christ's cataclysmic return; and since this event was imminent, Christians had to act quickly in order to prepare themselves to meet their God, while at the same time convincing others that purity was worth pursuing. Premillennialists of Simpson's ilk also stressed the pressing need for a multitude of strong, dynamic individuals who would take the gospel to the ends of the earth in order to make Christ's message known before his impending return. Bodies debilitated by disease, drunkenness, drug abuse, sexual delinquency, or other forms of impurity could not carry out the great commission to preach the good news to all nations.[32]

The Gospel for the Nations: Divine Healing and Foreign Missions

Throughout the nineteenth century, evangelical concern for spreading the message of Christian salvation to the "heathen" in foreign lands intensified as various denominations sent out missionaries across the globe and founded a host of missionary societies and publications designed to foster awareness and financial support for these endeavors among the domestic population. Caught up in the excitement of this broader missionary movement, many proponents of faith cure saw divine healing as a means for transforming helpless invalids into active workers for foreign fields as well as a tool for convincing the "pagan nations" of the truth of Christianity. While Simpson's fervor for preaching the gospel to "every creature" predated his healing at Old Orchard Beach, for example, his encounter with the Great Physician endowed him with the energy he needed to promote the cause of foreign missions. In January of 1882, several months after resigning his Presbyterian pulpit and launching the Gospel Tabernacle, Simpson published the first issue of *The Word, Work and World*, a journal that encouraged "the restoration of Apostolic purity, zeal and power in the Church of God, the speedy evangelization of the nations, and the preparation of the world for the coming of the Lord Jesus," and that also contained numerous articles endorsing divine healing. Over the course of the next several years, Simpson used this periodical to publicize the testimonies of many individuals whose healings prompted active engagement in the causes of both urban reform and missionary work abroad. In the fall of 1883, he founded the New York Missionary Training College "to aid those who were called to Mission or Evangelistic work, either at home or in the foreign field." One year later, seven students from the first class set sail for the Congo. This school became an important way-station for individuals like Carrie Bates, who went to New York to engage in city missions work after her healing at Judd's Faith-Rest Cottage. For three years prior to departing as a missionary to India, Bates studied at Simpson's college while also carrying out a ministry to residents of New York's tenement buildings.[33]

During the International Conference for Divine Healing and True Holiness held in London in June of 1885, Simpson articulated his conviction that divine healing and the cause of foreign missions were integrally related. "This gospel of healing is inseparably linked with the evangelizing of the world," he proclaimed to his fellow attendees. "God has given it to us as a testimony to the nations, and God's work wants thousands and thousands of men and women to go to Africa, and China, and India, and live Him there." This message resonated with a number of conference participants, including Elizabeth Baxter, who agreed to travel to the United States in the fall in order to assist Simpson in conducting a series of conventions on the topics of "Christian Life, Divine Healing, and Evangelistic and Missionary work." The first of these gatherings was held October 5–9, 1885, in New York City. From there the conveners, including Simpson, Baxter, Carrie Judd, and a number of others, went to Philadelphia to conduct a similar convention at the Kemuel Home from October 20 to 23. They then moved on to Buffalo, where they met in the local YMCA building. Over the next several weeks, the entourage journeyed to Pittsburgh, where they were hosted by the Third Presbyterian Church; to Chicago, where they gathered in the First Methodist Church; and finally to Detroit, where they convened at Woodward Avenue Congregational.[34]

At the Buffalo convention, Baxter gave an address on "The Gospel of Healing" that emphasized the connection between miracles of healing and "the great commission for missionary enterprise." Drawing on the text from Mark 16 in which Jesus commanded the disciples, "Go ye into all the world, and preach the gospel to every creature" and told them that "signs" such as the healing of the sick would follow them, Baxter argued that "wherever the Gospel should be preached, there should be healing, as a testimony that God is the living God, that He is among the people, that he is unchanged, that Jesus Christ is the same to-day and forever." Furthermore, Baxter contended, the commission to "preach the gospel" applied to every believer. Turning to the story of Pentecost in the book of Acts, Baxter noted that "the apostles, the laymen, the men and the women were sent out together to tell everybody of Jesus, the Savior for spirit, and for soul, and for body." All Christians, regardless of ministerial status or gender, were called to spread the good news, a message that, in her view, encompassed both spiritual salvation and physical restoration.[35]

Other speakers at the Buffalo convention corroborated Baxter's assertion that Jesus intended healing to play a crucial role in his disciples' efforts to proclaim the gospel "world-wide." In addition to revealing God's power to the unbelieving heathens and signifying that Christianity included good news for both soul and body, divine healing enabled believers "to rise up and go to work for Christ." If every Christian were "to go, and in some way or another preach the Gospel which God sends to every creature," as Baxter suggested, many would need an infusion of divine power in order to carry out this Great Commission. "That is why the Lord wants to heal you," Simpson declared. "He wants the service of your body; He is losing more than you by your long confinement." In fact, he maintained, God would withhold physical restoration from those who were unwilling to participate in "the good work" to which healing ought to lead. "He will not heal you on your back, you must arise, take up your bed, and walk, and go forth, and minister in His name," Simpson asserted. "Remember this! It is as you take it and use it for God's work that the healing is given to you." Healing, in other words, was equivalent with "the power to go forth and *minister*."[36]

While leaders such as Simpson and Baxter suggested that recipients of divine healing could fulfill their calling to preach the gospel and minister to others in a variety of ways, their zeal for foreign missions, coupled with the broader evangelical enthusiasm for spreading the good news to the nations, made this avenue of service an alluring one among former invalids seeking to employ their newfound health and strength for God. For some, like Helen Dawlly, healing provided an opportunity to fulfill a longstanding desire to become a missionary. Others attributed their calling to foreign fields more directly to an encounter with the Great Physician. One of the most celebrated beneficiaries of faith cure—Lucy Drake—admitted that she could never muster up much interest in "the heathen" prior to her healing, despite the fact that missions had been "a subject of daily conversation" during her childhood on account of her "father being a minister." One day, after years of suffering from ill-health while engaging in "evangelistic work," Drake recalled, "I went to my chamber to pour out my heart to my Saviour, and, as I was

doing so, the question came over me, 'Will you give your interest for a lost world?'"
Drake agreed, and several years following her healing was on her way to Basim,
India, where she established a mission station that eventually became the center of
operations for Cullis's "Faith-work" in India. After her marriage in 1879 to fellow
missionary and founder of the Ocean Grove Camp Meeting, Methodist minister
William B. Osborn, she eventually returned to the United States. In March of 1885,
she founded a missionary training school in Niagara Falls, Canada—just across the
border from Judd's Faith-Rest Cottage. Judd publicized this school in *Triumphs of
Faith* and also invited Drake Osborn to lead a monthly meeting on the subject of
foreign missions at her home in Buffalo. Invalids staying at Judd's faith home were
encouraged to attend these gatherings, which were also open to the wider public.
It was during her tenure as matron of Faith-Rest Cottage that Dawlly first encountered Drake Osborn and heard about the missionary training school. After spending a week with Drake Osborn, Dawlly decided to enroll. A little over one year later,
in the fall of 1887, she embarked for India.[37]

Dawlly departed on her mission under the auspices of two newly founded organizations: the Christian Alliance and the Evangelical Missionary Alliance. Conceived under Simpson's leadership at an Old Orchard Beach convention during
the summer of 1886 and formally established in the summer of 1887, these two
interrelated alliances were born out of a desire to "send the full gospel"—a message that included "four essential truths: Salvation, Complete sanctification, Divine
healing, Christ's personal and premillennial coming"—"to the neglected millions
of heathen lands." Although these two associations formally merged in 1897 and
adopted a denominational polity beginning in 1926, the founding members did
not aim to organize a separate denomination. "The Christian Alliance," Simpson
explained, "is designed to be a simple and fraternal union of all who hold in common the fullness of Jesus in His present grace and coming glory. It is not intended
in any way to be an engine of division or antagonism in the churches, but, on the
contrary, to embrace Evangelical Christians of every name who hold this common
faith and life." The Evangelical Missionary Alliance operated in tandem with the
Christian Alliance and was also interdenominational in character. While neither
group sought to promote separatism or disharmony, they did aspire to emphasize
what Simpson called the "special truths" that were "opposed by many conservative Christians" and to "cherish and deepen" the "chords of spiritual unity" among
those from different denominations who held these beliefs in common.[38]

By adopting an interdenominational organizational structure, the Christian
and Evangelical Missionary Alliances succeeded in incorporating many leaders of
the faith cure movement within a formal association that also affirmed the link

between divine healing, evangelistic work, and foreign missions. The roster of founding officers for the Christian Alliance included A. B. Simpson as president; Cullis's associate Dr. George Peck, Charles Ryder of Rhode Island, John Cookman, and R. K. Carter as vice presidents; Sarah Beck, the overseer of Kemuel Home in Philadelphia, and Mary Morehead, who ran Bethany Faith Home in Pittsburgh as members of the executive committee; and Carrie Judd as recording secretary. Many of the other individuals on the officers list, such as John Haugh, Henry Naylor, and E. G. Selchow had also embraced God as the Great Physician. As the Christian and Evangelical Missionary Alliances expanded in the months and years following their founding, many additional supporters of divine healing participated in local branches. A. J. Gordon served as one of the main speakers alongside Simpson, Ryder, and Cookman at a three-day convention of the Christian Alliance in Boston in January of 1889, for example. Mrs. H. J. Furlong and Miss A. S. Jordan, both of whom had been "marvelously healed by the Lord," helped to preside over a "flourishing branch" of the Christian Alliance in Chicago. Anna Prosser joined Carrie Judd in conducting weekly meetings of the Alliance's Buffalo branch. In his text, *Twenty-Five Wonderful Years, 1889–1914: A Popular Sketch of the Christian and Missionary Alliance,* George Pardington, who was himself an early participant in the Alliance as well as an ardent supporter of divine healing, highlighted the overlap between the two movements. "Of the many Christians from evangelical churches who have become members of the Alliance perhaps the majority have come into the movement through a definite experience of physical healing," Pardington asserted. "Most of our missionaries on the foreign field and our leaders and workers at home have been healed of serious and in many instances incurable diseases. Indeed, there is scarcely an Alliance member throughout the world who does not know Christ as the Great Physician."[39]

From the day that Dawlly set sail for India, the Christian and Evangelical Missionary Alliances provided a network of support for many recipients of divine healing who believed they were being called to serve as foreign missionaries. By 1893, Pardington reported, the Alliance was supporting forty-seven missionaries in India, a team of pioneer evangelists in Japan, a number of workers in various parts of China, and several mission stations in the Sudan and Congo regions of Africa. A large number of these early Alliance missionaries, as Pardington's account shows, were women. Of the thirty-six missionaries to India that Pardington memorialized in his history, twenty-four were women, at least twelve of whom were unmarried when they left the United States. In part because of the urgency that their premillennialist eschatology conveyed on preaching the gospel to all nations, leaders of the Alliance did not require women to be married in order to serve in foreign locales. Nor did they restrict women's activities on the mission field to working exclusively with native women and children or to overseeing the domestic needs of missionary families. Although many early Alliance missionaries adopted the increasingly influential missions ideology that characterized women as uniquely suited for evangelizing native women whose families or cultures required them to remain secluded, the Alliance's official policy offered female missionaries equal opportunities to engage in the work of evangelism among indigenous populations. In fact, Simpson's conviction that God desired "to emphasize and utilize . . . the ministry of women . . . both in the home and foreign fields" represented one of the driving motivations behind his initial call for a new "undenominational alliance." When he first floated the idea for the Alliance at the Old Orchard Convention in the summer of 1886, for example, Simpson argued for an interpretation of the Bible that gave women an important role in spreading the gospel and exhorted participants to join him in his efforts to make the gathering "a place and time of liberty and freedom for our sisters in the Lord Jesus Christ." "I am inclined to think, dear brothers," he declared, "that both at home and on the field our sisters have the best of it."[40]

The Alliance's attitude toward female missionaries—both foreign and domestic, single and married—was good news for women such as Dawlly and Carrie Bates, whom the Alliance sent out to join Dawlly in India in the fall of 1889. Both of these women believed that God had raised them up from "years of suffering invalidism" in order to engage, first in urban reform and evangelistic efforts, and then in foreign missions work. Through their connection with the Christian and Evangelical Missionary Alliances, Dawlly, Bates, and many others like them gained access to a wide range of potential donors to fund their missionary endeavors as well as to a community of like-minded believers who endorsed their efforts to spread a gospel message that included both spiritual salvation and physical restoration. By formalizing the connection between divine healing, foreign missions, and belief in Christ's imminent return, these organizations offered women as well as men avenues for engaging in the energetic ministries on behalf of others that the devotional ethic of acting faith required.[41]

In his commemorative text, Pardington often praised God for preserving the health and vitality of Alliance workers who ministered to the residents of city slums as well as those who preached the good news to "the heathen" amid "dangerous" climates and "other perils and trying conditions." He also acknowledged, however, that many of these individuals—even those who had experienced miraculous healings through the Great Physician—struggled with ongoing bouts of illness and

The 1891 Graduating Class of the New York Missionary Training Institute, shows more female than male graduates. Courtesy of the Christian and Missionary Alliance National Archives.

sometimes even chronic pain. "Whatever the explanation," he stated, "it is a fact that of those who take Christ as their Healer some are not healed of their diseases or delivered from their infirmities in the sense that the diseases wholly disappear or the infirmities are entirely removed." For persons such as these, Pardington suggested, engaging in "aggressive work" among the urban masses or the foreign multitudes served as a strategy for rising "above the power of disease and the weight of infirmity." Some, he explained, have "a paradoxical experience. Instead of being bedridden or helpless invalids, they keep going in the strength of Jesus, not only carrying their own burdens but stretching out a helping hand to help others." In their efforts to mitigate the spiritual oppression and physical suffering of others, in other words, individuals often found a means for assuaging the ongoing pain that accompanied their attempt to claim divine healing for themselves.[42]

Despite her healing through the prayer of faith, for example, Helen Dawlly frequently "broke down" as the result of her "excessive work" on the mission field. Nevertheless, Dawlly pressed on for several years without relenting. After her death in February of 1893, Jennie Fuller wrote a tribute celebrating Dawlly's life, and especially her determination to serve God and others regardless of her own enduring struggles with ill-health. "She did all her work in much physical suffering," Fuller recalled. Her pain was so severe, Fuller attested, that "many a young woman in America or England who suffered as much as she did, would have felt it an excuse for idleness at home, and would not have dared to press into the needy fields abroad." For Dawlly, however, action proved more attractive than indolence as a strategy for coping with the persistence of bodily affliction. Working to ease the sufferings of others, as Fuller put it, "swallowed up her own life of pain."[43]

Conclusion

Jennie Smith died in 1924. For forty-six years following her healing, Smith had crisscrossed the nation as a "railroad evangelist," seeking to bring salvation and sobriety to those "phases of humanity" who had been "neglected spiritually." In the final installment of her autobiography, published four years before her death, Smith recounted the "incidents and experiences" that had marked her ministry after her cure in 1878. Although she briefly alluded to her remarkable recovery in the preface to this memoir, nearly all of the episodes she described in the text focused on the spiritual conversion of hardened sinners rather than the physical restoration of afflicted sufferers. Whenever invalids or sick persons appear in the narrative, they usually remain confined to their beds. Some, such as Smith's infant niece and her co-worker of more than fourteen years, died from their diseases. Smith herself struggled with attacks of rheumatism and bouts of illness on several occasions and often admitted to needing rest from her labors.[1]

Smith's relative silence on the subject of faith cure following her initial healing set her apart from her friend Carrie Judd Montgomery, who continued to advocate divine healing until her own death in 1946. Although Smith maintained cordial relations with leaders of the divine healing movement like Judd Montgomery, A. B. Simpson, and R. K. Carter and sometimes even spoke at their conventions, faith cure never became a central focus of her own ministry. While she sometimes prayed for healing when she fell sick and testified that the "the Holy Spirit" made her well so that she could accomplish the work God had given her to do, her efforts on behalf of others were primarily evangelistic. Her own cure in 1878, she explained at a New York Gospel Tabernacle gathering eight years later, prompted "a special baptism of the Holy Ghost for service, for my life work. . . . Since then I keep hearing the Macedonian cry. There is so much to do and we are doing so little." Although she never disavowed divine healing, Smith implied that the work of preaching the good news of salvation to lost souls took precedence over propagating the doctrines of faith cure.[2]

While Smith's tendency to elevate the gospel of spiritual redemption over the hope of bodily restoration distinguished her from many of her peers in the divine healing movement, she was not the only recipient of faith cure to adopt this position. Lucy Drake Osborn, whose experience of divine healing was perhaps even more celebrated than Smith's, devoted herself primarily to urban relief work and foreign missions after her recovery. Like Smith, Osborn maintained contact with advocates of faith cure such as her mentor Charles Cullis and later worked alongside Carrie Judd to promote the cause of missions, but she never embarked on a healing ministry of her own or directly endorsed the efforts of these colleagues to foster the spread of faith healing.[3]

By the mid-1880s, even some of faith cure's most vocal champions had begun to moderate their emphasis on the ministry of healing as they shifted their attention toward social reform, evangelism, and foreign missions. An article published in the October 1885 issue of Simpson's *Word, Work and World* indicated that "other departments" of the New York Gospel Tabernacle were of "greater importance" than the Berachah healing home. "The work of the Tabernacle," the author declared, "embraces a large amount of evangelistic and missionary work, and the work is thus kept from getting into a single groove, in the line of faith healing alone. Indeed, this is recognized as but a subordinate part of a much greater whole." The founding of the Christian Alliance in 1887 confirmed the status of divine healing as one of the "four great essential truths of the Gospel of Christ," but placed the doctrine third in the list, behind the more vital tenets of salvation and complete sanctification. "More than ever is it necessary to hold Divine healing in its true place in inseparable connection with personal union with our Lord Jesus, and personal faith and holiness," wrote a correspondent for *Word, Work and World* in a report of the events surrounding the Alliance's establishment. As the Alliance matured, leaders placed even greater stress on faith healing's tertiary standing. In 1896, Simpson himself stated that "the place of divine healing in the whole system of spiritual truth . . . is a very important place, but it is also a very subordinate place. It is not the prime truth of the gospel, nor is it even the first truth that we have to testify to in these days of witnessing. It is a supplementary truth."[4]

The experiences of the Alliance's early missionaries on the foreign field accounted in part for the growing tendency of leaders like Simpson to insist that divine healing take a "supplemental" and "subordinate" position in the preaching and practice of Christianity. Although R. K. Carter asserted that Simpson had always held that "spiritual matters" were more important than divine healing and argued that he "never allowed the subject to claim more than a fraction of time or attention," Carter also admitted that "the failure of the holiest missionaries to withstand the African fever purely by faith" had prompted Simpson to play down the importance of divine healing even more adamantly. Many of the Alliance's first missionaries, Carter noted, "passed away, one after another" because they refused to take medicine when they contracted malaria, believing that "the Lord would keep them." Eventually, the Alliance moderated its policy on remedies and began screening candidates to make sure that missionaries met "some sort of physical qualifications for the work." By the late 1890s, Carter reported, most missionaries "used quinine and other remedies freely." Although Simpson continued to advocate divine healing in this period, his "utterances and considerations of the subject," Carter contended, had "moderated greatly from his earlier deliverances."[5]

No case of a missionary's death after rejecting "means" and medical assistance provoked more outrage among faith cure's critics or more consternation among the movement's exponents than the demise of twenty-one-year-old Charlie Miller on May 7, 1885. Only several months after arriving in Africa to serve alongside prominent Holiness leader and Methodist Bishop William Taylor in his missionary effort, Miller contracted malaria. For three weeks, Miller fought the fever, "refusing aid of any kind, testifying freely and continually that his trust was only in God, asserting that 'a steady faith wins,' and declaring that he did not have the fever." Despite the mission doctor's insistence that his body temperature had reached 105 and the urgings of his comrades, including Bishop Taylor himself, Miller refused to allow the physician to prescribe remedies. When "typhoid set in," he finally took medicine, but by then it was too late. After a week of delirium, Miller died.[6]

For detractors of divine healing such as James Buckley, Miller's death proved that faith cure was a dangerous form of fanaticism. Characterizing Miller as "a martyr to superstition which he mistook for faith," Buckley blamed proponents of divine healing for "the suicide of this young man." Skeptics like Buckley were not the only ones who attributed Miller's death to misguided belief. Even staunch supporters of faith cure found Miller's uncompromising adherence to a particular formulation of divine healing deeply troubling. In a letter describing Miller's illness, decline, and death, Bishop Taylor lamented the loss of such a promising worker and expressed his conviction that Miller was the "innocent victim of an insidious error." Having embraced "extreme views of certain good men who claim to be expositors of faith healing," Taylor wrote, Miller ignored the medical care that might have preserved his life. Although Taylor confirmed his own belief "in the direct healing of the body by faith," he rejected the notion that "we are justified in refusing to trust God in the use of well-tested remedies by means of medical skill." Taylor also took aim at "extremists" who based their refusal of medicine on a conviction that Christ's atoning work on the cross provided for "a present 'full salvation' for the body as well as the soul." While he too believed that Christ's atonement included a provision for bodily as well as spiritual restoration, Taylor insisted that the work of physical redemption would not be completed until the resurrection. By arguing that the "perfect healing of the body" and the "perfect healing of the soul" were inseparably connected and available to all in this life, Taylor charged, certain proponents of divine healing made miraculous cures dependent on an individual's ability to exercise faith in the promises of God rather than on God's providential decision to heal according to "the Divine will."[7]

Taylor's disagreement with Charlie Miller and those he labeled "extremists" became increasingly common among proponents of faith cure who took issue with the idea that spiritual holiness and bodily wholeness were inseparable parts of the gospel message, universally applicable to all persons in every situation. The most forceful apologies for the controversial "healing in the atonement" theology, Robert L. Stanton's *Gospel Parallelisms: Illustrated in the Healing of Body and Soul* and R. K. Carter's *The Atonement for Sin and Sickness; or, A Full Salvation for Soul and Body,* both appeared in 1884, just prior to Miller's departure for Africa. Yet in the same year, William McDonald, a longtime supporter of Cullis who succeeded Inskip as the second president of the National Holiness Association, began to publish editorials in the Methodist paper *The Christian Witness and Advocate of Bible Holiness,* warning his constituency against putting "modern miracles" such as the "healing of the sick in answer to prayer . . . in the foreground." Not only was salvation from sin "a thousand times more important than the healing of the body," McDonald argued, but the notion that "bodily healing by faith sustains the same relation to the atonement that sin does" represented an "extravagant" and "illogical" error. It was precisely this kind of "unscriptural" reasoning, McDonald charged, that misled Charlie Miller and cost him his life. Echoing Bishop Taylor, McDonald affirmed his belief in divine healing but insisted that the blessing of health was a special privilege extended to human beings "under certain conditions," according to God's sovereign will rather than a general promise for all Christians.[8]

While the tragedy of Miller's death prompted leaders like McDonald and Taylor to rein in their theologies of divine healing, some had offered qualified positions prior to this heartrending event. In 1879 Daniel Steele wrote to Jennie Smith, who at that point was still confined to her invalid cot, "that the gift of healing has been in the Church for all ages"; nevertheless, he rejected the conclusion that lack of faith was the only adequate explanation for a failure to be healed through prayer. Warning Smith of the "danger of fanaticism" associated with divine healing, Steele suggested that restoring the sick to health was not always God's will. Distinguishing between "the grace of faith" for salvation, which was "required of every soul," and the "gift of faith" that accompanied healing, Steele asserted that the latter was not "a general promise of the Bible" available to all but an "occasional" gift that God "sovereignly bestowed" by the Holy Spirit "to every one severally as he will." For this reason, Steele insisted, Smith need not worry that she remained bedridden because of unbelief. Several years later, in an address to the Boston Methodist Preachers' Meeting, Steele clarified his position, stating that healing was "not the result of ordinary faith in God, but rather of an extraordinary faith inwrought by the Holy Spirit for this specific purpose."[9]

Although leading proponents of divine healing like Steele had articulated a more moderate position regarding the extent to which Christians ought to expect God to cure them in answer to prayer as early as 1879, theirs remained the minority viewpoint. Throughout the 1880s, more vocal advocates such as A. B. Simpson, Carrie Judd, and R. K. Carter vigorously promoted the idea that healing was available to everyone who asked for it, since God always willed the health of believers. That these two competing theologies remained in play during this decade reveals the multiformity of the divine healing movement and suggests that the lack of any kind of official governing body or formal authority structure to adjudicate core issues made the development of a coherent and consistent theological framework difficult to achieve. Like the larger Holiness and Higher Life movements out of which it emerged, divine healing attracted a broad range of followers from a wide variety of denominational and regional backgrounds. While this diversity generated productive ecumenical energy that helped to inspire unique avenues of ministry as well as new cooperative efforts in the areas of evangelism, missions, and relief work, it also spawned institutional strife within existing denominational bodies and produced theological tensions that ultimately destabilized the movement's cohesion.[10]

By the 1890s, the uneasy synthesis among disparate factions within the divine healing movement had begun to unravel. The deaths of Charles Cullis on June 18, 1892, and A. J. Gordon on February 2, 1895, both of whom had served as mediating figures in the debate between those who advocated the notion that healing was a provision of Christ's atonement and those who urged a more restrained view, eroded the tenuous middle ground that these two elder statesmen had helped to maintain. While both Cullis and Gordon had cautiously embraced the idea that healing was a universally and presently accessible benefit of Christ's salvific work on the cross, they tempered their endorsements with repeated affirmations of God's sovereignty and insisted on preserving a place for the inscrutability of the divine will as a strategy for coping with the dilemma of unanswered prayer.[11]

The passing of these two influential leaders coincided with the emergence of more "radical" and "aggressive" exponents of "the Atonement theory" of healing—none of them more controversial or divisive than John Alexander Dowie. After emigrating from Australia to California in 1888, Dowie spent two years promoting divine healing along the western seaboard. Wherever he went, he established branches of the International Divine Healing Association, an organization he had founded several years prior to his arrival in the United States. In marked contrast to Cullis's Faith Work, the Christian Alliance, and even periodicals such as Judd's *Triumphs of Faith*, all of which aimed to promote both healing *and* holiness as well as rescue work, evangelistic outreach, and foreign missions, Dowie intentionally and emphatically limited the focus of his association to the advancement of divine healing. Although he eventually established a new denomination (the Christian Catholic Church) and a utopian community (Zion City, Illinois), both of which endorsed a broader range of theological propositions and reformist objectives in the late 1890s, Dowie concentrated almost exclusively on divine healing during his first eight years in the United States, even going so far as to criticize organizations like the Christian Alliance for diluting the importance of healing by incorporating it under the umbrella of the fourfold gospel. Comparing Dowie's ministry with that of most American teachers of faith healing, R. K. Carter noted that Dowie's presentation of the subject was "quite radical," and observed that "he gave the whole of his time, or most of it, to this one theme."[12]

While several leaders of the divine healing movement, including Carrie Judd Montgomery and her husband, George, embraced Dowie, some found his radicalism disconcerting. Even Carter, one of the most forceful apologists for the idea that healing was an integral part of the gospel message, eventually concluded that Dowie's explication of this doctrine and his emphasis on healing in general went too far. After a bout with malarial fever in 1888 left him with "a certain mysterious underlying weakness and inability to endure exertion," Carter sought prayer from Cullis, Simpson, and several others, but "the full healing did not come." In crisis, Carter turned to Dowie in 1890. Although Dowie was confident that he "felt the power of God" while laying hands upon Carter and expressed his certainty that his prayer would be effective, Carter did not receive the restoration he sought. This experience pushed Carter into a terrible state of "mental depression of nervous prostration" that endured for six months, until at last a physician friend convinced him to try a medicinal remedy. "Purely as an experiment," Carter recounted, "the medicine was taken and forgotten until a week or two later, when the writer waked up to the fact that the awful depression had gone, and a renewed sense of life and vigor that was simply delightful had taken its place." He then entered a season of "work and usefulness . . . which surpassed any similar time in his experience."[13]

As a result of this transformation, Carter began to reconsider his former views on divine healing. Turning to the scriptures, he began to reread the passages that he had used to bolster his teaching in *The Atonement for Sin and Sickness; or, A Full Salvation for Soul and Body.* Concluding that he had misinterpreted the Bible, Carter issued a retraction of his early work in which he declared that his defense of the atonement theory of healing had been a mistake. Published in 1897, Carter's *"Faith Healing" Reviewed After Twenty Years* included a point-by-point rebuttal of his prior position. Without disclaiming God's ability to work miracles of cure in the modern period, Carter agreed with McDonald and Steele that God granted healing as a "special favor" rather than as a "general provision in the Atonement for all believers." God might choose to heal "directly as a miraculous or unusual putting forth of His power," but very often God did not work in this way. Healing was thus a "subordinate matter" to salvation, an "incidental" rather than an "integral" part of the gospel.[14]

Carter's reexamination of scripture also led him to repudiate his original conviction that healing was a matter of "exercising faith" without regard for circumstances, feelings, or symptoms. All of the miraculous cures recorded in the New Testament, he argued in his later work, "were cases of full and complete healing." Those who approached Jesus or the apostles seeking physical restoration "were made perfectly whole" instantaneously, not instructed to act as if they were well while still suffering from the effects of their diseases. This scriptural study, combined with his own "downright inability" to claim healing and act faith in spite of ongoing pain, prompted Carter to declare that this "plan of action" was "all a mistake." "It is purely will power to attempt to act faith and make believe we are healed," he argued. Not only was this course of behavior misguided, it was often injurious and sometimes even fatal. Citing Charlie Miller's "heroic" efforts to "act faith," Carter asserted that his death offered "a solemn object lesson" to all who held the atonement theory of healing and consequently encouraged individuals "to say I believe, and not I feel."[15]

Admitting his own sense of responsibility for having "helped Miller to take the position he did," Carter urged other leaders of the divine healing movement to learn from his past errors and to revise their teaching on this point. By adopting a more moderate stance, he argued, proponents of faith cure would help prevent needless deaths like Miller's while also freeing suffering individuals from the uncertainty, confusion, and doubt they felt when the prayer of faith failed to bring relief. Although he rejoiced that some did experience physical restoration "by the direct power of God," Carter contended that "the very great majority" of those who sought healing by faith did not "receive the literal answer." After twenty years of participating in meetings for healing the sick and observing the "after results in cases of claimed healing," Carter conceded that "only a small per cent of the seekers after heath are *really and positively cured.*" To blame these apparent failures on the seekers themselves—most of whom were sincere Christians who endeavored to "take hold by faith" with their full strength—was "worse than foolish." Although Carter singled out Dowie as the most obvious offender in this regard, he also challenged Carrie Judd Montgomery and A. B. Simpson to admit that the atonement theory of healing led to the "irresistible" conclusion that unanswered prayers resulted "from some deficiency on the part of the subject" rather from the mystery of divine sovereignty.[16]

Finally, Carter asserted that advocates of the "extreme theory" of healing undermined the devotional ethic of active service to God that they sought to promote. Carter's own experience had convinced him that in many cases the practice of acting faith depleted a person's strength and hindered her ability to carry out the work that God had called her to undertake. For years, Carter recalled, he had "sought healing through faith, and used only the 'scriptural means' of prayer and anointing with oil, and had 'acted his faith' so desperately as many times to calmly take the platform and preach when sound medical opinion regarded it as very doubtful whether he would live through the effort." When he finally compromised and tried medicine, he was "speedily lifted" out of his enervated condition "and at once began to preach and work, accomplishing more in six months than he had been able to do in three years."[17]

While Carter claimed that "most of the leading teachers" of divine healing were "gradually coming to see that God does as He pleases, and what He pleases, and acts when He pleases, and that it is best for us not to be too dogmatic, or attempt to limit Him within our narrow lines," Dowie remained recalcitrant. In the same year that Carter issued his retraction, Dowie publicly condemned pharmacists and physicians as "poisoners and murders." On October 18, 1899, he preached his notorious sermon "Doctors, Drugs and Devils," inciting over two thousand physicians and medical students from the University of Chicago to riot in protest. The publicity that these events generated, on top of the negative press Dowie had received in 1895, when both he and his wife had been arrested on charges of practicing medicine without a license at the Zion Divine Healing Home they had established in 1894, further exacerbated the friction between Dowie and the faith-healing movement's more moderate proponents. Within this highly charged context, maintaining a mediating position on divine healing became increasingly difficult.[18]

The establishment of independent Holiness groups such as the Church of God (Anderson) in the early 1880s and the Fire-Baptized Holiness Association and the Church of God (Holiness) in the late 1890s, many of which vigorously promoted the notion that divine healing was a universally available benefit of Christ's atonement and encouraged followers to eschew all forms of medical treatment, also contributed to declining support for faith cure among more mainstream advocates of Holiness. "For Methodist evangelicals who sought to remain within the fold," historian Jonathan Baer has written, "qualified support for divine healing had become untenable" in light of the "fractiousness" and "radicalism" of the "come-outer" organizations. Paving the way for Pentecostalism, leaders of these separatist groups stressed Satan's agency in sickness to a greater degree than earlier apologists for divine healing had, interpreting miraculous cures as victories in a larger eschatological battle that was reaching its climax as the second coming of Christ drew near. Because bodily healings served as visible signs of Christ's power and authority over the devil's minions, they were accompanied by vivid and instantaneous physical manifestations.[19]

With the emergence and growth of Pentecostalism in the early twentieth century, this conception of faith cure became increasingly widespread, prompting some long-standing supporters of divine healing to become all the more circumspect about the place and practice of healing through faith in their own ministries. While a number of faith cure's earliest exponents, including Carrie and George Montgomery and Elizabeth Sisson, eventually embraced Pentecostalism, others— notably A. B. Simpson, George Pardington, and Mary Mossman—maintained their distance from the new movement and strove to distinguish their understanding of divine healing from the theology and practices being promoted by Pentecostals. Several weeks after Pentecostal revival broke out at Azusa Street in Los Angeles, for example, Alliance leaders complained in their annual report that the "many forms of fanaticism and extravagance that the year has brought to light" had thrown "discredit" on "the work of Divine Healing." Although they vowed to "be more true than ever to the sane and Scriptural doctrine of Divine Healing" in light of Pentecostal extremism, subsequent publications suggest that fulfilling their pledge became increasingly challenging. In the 1909 report, leaders described divine healing as a "distinguishing feature" of the Alliance but insisted that "the work is less sensational and spectacular and more a matter of habitual experience and normal Christian living." Several years later, in his 1914 history of the Alliance's first twenty-five years, longtime member George Pardington asserted that "while the truth of Divine Healing is made of great importance, it is held in strict subordination to the pre-eminent truths of salvation and holiness." After Simpson's death in 1919, his successor, Paul Rader, reaffirmed the Alliance's commitment to the four fold gospel but stressed the primacy of missions and evangelism. By 1920, the Alliance had closed all of its houses of healing, many of which had previously been converted to missionary retreats or rest homes for Christian workers. Although some healing evangelists ministered under the auspices of the Alliance in the ensuing decade, most leaders continued to downplay the doctrine.[20]

As a result of this increasing reticence among Alliance leaders as well as among those evangelicals who remained within "mainstream" denominations, divine healing became primarily associated with independent Holiness and Pentecostal churches during the early decades of the twentieth century. The rapid spread of these groups reshaped the divine healing movement in significant ways. Whereas late-nineteenth-century faith healing was an international and interdenominational phenomenon that flourished in large cities along the Atlantic seaboard, Pentecostalism prospered primarily in Midwestern and southern states, transferring the locus of divine healing away from urban centers like Boston, London, New York, and Philadelphia, to rural areas and smaller cities. Although Pentecostals continued to promote healing practices such as united prayer, laying on of hands, and anointing, they also ardently adopted ecstatic forms of worship such as trances, falling down in the spirit, and especially speaking in tongues, which earlier advocates of divine healing had rejected. Similarly, Pentecostals accorded a more prominent place to "healers" in the curative process than their predecessors in the faith cure movement had allowed. While evangelists like Maria Woodworth-Etter, who embraced Pentecostalism in 1912, always gave credit to God for the miraculous cures that took place during their revivals, they believed that particular people possessed the spiritual "gift" of healing and were therefore especially equipped to act as conduits of God's healing power. Finally, because Pentecostals placed such heavy stress on the cosmic significance of miraculous physical restorations in answer to prayer, the idiom of "power for service" that permeated the rhetoric of divine healing in the late nineteenth century was a far less prominent theme in Pentecostal discourse. Although Pentecostals frequently prayed for an "enduement of power," embraced the cause of world-wide evangelism with zealous energy, and sometimes engaged in efforts to alleviate the sufferings of the poor, their emphasis on the eschatological import of divine healing overshadowed the associations between miraculous cures and ministries of service that proponents such as Cullis, Simpson, and Judd Montgomery had so assiduously maintained. While bodies restored from crippling illnesses or brought back from the brink of death might engage in more active forms of godly work, their primary meaning, within the highly charged context of early Pentecostalism, was to display God's triumph over Satan. Fully inverting the conception of sanctified suffering that shaped Mary Rankin's experience of physical pain, Pentecostals suggested that somatic affliction was a sign of unvanquished evil or lurking sin, rather than a marker of spiritual holiness. Whereas Rankin's suffering flesh offered evidence of afflictive providence, symbolizing the presence and prerogative of the Almighty, Pentecostal theology implied that only perfectly healthy bodies could incarnate God's purity and power.[21]

The teaching and practice of divine healing among early-twentieth-century Pentecostals provoked the indignation of a diverse assortment of critics. Members of the medical community, secular reporters, and spokespersons for liberal Protestantism all derided Pentecostalism in general, saving some of their harshest denunciations for the ways leaders and participants imagined the meanings of sickness, health, and healing. Many of the most ardent opponents of Pentecostal healing, however, came from the ranks of the emerging fundamentalist movement. While some fundamentalists, notably figures like Rueben Torrey who had their roots in the late-nineteenth-century Higher Life movement, continued to champion divine healing during the early decades of the twentieth century, others rejected healing wholesale. Although usually at odds with Protestant modernists, theologians such as Princeton Seminary's Benjamin Warfield found common cause with customary adversaries on the issue of modern miracles of healing. Like his liberal counterparts, Warfield argued that the psychological theory of suggestion explained the vast majority of seemingly supernatural cures. Reasserting the classic Reformed belief that biblical miracles ceased with the apostolic age, Warfield insisted that God worked healing through natural means, not through miraculous intervention. Although his primary targets were Pentecostals, Warfield also criticized advocates of divine healing like Dowie, and even A. J. Gordon, all of whom, in his view, promoted a flawed understanding of God's providence that threatened both the physical and spiritual health of those who embraced it. Going beyond moderate proponents of faith cure such as Carter, McDonald, and Steele, who maintained that God's will regarding sickness and healing remained a mystery but continued to resist the notion that God was the author of suffering, Warfield reaffirmed the doctrine of afflictive providence in unmitigated terms. "Sickness is often the proof of special favor from God," he wrote in his text, *Counterfeit Miracles*, "and it always comes to His children from His Fatherly hand, and always in His loving pleasure works together with all other things which befall God's children, for good."[22]

While Warfield championed the ideal of sanctified suffering with a zeal befitting a front-man for fundamentalism, his arguments against divine healing echoed the complaints of a steady stream of detractors who, throughout the movement's history, insisted that the doctrines and practices of faith cure imperiled the bodies, minds, and souls of its devotees. By uncoupling physical affliction from spiritual sanctification, critics such as Methodist minister George Milton Hammell charged, advocates of divine healing promoted false hopes "among innumerable invalids who lie in the weakness of chronic disease," and thereby endorsed a form of Christianity that "mocks suffering, patience and faith." Theologian George H. Hepworth asserted that faith cure relied on a "magical theory of religion," and complained that the movement's proponents played "on the imagination of the pious in a very dangerous fashion." By attempting to circumvent God's sovereignty in a presumptuous fashion, he claimed, faith cure fostered "incredible fanaticism" over against "a pure and undefiled religion." Even physicians complained about the theological and pastoral implications of rejecting the doctrine of afflictive providence and the devotional ethic of passive resignation to physical suffering. "To promise present cure, and brand the failure to obtain it as unbelief, is a shocking cruelty, which cannot be too strongly opposed; and the recoil of the shattered faith in which it often results is painful to contemplate," wrote British physician Alfred Schofield in the early 1890s. "It is good to feel our limitations, and patiently to bear our infirmities, to feel the advance of age and the approach of death; and better to cultivate a spirit of filial submission than to talk of claiming and demanding immediate cures."[23]

One of the most trenchant critiques of faith cure's attitude toward pain, illness, and healing came, not from a minister or a physician, but from a lay woman who had once wholeheartedly embraced Jesus as the Great Physician and encouraged others to claim the promises contained in James 5 rather than resorting to medical remedies. During the early years of Charles Cullis's ministry in Boston, Elizabeth Annabelle Needham had worked alongside her husband, Irish-born evangelist George C. Needham, who served as the first editor of Cullis's journal, *Times of Refreshing*. In 1881 Elizabeth indicated her own support for the teaching and practice of divine healing in an article entitled "Jehovah Rophi—The Lord Our

Healer," which was published in A. J. Gordon's periodical, *The Watchword*. After several years of observing the progress of faith cure in Boston, however, Needham withdrew her endorsement of the movement. In 1891, she published *Mrs. Whilling's Faith Cure*, a parody of divine healing based on her own interactions with leaders like Cullis and Gordon as well as with sick persons who had prayed for healing, given up medicines, and endeavored to act faith, but who remained plagued by disease and discomfort. As a result of encounters such as these, Needham concluded that faith cure, rather than bringing bodily health and spiritual wholeness to those who sought these blessings, "twisted the heads and disturbed the hearts of hundreds of Christians; and robbed more invalids of the glory and peace of acquiescence in God's sovereign will than any deceit the Devil has ever perpetrated." Renouncing "the theory that 'continual health of the body is the highest state of religious life,'" Needham insisted that "God's purposes in sickness are various and majestic" and lambasted the "faith-healers" who "degrade and despise and depreciate and dishonor this awful and effectual instrument in the hand of the Almighty God." Although she never discouraged ailing sufferers from praying for healing, Needham insisted that resigned endurance represented the proper Christian response to affliction. Pain, in her view, was an integral part of the spiritual life. "The Christian is encouraged to beat his [body] black and blue," she declared. "The Christian is encouraged to take pleasure in tribulations, in persecutions, in necessities, in distresses. . . . The Christian is glorified when he is made a spectacle to the world, to men, and to angels."[24]

Needham's robust reclamation of the significance of somatic suffering in the Christian life suggests that the question of how believers ought to interpret and cope with illness, infirmity, and pain remained an unsettled issue among Protestants in the late nineteenth century. Although many participants in the evangelical faith cure movement embraced and embodied a model of spiritual experience that valorized active service to God rather than passive acceptance of affliction, others found this approach to the dilemma of corporeal disease and distress deeply disturbing. Rather than resolving the tensions that arose over the meaning and practice of suffering in this period, the divine healing movement sparked a vigorous and ongoing debate about the relationship between physical illness and spiritual health that continued well into the twentieth and twenty-first centuries.

During the 1910s and 20s, Pentecostal evangelists such as Maria Woodworth-Etter, John G. Lake, Smith Wigglesworth, Fred F. Bosworth, and Aimee Semple McPherson proclaimed the promise of divine healing to thousands across the United States and beyond through their large-scale revival campaigns. Millions more heard about God's wonder-working healing power over the airwaves as pioneers like Bosworth and McPherson took advantage of radio technologies to broadcast their gospel message. Although Pentecostals suffered some setbacks during the Great Depression of the 1930s, they again rose to prominence after World War II, when the revival crusades of evangelists William T. Branham and Oral Roberts thrust Pentecostal divine healing back into the national spotlight. In 1955, Roberts began televising his healing services, endeavoring to introduce the Great Physician to audiences outside Pentecostal circles. According to historian Paul Chappell, Roberts' weekly broadcast was "the number one syndicated religious program on television for almost thirty years" and helped give birth to the charismatic revival that swept through many "mainline" Protestant and Roman Catholic churches in the 1960s. Through the ministries of individuals such as evangelist Kathryn Kuhlman and author-teacher Francis MacNutt, both influential figures in the ecumenical charismatic movement, the message of miraculous healing became widely accepted among believers from a broad range of denominational backgrounds. Since the mid-1970s, the growth of independent charismatic churches like those associated with the Vineyard Fellowship has prompted many "mainstream" evangelicals to embrace the notion that the supernatural gifts of the New Testament—including glossolalia and healing—remain available for contemporary believers who desire and are willing to claim them. During this same period, televangelists such as Benny Hinn and advocates of the "Word of Faith," or "Positive Confession" movement have persuaded large numbers of American Christians to lay hold of "all the rights and privileges" that are theirs as "children of God"—including prosperity, health, and healing.[25]

Practitioners of nineteenth-century faith cure lived in a vastly different social, cultural, and theological world than contemporary Pentecostal and charismatic proponents of faith healing, yet it is possible to discern some common themes across the historical divide. Like their predecessors, current champions of divine healing aim to provide Christians with a means for comprehending and contending with physical affliction. The dilemmas they face also echo those that troubled their forbears: how to explain various forms of "failure" such as recalcitrant invalidism, recurring illnesses, and repeated relapse; what to recommend in the way of medical treatment; how to define and defend what counts as "true" Christian healing amidst an array of doctrinal possibilities and devotional permutations. Finally, recent attempts to promote faith in the Great Physician, like those that flourished in the latter decades of the nineteenth century, have provoked an assortment of reactions, ranging from enthusiastic appreciation, to cautious curiosity, to utter hostility.

Were late-nineteenth-century advocates of divine healing able to assess their own legacy, it is likely that they would rejoice in the fact that faith in the Great Physician remains so strong in the postmodern world, yet bewail the flamboyant performances of some popular evangelists and wince at the tendency of certain prominent figures to link the "promises" of physical rejuvenation and financial success. Despite its prominence throughout most of the twentieth century, the "health and wealth" gospel was never a part of nineteenth-century faith cure. With the exception of Carrie Judd Montgomery, who married a moneyed man after her miraculous recovery, most leaders of divine healing ended up worse off financially as a result of their involvement with the movement. Although Baptist pastor Russell Conwell preached his famous sermon "Acres of Diamonds" numerous times in the 1880s and 1890s, it was not until well into the twentieth century that some proponents of faith healing began to proclaim that Christ's atoning work on the cross guaranteed eternal salvation, freedom from bodily pain, and abundant financial gain.[26]

But if individuals like Sarah Mix, Charles Cullis, and A. B. Simpson would, in all probability, reject the notion that believers have a right to expect material riches as part of their Christian inheritance, they would be hard-pressed to deny some resemblance between their own understanding of divine healing and the view advanced by champions of the prosperity gospel. By maintaining that physical health was a universal blessing accessible to all who offered the "prayer of faith" and acted according to their conviction, these late-nineteenth-century teachers unwittingly paved the way for the emergence of the more instrumental concept of prayer and healing associated with numerous figures over the course of the twentieth century, most recently with "faith movement" spokespersons such as Kenneth Hagin, Kenneth Copeland, and Frederick K. C. Price, all of whom insist that perfect health is available to anyone who will "name it and claim it."[27]

The remarkable popularity of these "Word of Faith" preachers suggests that their version of the gospel message resonates with many people who are longing to obtain the "promised" blessings of bodily healing and wholeness. As countless contemporary commentators have observed, modern individuals (and modern Americans in particular) have become increasingly preoccupied with physical fitness over the course of the twentieth century. For some, "fitness" connotes freedom from disabling forms of illness or infirmity. For others, it involves the pursuit of corporeal perfection through participation in diet and exercise regimens, experimentation with ever more innovative therapies and surgical techniques, partaking of pharmaceutical treatments that promise to augment athletic prowess or sexual performance, and the embrace of a constantly expanding array of products designed to improve personal hygiene or enhance physical attractiveness. At another level, the quest for healthier, even superior bodies has fueled the advancement of medical research aimed not only at eradicating crippling diseases and genetic conditions but also at developing technologies that would, among other things, allow for human cloning and the production of "designer children."

Clearly, many factors have contributed to this pervasive and multifaceted obsession with bodily fitness, corporeal health, and the prospect of genomic perfection: extraordinary scientific discoveries, faith in the ideal of progress, and the forces of consumer capitalism not least among them. But as Marie Griffith has so aptly argued in her own study of twentieth-century "body fixations" among American Christians, Protestant beliefs and practices—particularly those with roots in nineteenth-century health reform and healing movements—have played an "indispensable role" in shaping and continuously reshaping the "widespread cultural obsession with human health, longevity, and what has blandly been termed wellness." While Griffith focuses primarily on the ways in which New Thought teachings and devotional regimens contributed to the rise of modern evangelical diet and fitness culture and shows how these contemporary religious weight-loss programs are implicated in the tendency to esteem "slender, white bodies over other kinds," I would like to suggest that the faith cure movement of the late nineteenth century also bears some responsibility for promoting an ideal of physical fitness that has profoundly influenced American attitudes toward and experiences of corporeal infirmity and suffering. By espousing a devotional ethic that associated sanctity with able-bodied service rather than resigned endurance of affliction, proponents of divine healing inadvertently fueled the conviction that "God favors fitness over sickliness, healthy Christians over their ill or flaccid brethren."[28]

Examining the unintended consequences of late-nineteenth-century faith cure reminds us that coping with corporeal affliction is always a highly charged and inescapably complex enterprise. By exposing the connections between the devotional ethics of divine healing and subsequent valuations of sickness and health, I do not mean to cast the faith cure movement or its legacy in an entirely, or even primarily, negative light. Instead, I have endeavored to show that making sense of suffering involves a host of complicated negotiations that rarely, if ever, resolve the cultural, social, and theological tensions that arise whenever people confront the predicaments of illness, pain, and death. Certainly, the ideal of sanctified suffering that proponents of divine healing worked so hard to modify had its downsides too—especially for women such as Carrie Judd who found the prescription of patient submission physically excruciating, professionally stifling, and spiritually oppressive. As this study has demonstrated, participating in faith cure helped individuals like

Judd and many others to overcome unbearable illnesses and to engage in admirable efforts to reform the meaning and experience of affliction in the lives of others. In so doing, they made possible new modes of being and acting that carried with them both beneficial advantages and troubling costs.

Acknowledging both the positive contributions and the distressing repercussions of divine healing will, I hope, alert contemporary interlocutors to the potential rewards and risks that accompany any attempt to deal with the dilemmas of sickness and suffering. As I indicated in the introduction, current debates about the role of religious belief and practice in promoting bodily health and healing reveal that the experience of physical affliction remains a challenging and perplexing issue for people of all faiths. By exploring how a specific cadre of believers in another time and place coped with the problem of pain, I have attempted to put present efforts to address the crises of illness and infirmity in broader historical context.

In recounting the stories of women and men like Jennie Smith, A. B. Simpson, and R. K. Carter, I have also aimed to encourage critical reflection on the kinds of theological, cultural, and social forces that shape the ways in which people interpret and respond to corporeal sickness and distress. Pain, according to a number of contemporary theorists, is more than a physiological phenomenon. While physical discomfort itself is rooted in biological and neurological mechanisms, the meanings that human beings assign to their pain, as well as the strategies they employ for coping with it, are influenced by the interaction of personal conviction and broader environmental factors. Suffering and healing, from this perspective, are "hermeneutical" processes, mediated through the symbols, metaphors, and categories of culture and belief. Drawing on this understanding of pain as a "culturogenic" or "psychosocial" phenomenon, some researchers have argued that human beings have the capacity to transform their experiences of bodily injury, disease, and distress. By altering their beliefs about affliction as well as their behavioral responses to it, scholars like David Morris have asserted, individuals can "completely reconstruct" the ways in which they suffer pain and experience healing. "Change the mind (powerfully enough) and it may well be that pain too changes," Morris has written. "When we recognize that the experience of pain is not timeless but changing, we may also recognize we can *act* to change or influence our own futures."[29]

Sarah Mix, Charles Cullis, Carrie Judd, and other advocates of faith cure would have agreed with Morris's reflections. The claims that these nineteenth-century devotees of divine healing forwarded regarding the power of faith and devotional disciplines to transform the meaning and experience of somatic affliction bear a striking resemblance to contemporary theories that stress the "interpretive" dimensions of pain and that promote various forms of practice—meditation, ritual engagement, "narrativization"—as means for alleviating bodily distress. By championing an alternative understanding of the relationship between physical suffering and spiritual blessing, and by adopting a set of devotional exercises that helped ailing individuals translate their faith into practice, proponents of divine healing endeavored to recast the present experience and future implications of corporeal pain for themselves and for the wider community of Christian saints of which they counted themselves a part.[30]

Participating in faith cure thus offered individuals means for pursuing both personal transformation and broader cultural reform. In addition to enabling believers to conquer illness and counteract its effects on their own flesh, the doctrines and rites of divine healing supplied strategies for navigating, and sometimes resisting or modifying, the complicated religious, cultural, historical, economic, and social circumstances that influenced the ways in which pain and suffering, illness and healing were understood and performed. To act faith was to defy a central premise of Reformation theology and to reject the authority of medical experts; to receive the laying on of hands was to close one's mind to rationalism and materialism while opening one's body to the incursion of supernatural power; to abandon one's self to God was to stretch certain normative constructions of gender without transgressing their limits.

Proponents of faith cure formulated their theology and practices within a historically and culturally contingent constellation of issues, but the solution they posed to the predicament of pain was applicable, they claimed, to a perennial problem in the history of Christianity. By declaring that healing was entirely the work of God, while at the same time instructing invalids to rise up and walk, ministers of faith cure were attempting to negotiate one of the thorniest dilemmas in Christian theology: deciphering the relationship between divine sovereignty, human volition, and spiritual practice in the processes of salvation and sanctification. For the evangelical Protestants who participated in the divine healing movement of the late nineteenth century, grace and faith; God's power and personal agency; devotional disciplines; and the redemption of body, mind, and soul were inextricably, if inexplicably intertwined. Invoking the Great Physician ultimately involved the acceptance, rather than the resolution, of the perplexing paradoxes and inscrutable enigmas that arise whenever human beings confront the mystery of bodily suffering and embrace the hope of divine healing.

Introduction

1. For Smith's story and the details of her illness and medical treatments, see Jennie Smith, *The Valley of Baca* (1876), esp. 19–22, 29–41, 48, 53, 57–63, 67–69, 92–95, 122–26, 153, 164, 212–15, 245–46, and 285–87; and Jennie Smith, *From Baca to Beulah* (1880).

2. Smith, *Valley of Baca*, 7, 32, 93–94, 142, and 285. The "valley of Baca" is an allusion to Psalm 84:5–7.

3. Thomas H. Pearne, introduction to Smith, *Valley of Baca*, 11. For examples of sermons commending patient endurance of sickness as a means for sanctification, see Sherrod, "That Great and Awful Change," 183–87. Sentimental novels in this vein included Susan Warner, *The Wide, Wide World* (1850); Harriet Beecher Stowe, *Uncle Tom's Cabin* (1852); and Elizabeth Prentiss, *Stepping Heavenward* (1869). For a discussion of the prevalence of the "piety of resignation" during the early nineteenth century, see Holifield, *Health and Medicine in the Methodist Tradition*, 72–73.

4. Smith, *Valley of Baca*, 203.

5. Smith, *Baca to Beulah*, 124.

6. Ibid., 124, 169, 181, 185–97, and 218. While some historians have argued that "faith cure" was a derogatory label, applied to the movement only by critics, I find evidence of its use among participants, especially during the first two decades of the movement's history. For example, two of the movement's key leaders, Charles Cullis and Sarah Mix, used this designation in the titles of their published collections of answered prayer narratives. As the movement came under increasing attack in the mid- to late-1880s, some of its defenders, such as A. B. Simpson, began to distance themselves from the phrase "faith cure" and argued that "divine healing" represented a more appropriate moniker. Given the enduring popularity of "faith cure" among many participants throughout the 1880s, I have chosen to use "divine healing," "faith cure," and "faith healing"—another idiom adopted by both proponents and detractors—interchangeably.

7. Ibid., 197–203.

8. For accounts of Jennie Smith's life and ministry following her healing, see Jennie Smith, *Ramblings in Beulah Land* (1886–1888); Jennie Smith, *Incidents and Experiences of a Railroad Evangelist* (1920); and Winters, *A Souvenir, Affectionately Inscribed to Miss Jennie Smith* (1889).

9. For an overview of Protestant beliefs regarding the miraculous in the nineteenth century, see Mullin, *Miracles and the Modern Religious Imagination*, esp. 9–30. On the circulation of healing testimonies in mid-nineteenth-century Britain, see *Dorothea Trudel, or, The Prayer of Faith*, 1.

10. Accounts of Cullis's Boston ministries to the sick can be found in William E. Boardman, *Faith Work under Dr. Cullis* (1874); and W. H. Daniels, ed., *Dr. Cullis and His Work* (1885). Daniels also included a chapter on Cullis's initial forays into the ministry of divine healing, see 339–52. For Cullis's own description of his encounter with Trudel and his interaction with Lucy Drake, see Charles Cullis, introduction to *Dorothea Trudel*, 5–12; and Cullis, *Ninth Annual Report of the Consumptives Home*, 44–55. The story of Drake's healing became so celebrated that Cullis and chroniclers of his work repeated it in numerous other publications. See, e.g., Boardman, *The Great Physician* (1881); W. H. Daniels, *Dr. Cullis and His Work*, 271–72; A. J. Gordon, *The Ministry of Healing* (1882), 170–73; and Patton, *Prayer and Its Remarkable Answers* (1885), 232–34. Drake's own account of her experience of healing is also included in Patton's volume, 256–58.

11. Cullis, *Ninth Annual Report*, 45. Scholarly debates about how to define the terms "evangelical," "evangelicals," and "evangelicalism" as they apply to any period, including the late nineteenth century, are ongoing and complicated. The problem has become increasingly complex as these designations have acquired new political, theological, and social meanings over the course of the twentieth and twenty-first centuries. The fourfold definition I employ here was first proposed by historian David Bebbington to describe evangelicalism in Britain from the late eighteenth century and has since been adopted by most scholars of nineteenth-century evangelicalism. For discussions of the "Bebbington quadrilateral" and the problem of definition in general, see Noll, Bebbington, and Rawlyk, eds., Introduction, in *Evangelicalism*; Bebbington, *Dominance of Evangelicalism*, esp. 21–81; Noll, *American Evangelical Christianity*; and Candy Gunther Brown, *The Word in the World*, esp. 1–18.

12. For the development of the Methodist Holiness and Reformed Higher Life movements, see Blumhofer, *Restoring the Faith*, esp. 11–42; Dayton, *Theological Roots of Pentecostalism*; Dieter, *Holiness Revival of the Nineteenth Century*; Hardesty, *Faith Cure*, esp. 27–40; Marsden, *Fundamentalism and American Culture*, esp. 72–85; and Wacker, *Heaven Below*, esp. 2–5.

13. Marsden argues that "by 1870, holiness teachings of one sort or another seemed to be everywhere in American revivalist Protestantism" (*Fundamentalism and American Culture*, 74–75). On the formation of extra-ecclesial organizations such as the Tuesday Meeting, Camp Meeting Associations, and Keswick Conventions, see Dieter, *Holiness Revival*, esp. 15–128; Figgis, *Keswick from Within* (1914); Pierson, *The Keswick Movement* (1903); Barnabas, *So Great Salvation*; and Pollock, *The Keswick Story*.

14. Inskip's testimony of healing may be found in Cullis, *More Faith Cures* (1881), 28–32, and Boardman, *Great Physician*, 201–207. For Inskip's biography, see McDonald and Searles, *Life of the Rev. John S. Inskip* (1885).

15. Boardman, *Great Physician*, 13–14. For Boardman's biography, see Mrs. [Mary M. Adams] Boardman, *Life and Labours of the Rev. W. E. Boardman* (1887). For Baxter's embrace of divine healing and her subsequent ministry, see Wiseman, ed., *Elizabeth Baxter* (1928).

16. For Gordon's endorsement of Cullis, see Gordon, *Ministry of Healing*, 170–73. Steele in-

dicated his support for Cullis's work through his ongoing participation in Cullis's enterprise as well as in written publications. See, e.g., Gracey and Steele, *Healing by Faith* (1882); and Steele, "Faith Healing and Broken Legs," *Zion's Herald,* quoted in Townsend, *"Faith Work," "Christian Science," and Other Cures* (1885), 163. Carter's testimony of healing is included in Cullis, *More Faith Cures,* 44–46; and also in Russell Kelso Carter, *"Faith Healing" Reviewed after Twenty Years* (1897), 153–61. Simpson recounts his healing in numerous places. For one version of his experience at Old Orchard Beach, see "Document 13—A. B. Simpson: extract from A. B. Simpson, *The Gospel of Healing,"* in Nienkirchen, "The Man, the Movement, and the Mission," 107–11. For fuller biographical treatments of these figures and discussions of their participation in divine healing, see Hardesty, *Faith Cure.* Contemporary biographies and autobiographies are also available for many prominent proponents of divine healing. See, esp., Ernest B. Gordon, *Adoniram Judson Gordon* (1896); Maria Hale and Adoniram J. Gordon, *Journal of Our Journey,* ed. John Beauregard; and A. E. Thompson, *Life of A. B. Simpson* (1920). For more recent treatments, see Gibson, "Adoniram Judson Gordon"; and Evearitt, *Body and Soul: Evangelism and the Social Concern of A. B. Simpson.*

17. Like their male counterparts, many female leaders also authored accounts of their own experiences, and some inspired biographies. See, e.g., Carrie F. Judd, *The Prayer of Faith* (1880); Carrie Judd Montgomery, *Under His Wings* (1936); Mary H. Mossman, *Steppings in God* (1909); and Sarah Freeman Mix, *Life of Mrs. Edward Mix, Written by Herself* (1884). For more recent treatments, see Albrecht, "Carrie Judd Montgomery"; Albrecht, "Life and Ministry of Carrie Judd Montgomery"; and Storms, "A Theology of Heaing Based on the Writings of Carrie Judd Montgomery."

18. On the Mixes' leadership and the participation of African Americans in late-nineteenth-century divine healing, see Gooden, introduction to Mrs. Edward [Sarah] Mix, *Faith Cures, and Answers to Prayer,* esp. xlii–xlvi. For Smith's involvement, see Robert L. Stanton, "Healing Through Faith," *The Presbyterian Review* 5 (1884): 55; and Amanda Berry Smith, *An Autobiography* (1893). Because evangelical divine healing was such a broad and diverse movement, generalizing about its constituency is difficult. In the southern and western regions of the United States, for example, divine healing evangelists often hailed from impoverished backgrounds and were rarely well educated. For a fuller treatment of divine healing in these geographical areas, consult Baer, "Perfectly Empowered Bodies," esp. chap. 3.

19. Allen, *Faith Healing* (1881).

20. *Record of the International Conference on Divine Healing* (1885).

21. For a contemporary account of the extensive coverage divine healing received in the "daily press," see Carter, *"Faith Healing" Reviewed,* 16. Historians have also documented the widespread attention faith cure garnered in both secular and religious publications in the 1880s. See, e.g., Chappell, "The Divine Healing Movement in America," 152–55. Taylor recorded his views on divine healing in a letter to Holiness leader William McDonald on May 15, 1885. The correspondence is reprinted as "Latest From Bishop Taylor: Death of One of His Missionaries," in *The Christian Witness and Advocate of Bible Holiness* 3, 2 July 1885, 1. Although many proponents of divine healing took part in Moody's revivals, and numerous healings (especially from addiction) took place during these events, Moody himself refrained from publicly embracing the doctrines or practices of faith cure. Instead, he tended to affirm a more conventional view of suffering as a blessing intended for the soul's sanctification. For

a helpful summary of Moody's views on suffering and healing, consult Baer, "Perfectly Empowered Bodies," 118–19.

22. Bell, *Ritual Theory, Ritual Practice*, 81; David D. Hall, ed., *Lived Religion in America*, xi. My use of practice theory as a tool for interpreting divine healing has been inspired by the following works: Bourdieu, *Outline of a Theory of Practice*; Bell, *Ritual Theory, Ritual Practice*; Certeau, *The Practice of Everyday Life*; Hall, *Lived Religion*; Orsi, "Everyday Miracles: The Study of Lived Religion"; Ortner, "Theory in Anthropology since the Sixties"; and Tambiah, *A Performative Approach to Ritual*. For a useful overview of practice theory and its application to historical scholarship in American religion, see Maffly-Kipp, Schmidt, and Valeri, Introduction, in *Practicing Protestants*, 1–15.

23. Hall, *Lived Religion*, vii.

24. Scholarship on the waning influence of Calvinism throughout the nineteenth century is voluminous. On the specific issue of challenges to the limited age of miracles theology, see Mullin, *Miracles*, esp. 31–82; and Ostrander, *Life of Prayer in a World of Science*, 35–38. For the rise of the "cult of benevolence," consult Turner, *Reckoning with the Beast*, 1–14. On the connection between millennialism, missionary fervor, and social reform, see especially, Timothy L. Smith, *Revivalism and Social Reform in Mid-Nineteenth-Century America*; and Wacker, "The Holy Spirit and the Spirit of the Age."

25. Glucklich, *Sacred Pain*, 195. The literature on "heroic" medicine and challenges to this form of therapy is extensive. For one classic treatment, see Rosenberg, "The Therapeutic Revolution." On the history of anesthesia, see especially, Pernick, *A Calculus of Suffering*.

26. On the waning attraction of self-restraint as a mark of character during the late nineteenth century, see Bederman, *Manliness and Civilization*. Jackson Lears, in *No Place of Grace*, also charts the growing ambivalence over proper Protestant character and behavior, particularly in relation to the "crisis" of neurasthenia.

27. See Bederman, *Manliness and Civilization*, esp. 10–15; and Bederman, "The Men and Religion Forward Movement." The literature on late-nineteenth-century manhood is extensive and growing. In addition to Bederman's important work, recent studies include Carnes and Griffen, eds., *Meanings for Manhood*; Davidoff and Hall, *Family Fortunes*; Griffith, "Apostles of Abstinence"; Donald E. Hall, ed. *Muscular Christianity*; Hilkey, *Character Is Capital*; Mangan and Walvin, eds., *Manliness and Morality*; Putney, *Muscular Christianity*; Rotundo, *Transformations in Masculinity*; and Vance, *Sinews of the Spirit*.

28. Associations between true womanhood and suffering have been assiduously documented. Classic studies of the domestic ideology include Barbara Welter, "The Cult of True Womanhood, 1820–60"; Cott, *The Bonds of Womanhood*; Sklar, *Catherine Beecher*; Smith-Rosenberg, *Disorderly Conduct*; and Theriot, *Mothers and Daughters in Nineteenth-Century America*.

29. Theriot, *Mothers and Daughters*, esp. 77–136. Martha H. Verbrugge, in *Able-Bodied Womanhood*, has also made a case for the importance of the physical education movement in promoting an alternate view of female health.

30. On the revisionist agenda of antebellum health reform movements, see Albanese, *Nature Religion in America*; Cayleff, *Wash and Be Healed*; Donegan, "*Hydropathic Highway to Health*"; Fuller, *Alternative Medicine and American Religious Life*; Gevitz, ed. *Other Healers*; Nissenbaum, *Sex, Diet, and Debility in Jacksonian America*; Sokolow, *Eros and Moderniza-*

tion; and Whorton, *Crusaders for Fitness.* For analyses of the relationship between "orthodox" Protestant notions of suffering and the alternatives posed by Spiritualism, Christian Science, and New Thought, respectively, see Braude, *Radical Spirits;* Gottschalk, *Emergence of Christian Science in American Religious Life;* and Satter, *Each Mind a Kingdom.* Also useful in this regard is Rennie B. Schoepflin's recent work, *Christian Science on Trial.*

31. While some scholars of health reform and religious healing movements have highlighted the continuities between their subjects and American evangelical religion more generally, the tendency to characterize Adventism, Spiritualism, Christian Science, and New Thought as "alternative" or "outsider" sects—as opposed to "mainstream" Protestant evangelicalism—remains strong. The classic statement of this categorization is Sydney Ahlstrom's chapter, "Harmonial Religion since the Later Nineteenth Century," in his seminal text, *A Religious History of the American People.* R. Laurence Moore reinforced this reading in his discussion of "Christian Science and American Popular Religion" in *Religious Outsiders and the Making of Americans.* Stephen J. Stein's recent work, "Healers and Occultists: Women of Spiritual Means," in *Communities of Dissent: A History of Alternative Religions in America,* also reproduces this dichotomy. Although Ann Taves has recently drawn attention to the parallels between evangelical divine healing and "new religious movements" such as Adventism, Spiritualism, New Thought, Christian Science, and Theosophy, in her sweeping oeuvre *Fits, Trances, and Visions,* there is yet to be a book-length interpretive study that places divine healing within the broader context of late-nineteenth-century efforts to revise traditional Protestant assumptions about physical suffering and the spiritual life.

32. For analyses of women's leadership in Adventism, Spiritualism, Christian Science, and New Thought, see Numbers, *Prophetess of Health;* Braude, *Radical Spirits;* Gill, *Mary Baker Eddy;* Peel, *Mary Baker Eddy;* Satter, *Each Mind a Kingdom;* and Thomas, *Bleeding Footsteps.* The only published studies that explicitly address the role of gender in divine healing are Opp, "Healing Hands, Healthy Bodies," and *The Lord for the Body;* and Gooden, introduction to *Faith Cures, and Answers to Prayer,* xxxii–xxxv and xlii–xlvi.

33. One study that begins the project of comparative analysis is Cunningham, "Ministry of Healing: The Origins of the Psychotherapeutic Role of the American Churches," which charts the emergence of various healing movements in the 1880s through the 1930s, beginning with divine healing and Christian Science.

34. For the term "retrospective ethnography," I am indebted to Leigh Eric Schmidt, *Holy Fairs,* 6. Several synoptic histories of divine healing in North America offer overviews of the movement's emergence, development, demographics and geography: Baer, "Perfectly Empowered Bodies"; Chappell, "Divine Healing Movement;" Cunningham, "From Holiness to Healing" and "Ministry of Healing"; Dayton, "The Rise of the Evangelical Healing Movement in Nineteenth-Century America"; Hardesty, *Faith Cure;* and Opp, *Lord for the Body.*

35. For discussions of how "come-outer" groups within Methodism and Pentecostalism transformed divine healing, see Baer, "Perfectly Empowered Bodies," esp. iii, 6–7, 170–202, 254–56, and 327–30; Hardesty, *Faith Cure,* 1 and 106–10; Mullin, *Miracles,* 91; and Opp, *Lord for the Body,* 121–45. On the effects of biblical criticism, medical professionalization, and legal challenges to various forms of religious healing in the 1890s and early twentieth century, see Hardesty, *Faith Cure,* 134–45; Mullin, *Miracles,* 138 and 179–220; and Opp, *Lord for the Body,* 92 and 119–20.

36. For overviews of studies that attempt to chart the connection between religious faith, spiritual practice, and health or healing, see Koenig and Kohen, eds. *The Link between Religion and Health;* Koenig, McCullough, and Larson, *Handbook of Religion and Health;* Koenig, *The Healing Power of Faith* and *Faith and Mental Health;* and Dossey, *Reinventing Medicine.* One of the most prominent and tenacious proponents of a positive correlation between spiritual practice and health is Herbert Benson, whose work *The Relaxation Response* (1975), helped pioneer studies of prayer and well-being. See also, Benson, *Beyond the Relaxation Response* and *Timeless Healing.* For a critique of Benson and other works of this genre, see Coakley and Shelemay, eds. *Pain and Its Transformations.*

37. On the challenges of diagnosis, see Kleinman, *Illness Narratives;* and Good et al., eds. *Pain as Human Experience.* Elaine Scarry, *The Body in Pain* is also relevant.

38. On the history of suffering and the status of the sick person or invalid in North America in the twentieth and twenty-first centuries, I have been helped by Robert Orsi's essay, "'Mildred, Is It Fun to Be a Cripple?'" in *Between Heaven and Earth,* 19–47.

Chapter One • A Thorn in the Flesh

1. Rankin, *Daughter of Affliction* (1871), 41–46.

2. Ibid., 42–45.

3. Ibid., 17–19, 23, and 28–29.

4. Ibid., 23, 29, 31, and 32. On the cutthroat and financially frustrating nature of the medical profession in this period, see Donegan, *Hydropathic Highway,* xii; and Rosenberg, Prologue to *Structure of American Medical Practice,* 3–6. A seton, according to the *Oxford English Dictionary,* 2nd ed. (1989), is "a thread, piece of tape, or the like, drawn through a fold of skin so as to maintain an issue or opening for discharges . . . or the issue so formed."

5. The literature on the rise of "heroic" medicine is vast. E.g., see Rosenberg, "Therapeutic Revolution," 3–25; and Donegan, *Hydropathic Highway,* 10–13. Another helpful treatment of the "reflex irritation" model of disease may be found in Smith-Rosenberg and Rosenberg, "The Female Animal."

6. Pernick, *Calculus of Suffering,* 13; and Rosenberg, "Therapeutic Revolution," 6. Numerous historians have discussed Rush's pivotal role in the history of American medical practice. I am particularly indebted to Pernick, *Calculus of Suffering;* Donegan, *Hydropathic Highway,* 10; and Stage, *Female Complaints,* 47–48.

7. Rankin, *Daughter of Affliction,* 32. Rosenberg, Donegan, and others have argued persuasively that heroic therapeutics remained popular in practice well into the second half of the nineteenth century, despite protests from sectarian physicians and health reformers. See Rosenberg, "Therapeutic Revolution," 15–19; and Donegan, *Hydropathic Highway,* 10–11. For Rosenberg's analysis of the persuasive effects that heroic remedies produced for doctors, patients, and families alike, see "Therapeutic Revolution," 8–10. On this point, see also Rothstein, "Botanical Movements and Orthodox Medicine." The processes of cupping and bleeding are described in Haller, *American Medicine in Transition,* 36–47.

8. Pernick, *Calculus of Suffering,* 44–45. For a helpful discussion of the Victorian tendency to associate insensibility with death and pain with vitality, see Winter, *Mesmerized,* chap. 7, esp. 171–72.

9. Rankin, *Daughter of Affliction,* 32 and 36. On the use of drugs and their purported effects, see Rosenberg, Prologue to *Structure of American Medical Practice,* 8; and Stage, *Female Complaints,* 45–63, who characterized the 1900s as the "poisoning century."

10. Rankin, *Daughter of Affliction,* 32, 38, and 39–40.

11. Ibid., 87 and 23. On the United Brethren in Christ, see Ahlstrom, *Religious History,* 439–41.

12. Rankin, *Daughter of Affliction,* 99–100.

13. Ibid., 34, and 137–38.

14. Ibid., 134, 36–37, and 31.

15. Ibid., 156–57 and 4. The twenty male testimonial signers included six physicians from Pennsylvania, one seminary principal, and ministers representing four different denominations: five United Brethren pastors, four Presbyterians, three Lutherans, and one German Reformed minister.

16. Rankin, *Daughter of Affliction,* 174, 34, and 4. For a discussion of the evangelical penchant for "usefulness" and "influence" in the nineteenth century, see Brown, *Word in the World,* esp. 1–9. Brown also provides a helpful overview of the history of Christian hagiography and argues for the expansion of this genre as a result of evangelical publishing efforts throughout the nineteenth century (pp. 88–95). On the nineteenth-century etymology of the word "interesting," see Brown, *Word in the World,* 92; and Pernick, *Calculus of Suffering,* 47.

17. The history of Christian spirituality, and particularly of the relationship between physical suffering and personal sanctity, is better developed for the periods of early Christianity through the Protestant Reformation than for the modern and postmodern eras. Some of the most influential studies among this vast literature that have influenced my own thinking include: Peter Brown, *The Body and Society* and *The Cult of the Saints;* Bynum, *Holy Feast and Holy Fast;* Clark, *Reading Renunciation;* Hollywood, "Inside Out: Beatrice of Nazareth and Her Hagiographer" and "Suffering Transformed: Marguerite Porete, Meister Eckhart, and the Problem of Women's Spirituality"; Kieckhefer, *Unquiet Souls;* McGinn, *The Foundations of Mysticism, The Growth of Mysticism,* and *The Flowering of Mysticism;* and Vauchez, *Sainthood in the Later Middle Ages.*

18. For general overviews of Protestant challenges to pre-Reformation models of sanctity, see Bossy, *Christianity in the West;* Kolb, *For All the Saints;* Raitt, McGinn, and Meyerhoff, *Christian Spirituality: High Middle Ages and Reformation;* Richard, *The Spirituality of John Calvin;* and White, *Tudor Books of Saints and Martyrs.*

19. Helpful studies of Protestant martyrdom and the development of Protestant hagiographical literature include Fairfield, "John Bale and the Development of Protestant Hagiography in England"; Green, *Print and Protestantism in Early Modern England;* Gregory, *Salvation at Stake;* Hambrick-Stowe, *The Practice of Piety;* and Watt, *Cheap Print and Popular Piety.* See also Brown, *Word in the World,* esp. 88–95.

20. Brumberg, *Mission for Life,* esp. 1–19 and 107–109.

21. Edwards, *Life of David Brainerd,* 3 and 436.

22. Brumberg, *Mission for Life,* 102–104.

23. On the somatic and visionary pieties of certain late-medieval mystics, especially as presented by their male hagiographers, see esp. Hollywood, "Inside Out," 78–98; Bynum, *Holy Feast and Holy Fast;* and McGinn, *Flowering of Mysticism.*

24. McGinn, *Flowering of Mysticism*, 308; and Ebner, *Major Works*. In *Holy Feast and Holy Fast*, Bynum argues for a link between illness and sanctity most forcefully; see esp. 199–200, and 209. It should be noted, however, that Hollywood seeks to modify this characterization of late-medieval female mysticism in "Inside Out" and "Suffering Transformed," by arguing that somatic and visionary piety was the construction of male hagiographers rather than a concern of women mystics themselves. For her comments regarding the incarnational function of women's bodies, see Hollywood, "Inside Out," 78–98.

25. Barbara Welter was among the first to analyze the cults of domesticity and true womanhood in her now-classic article, "The Cult of True Womanhood," 151–74. Of the many subsequent studies, I have found the following works especially useful: Cott, *Bonds of Womanhood*; Sklar, *Catherine Beecher*; Smith-Rosenberg, *Disorderly Conduct*; and Theriot, *Mothers and Daughters.*

26. Rotundo, *Transformations in Masculinity*, 245. While the literature assessing nineteenth-century ideals of manhood and masculinity among American and English Protestants is not as voluminous as that which analyzes female gender norms in the same period, a number of excellent studies have appeared in recent years. See, e.g., Bederman, *Manliness and Civilization* and "The Men and Religion Forward Movement"; Carnes and Griffen, eds., *Meanings of Manhood*; Davidoff and Hall, *Family Fortunes*; Griffith, "Apostles of Abstinence"; Hall, *Muscular Christianity*; Hilkey, *Character Is Capital*; Mangan and Walvin, eds., *Manliness and Morality*; Putney, *Muscular Christianity*; and Vance, *Sinews of the Spirit.*

27. Grimke, *Letters on the Equality of the Sexes and the Condition of Woman* (1838). For this interpretation of Catharine Beecher's position and her debate with the Grimke sisters, I am indebted to Sklar, *Catharine Beecher*, 132–37.

28. Sklar, *Catharine Beecher*, 132–37.

29. Rankin, *Daughter of Affliction*, 174.

30. Ibid., 278.

31. Ibid., 59 and 89–91.

32. Numerous historians have charted the increasing trend among nineteenth-century physicians toward focusing on the reproductive organs as the main determinants of female health. Classic studies include Smith-Rosenberg and Rosenberg, "Female Animal," 332–56; Douglas Wood, "'The Fashionable Diseases'"; and Stage, *Female Complaints*, 64–88. For more recent analyses, see Braude, *Radical Spirits*, 142–61; and Satter, *Each Mind a Kingdom*, 21–56. As Satter, Braude, and others have shown, even under the best of circumstances, menstruation was seen as fundamentally pathological. E. H. Dixon's *Woman and Her Diseases*, 195–97, quoted in Price Herndl, *Invalid Women*, 35; John Wiltbank, *Introductory Lecture for the Session* (1854), 7, quoted in Smith-Rosenberg, *Disorderly Conduct*, 183–84; and Smith-Rosenberg, *Disorderly Conduct*, 207.

33. Stephen Tracy, *The Mother and Her Offspring* (1860), xv, quoted in Smith-Rosenberg and Rosenberg, "Female Animal," 334; Morrill Wyman, *Progress in School Discipline* (1866), 6, quoted in Pernick, *Calculus of Suffering*, 149; and Marshall Hall, *Commentaries on Some of the More Important of the Diseases of Females* (1827), 2, quoted in Smith-Rosenberg and Rosenberg, "Female Animal," 334. On medical theories regarding the inherent delicacy of women, see also Smith-Rosenberg, *Disorderly Conduct*, 182–96; and Pernick, *Calculus of Suffering*, 150. Also useful in this regard are Duffin, "Conspicuous Consumptive"; Ehrenreich and English,

For Her Own Good; Fellman and Fellman, *Making Sense of Self;* Jacobus and Shuttleworth, *Body/Politics;* Leavitt, *Women and Health in America;* Leavitt, *Women and Health in America,* 2nd ed.; Shorter, *A History of Women's Bodies;* and Vicinus, *Suffer and Be Still.*

34. For an example of this genre, see Leonard Trask, *A Brief Historical Sketch of the Life and Sufferings of Leonard Trask, the Wonderful Invalid* (ca. 1857). Although Miriam Bailin (*The Sickroom in Victorian Fiction,* 2) has argued that Victorian literature includes numerous examples of male invalids, these figures are rarely presented as exemplary. The literature on male illness and therapy is less developed than the corresponding literature on female invalidism. The best treatments focus primarily on the late nineteenth century, with an emphasis on the diagnosis and treatment of male neurasthenia. See, e.g., Hilkey, *Character Is Capital,* 76–68; Lutz, *American Nervousness,* 31–37; and Rotundo, *American Manhood,* 185–93.

35. Stage, *Female Complaints,* 74–5. Numerous historians have confirmed the immense influence of the literary "cult of female invalidism" in this period. Martha Verbrugge seems to have been among the first to use this phrase in her study, *Able-Bodied Womanhood,* 16. For a summary of debates over the meaning of this phenomena, see Price Herndl, *Invalid Women,* 20–30. Jane Tompkins's analysis of the sentimental ethic of submission promoted in nineteenth-century evangelical literature has shaped my own reading of these texts. See Tompkins, *Sensational Designs,* esp. chaps. 5–6. Warner, *Wide, Wide World,* 427.

36. Prentiss, *Stepping Heavenward,* 69, 182, and 149.

37. Ibid., 192 and 259.

38. George L. Prentiss, *The Life and Letters of Elizabeth Prentiss* (1882), 157.

39. Tompkins, *Sensational Designs,* esp. 160–65 and 172–81.

40. On the unparalleled popularity of these works, see Tompkins, *Sentimental Designs,* 124–25, and 148.

41. Rankin, *Daughter of Affliction,* 276; Price Herndl, *Invalid Women,* 54; and Rankin, *Daughter of Affliction,* 34.

42. Atwell, *Chloe Lankton* (1859), preface, 151, 161, and 263. Evidence for the lasting and widespread popularity of Rankin's text may be found in Smith, *Valley of Baca,* 197–98. For another example of this genre, see Webb, *Memoir of Miss Charity Richards* (1845).

43. Rankin, *Daughter of Affliction,* 4 and 132. The testimonial and introduction to *Daughter of Affliction* indicate that the work was intended for both male and female audiences. In addition to the numerous male patrons who sponsored Rankin's autobiography, evidence that the book was actually read by men may be found in Smith, *Valley of Baca,* 197–98, and in Young, *Sunny Life of an Invalid* (1897), 9.

44. Rankin, *Daughter of Affliction,* 13–14.

45. Mary H. Lamb to Carrie F. Judd, August 1884, *Triumphs of Faith* 4 (October 1884): 236–38; and Mrs. L. W. Bush, "Experiences of Spiritual and Physical Healing," *Triumphs of Faith* 5 (August 1885): 190–92.

46. For Moore's testimony, see Judd, *Prayer of Faith,* 136–38. "John Haugh," in *A Cloud of Witnesses for Divine Healing,* ed. Albert B. Simpson (1887), 44–45.

47. Rankin, *Daughter of Affliction,* 99–100 and 278.

Chapter Two • Resisting Resignation

1. Smith, *Valley of Baca,* 169–70.

2. Cullis, *Ninth Annual Report,* 50–52.

3. Cullis, *Faith Cures* (1879), 81; W. A. B. to Charles Cullis, 4 March 1880, *More Faith Cures,* ed. Charles Cullis, 70–72; W. M. H. to Charles Cullis, 18 February 1883, *More Faith Cures,* ed. Charles Cullis, 82–85; and Cullis, *Other Faith Cures; or Answers to Prayer in the Healing of the Sick* (1885), 51–59.

4. Cullis, *Faith Cures,* 81.

5. W. A. B. to Charles Cullis, 4 March 1880, *More Faith Cures,* ed. Charles Cullis, 70–72; and Cullis, *Faith Cures,* 81.

6. "Mrs. Kath. H. Brodie," in *A Cloud of Witnesses,* ed. A. B. Simpson, 15–32; and Belle Lewis, "Experiences of Spiritual and Physical Healing," *Triumphs of Faith* 5 (June 1885): 136–39.

7. A. J. Gordon, *Ministry of Healing,* 127 and 195–97.

8. Russell Kelso Carter, *Atonement for Sin and Sickness* (1884), 292 and 180–82.

9. A. B. Simpson, "The Gospel of Healing: Common Objections," *Word, Work and World* 5:3 (November and December 1883): 172; and "The I Wills of God," *Triumphs of Faith* 4 (October 1884): 232–33.

10. Simpson, "The Gospel of Healing: Common Objections," *Word, Work and World,* 172. See also A. B. Simpson, *Inquiries and Answers* (1887), 5–7.

11. S. L. Brown, "Christ's Healing Mercy," *Triumphs of Faith* 2 (November 1882): 161; and L. H. C., "Experiences of Spiritual and Physical Healing," *Triumphs of Faith* 1 (March 1881): 47–8.

12. Whorton, *Crusaders for Fitness,* 54; and Albanese, *Nature Religion,* 126.

13. Julia A. Norcross Crafts Smith, *The Reason Why; or, Spiritual Experiences of Mrs. Julia Crafts Smith* (1881), 60–62; and Braude, *Radical Spirits,* 144 and 34.

14. Gottschalk, *Emergence of Christian Science,* 48 and 235–37.

15. Laura C. Nourse, "Reminiscences," *Christian Science Journal* 9:10 (January 1891): 413–18.

16. S. E. A., "From Trinitarianism to Christian Science," *Christian Science Journal* 10:3 (June 1892): 104–107.

17. Cullis, *Other Faith Cures,* 4.

18. Boardman, *Faith-Work Under Dr. Cullis,* 13–17; and W. H. Daniels, *Dr. Cullis and His Work,* 3–5.

19. On homeopathy, see Kaufman, "Homeopathy in America"; Fuller, *Alternative Medicine,* 22–26; and Albanese, *Nature Religion,* 132–36.

20. Quoted in Albanese, *Nature Religion,* 134.

21. Whorton, *Crusaders for Fitness,* 15; and Whorton, "Patient, Heal Thyself."

22. W. H. Daniels, *Dr. Cullis and His Work,* esp. 64–65, 74, 91, 185–99, 233–51, and 252–70; Boardman, *Faith Work under Dr. Cullis,* esp. 28–29 and 33–34; and Chappell, "The Divine Healing Movement in America," 104–91.

23. For a fuller discussion of the distinctions between and interactions among various nineteenth-century "holiness" movements and especially their understandings of sanctification and their "Arminian" leanings, see Dieter, *Holiness Revival;* Hardesty, *Faith Cure,* 1

and 27–40; and Timothy L. Smith, *Revivalism and Social Reform,* esp. 80–94 and 103–47. For an insider's rendering of this view of sanctification, see Pardington, *Twenty-Five Wonderful Years* (1914), 53–55.

24. Gordon, *Ministry of Healing,* 194–96; Carter, *Atonement for Sin and Sickness,* 83. For a discussion of Mahan's involvement in divine healing, see Baer, "Perfectly Empowered Bodies," 128; and Hardesty, *Faith Cure,* 32. Cookman's testimony of healing is included in Simpson, *A Cloud of Witnesses,* 1–10; and a brief sketch of his life and involvement in the divine healing movement may be found in George P. Pardington, *Twenty-Five Wonderful Years* (1919), 214–17. For Platt's testimony of healing, see Smith H. Platt, *My 25th Year Jubilee* (1875). More information on his participation in the wider divine healing movement may be found in Baer, "Perfectly Empowered Bodies," 157–59; and Hardesty, *Faith Cure,* 60–62 and 97.

25. Smith, *Valley of Baca,* esp. 169–70 and 203; Smith, *Baca to Beulah,* esp. 133–49, 205, 211, 238, 247, 281–83, and 353–55.

26. "Mrs. Kath. H. Brodie," *Cloud of Witnesses,* ed. A. B. Simpson, 15–32. For a brief history of *The Guide to Holiness* and its role in disseminating testimonies of divine healing, see Dieter, *Holiness Revival,* 42; and Hardesty, *Faith Cure,* 22–23 and 35. Simpson published the first issue of *Word, Work and World* in January of 1882. The version of Jennie Smith's testimony that was published in the Dayton, Ohio *Democrat* is reprinted in Smith, *From Baca to Beulah,* 211–13.

27. Smith, *Valley of Baca,* 33–34 and 57–63; and Smith, *From Baca to Beulah,* 154–65.

28. Cullis, *Other Faith Cures,* 14; Carter, *Atonement for Sin and Sickness,* 107; Thomas W. Whitehall, "Experiences of Spiritual and Physical Healing," *Triumphs of Faith* 3 (September 1883): 215; and Edward Ryder "Ordinary Grace," *Triumphs of Faith* 5 (June 1885): 134–35.

29. W. T. Vail, quoted in Albanese, *Nature Religion,* 137; and Anna W. Prosser, "Jesus Only," *Triumphs of Faith* 8 (February 1888): 31–34.

30. Helen F. Dawlly, "In An Acceptable Time," *Triumphs of Faith* 1 (November 1881): 165–68; and S. G. C., "My Help and My Deliverer," *Triumphs of Faith* 1 (October 1881): 153–56. For another example, see Mrs. J. B. Safford, "Experiences of Spiritual and Physical Healing," *Triumphs of Faith* 4 (November 1884): 264.

31. Spencer R. Wells, "Experiences of Spiritual and Physical Healing," *Triumphs of Faith* 4 (August 1884): 189–90; M. H. T. to Carrie Judd, *Triumphs of Faith* 3 (February 1883): 44–46; Libbie Osborn to Carrie Judd, *Triumphs of Faith* 7 (April 1887): 91–96; and Agnes N. Ormsbee to Carrie Judd, *Triumphs of Faith* 8 (July 1888): 188–89.

32. Osborn to Judd, *Triumphs of Faith,* 91–96; L. E. E., "Healed by the Great Physician," *Triumphs of Faith* 2 (March 1882): 56–59. For more on Foster, see Donegan, *"Hydropathic Highway to Health,"* 50. For another example of Foster's support for divine healing, and for Charles Cullis's ministry in particular, see A. G. B. to Charles Cullis, 12 August 1879, *More Faith Cures,* ed. Charles Cullis, 38–40.

33. Osborn to Judd, *Triumphs of Faith,* 91–96; and Ormsbee to Judd, *Triumphs of Faith,* 188–89.

34. Cullis, preface to *Faith Cures;* and Ryder, "Ordinary Grace," *Triumphs of Faith,* 134–35.

35. Mullin's *Miracles* offers a thorough account of both Protestant and Catholic attitudes toward miracles, particularly toward claims of miraculous healing, leading up to and during the nineteenth century. Chapter 4, "The Question of Healing," pp. 83–107, is especially useful.

36. F. P. Church to Charles Cullis, 16 July 1884, *Other Faith Cures,* ed. Charles Cullis, 137–38; S. H. Wasgatt to Carrie Judd, 23 October 1884, *Triumphs of Faith* 4 (November 1884): 260–61; George F. Donaldson, "Experiences of Spiritual and Physical Healing," *Triumphs of Faith* 4 (April 1884): 95–96; and Alford H. McClellan, "Experiences of Spiritual and Physical Healing," *Triumphs of Faith* 4 (January 1884): 22–24.

37. Lansing Van Shoonhoven to Carrie Judd, 27 May 1882, *Triumphs of Faith* 2 (July 1882): 110–11; S. G. C., "My Help and My Deliverer," *Triumphs of Faith,* 154; Mrs. Thomas H. Davy, "Out of Darkness into Light," *Triumphs of Faith* 4 (February 1884): 43–45.

38. Cullis, *Ninth Annual Report,* 44–45 and 55; A. P. Moore, "Healing Faith," *Triumphs of Faith* 1 (April 1881): 55–56; and "For Us, Or For the Apostles?" *Word, Work and World* 1 (July 1882): 245. On the fascination with the work of the Holy Spirit that characterized late-nineteenth-century evangelicals and liberals, see Wacker's classic article, "The Holy Spirit and the Spirit of the Age," 45–62.

39. Gordon, *Ministry of Healing,* esp. 1–2 and 58–86.

40. Ibid., esp. 1–13.

41. Ibid., 1–13.

42. Gordon, *Ministry of Healing,* 2; "For Us, Or For the Apostles?" *Word, Work and World,* 245; Robert L. Stanton, "Healing Through Faith," *Presbyterian Review* 5 (1884): 51; and Gordon, *Ministry of Healing,* 175.

43. Ostrander, *Life of Prayer,* 44–53. A. B. Simpson, "The Gospel of Healing," *Word, Work and World* 3 (April 1883): 57–60; and A. B. Simpson, "The Gospel of Healing; Divine Healing and Demonism Not Identical. A Protest and Reply to Dr. Buckley in the Century Magazine. Concluded." *Word, Work and World* 7 (August 1886): 114–22.

44. A. B. Simpson, "The Power of the Resurrection, *Word, Work and World* 3 (April 1883): 54–55. On Blumhardt, see Russell Kelso Carter, *Pastor Blumhardt* (1883); and Hardesty, *Faith Cure,* 19–20.

45. Simpson, "The Power of His Resurrection," *Word, Work and World,* 54–55; and A. B. Simpson, "The Gospel of Healing, No. III, Objections," *Word, Work and World* 3 (October 1883): 150–52. The hymn that Simpson quoted was "Jesus wept! Those Tears Are Over," written in 1853 by Scottish minister John R. Macduff.

46. Horace Bushnell, *Nature and the Supernatural* (1858). I am deeply indebted to Bruce Mullin's astute analysis of Bushnell's position on modern miracles: see Mullin, *Miracles,* esp. 66–75. See also Ostrander, *Life of Prayer,* 36.

47. Bushnell, *Nature and the Supernatural,* new ed. (1871), 521, 448, quoted in Mullin, *Miracles,* 73 and 69.

48. Ostrander, *Life of Prayer,* 44. See also Paul A. Carter, *The Spiritual Crisis of the Gilded Age;* Lears, *No Place of Grace;* and Turner, *Without God, Without Creed.*

49. On the primitivist impulse in American Protestantism, see Hughes, ed. *The American Quest for a Primitive Church;* Hughes, *Illusions of Innocence;* and Mead, *The Lively Experiment,* 108–11. On Christian Science healing as a primitivist impulse, see Gottschalk, *Emergence of Christian Science,* esp. 23–24, 210–11, and 237–38. On the anti-clerical strain within nineteenth-century Spiritualism, see Braude, *Radical Spirits,* 143–44. Smith, *Reason Why,* 23–24.

50. Bushnell, *Nature and the Supernatural,* quoted in Gordon, *Ministry of Healing,* 110–15.

51. Marvin R. Vincent, "Modern Miracles," *Presbyterian Review* 4 (July 1883): 473–502 and

Marvin R. Vincent, "Dr. Stanton on 'Healing Through Faith," *Presbyterian Review* 5 (April 1884): 305–29. For Vincent's biography, see Baer, "Perfectly Empowered Bodies," 133.

52. Townsend, *"Faith-Work," "Christian Science," and Other Cures*, 24–51.

53. Vincent, "Modern Miracles," *Presbyterian Review*, 487.

54. A. J. Gordon, "'Christian Science' Tested by Scripture," *Triumphs of Faith* 6 (December 1886): 276–80, and Gordon, *Ministry of Healing*, 131–43. R. K. Carter offers a much more charitable reading of Roman Catholic miracle claims in *Atonement for Sin and Sickness*, 176–77. For evidence of the ill-repute in which advocates of divine healing held Christian Science and other movements of mental healing, see, e.g., E. P. Marvin, "'Christian Science' (not Christian and not Science)," *Triumphs of Faith* 9 (March 1889): 52–54; W. T. Hogg, "'Christian Science' Unmasked," parts 1–4, *Triumphs of Faith* 10 (1890): 196–200, 224–27, 252–55, and 265–68; W. T. Hogg, "'Christian Science' Unmasked," part 5, *Triumphs of Faith* 11 (1891): 4–7; and Anna Prosser, "So-Called 'Christian Science,'" *Triumphs of Faith* 10 (March 1890): 49–52.

55. A. B. Simpson, "The Gospel of Healing, No. III, Objections," *Word, Work and World* 3 (October 1883): 150–52.

56. Pardington, *Twenty-Five Wonderful Years*, 61–64, and 103. Studies of the development of premillennialist eschatology following the American Civil War include Marsden, *Understanding Fundamentalism and Evangelicalism*, 39–41; Marsden, *Fundamentalism and American Culture*, esp. 48–93; Moorhead, *World Without End*; Sandeen, *The Roots of Fundamentalism*; and Weber, *Living in the Shadow of the Second Coming*. Grant Wacker has persuasively argued that early premillennialists like A. J. Gordon interpreted the doctrine as "an efficient instrument for mobilizing religious energies" rather than as "an ideology of despair." On this point, see Wacker, "The Holy Spirit and the Spirit of the Age," 57–58.

57. A. B. Simpson, "Editorial Paragraphs," *Word, Work and World* 3 (March 1883): 47. For a discussion of the diversity of eschatological views held by supporters of divine healing, see Dieter, *Holiness Revival*, 254, and Dayton, *Theological Roots*, 164–67. Daniel Steele was one prominent proponent of faith cure who rejected premillennialism.

58. Gordon, *Ministry of Healing*, 131–43; Simpson, "The Gospel of Healing, No. III, Objections," *Word, Work and World*, 151; "Meeting in Connection with Faith Healing," *Word, Work and World* 1 (May 1882): 215–16; and "Miss H. M. Barker," in *A Cloud of Witnesses*, ed. A. B. Simpson, 170–78.

Chapter Three • Acting Faith

1. Judd recounts the story of her illness and healing in "Have Faith in God," in Mix, *Faith Cures, and Answers to Prayer*, 32–45; and Judd, *Prayer of Faith*, esp. 9–21. She offers another version in her autobiography, Judd Montgomery, *Under His Wings*, 48–60.

2. Judd, *Prayer of Faith*, 14.

3. Ibid., 16–21. The letter, from C. F. R. Bielby, dated 13 March 1880, is reprinted in Judd, *Prayer of Faith*, 16–21.

4. Ibid., 16–21, and Judd Montgomery, *Under his Wings*, 54, 59, and 65–67.

5. Judd discusses her struggle to give up her ambitions at several points in her autobiography. See, e.g., Judd Montgomery, *Under His Wings*, 49, 53, and 61. The conversation with her mother is on page 53.

6. Judd Montgomery, *Under His Wings,* 32–35 and 48–54.

7. Mix, *Faith Cures,* 140–41, 72–74, and 107–10.

8. Ibid.

9. Smith, *Baca to Beulah,* 197–203.

10. Mix, *Faith Cures,* 180; Dawlly, "In An Acceptable Time," 166; and L. A. Baldwin, "Experiences of Spiritual and Physical Healing," *Triumphs of Faith* 2 (November 1882): 174–75.

11. Cullis, *Tenth Annual Report of the Consumptives Home* (1875), 89. For a similar statement, see Cullis, *Ninth Annual Report,* 55. Gordon, *Ministry of Healing,* 198 and 16.

12. Stanton's series of articles was published in the journal *Triumphs of Faith,* edited by Carrie Judd, from April 1883 to May 1884 and reprinted as a book by Judd's publishing office in 1884. Citations are taken from the volume: Stanton, *Gospel Parallelisms: Illustrated in the Healing of Body and Soul* (1884), 13–14. For biographical information on Stanton, see *Gospel Parallelisms;* Baer, "Perfectly Empowered Bodies," 133; and Hardesty, *Faith Cure,* 139. Carter, *Atonement for Sin and Sickness,* 32 and 36.

13. R. L. Stanton, "Health for Body and Soul—Two Experiences," *Triumphs of Faith* 3 (March 1883): 61; and Stanton, *Gospel Parallelisms,* 30.

14. Carter, *Atonement for Sin and Sickness,* 210, 234, 237, 231, 182, and 234.

15. Mrs. L. E. P. to Charles Cullis, 8 October 1879, *More Faith Cures,* ed. Charles Cullis, 49–51; and Cullis, *Tenth Annual Report,* 81.

16. Cullis, *Other Faith Cures,* 4 and 9.

17. H. A. Steinhauer, "Views of Faith-Healing" *Triumphs of Faith* 3 (September 1883): 197–99.

18. Carrie F. Judd, "Faith Without Works," *Triumphs of Faith* 1 (October 1881): 145–46; and Judd, *Prayer of Faith,* 16–18.

19. Judd, *Prayer of Faith,* 94, 42, 102–103, and 100.

20. For Palmer's "altar phraseology," see Wheatley, *The Life and Letters of Mrs. Phoebe Palmer* (1876), 525–40. Carrie F. Judd, "Faith's Reckonings," *Triumphs of Faith* 1 (January 1881): 1–4.

21. Judd, "Faith's Reckonings," *Triumphs of Faith,* 1–4.

22. Mrs. Sara Burdge, "Experiences of Spiritual and Physical Healing," *Triumphs of Faith* 6 (October 1886): 236–37; Anna W. Prosser, *From Death to Life: An Autobiography* (1901), 127–28; and Prosser, "Jesus Only," *Triumphs of Faith* 8 (February 1888): 31–34.

23. Mrs. M. [Elizabeth] Baxter, "I Am Come Down to Deliver Them," *Triumphs of Faith* 6 (December 1886): 267–70.

24. A. B. Simpson, "The Gospel of Healing," *Triumphs of Faith* 3 (November 1883): 257–60.

25. A. B. Simpson, "Himself," *Triumphs of Faith* 5 (November 1885): 204–209; A. B. Simpson, "Gospel of Healing," *Triumphs of Faith,* 257; and A. B. Simpson, "How to Receive Divine Healing," *Triumphs of Faith* 8 (February 1888): 35–40.

26. Judd, *Prayer of Faith,* 18; and Mrs. [Elizabeth] Baxter, "The Sentence of Death," *Triumphs of Faith* 5 (October 1885): 217–19.

27. A. B. Simpson, "Principles of Divine Healing," *Triumphs of Faith* 7 (August 1887): 171–78.

28. Carrie Judd, "Abide in Me," *Triumphs of Faith* 3 (September 1883): 201–202.

29. Ibid.; Carrie Judd, "If Any Man Draw Back," *Triumphs of Faith* 6 (July 1886): 145; and Carrie Judd, "Kept by the Power of God," *Triumphs of Faith* 3 (February 1883): 37–38.

30. Mrs. Violet Edmunds, "Experiences of Spiritual and Physical Healing," *Triumphs of Faith* 9 (April 1889): 92–94.

31. W. T. Hogg, "'Christian Science' Unmasked," *Triumphs of Faith* 11 (January 1891): 4; and K. Mackenzie Jr. "The Devil," *Triumphs of Faith* 9 (April 1889): 78. On the rise of mind cure and mental therapeutics over the course of the nineteenth century, see Rosenberg, "Therapeutic Revolution," 3–25; Gosling, *Before Freud;* and Taves, *Fits, Trances and Visions,* 122–26.

32. Gordon, *Ministry of Healing,* 191–92.

33. Annie Van Ness Blanchet to Carrie Judd, 15 December 1884, *Triumphs of Faith* 5 (January 1885): 22–23; and Mrs. M. [Elizabeth] Baxter, "Blind Bartimaeus," *Triumphs of Faith* 8 (August 1888): 184–87.

34. A. J. Gordon, "'Christian Science' Tested by Scripture," *Triumphs of Faith,* 276–80; this article originally appeared in *The Congregationalist* in the spring of 1885 and was subsequently reprinted as a tract as well as in periodicals such as *Triumphs of Faith.* James Monroe Buckley, "Faith-Healing and Kindred Phenomena," *Century Illustrated Monthly Magazine* 32 (June 1886): 221–36. See also James Monroe Buckley, "Faith-Healing and Kindred Phenomena (Supplementary Article)," *Century Illustrated Monthly Magazine* 33 (March 1887): 781–87. Both of these articles were reprinted along with two essays on what Buckley considered "kindred phenomena"—"Christian Science and 'Mind-Cure'" and "Dreams, Nightmares and Somnambulism"—as *Faith-Healing, Christian Science and Kindred Phenomena* (1898). For biographical information on Buckley, see Mains, *James Monroe Buckley* (1917); Baer, "Perfectly Empowered Bodies," 165–69; Cunningham, "Ministry of Healing," 26; Hardesty, *Faith Cure,* 139; Holifield, *Health and Medicine in the Methodist Tradition,* 40; and Mullin, *Miracles,* 101–102.

35. A. B. Simpson, "The Gospel of Healing; Divine Healing and Demonism Not Identical," *Word, Work and World* 7 (August 1886): 114–22.

36. Marvin, "'Christian Science,'" *Triumphs of Faith,* 52–54; Hogg, "'Christian Science' Unmasked," parts 1–5, *Triumphs of Faith;* Prosser, "So-Called 'Christian Science,'" *Triumphs of Faith,* 49–52; and Gordon, "'Christian Science' Tested by Scripture," *Triumphs of Faith,* 276–80.

37. Elizabeth V. Baker, "My Saviour and Healer," *Triumphs of Faith* 11 (September 1891): 193–99.

38. Prosser, "So-Called 'Christian Science,'" *Triumphs of Faith,* 49; and Gordon, "'Christian Science' Tested by Scripture," *Triumphs of Faith,* 277.

39. Mary Baker Glover (Eddy), *Science and Health* (1875), 453–54; Carrie Judd, "How to Resist the Devil," quoted in Chappell, *Divine Healing Movement,* 239; C. S., "Healing Through the Atonement," *Triumphs of Faith* 2 (August 1882): 124–25; and Simpson, "Gospel of Healing," *Triumphs of Faith,* 258.

40. Clarke, *Sex in Education* (1873). For discussions of "scientific" discourses on women's physiology and pathology, especially with reference to late-nineteenth-century gender norms, see: Braude, *Radical Spirits,* 142–61; Wood, "'The Fashionable Diseases'"; Satter, *Each Mind a Kingdom,* 21–56; Smith-Rosenberg, *Disorderly Conduct,* 197–216; Stage, *Female Complaints,* 64–88; Theriot, *Mothers and Daughters,* 86; and ch. 1, n. 33 above. On mounting fears of "race suicide" and concerns about the advancement of civilization, see Smith-Rosenberg and Rosenberg, "The Female Animal"; and Satter, *Each Mind a Kingdom.*

41. On Mitchell and the "rest cure," see Bassuk, "The Rest Cure"; and Satter, *Each Mind a Kingdom,* 54–55. Bassuk notes that while the rest cure was "theoretically used to treat

both men and women, most patients described in the literature were nervous females" (141).

42. L. Etta Avery, "His Name, Through Faith in His Name," *Triumphs of Faith* 4 (March 1884): 49–53; Almena J. Cowles, "Made Every Whit Whole," *Triumphs of Faith* 2 (May 1882): 65–66; and Almena J. Cowles to Sarah Mix, August 1881, in Mrs. Edward [Sarah] Mix, *Faith Cures, and Answers to Prayer* (1882), 58.

43. On women's proclivity to hysteria, see Smith-Rosenberg, *Disorderly Conduct,* 197; and Rosenberg and Rosenberg, "The Female Animal," 332–56. For the comment on mind cure, see Hogg, "'Christian Science' Unmasked," *Triumphs of Faith,* 199.

44. Cowles, "Made Every Whit Whole," *Triumphs of Faith,* 66.

45. George M. Beard, *American Nervousness* (1881). On the treatment of male neurasthenia, see, e.g., Hilkey, *Character Is Capital,* 76–68; Lutz, *American Nervousness,* 31–37; and Rotundo, *American Manhood,* 185–93.

46. Buckley, "Faith-Healing and Kindred Phenomena," *Century Magazine,* 236; and George H. Hepworth, "The Faith Cure," *The Independent,* 19 October 1882, 1.

47. Sophia Nugent, "Where Is the Guest-Chamber?" *Triumphs of Faith* 4 (May 1884): 108; Sophia Nugent, "He Shall Live," *Triumphs of Faith* 5 (April 1885): 89–92; A. P. Moore, "The Walk on the Waves" *Triumphs of Faith* 4 (January 1884): 10; and Simpson, "How to Receive Divine Healing," *Triumphs of Faith,* 36.

48. "Rev. T. C. Easton, D.D." in *A Cloud of Witnesses,* ed. A. B. Simpson, 63–66; "Geo. P. Pardington," in *A Cloud of Witnesses,* ed. A. B. Simpson, 118–28; and "Rev. Henry Wilson, D.D.," in *A Cloud of Witnesses,* ed. A. B. Simpson, 10–14.

49. In one measure of women's predominance in the movement, James Opp has found that women authored more than eight of every ten testimonials that appeared in *Triumphs of Faith* from 1890 to 1898; see Opp, *Lord for the Body,* 39 and 218.

50. Mrs. R. W. Fuller to Carrie Judd, 14 June 1883, *Triumphs of Faith* 3 (September 1883): 214.

51. Mrs. Mattie E. Littell, "Experiences of Spiritual and Physical Healing," *Triumphs of Faith* 5 (May 1885): 118–20; Alice M. Ball, "Following On," *Triumphs of Faith* 7 (October 1887): 224–26; Urwin D. Sterry to Carrie Judd, 11 February 1884, *Triumphs of Faith* 4 (July 1884): 164–66; and Ruth Whitney, "Honey from the Rock," *Triumphs of Faith* 3 (April 1883): 82–83.

52. Mrs. Sara Burdge, "Experiences of Spiritual and Physical Healing," *Triumphs of Faith* 6 (October 1886): 236–37; Mrs. J. B. Safford, "Experiences of Spiritual and Physical Healing," *Triumphs of Faith* 4 (November 1884): 264; and Simpson, "The Gospel of Healing," *Triumphs of Faith,* 258–59.

53. Carter, *Atonement for Sin and Sickness,* 211 and 206.

Chapter Four • The Use of Means

1. Mrs. Sidney [Emma] Whittemore, "Made Perfectly Whole," in *A Cloud of Witnesses,* ed. A. B. Simpson, 94–108; and Robinson, ed. *Mother Whittemore's Records of Modern Miracles* (1931), 27.

2. Whittemore, "Made Perfectly Whole," *A Cloud of Witnesses,* 94–108.

3. Ibid.

4. Lindenberger, *Streams from the Valley of Berachah* (1893), 82–83.

5. Elizabeth Sisson, "Faith, Fasting and Prayer," *Triumphs of Faith* 7 (January 1887): 14. Proponents of divine healing often cited Romans 12:2, 2 Corinthians 4:18, and 2 Corinthians 5:7 in support of their position. In her autobiography, *Steppings in God*, 107, Mary H. Mossman mentions a fourth biblical "means": walking in the Spirit (Gal. 5:16), but the tripartite formulation is much more common. See, e.g., Frederick C. Seely, "The Heritage of the Church of Christ," *Triumphs of Faith* 3 (April 1883): 78–79, which mentions these three practices along with the corresponding scripture passages.

6. T. F. Thiselton Dyer, "Faith-Healing," *Gentleman's Magazine* 259 (July-December 1885): 61–74. Critiques of the divine healing movement were ubiquitous throughout the 1880s and 1890s. For additional examples of critical reviews and commentaries from this period, see, e.g.: Leonard Woolsey Bacon, "The Faith Cure Delusion," *Forum* 5 (March 1888): 691–98; Meredith Clymer, "Creed, Craft and Cure," *Forum* 5 (April 1888): 192–206; Frances Power Cobbe, "Faith Healing and Fear Killing," *Littell's Living Age* 174 [5th series, vol. 59], 16 July 1887, 131–42; "Exit—The Faith Cure," *Journal of the American Medical Association* 10 (June 16, 1888): 749; William I. Gill, "Isms. The Faith-Cure," *New-England Magazine and Bay State Monthly* 5 (March 1887): 438–39; William Hammond, "The Scientific Relations of Modern Miracles," *International Review* 10 (March 1881): 225–42; William E. Hull, "Divine Healing or Faith Cure," *Lutheran Quarterly* 27 (April 1897): 263–76; James Hendrie Lloyd, "Faith-Cures," *Medical Record: A Weekly Journal of Medicine and Surgery* 29 (March 27, 1886): 349–52; C. F. Nichols, "Divine Healing," *Science* 19 (January 22, 1892): 43–44; Lucius E. Smith, "Are Miracles to Be Expected?" *Bibliotheca Sacra* 48 (January 1891): 1–26; Samuel T. Spear, "The Faith Cure," *Independent* 34 (September 14, 1882): 7–8; Lloyd Tuckley, "Faith-Healing as a Medical Treatment," *Nineteenth Century* 24 (December 1888): 839–50; and Clyde W. Votaw, "Christian Science and Faith Healing," *New Englander and Yale Review* 54 (March 1891): 249–59.

7. Townsend, *"Faith-Work," "Christian Science," and Other Cures*, 57. A. F. Schauffler, "Faith-Cures: A Study in Five Chapters," *Century Magazine* 31 (December 1885): 274–78.

8. Walter Moxon, "Faith Healing," *Contemporary Review* 48 (November 1885): 707–22.

9. Lindenberger, *Streams from the Valley*, 82; and Mossman, *Steppings in God*, 17–22, 25, and 110–19.

10. Mossman, *Steppings in God*, 78; Otto Stockmayer, "The 'Look on Jesus,'" *Words of Faith* 11:8 (August 1885): 93–96; and Prosser, *From Death to Life*, 198.

11. Mossman, *Steppings in God*, 46.

12. Stockmayer, "The 'Look on Jesus,'" *Words of Faith*, 93; and Mossman, *Steppings in God*, 21–22.

13. Judd, *Prayer of Faith*, 126–28.

14. A. B. Simpson, *The Lord for the Body* (1925), 52; "The Work and the Workers: Christian Alliance Meeting and Ordination Service," *Triumphs of Faith* 13 (September 1893): 211–12; and Mossman, *Steppings in God*, 42.

15. Judd, *Prayer of Faith*, 130–31; and Carrie F. Judd, "The Temple of the Body," *Triumphs of Faith* 4 (February 1884): 25–27.

16. A. B. Simpson, "Principles of Divine Healing," *Triumphs of Faith* 7 (August 1887): 173.

17. John Salmon, "Trusting in the Lord," *Triumphs of Faith* 7 (January 1887): 13–16; Mrs. M. [Elizabeth] Baxter, "Deliverance from Sickness," *Triumphs of Faith* 1 (August 1881): 113–14; and Cullis, *Other Faith Cures*, 4–5.

18. Edward Ryder, "Healing Through Christ," *Triumphs of Faith* 5 (March 1885): 54.

19. Mrs. W. J. Starr, "Touching the Hem of His Garment," *Triumphs of Faith* 2 (March 1882): 39–41; Sarah Battles, "Experiences of Spiritual and Physical Healing," *Triumphs of Faith* 2 (April 1882): 63–64; Ruth S. King to Carrie F. Judd, *Triumphs of Faith* 3 (December 1883): 285–87; and *Record of the International Conference*, 22–23.

20. R. L. Stanton, "Did Christ Ever Use Means in Healing?" *Triumphs of Faith* 3 (August 1883): 177–79; and A. B. Simpson, "Divine Healing, Inquiries and Answers. Concluded," *Word, Work and World* 7:6 (December 1886): 338–42. This piece, along with the several articles on the same topic that preceded it, were reprinted in book form: *Inquiries and Answers* (1887).

21. Gordon, *Ministry of Healing*, 32; Judd, *Prayer of Faith*, 75; and "Rev. John E. Cookman, D.D.," in *A Cloud of Witnesses*, ed. A. B. Simpson, 7.

22. Gordon, *Ministry of Healing*, 32; Judd, *Prayer of Faith*, 71; C[harlotte] C. Murray, "Anointing Him With Oil," *Triumphs of Faith* 5 (May 1885): 97–100, also printed in *Words of Faith* 9 (May 1885): 49–51; R. K. Carter, "The Means of Faith," *Triumphs of Faith* 13 (April 1893): 85–91; and A. B. Simpson, *Gospel of Healing*, rev. ed (1915), 19.

23. Gordon, *Ministry of Healing*, 32–33; Elizabeth V. Baker, "My Savior and Healer," *Triumphs of Faith* 91 (September 1891): 193–99; Carter, "Means of Faith," *Triumphs of Faith*, 85–91.

24. Carra H. Close, "Taking God at His Word," *Triumphs of Faith* 5 (January 1885): 6–11; "The Living Word and the Vital Touch," *Triumphs of Faith* 11 (July 1891): 164; and "Testimonies of Divine Healing: Rev. F. C. A. Jones," *Word, Work and World* 8 (February 1887): 81–82.

25. Ryder, "Healing Through Christ," *Triumphs of Faith*, 54; and A. P. Moore, "Healing Faith," *Triumphs of Faith* 1 (April 1881): 55–6.

26. E. P. M., "Faith Healing," *Triumphs of Faith* 1 (September 1881): 129–31; Seely, "Heritage of the Church of Christ," *Triumphs of Faith*, 78; and Simpson, *Gospel of Healing*, 19.

27. A. B. Simpson, "The Conferences in Great Britain," *Word, Work and World* 5 (September 1885): 233–40; A. B. Simpson, "True and False Teaching Concerning Divine Healing," *Word, Work and World* 5 (November 1885): 293–94; and Simpson, "Divine Healing, Inquiries and Answers," *Word, Work and World*, 338–42.

28. Cullis, *More Faith Cures*, 7; Carrie F. Judd, "Holding Forth the Word of Life," *Triumphs of Faith* 3 (May 1883): 97; and Mrs. M. [Elizabeth] Baxter, "Questions Concerning Healing," *Word, Work and World* 5 (November 1885): 297–98.

29. Prosser, "Jesus Only," *Triumphs of Faith* 8, 31–34; Baxter, "Questions Concerning Healing," *Word, Work and World*, 297–98; and Simpson, "Conferences in Great Britain," *Word, Work and World*, 238.

30. Simpson, "True and False Teaching," *Word, Work and World*, 293–94.

31. Dyer, "Faith-healing," *Gentleman's Magazine*, 73. For discussions of the professionalization of medicine in this period, and particularly the tendency of "regular" or "orthodox" physicians to critique "sectarian" practitioners and "quacks," see, e.g., Burrow, *Organized Medicine in the Progressive Era*; Haller, *American Medicine in Transition*; Rosenberg, Prologue to *The Structure of American Medical Practice, 1875–1941*, by George Rosen; Rosenberg, "Therapeutic Revolution," 2–35; and Starr, *Social Transformation of American Medicine*. On the popularity and social geography of "quack" medicine, see Armstrong and Metzger Armstrong, *The Great American Medicine Show*, 173–84.

32. A. B. Simpson, editor's notes, *Word, Work and World* 3 (February 1883): 1.

33. A. B. Simpson, "The Gospel of Healing; Divine Healing and Demonism Not Identical. A Protest and Reply to Dr. Buckley in the Century Magazine," *Word, Work and World* 7 (July 1886): 52–58.

34. *Record of the International Conference,* 86.

35. "The Philadelphia Convention," *Words of Faith,* 11 (December 1885): 141–43; and Cullis, *Other Faith Cures,* 1.

36. *Dorothea Trudel,* 56.

37. Mossman, *Steppings in God,* 55–56.

38. Editorial reply to L. Baxter, *The Christian,* 16 July 1885, 13; and "Notes and Comments," *The Christian,* 25 June 1885, 12.

39. *Record of the International Conference,* 124.

40. Ibid.

41. Ibid.; and "Notes and Comments," *The Christian,* 11 June 1885, 15.

42. Buckley, "Faith-Healing and Kindred Phenomena," *Century Magazine,* 221–36; Simpson, "The Gospel of Healing; Divine Healing and Demonism Not Identical," *Word, Work and World,* 52–58; and Simpson, "The Gospel of Healing; Divine Healing and Demonism Not Identical. Concluded," *Word, Work and World,* 114–22.

43. Simpson, "The Gospel of Healing; Divine Healing and Demonism Not Identical. Concluded," *Word, Work and World,* 114.

44. Ibid., 116–17.

45. Ibid., 117.

46. Carrie F. Judd, "Ancient and Modern Spiritualism Considered in the Light of God's Word," *Triumphs of Faith* 6 (October 1886): 231–33.

47. Simpson, "The Gospel of Healing: Divine Healing and Demonism Not Identical," *Word, Work and World,* 57; and "The Gospel of Healing; Divine Healing and Demonism Not Identical. Concluded," *Word, Work and World,* 118.

48. *Kokomo (IN) Dispatch* 5 February 1885, 5; and "Woodworth's Wand," *Muncie (IN) Daily News* 21 September 1885, 4. Woodworth recounts her experiences and her entrance into the ministry of healing in Maria Woodworth-Etter, *Signs and Wonders God Wrought in the Ministry of Forty Years* (n.d.). See also, Maria B. Woodworth, *Life and Experiences of Maria B. Woodworth* (1885); M[aria] B. Woodworth, *Trials and Triumphs of Mrs. M. B. Woodworth* (1886); Maria Woodworth-Etter, *Life and Experiences* (1904); Maria Woodworth-Etter, *Acts of the Holy Ghost* (1912); and Maria Woodworth-Etter, *Life and Testimony of Mrs. M. B. Woodworth-Etter* (1925). For secondary accounts of Woodworth's life and ministry, see Wayne E. Warner, *The Woman Evangelist;* Hardesty, *Faith Cure,* 122–23; and Baer, "Perfectly Empowered Bodies," 203–12. For additional examples of press coverage highlighting the ecstatic features of Woodworth's revival meetings and comparing her healing work with magnetism, mesmerism, hypnotism, and magic see, e.g., "Sister Woodworth: She Knocks 'Em Cold," *Ft. Wayne (IN) Gazette,* 23 January 1885; "Trance Evangelism," *Cincinnati Enquirer,* 27 January 1885; "Religious Craze in Indiana," *New York Times,* 30 January 1885; "The Great Revival," *Cincinnati Enquirer,* 17 February 1885; "A Farcical Religion," *Indianapolis (IN) Times,* 11 May 1885, 1; Halleck Floyd, "Mrs. Woodworth's Work," *Christian Conservator,* 15 July 1886, 2; "Riotous Religion," *Indianapolis Sentinel,* 14 September 1886; "A Season of Trances," *Indianapolis (IN) Sentinel,* 9 December 1886; "The Camp Meeting," *The Champaign County (IL) Herald,*

24 August 1887; "Cancer Cured by Faith," *St. Louis (MO) Globe Democrat*, 3 September 1887, 12; "A Form of Emotional Religion," *Oakland (CA) Daily Evening Tribune*, 5 December 1889; "The Power," *Oakland Daily Evening Tribune*, 9 January 1890, 4; "Ring the Riot Alarm!" *San Francisco Examiner*, 9 January 1890; "Dangerous Hysteria," *Oakland Daily Evening Tribune*, 10 January 1890; "Victims of Hypnotism: Religious Frenzy Inspired by an Insane Evangelist," *New York Times*, 1 September 1890; "Quackery and Emotional Religion," *St. Louis (MO) Republic*, 3 September 1890; and "Magnetic Phenomena," *St. Louis (MO) Post-Dispatch*, 21 September 1890. I am deeply grateful to Jonathan Baer for sharing his file of newspaper clippings on Woodworth's ministry with me.

49. Three articles on Woodworth's revivals appeared in the *New York Times* in January of 1885: "Said to be Religion: Strange Scenes at 'Revival Meetings' Held in Indiana," *New York Times*, 24 January 1885; "An Evangelist at Work: A Revival in Indiana Conducted by Mrs. Woodworth," *New York Times*, 26 January 1885; and "Religious Craze in Indiana," *New York Times*, 30 January 1885. For Judd's initial reaction to Woodworth's revival meetings, see Carrie F. Judd, "The Work and the Workers," *Triumphs of Faith* 10 (January 1890), 19–23. For Sisson's own account of her involvement in Woodworth's ministry, see Elizabeth Sisson, *Foregleams of Glory* (1912), esp. 138–41. See also Wayne E. Warner, *Woman Evangelist*, 105 and 108–109. For Sisson's positive assessment of trance as a legitimate spiritual experience, see Elizabeth Sisson, "The Spiritual Priesthood Illustrated in Levi," *Triumphs of Faith* 19 (February 1890): 30–33.

50. Sisson expresses remorse for her role in promulgating false prophesies in several places. See, e.g., Carrie F. Judd, "The Work and the Workers," *Triumphs of Faith* 10 (May 1890): 116; and Elizabeth Sisson, "The Holy Ghost and Fire," *The Latter Rain Evangel* (May 1909): 9, quoted in Warner, *Woman Evangelist*, 109. Warner offers a full discussion of Woodworth's Oakland ministry, the scandal surrounding the doomsday prophesies, and the subsequent fallout in *Woman Evangelist*; see esp. 98–129 and 314–19. For a detailed account of the 1890 insanity trial, see Taves, *Fits, Trances and Visions*, 241–47.

51. Carrie F. Judd, "The Work and the Workers," *Triumphs of Faith* 10 (April 1890): 90–91; Judd, "The Work and the Workers," *Triumphs of Faith* 10 (May 1890): 116; and Carrie Judd Montgomery, "The Work and the Workers," *Triumphs of Faith* 10 (September 1890): 212–16.

52. John Alexander Dowie, "Trance Evangelism," *Leaves of Healing* 1 (January 1890): 98; reprinted 8 March 1895, 382. On Dowie's interactions with Woodworth, see "Diabology. Brother Dowie's War on Mankind. Sister Woodworth on the Side," *Oakland (CA) Daily Evening Tribune*, 1 February 1890, 1; and Warner, *Woman Evangelist*, 80–82, 94, 99, and 149. For a fuller history of Dowie's controversial ministry, see Baer, "Perfectly Empowered Bodies," 212–19; Chappell, "Divine Healing Movement," 283–339; Cook, *Zion City, Illinois*; Hardesty, *Faith Cure*, 51–53, 67–68, and 110–13; Mullin, *Miracles*, 203–208; John Swain, "John Alexander Dowie: The Prophet and His Profits. A Study, at First Hand, of 'A Modern Elijah,'" *Century Magazine* 64:7 (October 1902): 933–44; and Wacker, "Marching to Zion."

53. Simpson, "True and False Teaching," *Word, Work and World*, 294. While Simpson does not mention Woodworth directly, there is evidence to suggest that he may have had her in mind. As noted above, the *New York Times* had begun reporting on Woodworth's revival activities in January of 1885. Later that same year, Woodworth traveled to New York City and

attended one of Simpson's Gospel Tabernacle meetings; see Woodworth-Etter, *Acts of the Holy Ghost*, 118, quoted in Warner, *Woman Evangelist*, 31 and 155.

54. James M. Buckley, "Concluding Editorial on the West," *Christian Advocate*, 30 April 1891, 2. Buckley was also highly critical of Dowie's ministry. See, e.g., James M. Buckley, "Dowie, Analyzed and Classified," *Century Illustrated Monthly Magazine* 64 (October 1902): 928–32.

55. Dowie, "Trance Evangelism," *Leaves of Healing*, 98.

56. *Record of the International Conference*, 150.

57. Cullis, *Other Faith Cures*, 4; Simpson, "The Gospel of Healing; Divine Healing and Demonism Not Identical. Concluded," *Word, Work and World*, 114–22; Whittemore, "Made Perfectly Whole," in *A Cloud of Witnesses*, ed. A. B. Simpson, 96–97.

58. A. B. Simpson, editor's notes, *Word, Work and World* 3 (February 1883): 1; and "Rev. G. O. Barnes," *Word, Work and World* 1 (July 1882): 267. Barnes had visited New York in December of 1882 and assisted Simpson in a healing service. See W. T. Price, *Without Purse or Scrip* (1883), esp. 478–531, and 511. For more contemporary accounts of Barnes's ministry, see Mrs. L. A. Baldwin, "Faith in Jesus," *Triumphs of Faith* 2 (May 1882): 69–70; Thomas C. Barnum to Carrie F. Judd, 28 August 1883, *Triumphs of Faith* 3 (October 1883): 239; James M. Buckley, "George O. Barnes, Evangelist," *Christian Advocate* 58, 11 January 1883, 17–18; James M. Buckley, "George O. Barnes, Evangelist," *Christian Advocate* 58, 18 January 1883, 33–34; George O. Barnes, "Hallelujah," *Thy Healer* 1 (1884): 29–30; "A Young Lady's Faith," *New York Times*, 30 September 1882, 4; *New York Tribune*, 6 August 1882, 9; "The 'Mountain Evangelist,'" *New York Tribune*, 20 August 1882, 9; and "The 'Mountain Evangelist,'" *New York Tribune*, 10 June 1883, 10. For a helpful overview of Barnes's divine healing ministry, see Baer, "Perfectly Empowered Bodies," 149–50.

59. Baldwin, "Faith in Jesus," *Triumphs of Faith*, 69–70; Simpson, editor's notes, *Word, Work and World* 3 (February 1883): 1; "Rev. G. O. Barnes," *Word, Work and World*, 267; Buckley, "Faith Healing and Kindred Phenomena (Supplementary Article)," *Century Magazine*, 781–87; Townsend, *"Faith-Work," "Christian Science," and Other Cures*, 40; and A. B. Simpson, "Divine Healing. Reply to Rev. A. F. Schauffler," in *Inquiries and Answers* (1887), 21.

Chapter Five • Houses of Healing

1. "Miss H. M. Barker," in *A Cloud of Witnesses*, ed. A. B. Simpson, 170–78. See also Nettie M. Barker, "Made Whole in Christ," *Word, Work and World* 5 (April 1885): 124–25.

2. "H. M. Barker," in *A Cloud of Witnesses*, ed. A. B. Simpson, 170–78.

3. Ibid.

4. Ibid.

5. *Record of the International Conference*, 151–63. See also A. B. Simpson, "The Conferences in Great Britain," *Word, Work and World* 5 (September 1885): 233–40.

6. Mrs. M. [Elizabeth] Baxter, "American Faith Homes," *Thy Healer* 2 (1885): 350–54; Carrie F. Judd, "Faith-Work Abroad: Bethshan," *Triumphs of Faith* 2 (November 1882): 165–66. See also Wiseman, *Elizabeth Baxter*, 136.

7. A. B. Simpson, "The New Berachah Home," *Word, Work and World* (September 1886): 186–87.

8. Eliza J. Robertson to Carrie F. Judd, 12 November 1881, *Triumphs of Faith* 2 (April 1882): 62–63; and W. H. Daniels, *Dr. Cullis and His Work,* 349–52.

9. Boardman, *Life and Labours of the Rev. W. E. Boardman,* 234–35; "Faith-Healing," *The Christian,* 5 October 1882, 8; and Wiseman, *Elizabeth Baxter,* 133–34.

10. Carrie F. Judd, "Faith-Rest Cottage," *Triumphs of Faith* 2 (February 1882): 19–20; Judd Montgomery, *Under His Wing,* 83; Carrie F. Judd, "Faith-Rest Cottage," *Triumphs of Faith* 2 (March 1882): 45; Carrie F. Judd, "Faith-Rest Cottage," *Triumphs of Faith* 2 (May 1882): 71–72; and Carrie F. Judd, "Faith-Work," *Triumphs of Faith* 4 (December 1884): 265–69.

11. McClellan's testimony may be found in "Experiences of Spiritual and Physical Healing," *Triumphs of Faith* 4 (January 1884): 22–24. For Warner's testimony, see Mrs. S. J. Warner to Carrie F. Judd, 15 February 1885, *Triumphs of Faith* 5 (April 1885): 93–94.

12. Carrie F. Judd, "'Faith Rest,' Buffalo, N.Y.," *Triumphs of Faith* 8 (April 1884): 96; Carrie Judd Montgomery, "The Present Outlook of Our Work," *Triumphs of Faith* 10 (July 1890): 147–48.

13. *Record of the International Conference,* 27; Mrs. C. E. Chancey, "Healed by Power Divine," *Triumphs of Faith* 8 (August 1888): 178; and Simpson, "The New Berachah Home," *Word, Work and World,* 186.

14. "The Rest," *Triumphs of Faith* 3 (April 1883): 92–93; "Homes of Divine Healing," *Word, Work and World* 5 (October 1885): 253–54; Carrie F. Judd, "Bethany Home in Pittsburgh, PA," *Triumphs of Faith* 8 (March 1883): 98; and Carrie F. Judd, "'Beulah,' A New Faith Home," *Triumphs of Faith* 7 (March 1887): 60–61; Baxter, "American Faith Homes," *Thy Healer,* 350–54.

15. A. B. Simpson, "Editorial Paragraphs," *Word, Work and World* 3 (May and June 1883): 93; Judd, "Faith-Rest Cottage," *Triumphs of Faith* 2 (May 1882): 71–72; M.M.S., "Faith-Rest Cottage," *Triumphs of Faith* 2 (October 1882): 152; and Judd, "Beulah," *Triumphs of Faith,* 60–61.

16. Carrie F. Judd, "Faith-Rest Cottage," *Triumphs of Faith* 2 (April 1882): 59–60; Mrs. L. A. Fouke, "Faith-Rest Cottage," *Triumphs of Faith* 3 (June 1883): 139–40; and Baxter, "American Faith Homes," *Thy Healer,* 350.

17. Elizabeth Sisson, "Thoughts on 1 Peter, V," *Triumphs of Faith* 9 (February 1889): 35–38.

18. "Letter from Miss Carrie Bates, Missionary to India," *Triumphs of Faith* 9 (January 1889): 11–14; "Homes of Divine Healing," *Word, Work and World,* 253–54; and A. B. Simpson, "In Memoriam: Miss E. A. Griffin," *Word, Work and World* 8 (February 1887): 94–98.

19. Judd, "Faith-Rest Cottage," *Triumphs of Faith* (April 1882): 59–60; Baxter, "American Faith Homes," *Thy Healer,* 351.

20. George Muller, *The Life of Trust* (1873). On Mueller's ministry and influence on both British and American evangelicals, see Ostrander, *Life of Prayer,* 40–43. For an example of a critique of church fund-raising methods, see Prosser, *From Death to Life,* 197. On the "terms" that various faith houses established, see Judd, "Faith-Work," *Triumphs of Faith* 4 (December 1884): 265–69; W. H. Daniels, *Dr. Cullis and His Work,* 352; Carrie F. Judd, "Faith-Work Abroad: Bethshan," *Triumphs of Faith,* 165–66; and Kittie A. Sloan, "Faith Work in Stratford," *Triumphs of Faith* 4 (August 1884): 185–88.

21. For a critique of this financing method, see Buckley, "Faith-Healing and Kindred Phenomena (Supplementary Article)," *Century Magazine,* 781–87. Judd, "Faith-Work," *Triumphs of Faith,* 265–69; and "The Rest," *Triumphs of Faith,* 92–93.

22. For examples of individuals who compared themselves with the woman in Mark 5, see Alice Lancaster's testimony, in "Experiences of Physical and Spiritual Healing," *Triumphs*

of Faith 1 (February 1881): 30–31; and Elizabeth Baptist's account of her healing in Mix, *Faith Cures, and Answers to Prayer,* 72.

23. Beryl Satter discusses the rate policies of Christian Science healers in *Each Mind a Kingdom,* 85–86. Divine healing advocates contrasted their policies to magnetic, clairvoyant, orthodox, and Christian Science practitioners on many occasions and also confirmed that operating faith homes was not a profitable enterprise. See, e.g., Carrie F. Judd, "'He That Receiveth You Receiveth Me,'" *Triumphs of Faith* 6 (November 1886): 260; Cullis, *Faith Healing* (tract, n.d), 36; Judd, "Faith-Work," *Triumphs of Faith* 4 (December 1884): 265–69; and Prosser, *From Death to Life,* 164–69.

24. Libbie Osborn to Carrie Judd, *Triumphs of Faith* 7 (April 1887): 91–96; Carrie Judd Montgomery, "The Lord Our Healer," *Triumphs of Faith* 13 (January 1893): 8.

25. Carrie F. Judd, "Our Faith Meetings," *Triumphs of Faith* 1 (January 1881): 12.

26. Charlotte C. Murray, "Bethshan," *Triumphs of Faith* 2 (July 1882): 97–100; Judd, "Faith-Work Abroad: Bethshan," *Triumphs of Faith,* 165–66; Simpson, "The New Berachah Home," *Word, Work and World,* 186; Carrie F. Judd, "The Work and the Workers," *Triumphs of Faith* 9 (March 1889): 70–71; and (Rev.) J. A. Ivison to Carrie F. Judd, 2 October 1882, *Triumphs of Faith* 2 (December 1882): 192.

27. *Dorothea Trudel,* 9 and 58–59.

28. Wiseman, *Elizabeth Baxter,* 136; and Judd, "Faith-Work Abroad: Bethshan," *Triumphs of Faith,* 165–66. For more on Barnett's embrace of divine healing and her work at Berachah, see "Dr. A. Barnett," in *A Cloud of Witnesses,* ed. A. B. Simpson, 41–43; and Pardington, *Twenty-Five Wonderful Years,* 212–13.

29. Moxon, "Faith Healing," *Contemporary Review,* 707–22.

30. Townsend, *"Faith Work," "Christian Science," and Other Cures,* 140.

31. Ibid., 133–53.

32. "The Faith Cure in Court. A Minister Forced to Substitute Physicians for Prayers," *New York Times,* 6 June 1884, 8; and Townsend, *"Faith Work," "Christian Science," and Other Cures,* 164.

33. Charles Cullis, quoted in Townsend, *"Faith Work," "Christian Science," and Other Cures,* 160–61; and Daniel Steele, "Faith Healing and Broken Legs," *Zion's Herald,* quoted in Townsend, *"Faith Work," "Christian Science," and Other Cures,* 163.

34. Cullis, *Faith Healing,* 16.

35. Townsend, *"Faith Work," "Christian Science," and Other Cures,* 164–66; and Cullis, *Faith Healing,* 15. A. J. Gordon also included the case in question in his influential text, *The Ministry of Healing,* 184–85.

36. Cullis, *Faith Healing,* 26; and preface to *Faith Cures.*

37. Cullis, *Faith Healing,* 26; and *Dorothea Trudel,* 63.

38. R. K. Carter, "Divine Healing, or 'Faith Cure,'" *Century Illustrated Monthly Magazine* (November 1886 to April 1887): 780.

39. A. B. Simpson, "Divine Healing: Reply to Rev. A. F. Schauffler," in *Inquiries and Answers,* part II (1887), 3.

40. Alfred T. Schofield, *A Study of Faith-Healing* (ca. 1892), 117. Hodge's lecture is quoted in A. B. Simpson, "Prayer and the Prayer Cure. A Reply to Dr. Hodge," in *Inquiries and Answers,* part II, 44–45.

41. A. B. Simpson, "Divine Healing, Inquiries and Answers. Concluded," *Word, Work and World* 7:6 (December 1886): 338–42; Simpson, "Prayer and the Prayer Cure," *Inquiries and Answers*, 45.

42. Simpson, "Prayer and the Prayer Cure," *Inquiries and Answers*, 45; Simpson, "Divine Healing. Reply to Rev. A. F. Schauffler," *Inquiries and Answers*, 4; and Carrie F. Judd, "Faith Without Works," *Triumphs of Faith* 4 (October 1884): 145–46.

43. Judd, "Faith Without Works," *Triumphs of Faith*, 145–46; Carrie F. Judd, "The Lord Our Healer," *Triumphs of Faith* 5 (December 1885): 269–73; Simpson, "Divine Healing, Inquiries and Answers. Concluded," *Word, Work and World*, 338–42; and Cullis, *Faith Healing*, 24.

44. Charles Ryder, "The Gospel of Healing," *Triumphs of Faith* 8 (January 1888): 16–21; and Frederick C. Seely, "The Heritage of the Church of Christ," *Triumphs of Faith* 3 (April 1883): 78–80.

45. George Milton Hammell, "Religion and Fanaticism," *Methodist Review* 70 (July 1888): 530–38; and "Discussing Faith Cures: Contradictory Opinions of Baptist Ministers," *New York Times*, 5 May 1885, 8. The accusation described in the *New York Times* article was likely leveled against J. C. Young, a former superintendent of Cullis's work in Boston who opened a faith home in Brooklyn in 1882. For Young's story, see J. C. Young, "God's Testimony to His Word Through Faith Healing," *Word, Work and World* 1 (May 1882): 149–51.

46. Mrs. M. [Elizabeth] Baxter, "Spoken in a Son," *Triumphs of Faith* 9 (April 1889): 73–74.

47. Simpson, "Divine Healing. Reply to Rev. A. F. Schauffler," *Inquiries and Answers*, 9.

48. Maggie Mitchell, "Experiences of Spiritual and Physical Healing," *Triumphs of Faith* 2 (September 1882): 144.

49. Mrs. J. K. Brinkerhoff, "An Instance of God's Healing Power," *Triumphs of Faith* 3 (January 1883): 1–5.

50. "Mrs. J. C. Barrett," in *A Cloud of Witnesses*, ed. A. B. Simpson, 161–65.

51. Mrs. T. L. Mansfield to Carrie F. Judd, 21 August 1882, *Triumphs of Faith* 2 (October 1882): 158.

52. Buckley, "Faith-Healing and Kindred Phenomena. (Supplementary Article)," *Century Magazine*, 781–87.

53. Ibid.

54. Prosser, *From Death to Life*, esp. 8–12, 30–40, 53–61, and 68–69.

55. For Bates's story, see Carrie B. Bates to Carrie F. Judd, 22 November 1884, *Triumphs of Faith* 4 (December 1884): 286–88; Bates, "The Lord My Healer and Keeper," *Triumphs of Faith* 2 (February 1889): 25–29; and Pardington, *Twenty-Five Wonderful Years*, 172–73.

56. Dawlly's testimony is included in Carrie F. Judd, "Convention Notes," *Triumphs of Faith* 7 (December 1887): 265–62.

Chapter Six • The Lord of the Body

1. Helen F. Dawlly, "In An Acceptable Time," *Triumphs of Faith* 1 (November 1881): 165–68; Carrie F. Judd, "Convention Notes," *Triumphs of Faith* 7 (December 1887): 265–69; and Jennie Fuller, *White Fields: Sketch of Helen Dawlly*, esp. 9, 11, and 15–24.

2. Dawlly, "In An Acceptable Time," *Triumphs of Faith*, 165–68; Judd, "Convention Notes," *Triumphs of Faith*, 265–69; and Fuller, *White Fields*, 17–32.

3. A. B. Simpson, "The First Promise of Physical Healing," *Word, Work, and World* 3 (February 1883): 23.

4. The literature on late-nineteenth-century Protestant reform efforts is well developed. For helpful discussions of the relationship between Holiness and Higher Life evangelicalism and social reform, see Long, *The Revival of 1857–1858;* Magnuson, *Salvation in the Slums;* Marsden, *Fundamentalism and American Culture,* esp. 72–85; McLoughlin, *Revivalism, Awakenings, and Reform;* Jean Miller Schmidt, *Souls or the Social Order;* and Smith, *Revivalism and Social Reform.* For a more contemporary account of evangelical social efforts, see Pierson, *Forward Movements of the Last Half Century* (1905). The best analysis of the overlap between evangelicalism, progressivism, and the emerging Social Gospel is still Grant Wacker's influential article, "The Holy Spirit and the Spirit of the Age," 45–62.

5. The following account of A. B. Simpson's ministry and healing is drawn from several biographical and autobiographical sources, including an anthology of primary sources edited by Charles Nienkirchen, "The Man, the Movement, and the Mission"; an unpublished collection of primary documents compiled by C. Donald McKaig, "Simpson Scrapbook"; J. S. Sawin, "Alliance History—Simpson: The Man and the Movement"; A. E. Thompson, *The Life of A. B. Simpson: Official Authorized Edition* (1920); and A. W. Tozer, *Wingspread.* For a version of Simpson's own account of his illness and experience at Old Orchard Beach, see "Document 13—A. B. Simpson: extract from A. B. Simpson, *Gospel of Healing,*" in Nienkirchen, "Man, Movement, and Mission," 107–11; and "Document No. 12—Newspaper Reports (n.d.) taken from McKaig, ed., "Simpson Scrapbook," in Nienkirchen, "Man, Movement, and Mission," 100. See also Evearitt, *Body and Soul: Evangelism and the Social Concern of A. B. Simpson.*

6. For Simpson's discussion of his emotional state during the summer of 1881, see "Document 13," in Nienkirchen, "Man, Movement, and Mission," 107. Extracts from Simpson's journal included in both Nienkirchen's "Man, Movement, and Mission" and McKaig's "Simpson Scrapbook" attest to his tendency to work without sleeping; see, e.g., McKaig, "Simpson Scrapbook," 176. For the Simpsons' reservations about New York City, see Nienkirchen, "Man, Movement, and Mission," 93. Simpson expressed his interest in reaching the masses in a journal entry dated 22 February 1880, in McKaig, "Simpson Scrapbook," 176.

7. "Document 13," in Nienkirchen, "Man, Movement, and Mission," 107–11.

8. On Simpson's relationship with his congregation, see, e.g., "Quitting the Pulpit to Go Among the Churchless," in Nienkirchen, "Man, Movement, and Mission," 103–105; "Retiring from the Pulpit: A Presbyterian Preacher's Changed View of Baptism," ibid., 105–106; "Document No. 15—A. B. Simpson: The Work of the Christian and Missionary Alliance" (1916), ibid., 116–22; and "Document No. 16—A. B. Simpson: A Story of Providence" (1907), ibid., 122–31. Simpson also changed his views on infant baptism and no longer felt able to administer the sacrament within the context of his Presbyterian church in good conscience. In his farewell address to his congregation as well as in his meeting with his church and denominational officers, however, he indicated that his opinion regarding baptism was secondary to his sense of calling to the work of urban and foreign missions. See, e.g., "Quitting the Pulpit," and "Retiring from the Pulpit," in Nienkirchen, "Man, Movement, and Mission," 103–105 and 105–107.

9. "The Work of the Christian and Missionary Alliance," in Nienkirchen, "Man, Movement, and Mission," 118.

10. "Quitting the Pulpit," 103–105.

11. Ibid.; "How the Church Can Reach the Masses," *Word, Work and World* 1 (January 1882): 24–25; "The Rich and the Poor Meet Together," *Word, Work and World* 1 (January 1882): 25; and "The Religious Wants of New York," *Word, Work and World* 1 (January 1882): 26–28.

12. "Religious Wants of New York," *Word, Work and World*, 27.

13. "Quitting the Pulpit," 103–105; "The Rich and the Poor," *Word, Work and World*, 25.

14. "Religious Wants of New York," *Word, Work and World*, 27–28.

15. "The Gospel Tabernacle, New York," *Word, Work and World* 3 (March 1883): 45–46; and "A. B. Simpson: A Story of Providence," in Nienkirchen, "Man, Movement, & Mission," 123.

16. "The Gospel Tabernacle," *Word, Work and World*, 45; "A. B. Simpson: A Story of Providence," 123; and "The Rich and the Poor," *Word, Work and World*, 25.

17. "How the Church Can Reach the Masses," *Word, Work and World*, 24.

18. Ibid., 25; and "Quitting the Pulpit," 104.

19. McKaig's "Simpson Scrapbook" contains various articles describing the Gospel Tabernacle's early meeting locations; see pp. 192–98. For the reasoning behind the decision to meet in secular locations, see, e.g., "Quitting the Pulpit," 104.

20. "The Flesh and the Spirit: A Sermon Preached by Rev. A. B. Simpson, New York, April 29, 1883," *Word, Work and World*, 3 (May and June, 1883): 73–74; Pardington, *Twenty-Five Wonderful Years*, 26–29; and "A Church in Salmi Morse's Theatre," in McKaig, "Simpson Scrapbook," 201–203.

21. Pardington, *Twenty-Five Wonderful Years*, 28; and "The Gospel Tabernacle," *Word, Work and World*, 46.

22. "The Gospel Tabernacle," *Word, Work and World*, 6; Robinson, *Mother Whittemore*, 156, 162, and 164; and R. Wheatley, "Gospel Work among the Masses," *Word, Work and World* 5 (October 1885): 264.

23. Robinson, *Mother Whittemore*, 180–85.

24. Ibid., 48–53. For the broader context of anti-prostitution efforts in North American cities leading up to and during the late nineteenth century, see Smith-Rosenberg, *Disorderly Conduct*, 109–28; and Smith-Rosenberg, *Religion and the Rise of the American City*.

25. Robinson, *Mother Whittemore*, 41–47.

26. For illustrations, see Robinson, *Mother Whittemore*, 128, 208, and 209. Interestingly, before and after photographs were rarely (if ever) produced as a means of legitimating or illustrating a testimony of divine healing of disease, perhaps because "manifestations" and symptoms often failed to disappear.

27. Robinson, *Mother Whittemore*, 155–56.

28. Ibid., 155–56.

29. Magnuson, *Salvation in the Slums*, 79–90.

30. Reformers did recognize that women were also susceptible to the corrupting effects of alcohol, noting that most "fallen women" were also heavy drinkers. Although treatment for alcoholism was part of the program in rescue homes for these women, workers conceived of their clientele primarily in terms of their sexual degradation. Substance abuse abetted prostitution, but it was not the principal problem. For a discussion of the relationship between temperance and anti-prostitution efforts, as well as temperance efforts aimed primarily at men, see Magnuson, *Salvation in the Slums*, 132–42. On the involvement of divine healing

leaders in various temperance and reform movements, see, e.g., Judd Montgomery, *Under His Wings,* 89; Prosser, *From Death to Life,* esp. 44–47 and 69–79; Robinson, *Mother Whittemore,* 21–25; and Jennie Smith, *Ramblings in Beulah Land* and *Incidents and Experiences.*

31. Magnuson, *Salvation in the Slums,* 132–42. See also Walters, *American Reformers.*

32. Pardington, *Twenty-Five Wonderful Years,* 61. On the social implications of the pre-millennialist position, see, e.g., Marsden, *Fundamentalism and American Culture,* esp. 48–93; Marsden, *Understanding Fundamentalism and Evangelicalism,* 39–41; and Wacker, "The Holy Spirit and the Spirit of the Age," 58. On premillennialist eschatology in general, see chap. 2, n. 56 above.

33. For a historical overview of the burgeoning interest in foreign missions among late-nineteenth-century evangelicals, see Robert, *American Women in Mission.* On the founding of *The Word, Work and World* and the Missionary Training College, see A. B. Simpson, "End of Vol. 1," *Word, Work and World* 1 (July 1882): 242; Pardington, *Twenty-Five Wonderful Years,* 30; and "The Work. The Dedication Services," *Word, Work and World* 7 (October 1886): 234. Carrie B. Bates recounts her missions work and her association with the New York Missionary Training College in "The Lord My Healer and Keeper," *Triumphs of Faith* 9 (February 1889): 25–29. For more on the founding and development of missionary training schools in this period, see Brereton, *Training God's Army.*

34. *Record of the International Conference,* 69. Announcements and descriptions of the North American conferences may be found in *Triumphs of Faith* 5 (September 1885): 216; "A Christian Convention in Philadelphia," *Triumphs of Faith* 5 (October 1885): 240; "Report of the Christian Convention in Buffalo, N.Y.," *Triumphs of Faith* 5 (November 1885): 241; and Carrie F. Judd, "Convention Report," *Triumphs of Faith* 5 (December 1885): 265.

35. Mrs. M. [Elizabeth] Baxter, "The Gospel of Healing," *Triumphs of Faith* 5 (December 1885): 274–75.

36. Baxter, "The Gospel of Healing," *Triumphs of Faith,* 274–75; and A. B. Simpson, "Divine Healing," *Triumphs of Faith* 5 (December 1885): 276–79.

37. Mrs. Rev. Wm. B. [Lucy Drake] Osborne, "Missions in Foreign Lands," *Triumphs of Faith* 5 (December 1885): 279–84. Drake set sail for India in early November, 1875. For accounts of her missionary activities, see her autobiography, *Heavenly Pearls Set in a Life* (1893); W. H. Daniels, *Dr. Cullis and His Work,* 245 and 300–302; "Missionary Training School," *Triumphs of Faith* 5 (October 1885): 221–23; Patton, *Prayer and Its Remarkable Answers,* 190–95; and Amanda Berry Smith, *An Autobiography* (1893), 308. For Dawlly's encounter with Drake Osborn see Judd, "Convention Notes," *Triumphs of Faith,* 266–68.

38. "A New Missionary Alliance," *Word, Work and World* 8 (June 1887): 365–68; A. B. Simpson, "Editorial Paragraphs," *Word, Work and World* 9 (August and September 1887): 110–11; and Pardington, *Twenty-Five Wonderful Years,* esp. 34–46. See also Ekvall, *After Fifty Years: A Record of God's Working Through the Christian and Missionary Alliance;* and Niklaus, Sawin, and Stoesz, *All for Jesus: God at Work in the Christian and Missionary Alliance.*

39. For a list of founding officers, see Simpson, "Editorial Paragraphs," *Word, Work and World,* 110–11; and "The Christian Alliance," *Triumphs of Faith* 8 (February 1888): 48. On the involvement of A. J. Gordon, Anna Prosser, and others in local Alliance conventions, see, e.g., Carrie F. Judd, "The Work and the Workers," *Triumphs of Faith* 9 (February 1889): 46–47; Carrie F. Judd, "The Work and the Workers," *Triumphs of Faith* 9 (January 1889): 21–24; and

Carrie F. Judd, "The Work and the Workers," *Triumphs of Faith* 9 (June 1889): 138–40. Pardington, *Twenty-Five Wonderful Years,* 58.

40. Pardington, *Twenty-Five Wonderful Years,* esp. 107–39 and 161–204. On the Alliance's policies toward women in foreign missions, see Robert, esp. 25–137, 167–69, and 189–205. Simpson articulates his views in "A New Missionary Alliance," *Word, Work and World,* 367; and "The Old Orchard Convention. Opening Address," *Word, Work and World* 7 (September 1886): 130–32.

41. Carrie B. Bates, "Missionary Address," *Triumphs of Faith* 8 (November 1888): 249–51.

42. Pardington, *Twenty-Five Wonderful Years,* 130 and 58–62.

43. Fuller, *White Fields,* 25, 31, 41, and 43–44.

Conclusion

1. Smith, *Incidents and Experiences,* see esp. 5, 51, 55, 66, 68–70, 160, and 189.

2. On Judd Montgomery's ongoing involvement with ministries of divine healing, including the founding of an interdenominational weekly meeting for divine healing in downtown Oakland in 1910 that continued for many years, see her autobiography, *Under His Wings,* and Storms, "A Theology of Healing Based on the Writings of Carrie Judd Montgomery," 77. Judd also describes her friendship with Jennie Smith in *Under His Wings.* For Smith's description of her own prayers for healing in the years following her dramatic cure, see Smith, *Incidents and Experiences,* 68–70 and 160. For her explanation of her call to ministry, see Jennie Smith, "The Promised Cities of Faith," *Word, Work and World* 7 (October 1886): 199–200.

3. For accounts of Lucy Drake Osborn's activities following her healing in 1871, see chap. 6, n. 37 above.

4. "Homes of Divine Healing," *Word, Work and World* 5, 253–54; A. B. Simpson, "Editorial Paragraphs," *Word, Work and World* 4 (August and September 1887): 110–11; "Summer Conventions," *Word, Work and World* 4 (August and September 1887): 65–68; A. B. Simpson, "Editorials," *Christian Alliance and Foreign Missionary Weekly* 16 (24 January 1896): 84.

5. Carter, *"Faith Healing" Reviewed,* 17 and 110–12. The Alliance's changing policy toward the use of medicine on the mission field as well as toward medical missionaries is discussed in Hardesty, *Faith Cure,* 137. See also Wilson, "The Christian & Missionary Alliance: Developments and Modifications of Its Original Objectives"; and Bedford, "'A Larger Christian Life': A. B. Simpson and the Early Years of the Christian and Missionary Alliance."

6. Carter, *"Faith Healing" Reviewed,* 126–27.

7. Buckley, "Faith-Healing and Kindred Phenomena," *Century Illustrated Monthly,* 221–36. William Taylor's letter to William McDonald, 15 May 1885, is reprinted in "Latest From Bishop Taylor: Death of One of His Missionaries," *Christian Witness and Advocate of Bible Holiness* 3:13, 2 July 1885, 1.

8. "Modern Miracles," *Christian Witness and Advocate of Bible Holiness* 2:4, 21 February 1884, 4; "Misplaced Faith," *Christian Witness and Advocate of Bible Holiness* 3:15, 16 July 1885, 4; "Faith-Healing in the Epistles," *Christian Witness and Advocate of Bible Holiness* 4:6, 18 March 1886, 1; and "Errors Respecting Faith-Healing," *Christian Witness and Advocate of Bible Holiness* 4:8, 15 April 1886, 1.

9. Daniel Steele to Jennie Smith, 9 June 1879, reprinted in *From Baca to Beulah,* 353–55; and Gracey and Steele, *Healing by Faith.* J. W. Hamilton makes this same distinction between

the grace of faith and the gift of faith in "The Faith Cure," *The Chautauquan* 11:2 (May 1890): 204–208.

10. For a lucid and detailed account of the discord that divine healing provoked within American Methodism, in particular, see Baer, "Perfectly Empowered Bodies," 152–99.

11. Charles Cullis, *The Twenty-Fifth Annual Report of the Consumptives Home, and Other Institutions Connected with a Work of Faith, to Sept 30, 1892* (1893), 28–30; Chappell, "Divine Healing Movement," 188–91; and Gordon, *Adoniram Judson Gordon: A Biography,* 367–86.

12. Carter, *"Faith-Healing" Reviewed,* 13, 18 and 117. For Dowie's criticism of Simpson and the Christian Alliance, see J. A. Dowie, "That Great Neglected Chapter," *Leaves of Healing* 3, 8 March 1895, 380–82. Helpful accounts of Dowie's healing ministry and his broader activities include Baer, "Perfectly Empowered Bodies," 212–19; Chappell, "Divine Healing Movement," 284–340; and Hardesty, *Faith Cure,* 51–53 and 67–68. See also chap. 4, n. 52, above.

13. George Montgomery had been healed of diabetes through Dowie's ministry in 1888; see Rev. John Alexander Dowie and Jane Dowie, *American First-fruits* (1895), 140–41. Carter, *"Faith-Healing" Reviewed,* esp. 86–87, 89–91, and 153–61.

14. Carter, *"Faith-Healing" Reviewed,* esp. 12–13, 21, 51, 54, 74, 105, and 117.

15. Ibid., esp. 107, 89–90, 126–27, and 34.

16. Ibid., esp. 126–27, 63, 86–91, and 118–21.

17. Ibid., 128.

18. Ibid., 121; and *Leaves of Healing* 2 (28 August 1897): 697. For more detailed accounts of Dowie's tirade against physicians and medicine, and the riot that his sermon provoked, see Chappell, "Divine Healing Movement," esp. 286–87 and 330–32; and Mullin, *Miracles,* 203–205.

19. Baer, "Perfectly Empowered Bodies," 173–74. On the tendency of these independent holiness or "come outer" groups to emphasize the cosmological significance of divine healing, and especially Satan's agency in sickness, see Baer, "Perfectly Empowered Bodies," 149–50.

20. On the divergent reactions to Pentecostalism among various proponents of divine healing, see Hardesty, *Faith Cure,* 106–10. For Judd Montgomery's embrace of Pentecostalism, see Judd Montgomery, *Under His Wings,* esp. 150–51, 159–61, and 164–69. Historians agree that Simpson's discomfort with Pentecostalism prompted him to moderate his emphasis on divine healing. See, e.g., Baer, "Perfectly Empowered Bodies," 95–96; Hardesty, *Faith Cure,* 144–45; Nienkirchen, *A. B. Simpson and the Pentecostal Movement;* and Opp, *Lord for the Body,* 127–34. Mossman discusses her reaction to Pentecostalism in *Steppings in God,* 149–69. On the Alliance's changing stance, see *President's Report of the Christian and Missionary Alliance for the year 1905–6* (30 May 1906): 7; *Twelfth Annual Report of the Christian and Missionary Alliance (Reorganized)* (Nyack, NY: 25 May 1909): 50 and 11; Pardington, *Twenty-Five Wonderful Years,* 50; and Opp, *Lord for the Body,* 133 and 151–53.

21. Historians of divine healing debate the extent to which Pentecostalism represented a "break" from earlier forms of faith healing embraced by Holiness and Higher Life evangelicals. Paul Chappell argues most forcefully for the continuity between these various movements in "Divine Healing Movement," see esp. v–vi and 192. While I concur with Chappell's conviction that divine healing and Holiness in many ways presaged Pentecostalism and promoted theological doctrines that Pentecostals would embrace, I also agree with scholars such as Baer, Hardesty, Mullin, and Opp, who insist that Pentecostalism transformed divine heal-

ing in fundamental ways. For overviews of the characteristics of Pentecostal healing and the ways Pentecostalism reshaped the late-nineteenth-century divine healing movement, see Baer, "Perfectly Empowered Bodies," esp. 6, 95–96, 254–56, and 327–30; Hardesty, *Faith Cure,* 106–10; and Opp, *Lord for the Body,* 94 and 120–45. For Pentecostalism's preoccupation with the supernatural world, and especially with Satan, alongside a relative disinterest in social reform, see Wacker, *Heaven Below,* 59, 62–65, and 223–25.

22. Warfield, *Counterfeit Miracles* (1918), 193–95. For more on Warfield and the reaction of fundamentalists to Pentecostalism, see Baer, "Perfectly Empowered Bodies," 303–26; Hardesty, *Faith Cure,* 139–44; and Mullin, *Miracles,* 210–13.

23. Hammell, "Religion and Fanaticism," *Methodist Review,* 535; Hepworth, "The Faith Cure," *The Independent,* 1; and Schofield, *Study of Faith Healing,* 127–28.

24. Mrs. George C. [Elizabeth Annabelle] Needham, *Mrs. Whilling's Faith Cure* (1891), esp. 93, 111, 95–96, and 99. See also her "Jehovah-Rophi—The Lord Our Healer," *Watchword* 4:3 (December 1881): 57–58; and Alfred W. Needham, *Events and Experiences in the Life of George C. Needham, Evangelist* (1900).

25. For overviews of twentieth-century Pentecostal and charismatic healing movements, see Chappell, "Healing Movements," 353–74; Harrell, *All Things Are Possible;* and Hardesty, *Faith Cure,* 101–28. For the Word of Faith, or Positive Confession movement, see Lovett, "Positive Confession Theology," in *Dictionary of Pentecostal and Charismatic Movements,* 718–20.

26. On Conwell, see R. H. Conwell, *Acres of Diamonds* (1943).

27. Lovett, "Positive Confession Theology," 718–20. Frederick K. C. Price published a book with the title *Name It and Claim It: The Power of Positive Confession* (Los Angeles, CA: Faith One Pub., 1992).

28. Griffith, *Born Again Bodies,* 248 and viii.

29. Morris, *The Culture of Pain,* 1–2, 20 and 4; and "Placebo: Conversations at the Disciplinary Borders," 188 and 190–91. For the term "culturogenic," see Harrington, *Placebo Effect,* 9. Other recent discussions of the relationship between culture, personal belief, and the experience of pain include: Coakley and Shelemay, eds. *Pain and Its Transformations;* Csordas, *Body/Meaning/Healing;* Glucklich, *Sacred Pain;* Good et al., *Pain as Human Experience;* Kleinman, *Illness Narratives;* and Mattingly and Garro, eds., *Narrative and the Cultural Construction of Illness and Healing.*

30. On the "hermeneutical," "interpretive," and "narrative" dimensions of pain, see esp. Coakley and Shelemay, *Pain and Its Transformations;* and Kleinman, *Illness Narratives.*

Primary Sources

ARCHIVAL COLLECTIONS

Cullis, Charles. *Annual Reports of the Consumptives' Home.* Boston, 1865–1895. Bound as *A Work of Faith,* v. 1–6. Simmons College Archives, Boston, MA.

Gordon, Adoniram Judson. Papers. Archives, Jenks Library and Learning Resource Center, Gordon College, Wenham, MA.

Gordon, Adoniram Judson. Papers. Archives, Goddard Library, Gordon-Conwell Theological Seminary, South Hamilton, MA.

Montgomery, Carrie Judd. Papers. Flower Pentecostal Heritage Center, Assemblies of God Headquarters, Springfield, MO.

Simpson, Albert Benjamin. Papers. Christian and Missionary Alliance Archives, Colorado Springs, CO.

Smith, Jennie. Papers. Alice Marshall Women's History Collection, Penn State Harrisburg Library, Middletown, PA.

Woodworth-Etter, Maria B. Papers. Flower Pentecostal Heritage Center, Assemblies of God Archives, Springfield, MO.

PERIODICALS

Bibliotheca Sacra. Andover, MA. 1891.

Century Illustrated Monthly Magazine. New York. 1885–1887, 1902.

Champaign County Herald. Urbana, IL. 1887.

Chautauquan. Jamestown, NY. 1890.

Christian. London. 1882–1889.

Christian Advocate. New York. 1883, 1891.

Christian Alliance. New York. 1887–1891.

Christian Alliance and Foreign Missionary Weekly. New York. 1894–1896.

Christian Alliance and Missionary Weekly. New York. 1891–1893.

Christian and Missionary Alliance. New York. 1897–1911.

Christian Conservator. Dayton, OH. 1886.

Christian Science Journal. Boston. 1883–1893.

Christian Witness and Advocate of Bible Holiness. Boston. 1883–1886.

Cincinnati Enquirer. Cincinnati, OH. 1885.

Congregationalist. Boston. 1885.

Contemporary Review. London. 1885.

Fort Wayne Gazette. Fort Wayne, IN. 1885.

Forum. New York. 1888.

Gentleman's Magazine. London. 1885.

Guide to Holiness. New York. 1864–1901.

Independent. New York. 1882.

Indianapolis Sentinel. Indianapolis, IN. 1886.

Indianapolis Times. Indianapolis, IN. 1885.

International Review. New York. 1881.

Journal of the American Medical Association. Chicago. 1888.

Kokomo Dispatch. Kokomo, IN. 1885.

Latter Rain Evangel. Chicago. 1909.

Leaves of Healing. Chicago. 1894–1906.

Littell's Living Age. Boston. 1887.

Lutheran Quarterly. Gettysburg, PA. 1897.

Medical Record: A Weekly Journal of Medicine and Surgery. New York. 1886.

Methodist Review. New York. 1888.

Muncie Daily News. Muncie, IN. 1885.

New England Magazine and Bay State Monthly. Boston. 1887.

New York Times. New York. 1880–1890.

New York Tribune. New York. 1882.

Nineteenth Century. London. 1888.

Oakland Daily Evening Tribune. Oakland, CA. 1890.

Presbyterian Review. New York. 1883–1884.

St. Louis Globe Democrat. St. Louis, MO. 1887.

St. Louis Republic. St. Louis, MO. 1890.

St. Louis Post-Dispatch. St. Louis, MO. 1890.

Thy Healer. London. 1884–1885.

Times of Refreshing. Boston. 1869–1871.

Triumphs of Faith. Buffalo, NY and Oakland, CA. 1881–1905.

Victory Through Faith. Torrington, CT. 1884.

Watchword. Boston. 1878–1896.

Word, Work and World. New York. 1882–1887.

Words of Faith. Philadelphia. 1884–1885.

SELECTED BOOKS AND TRACTS

Allen, Ethan O. *Faith Healing; or, What I Have Witnessed of the Fulfillment of James V: 14, 15, 16.* Philadelphia: G. W. McCalla, 1881.

Atwell, Harriet G. *Chloe Lankton; or, Light Beyond the Clouds. A Story of Real Life.* Philadelphia: American Sunday School Union, 1859.

Baker, Elizabeth V., et. al. *Chronicles of a Faith Life.* Reprint, New York: Garland Publishing, 1984.

Baxter, Mrs. M. [Elizabeth]. *Divine Healing.* Brighton: Christian Herald Co., n.d.

———. *Holy Ghost Days.* London: Christian Herald, 1888.

Beard, George M. *American Nervousness, Its Causes and Consequences: A Supplement to Nervous Exhaustion (neurasthenia).* New York: Putnam, 1881.

Beecher, Catharine Esther. *Essay on Slavery and Abolitionism with Reference to the Duty of American Females.* Philadelphia: Henry Perkins, 1837.

———. *Letters to the People on Health and Happiness.* New York: Harper and Bros, 1855.

Boardman, Mrs. [Mary M. Adams]. *Life and Labours of the Rev. W. E. Boardman.* New York: D. Appleton and Co., 1887.

Boardman, William E. *Faith-Work under Dr. Cullis, in Boston.* Boston: Willard Tract Repository, 1874.

———. *The Great Physician (Jehovah Rophi).* Boston: Willard Tract Repository, 1881.

———. *The Higher Christian Life.* Chicago: Wm. Tomlinson, 1858.

Buckley, James Monroe. *An Address on Supposed Miracles.* New York: Hurd and Houghton, 1875.

———. *Faith-Healing, Christian Science and Kindred Phenomena.* New York: Century Co., 1887.

Bushnell, Horace. *Nature and the Supernatural as Together Constituting the One System of God.* New York: C. Scribner, 1858.

Carter, Russell Kelso. *The Atonement for Sin and Sickness; or A Full Salvation for Soul and Body.* Boston: Willard Tract Repository, 1884.

———. *"Faith Healing" Reviewed After Twenty Years.* Boston and Chicago: Christian Witness Company, 1897.

———. *Pastor Blumhardt: A Record of the Wonderful Spiritual and Physical Manifestations of God's Power in Healing Souls and Bodies.* Boston: Willard Tract Repository, 1883.

Carter, Russell Kelso, and Albert Benjamin Simpson. *Hymns of the Christian Life, New and Standard Songs for the Sanctuary, Sunday Schools, Prayer Meetings, Mission Work and Revival Services.* New York: Christian Alliance, 1891.

Clarke, Edward. *Sex in Education; or, A Fair Chance for the Girls.* Boston: J. R. Osgood, 1873.

Close, Carra H., comp. *God's Word on Divine Healing: Containing Instances and Promises Recorded Therein.* Oakland, CA: Triumphs of Faith, n.d.

Conwell, R. H. *Acres of Diamonds, by Russell H. Conwell . . . His Life and Achievements, by Robert Shackleton.* New York: Harper and Brothers, 1943.

Cullis, Charles. *Annual Reports of the Consumptives' Home, and Other Institutions Connected with a Work of Faith.* Boston: Willard Tract Repository, 1864–1892.

———. ed. *Dorothea Trudel, or, The Prayer of Faith. With Some Particulars of the Remarkable Manner in Which Large Numbers of Sick Persons Were Healed in Answer to Special Prayer.* 3rd rev. ed. Boston: Willard Tract Repository, 1872.

———. *Faith Cures; or, Answers to Prayer in the Healing of the Sick.* Boston: Willard Tract Repository, 1879.

———. *Faith Healing.* Tract. Boston: Willard Tract Repository, n.d.

————. *Faith Hymns*. Boston: Willard Tract Repository, 1882.

————. *More Faith Cures; or, Answers to Prayer in the Healing of the Sick*. Boston: Willard Tract Repository, 1881.

————. *Other Faith Cures; or, Answers to Prayer in the Healing of the Sick*. Boston: Willard Tract Repository, 1885.

————. *Songs of Victory*. Boston: Willard Tract Repository, 1889.

————. *Tuesday Afternoon Talks*. Boston: Willard Tract Repository, 1892.

————. *Work for Jesus: The Experience and Teachings of Mr. and Mrs. Boardman*. Boston: Willard Tract Repository, 1875.

Daniels, Morris S. *The Story of Ocean Grove: Related in the Year of its Golden Jubilee, 1869–1919*. New York: Methodist Book Concern, 1919.

Daniels, W. H., ed. *Dr. Cullis and His Work: Twenty Years of Blessing in Answer to Prayer*. Boston: Willard Tract Repository, 1885.

Dixon, E. H. *Woman and Her Diseases, from the Cradle to the Grave: Adapted Exclusively to Her Instruction in the Physiology of Her System, and All the Diseases of Her Critical Periods*. 10th ed. New York: A. Ranney, 1855.

Dorothea Trudel; or, The Prayer of Faith. With Some Particulars of the Remarkable Manner in Which Large Numbers of Sick Persons Were Healed in Answer to Special Prayer. London: Morgan and Chase, n.d.

Dowie, John Alexander. *The Personal Letters of John Alexander Dowie*. Compiled by Edna Sheldrake. Zion City, IL: Wilbur Glenn Voliva, 1912.

Dowie, John Alexander and Jane Dowie. *American First-fruits: Being a Brief Record of Eight Months' Divine Healing Missions in the State of California*. 4th ed. Chicago: Zion Publishing House, 1895.

————. *Our Second Year's Harvest, Being a Brief Record of a Year of Divine Healing Mission on the Pacific Coast of America. . . .* Chicago: International Divine Healing Association, 1891.

Dudley, Dora G. *Beulah: Or Some of the Fruits of One Consecrated Life*. Rev. ed. Grand Rapids, MI: Author, 1896.

————. *Beulah, or Two and One-Half Years of Consecrated Life, Showing That "All Things Are Possible to Him that Believeth."* Grand Rapids, MI: Candee and Co., 1888.

Ebner, Margaret. *Major Works*. Translated and edited by Leonard P. Hindsley. New York: Paulist Press, 1993.

Eddy, Mary Baker. *Science and Health*. Boston: Christian Scientist Publishing Co., 1875.

Edwards, Jonathan. *The Life of David Brainerd*. Edited by Norman Pettit. New Haven, CT: Yale University Press, 1985.

Eggleston, Edward. *The Faith Doctor: A Story of New York*. 1891. Reprint, Ridgewood, NJ: Gregg Press, 1968.

Figgis, J. B. *Keswick From Within*. 1914. Reprint, New York: Garland Publishing, 1984.

Fuller, Jennie. *White Fields: Sketch of Helen Dawlly*. New York: Christian Alliance Publishing Company, n.d.

Gainsforth, Mary E. *Divine Healing Secrets*. Oakland, CA: Office of Triumphs of Faith, n.d.

Glaser, Mary A. *Wonderful Leadings*. Allentown, PA: Haines and Worman, 1893.

Gordon, Adoniram Judson. *Brief history of the Clarendon St. Baptist Church: (formerly Federal Street, afterwards Rowe Street, Church) Boston*. Boston: Gould and Lincoln, 1872.

———. *Christian Science Not Scriptural.* Los Angeles: Bible House, 187-?.

———. *Christian Science Tested by the Scriptures.* Dayton, OH: Standard Bearer, 1903.

———. *The Ministry of Healing; or, Miracles of Cure for All ages.* Boston: H. Gannett, 1882.

Gordon, Ernest B. *Adoniram Judson Gordon: A Biography.* New York: Fleming H. Revell, 1896.

Gordon, Maria Hale, and Adoniram Judson Gordon. *Journal of Our Journey.* Edited by John Beauregard. Wenham, MA: Gordon College Archives, 1989.

Gracey, Samuel L. and Daniel Steele, *Healing by Faith: Two Essays.* Boston: Willard Tract Repository, 1882.

Grimke, Sarah Moore. *Letters on the Equality of the Sexes and the Condition of Woman.* Boston: I. Knapp, 1838.

Hall, Marshall. *Commentaries on Some of the More Important of the Diseases of Females: in three parts.* London: Longman, Rees, Orme, Brown and Green, 1827.

Hodge, Archibald Alexander. *Popular Lectures on Theological Themes.* Philadelphia: Presbyterian Board of Publications, 1887.

Hussey, A. H. *Divine Healing in Mission Work.* Nyack, NY: Christian Alliance Publishing Co., n.d. [ca. 1902].

Judd, Carrie F. *The Prayer of Faith.* 1881. Reprinted in *The Life and Teachings of Carrie Judd Montgomery.* New York: Garland Publishing, 1985.

Judd Montgomery, Carrie. Christian Life Pamphlets. Oakland, Calif.: Triumphs of Faith, n.d.

———. *"Under His Wings": The Story of My Life.* 1936. Reprinted in *The Life and Teachings of Carrie Judd Montgomery.* New York: Garland Publishing, 1985.

Lindenberger, S. A., *A Cloud of Witnesses: Testimonies of Divine Healing New and Old.* Nyack, NY: Christian Alliance Publishing Co., 1900.

———. *Streams from the Valley of Berachah.* New York: Christian Alliance Publishing Co., 1893.

Mains, George Preston. *James Monroe Buckley.* New York: Methodist Book Concern, 1917.

Mallory, E. F., ed. *Touching the Hem: A Record of Faith Healing.* Montreal: F. E. Grafton, 1884.

Marsh, R. L. *"Faith Healing": A Defense or, The Lord Thy Healer.* New York: Fleming H. Revell, 1889.

McDonald, William, and John E. Searles. *The Life of the Rev. John S. Inskip, President of the National Association for the Promotion of Holiness.* 1885. Reprint, New York: Garland Publishing, 1985.

McKaig, Donald, comp. A. B. Simpson Scrapbook. Unpublished collection of primary documents, deposited at Christian and Missionary Alliance National Archives, Colorado Springs, CO.

Mix, Mrs. Edward [Sarah Freeman]. *Faith Cures, and Answers to Prayers.* Springfield, Mass: Press of Springfield Printing Co., 1882.

———. *The Life of Mrs. Edward Mix Written by Herself in 1880.* Torrington, CT: Press of the Register Printing Co., 1884.

M.H.M. [Mary H. Mossman]. *Steppings in God; or, the Hidden Life Made Manifest.* 6th ed., rev. New York: Eaton and Mains, 1909.

Muller, George. *The Life of Trust: Being a Narrative of the Lord's Dealings with George Muller, Written by Himself.* Rev. ed. New York: Sheldon and Co., 1873.

Murray, Andrew. *Divine Healing: A Series of Addresses.* New York: Alliance Press Co., 1900.

Needham, Albert W. *Events and Experiences in the Life of George C. Needham, Evangelist.* Philadelphia: Narberth, 1900.

Needham, Mrs. George C. [Elizabeth Annabelle]. *Mrs. Whilling's Faith Cure.* Boston: Bradley and Woodruff, 1891.

Osborn, Lucy Drake. *Heavenly Pearls Set in a Life: A Record of Experiences and Labors in America, India and Australia.* New York: Fleming H. Revell, 1893.

Palmer, Phoebe. *The Devotional Writings of Phoebe Palmer.* New York: Garland Press, 1985.

Pardington, George P. *The Crooked Made Straight.* 3rd ed., rev. Nyack, NY: Author, 1898.

———. *Twenty-Five Wonderful Years: A Popular Sketch of the Christian and Missionary Alliance.* 1919. Reprint, New York: Garland Publishing, 1984.

Patton, William W. *Prayer and Its Remarkable Answers; Being a Statement of Facts in the Light of Reason and Revelation.* New York: Funk and Wagnalls, 1885.

Peck, George Clarke. *The Method of the Master: A Study of the Clinics of Jesus.* New York: Fleming H. Revell, 1912.

Pierson, Arthur T. *Forward Movements of the Last Half Century.* 1905. Reprint, New York: Garland Publishing, 1984.

———. *The Keswick Movement: In Precept and Practice.* New York: Funk and Wagnalls, 1903.

Pitt, F. W. *Faith Healing Tragedies.* London: Pickering and Inglis, n.d.

Platt, Smith H. *My 25th Year Jubilee: or, Cure by Faith after Twenty-five Years of Lameness.* Brooklyn, NY: S. Harrison, 1875.

———. *The Secrets of Health: or How Not to Be Sick and How to Get Well from Sickness.* New York: Orange Judd Co., 1895.

Prentiss, George L. *The Life and Letters of Elizabeth Prentiss.* 1882. Reprint, New York: Garland Publishing Co., 1987.

Prentiss, Elizabeth. *Stepping Heavenward.* 1869. Reprint, Sterling, VA: GAM Publications, 1996.

Price, W. T. *Without Purse of Scrip; or, "The Mountain Evangelist," George O. Barnes.* Louisville, KY: W. T. Price, 1883.

Prosser, Anna W. *From Death to Life: An Autobiography.* Buffalo, NY: McGerald Publishing Co., 1901.

Rankin, Mary. *The Daughter of Affliction: A Memoir of the Protracted Sufferings and Religious Experience of Miss Mary Rankin.* 2nd ed. Dayton, OH: United Brethren Printing Establishment, 1871.

Record of the International Conference on Divine Healing and True Holiness held at Agricultural Hall, London, June 1 to 5, 1885. London: J. Snow and Co. and Bethshan, 1885.

Robinson, F. A. ed. *Mother Whittemore's Records of Modern Miracles.* Toronto, Canada: Missions of Biblical Education, 1931.

Schofield, Arthur T. *A Study of Faith Healing.* New York: Fleming H. Revell, n.d. [ca. 1892].

Simpson, Albert Benjamin, ed. *The Christian Alliance Yearbook.* New York: Word, Work and World Publishing Co., 1888.

———. *Christian Science Unchristian.* New York: Alliance Press Co., n.d. [ca. 1907].

———. ed. *A Cloud of Witnesses for Divine Healing.* 2nd ed. New York: Word, Work and World Publishing Co., 1887.

———. *Discovery of Divine Healing.* New York: Alliance Press Company, 1903.

———. *Friday Meeting Talks: Or Divine Prescriptions for the Sick and Suffering.* New York: Christian Alliance Publishing Co., 1894.

———. *Friday Meeting Talks: Or Divine Prescriptions for the Sick and Suffering,* No. 2. Nyack, NY: Christian Alliance Publishing Co., 1894.

———. *Friday Meeting Talks: Or Divine Prescriptions for the Sick and Suffering,* No. 3. Nyack, NY: Christian Alliance Publishing Co., 1900.

———. *The Gospel of Healing.* 1888. Rev. ed. London: Morgan and Scott, 1915.

———. *Inquiries and Answers.* New York: Word, Work and World Publishing Co., 1887.

———. *The Lord for the Body with Questions and Answers on Divine Healing.* New York: Christian Alliance Publishing Co., 1925.

Simpson, Albert Benjamin, and Russell Kelso Carter, eds. *Hymns of the Christian Life.* Harrisburg, PA: Christian Publications, n.d. [1891].

Sisson, Elizabeth. *Foregleams of Glory: Resurrection Papers, Faith Reminiscences in Trinity College.* Chicago: Evangel Publishing House, 1912.

Smith, Amanda Berry. *An Autobiography: The Story of the Lord's Dealings with Mrs. Amanda Smith, the Colored Evangelist.* 1893. Reprint, New York: Garland Publishing, 1987.

Smith, Hannah Whitall. *The Christian's Secret of a Happy Life.* Rev. ed. Boston: Willard Tract Repository, 1885.

Smith, Jennie. *From Baca to Beulah: Sequel to 'Valley of Baca.'* Philadelphia: Garrigues Brothers, 1880.

———. *Incidents and Experiences of a Railroad Evangelist.* Washington, D.C.: n.p., 1920.

———. *Ramblings in Beulah Land: A Continuation of Experiences in the Life of Jennie Smith.* 2 vols. Philadelphia: Garrigues Brothers, 1886–1888.

———. *The Valley of Baca: A Record of Suffering and Triumph.* Cincinnati: Hitchcock and Walden, 1876.

Smith, Julia A. Norcross Crafts. *The Reason Why; or, Spiritual Experiences of Mrs. Julia Crafts Smith, Physician, Assisted by Her Spirit Guides.* Boston: The Author, 1881.

Spiher, H. H. *The World's Physician, Christ the Lord: Or Five-Hundred Testimonials of Divine Healing in Answer to Prayer Through the Ages.* St. Louis: n.p., 1895.

Stanton, Robert Livingston. *Gospel Parallelisms: Illustrated in the Healing of Body and Soul.* Buffalo, NY: Office of Triumphs of Faith, 1884.

———. *"Healing Through Faith," Again: A Paper Prepared for "The Presbyterian (Quarterly) Review," But Its Publication Declined. . . .* Buffalo, NY: Baker, Jones and Co., 1884.

Stockman, E. A. *Faith Healing versus Fanaticism.* Boston: Adventist Christian Publication Society, 1880.

Stockmayer, Otto. *Sickness and the Gospel.* 2nd ed., rev. London: Bemrose and Sons, 1887.

Stowe, Harriet Beecher, *Uncle Tom's Cabin; or Life Among the Lowly,* 1852. Reprint, New York: Penguin Books, 1981.

Thompson, Albert E. *The Life of A. B. Simpson: Official Authorized Edition.* Harrisburg, PA: Christian Publications Inc., 1920.

Townsend, Luther T. *"Faith-work," "Christian Science," and Other Cures.* Boston: W. A. Wilde, 1886.

Tracy, Stephen. *The Mother and Her Offspring.* 3rd ed. New York, Harper and Bros., 1860.

Trask, Leonard. *A Brief Historical Sketch of the Life and Sufferings of Leonard Trask, the Wonderful Invalid.* Portland, ME: printed by David Tucker, 1858 [ca. 1857].

Warfield, Benjamin B. *Counterfeit Miracles.* New York: Charles Scribner's, 1918.

Warner, Susan. *The Wide, Wide World.* 1850. Reprint, New York: The Feminist Press at the City University of New York, 1987.

Webb, Rev. J. M. *Memoir of Miss Charity Richards; Or, Grace Reigning and Triumphant Under Complicated and Protracted Sufferings.* Adams, N.Y.: J. C. Hatch, 1845.

Wheatley, Richard, ed. *The Life and Letters of Mrs. Phoebe Palmer.* New York: W. C. Palmer Jr., 1876.

Winters, Susan L. *A Souvenir, Affectionately Inscribed to Miss Jennie Smith.* Dayton, OH: United Brethren Publishing House, 1889.

Wiseman, Nathaniel, ed. *Elizabeth Baxter (Wife of Michael Paget Baxter), Saint, Evangelist, Preacher, Teacher, and Expositor.* London: The Christian Herald Co., 1928.

Woodworth, Maria B. *Life and Experiences of Maria B. Woodworth.* Dayton, OH: United Brethren Publishing House, 1885.

———. *Trials and Triumphs of Mrs. M. B. Woodworth.* Dayton, OH: United Brethren Publishing House, 1886.

Woodworth-Etter, Maria. *Acts of the Holy Ghost, or Life, and Experience, of Mrs. M. B. Woodworth-Etter.* Dallas, TX: John F. Worley Printing Co., 1912.

———. *Life and Experiences, Including Sermons and Visions of Mrs. M. B. Woodworth-Etter.* N.p.: n.p., 1904.

———. *Life and Testimony of Mrs. M. B. Woodworth-Etter, Evangelist: Finished Biography: Nearly Fifty Years of Ministry.* Indianapolis: n.p., 1925.

———. *Signs and Wonders God Wrought in the Ministry of Forty Years.* 1916. Reprint, Bartlesville, OK: Oak Tree Publications, n.d.

Wyman, Morrill. *Progress in School Discipline: Remarks by Dr. Morrill Wyman, of Cambridge, in Support of the Resolution to Abolish Corporal Punishment of Girls. . . .* Cambridge, MA: J. Cox, Printer, 1866.

Young, C. Howard. *Sunny Life of an Invalid.* Hartford, CT: Press of the Case, Lockwood and Brainard Company, 1897.

Secondary Sources

Abell, Aaron Ignatius. *The Urban Impact on American Protestantism, 1865–1900.* 1943. Reprint: London, Archon, 1962.

Ahlstrom, Sydney E. *A Religious History of the American People.* New Haven, CT: Yale University Press, 1972.

Albanese, Catherine L. *Nature Religion in America: From the Algonkian Indians to the New Age.* Chicago: University of Chicago Press, 1990.

———. "The Poetics of Healing: Root Metaphors and Rituals in Nineteenth-Century America." *Soundings* 63 (Winter 1980): 390–94.

———. "Physic and Metaphysic in Nineteenth-Century America: Medical Sectarians and Religious Healing." *Church History* 55 (December 1986): 489–502.

Albrecht, Daniel E. "Carrie Judd Montgomery: Pioneering Contributor to Three Religious

Movements." *Pneuma: The Journal for the Society for Pentecostal Studies* 8 (Fall 1986): 101–19.

———. "The Life and Ministry of Carrie Judd Montgomery." M.A. thesis, Western Evangelical Seminary, 1984.

Armstrong, David, and Elizabeth Metzger Armstrong. *The Great American Medicine Show.* New York: Prentice Hall, 1991.

Baer, Jonathan R. "Perfectly Empowered Bodies: Divine Healing in Modernizing America." Ph.D. diss., Yale University, 2002.

———. "Redeemed Bodies: The Functions of Divine Healing in Incipient Pentecostalism." *Church History* 70 (December 2001): 735–71.

Bailin, Miriam. *The Sickroom in Victorian Fiction: The Art of Being Ill.* New York: Cambridge University Press, 1994.

Barnabas, Steven. *So Great Salvation: The History and Message of the Keswick Convention.* London: Marshal, Morgan and Scott, 1952.

Barnes, Linda L., and Susan S. Sered, eds. *Religion and Healing in America.* New York: Oxford University Press, 2004.

Bassuk, Ellen L. "The Rest Cure: Repetition or Resolution of Victorian Women's Conflicts?" In *The Female Body in Western Culture,* edited by Susan Rubin Suleiman, 141–43. Cambridge, MA: Harvard University Press, 1986.

Bebbington, David W. *The Dominance of Evangelicalism: The Age of Spurgeon and Moody.* Downers Grove, IL: Intervarsity Press, 2005.

———. *Evangelicalism in Modern Britain: A History from the 1730s to the 1980s.* Grand Rapids, MI: Baker Book House, 1989.

Bederman, Gail. *Manliness and Civilization: A Cultural History of Gender and Race in the United States, 1880–1917.* Chicago: University of Chicago Press, 1995.

———. "'The Women Have Had Charge of the Church Work Long Enough': The Men and Religion Forward Movement of 1911–1912 and the Masculinization of Middle-Class Protestantism." *American Quarterly* 41:3 (September 1989): 432–65.

Bedford, William Boyd, Jr. "'A Larger Christian Life': A. B. Simpson and the Early Years of the Christian and Missionary Alliance." Ph.D. dissertation, University of Virginia, 1992.

Bell, Catherine. *Ritual Theory, Ritual Practice.* New York: Oxford University Press, 1992.

Bendroth, Margaret Lamberts, and Virginia Lieson Brereton, eds. *Women and Twentieth-Century Protestantism.* Urbana: University of Illinois Press, 2002.

Benson, Herbert. *Timeless Healing: The Power and Biology of Belief.* New York: Scribner, 1996.

———. *Beyond the Relaxation Response: How to Harness the Healing Power of Your Personal Beliefs.* New York: Times Books, 1984.

———. *The Relaxation Response.* New York: Morrow Press, 1975.

Blumhofer, Edith. "Life on Faith Lines: Faith Homes and Early Pentecostal Values." *Assemblies of God Heritage* 10 (Summer 1990): 10–12, 22.

———. *Restoring the Faith: The Assemblies of God, Pentecostalism, and American Culture.* Urbana: University of Illinois Press, 1993.

Bossy, John. *Christianity in the West, 1400–1700.* New York: Oxford University Press, 1985.

Bourdieu, Pierre. *Outline of a Theory of Practice.* New York: Cambridge University Press, 1977.

Braude, Ann. *Radical Spirits: Spiritualism and Women's Rights in Nineteenth-Century America*. 2nd ed. Bloomington: University of Indiana Press, 2001.

Brereton, Virginia Lieson. *Training God's Army: The American Bible School, 1880–1940*. Bloomington: University of Indiana Press, 1990.

Brown, Candy Gunther. *The Word in the World: Evangelical Writing, Publishing, and Reading in America, 1789–1880*. Chapel Hill: University of North Carolina Press, 2004.

Brown, Peter. *The Body and Society: Men, Women and Sexual Renunciation in Early Christianity*. New York: Columbia University Press, 1988.

———. *The Cult of the Saints: Its Rise and Function in Latin Christianity*. Chicago: University of Chicago Press, 1981.

Brumberg, Joan Jacobs. *Mission for Life: The Story of the Family of Adoniram Judson, the Dramatic Events of the First American Foreign Mission, and the Course of Evangelical Religion in the Nineteenth Century*. New York: Free Press, 1980.

Burgess, Stanley M., and Gary B. McGee, eds. *Dictionary of Pentecostal and Charismatic Movements*. Grand Rapids, MI: Zondervan Publishing House, 1988.

Burrow, James G. *Organized Medicine in the Progressive Era: The Move Toward Monopoly*. Baltimore: Johns Hopkins University Press, 1977.

Bynum, Caroline Walker. *Fragmentation and Redemption: Essays on Gender and the Human Body in Medieval Religion*. New York: Zone Books, 1991.

———. *Holy Feast and Holy Fast: The Religious Significance of Food to Medieval Women*. Berkeley: University of California Press, 1987.

———. "Why All the Fuss About the Body? A Medievalist's Perspective." *Critical Inquiry* 22:1 (1995). 1–33.

Bynum, Caroline Walker, Steven Harrell, and Paula Richman. *Gender and Religion: On the Complexity of Symbols*. Boston: Beacon Press, 1986.

Carnes, Mark C., and Clyde Griffen, eds. *Meanings For Manhood: Constructions of Masculinity in Victorian America*. Chicago: University of Chicago Press, 1990.

Carter, Paul A. *The Spiritual Crisis of the Gilded Age*. DeKalb: Northern Illinois University Press, 1971.

Cayleff, Susan E. *Wash and Be Healed: The Water-Cure Movement and Women's Health*. Philadelphia: Temple University Press, 1987.

Certeau, Michel de. *The Practice of Everyday Life*. Translated by Steven F. Rendall. Berkeley: University of California Press, 1984.

Chappell, Paul G. "Healing Movements." *Dictionary of Pentecostal and Charismatic Movements*, ed. Stanley M. Burgess and Gary B. McGee, 353–74. Grand Rapids, MI: Zondervan, 1988.

———. "The Divine Healing Movement in America." Ph.D. diss., Drew University, 1983.

Clark, Elizabeth A. *Reading Renunciation: Asceticism and Scripture in Early Christianity*. Princeton, NJ: Princeton University Press, 1999.

Coakley, Sarah, ed. *Religion and the Body*. New York: Cambridge University Press, 1997.

Coakley, Sarah, and Kay Shelemay, eds. *Pain and Its Transformations: The Interface of Biology and Culture*. Cambridge, MA: Harvard University Press, forthcoming.

Cook, Philip L. *Zion City, Illinois: Twentieth-Century Utopia*. Syracuse, NY: Syracuse University Press, 1996.

Cott, Nancy F. *The Bonds of Womanhood: 'Woman's Sphere' in New England, 1780–1835.* New Haven, CT: Yale University Press, 1977.

Csordas, Thomas J. *Body/Meaning/Healing.* New York: Palgrave, 2002.

———. *The Sacred Self: A Cultural Phenomenology of Charismatic Healing.* Berkeley: University of California Press, 1994.

Cunningham, Raymond J. "From Holiness to Healing: The Faith Cure in America, 1872–1892." *Church History* 43 (December 1974): 499–513.

———. "Ministry of Healing: The Origins of the Psychotherapeutic Role of the American Churches." Ph.D. diss., Johns Hopkins University, 1965.

Davidoff, Leonore, and Catherine Hall. *Family Fortunes: Men and Women of the English Middle Class, 1780–1850.* Rev. ed. New York: Routledge, 2002.

Dayton, Donald W. "The Rise of the Evangelical Healing Movement in Nineteenth-Century America." *Pneuma: Journal for the Society of Pentecostal Studies* 4 (Spring 1982): 1–18.

———. *Theological Roots of Pentecostalism.* Metuchen, NJ: Scarecrow Press, 1987.

Dayton, Donald W., and Robert K. Johnson, eds. *The Variety of American Evangelicalism.* Knoxville: University of Tennessee Press, 1991.

Dieter, Melvin Easterday. *The Holiness Revival of the Nineteenth Century.* 2nd ed. Lanham, MD: Scarecrow Press, 1996.

Donegan, Jane B. *"Hydropathic Highway to Health": Women and Water-Cure in Antebellum America.* Westport, CT: Greenwood Press, 1986.

Dossey, Larry. *Reinventing Medicine: Beyond Mind-Body to a New Era of Healing.* San Francisco: HarperSanFrancisco, 1999.

Duffin, Lorna. "The Conspicuous Consumptive: Woman as an Invalid." In *The Nineteenth Century Woman: Her Cultural and Physical World,* edited by Sara Delamont and Lorna Duffin. New York: Barnes and Noble Books, 1978.

Duffy, John. *The Healers: A History of American Medicine.* Urbana: University of Illinois Press, 1979.

Ehrenreich, Barbara, and Deirdre English. *For Her Own Good: 50 Years of Experts' Advice to Women.* New York: Doubleday, 1978.

Ekvall, Robert B., et al. *After Fifty Years: A Record of God's Working through the Christian and Missionary Alliance.* Harrisburg, PA: Christian Publications, 1939.

Evearitt, Daniel J. *Body and Soul: Evangelism and the Social Concern of A. B. Simpson.* Camp Hill, PA: Christian Publications, 1994.

Fairfield, Leslie. "John Bale and the Development of Protestant Hagiography in England." *Journal of Ecclesiastical History* 24:2 (April 1973): 145–60.

Fellman, Anita Clair, and Michael Fellman. *Making Sense of Self: Medical Advice Literature in Late-nineteenth-century America.* Philadelphia: University of Pennsylvania Press, 1981.

Fichter, Joseph H. *Religion and Pain: The Spiritual Dimensions of Health Care.* New York: Crossroads, 1981.

Fuller, Robert C. *Alternative Medicine and American Religious Life.* New York: Oxford University Press, 1989.

Gallagher, Catherine, and Thomas Laqueur, eds. *The Making of the Modern Body: Sexuality and Society in the Nineteenth Century.* Berkeley: University of California Press, 1987.

Gardner, Martin. *The Healing Revelations of Mary Baker Eddy: The Rise and Fall of Christian Science*. Buffalo, NY: Prometheus Books, 1993.

Gevitz, Norman, ed. *Other Healers: Unorthodox Medicine in America*. Baltimore: Johns Hopkins University Press, 1988.

Gibson, Scott M. "Adoniram Judson Gordon, D.D. (1836–1895): Pastor, Premillennialist, Moderate Calvinist, and Missionary Statesman." Ph.D. dissertation, Oxford University, 1997.

Gill, Gillian. *Mary Baker Eddy*. Reading, MA: Perseus Books, 1998.

Glucklich, Ariel. *Sacred Pain: Hurting the Body for the Sake of the Soul*. New York: Oxford University Press, 2001.

Good, Mary-Jo DelVecchio, et. al. *Pain as Human Experience: An Anthropological Perspective*. Berkeley: University of California Press, 1994.

Gooden, Rosemary D. Introduction to *Faith Cures, and Answers to Prayer*, by Mrs. Edward [Sarah Freeman] Mix. 1882. Reprint, Syracuse, NY: Syracuse University Press, 2002.

Gosling, F. G. *Before Freud: Neurasthenia and the American Medical Community, 1870–1910*. Urbana: University of Illinois Press, 1987.

Gottschalk, Stephen. *The Emergence of Christian Science in American Religious Life*. Berkeley: University of California Press, 1973.

Green, Ian. *Print and Protestantism in Early Modern England*. New York: Oxford University Press, 2000.

Gregory, Brad. *Salvation at Stake: Christian Martyrdom in Early Modern Europe*. Cambridge, MA: Harvard University Press, 1999.

Griffith, R. Marie. "Apostles of Abstinence: Fasting and Masculinity During the Progressive Era." *American Quarterly* 52:4 (December 2000): 599–638.

———. *Born Again Bodies: Flesh and Spirit in American Christianity*. Berkeley: University of California Press, 2004.

———. "Female Suffering and Religious Devotion in American Pentecostalism." In *Women in American Protestantism*, edited by Margaret Bendroth and Virginia L. Brereton, 393–439. Bloomington: Indiana University Press, 2002.

Hall, David D. *Lived Religion: Towards a History of Practice*. Princeton, NJ: Princeton University Press, 1997.

Hall, Donald E., ed. *Muscular Christianity: Embodying the Victorian Age*. New York: Cambridge University Press, 1994.

Haller, John S. *American Medicine in Transition, 1840–1910*. Chicago: University of Illinois Press, 1981.

Haley, Bruce. *The Healthy Body and Victorian Culture*. Cambridge, MA: Harvard University Press, 1978.

Hambrick-Stowe, Charles. *The Practice of Piety: Puritan Devotional Disciplines in Seventeenth-Century New England*. Chapel Hill: University of North Carolina Press, 1982.

Hardesty, Nancy. *Faith Cure: Divine Healing in the Holiness and Pentecostal Movements*. Peabody, MA: Hendrickson Publishers, 2003.

Harrell, David Edwin. *All Things Are Possible: The Healing and Charismatic Revivals in Modern America*. Bloomington: Indiana University Press, 1975.

Harrington, Anne, ed. *The Placebo Effect: An Interdisciplinary Exploration*. Cambridge, MA: Harvard University Press, 1997.

Harris, Ruth. *Lourdes: Body and Spirit in the Secular Age.* New York: Penguin Compass, 1999.

The Higher Christian Life: A Bibliographical Overview. New York: Garland Publishing, 1985.

Hilkey, Judy. *Character Is Capital: Success Manuals and Manhood in Gilded Age America.* Chapel Hill: University of North Carolina Press, 1997.

Holifield, E. Brooks. *Health and Medicine in the Methodist Tradition: Journey Toward Wholeness.* New York: Crossroad, 1986.

Hollywood, Amy M. "Inside Out: Beatrice of Nazareth and Her Hagiographer." In *Gendered Voices: Medieval Saints and Their Interpreters,* edited by Catherine Mooney, 78–98. Philadelphia: University Press, 1999.

———. "Suffering Transformed: Marguerite Porete, Meister Eckhart, and the Problem of Women's Spirituality." In *Meister Eckhart and the Beguine Mystics,* edited by Bernard McGinn, 87–113. New York: Continuum, 1994.

Hughes, Richard T., ed. *The American Quest for a Primitive Church.* Urbana: University of Illinois Press, 1988.

———. *Illusions of Innocence: Protestant Primitivism in America, 1630–1875.* Chicago: University of Chicago Press, 1988.

Israel, Adrienne M. *Amanda Berry Smith: From Washerwoman to Evangelist.* Lanham, MD: Scarecrow Press, 1998.

Jacobus, Mary, Evelyn Fox Keeler, and Sally Shuttleworth, *Body/Politics: Women and the Discourses of Science.* New York: Routledge, 1990.

Kaufman, Martin. "Homeopathy in America: The Rise and Fall and Persistence of a Medical Heresy." In *Other Healers: Unorthodox Medicine in America,* edited by Norman Gevitz, 99–123. Baltimore: Johns Hopkins University Press, 1988.

Kelsey, Morton. *Healing and Christianity: A Classic Study.* Minneapolis, MN: Augsburg Press, 1995.

Kieckhefer, Richard. *Unquiet Souls: Fourteenth-Century Saints and their Religious Milieu.* Chicago: University of Chicago Press, 1984.

Kleinman, Arthur. *The Illness Narratives: Suffering, Healing and the Human Condition.* New York: Basic Books, 1988.

Knee, Stuart E. *Christian Science in the Age of Mary Baker Eddy.* Westport, CT: Greenwood Press, 1994.

Knox, Ronald A. *Enthusiasm: A Chapter in the History of Religion.* Rev. ed. Oxford: Clarendon Press, 1959.

Koenig, Harold G. *Faith and Mental Health: Religious Resources for Healing.* Philadelphia, PA: John Templeton Foundation Press, 2005.

———. *The Healing Power of Faith: Science Explores Medicine's Last Great Frontier.* New York: Simon and Schuster, 1999.

Koenig, Harold G., and Harvey J. Kohen, eds. *The Link between Religion and Health: Psychoneuroimmunology and the Faith Factor.* New York: Oxford University Press, 2002.

Koenig, Harold G., Michael E. McCullough, and David B. Larson, eds. *Handbook of Religion and Health.* New York: Oxford University Press, 2001.

Kolb, Robert. *For all the Saints: Changing Perceptions of Martyrdom and Sainthood in the Lutheran Reformation.* Macon, GA: Mercer University Press, 1987.

Lears, Jackson. *No Place of Grace: Antimodernism and the Transformation of American Culture, 1880–1920*. New York: Pantheon Books, 1981.

Leavitt, Judith Walzer. *Women and Health in America: Historical Readings*. Madison: University of Wisconsin Press, 1984.

———. *Women and Health in America*. 2nd. ed. Madison: University of Wisconsin Press, 1999.

Leavitt, Judith Walzer, and Ronald L. Numbers, eds. *Sickness and Health in America: Readings in the History of Medicine and Public Health*. Madison: University of Wisconsin Press, 1978.

———. *Sickness and Health in America: Readings in the History of Medicine and Public Health*. 2nd rev. ed. Madison: University of Wisconsin Press, 1985.

———. *Sickness and Health in America: Readings in the History of Medicine and Public Health*. 3rd rev. ed. Madison: University of Wisconsin Press, 1997.

Long, Kathryn T. *The Revival of 1857–1858: Interpreting a Religious Awakening*. New York: Oxford University Press, 1988.

Lovett, L. "Positive Confession Theology." In *Dictionary of Pentecostal and Charismatic Movements,* ed. Stanley M. Burgess and Gary B. McGee, 718–20. Grand Rapids, MI: Zondervan, 1988.

Lutz, Tom. *American Nervousness, 1903: An Anecdotal History*. Ithaca, NY: Cornell University Press, 1991.

Maffly-Kipp, Laurie F., Leigh E. Schmidt, and Mark Valeri, eds. Introduction to *Practicing Protestants: Histories of Christian Life in America, 1630–1965*. Baltimore: Johns Hopkins University Press, 2006.

Magnuson, Norris. *Salvation in the Slums: Evangelical Social Work, 1865–1920*. Metuchen, NJ: Scarecrow Press, 1977.

Mangan, J. A., and James Walvin, eds. *Manliness and Morality: Middle-class Masculinity in Britain and America*. Manchester: Manchester University Press, 1987.

Marsden, George M. *Fundamentalism and American Culture: The Shaping of Twentieth-Century Evangelicalism, 1870–1925*. New York: Oxford University Press, 1980.

———. *Understanding Fundamentalism and Evangelicalism*. Grand Rapids, MI: Eerdmans, 1991.

Mattingly, Cheryl, and Linda C. Garro, eds. *Narrative and the Cultural Construction of Illness and Healing*. Berkeley: University of California Press, 2000.

Mead, Sidney. *The Lively Experiment: The Shaping of Christianity in America*. New York: Harper and Row, 1963.

McGinn, Bernard. *The Flowering of Mysticism: Men and Women in the New Mysticism, 1200–1350*. New York: Crossroad, 1998.

———. *The Foundations of Mysticism*. New York: Crossroad, 1991.

———. *The Growth of Mysticism*. New York: Crossroad, 1994.

McLoughlin, William G., Jr. *Modern Revivalism: Charles Grandison Finney to Billy Graham*. New York: Ronald Press Company, 1959.

Meyer, Donald B. *The Positive Thinkers: Popular Religious Psychology from Mary Baker Eddy to Norman Vincent Peale and Ronald Reagan*. Rev. ed. Middletown, CT: Wesleyan University Press, 1988.

Moore, R. Laurence. *Religious Outsiders and the Making of Americans.* New York: Oxford University Press, 1986.

Moorhead, James H. *World Without End: Mainstream American Protestant Visions of the Last Things, 1880–1925.* Bloomington: Indiana University Press, 1999.

Morantz-Sanchez, Regina Markell. *Sympathy and Science: Women Physicians in American Medicine.* New York: Oxford University Press, 1985.

Morris, David B. *The Culture of Pain.* Berkeley: University of California Press, 1991.

———. *Illness and Culture in the Postmodern Age.* Berkeley: University of California Press, 1998.

———. "Placebo: Conversations at the Disciplinary Borders." In *The Placebo Effect: An Interdisciplinary Exploration,* edited by Anne Harrington. Cambridge, Mass: Harvard University Press, 1997.

Mullin, Robert Bruce. "The Debate Over Religion and Healing in the Episcopal Church: 1870–1930." *Anglican and Episcopal History* 60 (June 1991): 213–34.

———. *Miracles and the Modern Religious Imagination.* New Haven, CT: Yale University Press, 1996.

Nienkirchen, Charles. "The Man, the Movement, and the Mission: A Documentary History of the Christian and Missionary Alliance." Canadian Theological Seminary, 1987. Unpublished research paper, deposited at Christian and Missionary Alliance National Archives, Colorado Springs, CO.

———. *A. B. Simpson and the Pentecostal Movement: A Study in Continuity, Crisis and Change.* Peabody, MA: Hendrickson Publishers, 1992.

Niklaus, Robert L., John S. Sawin, and Samuel J. Stoesz. *All for Jesus: God at Work in the Christian and Missionary Alliance Over One Hundred Years.* Camp Hill, PA: Christian Publications, 1986.

Nissenbaum, Stephen. *Sex, Diet, and Debility in Jacksonian America: Sylvester Graham and Health Reform.* Westport, CT: Greenwood Press, 1980.

Noll, Mark A. *American Evangelical Christianity: An Introduction.* Oxford: Blackwell Publishers, 2001.

Noll, Mark A., David W. Bebbington, and George A. Rawlk, eds. *Evangelicalism: Comparative Studies of Popular Protestantism in North America, the British Isles, and Beyond, 1700–1990.* New York: Oxford University Press, 1994.

Numbers, Ronald L. *Prophetess of Health: Ellen G. White and the Origins of Seventh-Day Adventist Health Reform.* Knoxville: University of Tennessee Press, 1992.

Numbers, Ronald L., Darrel W. Amundsen, and Carter Lindberg, eds. *Caring and Curing: Health and Medicine in the Western Religious Traditions.* Baltimore: Johns Hopkins University Press, 1998.

Opp, James W. *The Lord for the Body: Religion, Medicine, and Protestant Faith Healing in Canada, 1880–1930.* Montreal: McGill-Queen's University Press, 2005.

———. "Healing Hands, Healthy Bodies: Protestant Women and Faith Healing in Canada and the United States, 1880–1930." In *Women and Twentieth-Century Protestantism,* edited by Margaret Bendroth and Virginia Brereton, 236–56. Urbana: University of Illinois Press, 2002.

Orsi, Robert A. *Between Heaven and Earth: The Religious Worlds People Make and the Scholars Who Study Them.* Princeton, NJ: Princeton University Press, 2005.

———. "Everyday Miracles: The Study of Lived Religion." In *Lived Religion in America: Toward a History of Practice,* edited by David D. Hall, 3–21. Princeton, NJ: Princeton University Press, 1997.

Ortner, Sherry B. "Theory in Anthropology since the Sixties." *Comparative Studies in Society and History* 26 (1984): 126–66.

Ostrander, Rick. *The Life of Prayer in a World of Science: Protestants, Prayer, and American Culture, 1870–1930.* New York:257 Oxford University Press, 2000.

Parker, Gail Thain. *Mind Cure in New England from the Civil War to World War I.* Hanover, NH: University Press of New England, 1973.

Pearce, Kimber Charles. "Rhetorical Polysemy in Mary Baker Eddy's 'Christian Science in Tremont Temple.'" *Journal of Communication and Religion* 23 (September 2000): 73–94.

Peel, Robert. *Mary Baker Eddy.* 3 vols. New York: Holt, Rinehart and Winston, 1966–1977.

Pernick, Martin S. *A Calculus of Suffering: Pain, Professionalism and Anesthesia in Nineteenth-Century America.* New York: Columbia University Press, 1985.

Pollock, J. C. *The Keswick Story: The Authorized History of the Keswick Convention.* London: Hodder and Stoughton, 1964.

Porterfield, Amanda. *Healing in the History of Christianity.* New York: Oxford University Press, 2005.

Price Herndl, Diane. *Invalid Women: Figuring Feminine Illness in American Fiction and Culture, 1840–1940.* Chapel Hill: University of North Carolina Press, 1993.

Putney, Clifford. *Muscular Christianity: Manhood and Sports in Protestant America, 1880–1920.* Cambridge, MA: Harvard University Press, 2001.

Raitt, Jill, Bernard McGinn, and John Meyerhoff, eds. *Christian Spirituality: High Middle Ages and Reformation.* New York: Crossroad, 1987.

Reid, George W. *A Sound of Trumpets: Americans, Adventists, and Health Reform.* Washington, DC: Review and Herald Publishing Co, 1982.

Rey, Roselyne. *The History of Pain.* Translated by Louise Elliot Wallace, J. A. Cadden, and S. W. Cadden. Cambridge, MA: Harvard University Press, 1995.

Richard, Lucien. *The Spirituality of John Calvin.* Atlanta: John Knox Press, 1974.

Robert, Dana L. *American Women in Mission: A Social History of Their Thought and Practice.* Macon, GA: Mercer University Press, 1997.

Rosen, George. *The Structure of American Medical Practice, 1875–1941.* Philadelphia: University of Pennsylvania Press, 1983.

Rosenberg, Charles E. Prologue to *The Structure of American Medical Practice, 1875–1941,* by George Rosen. Philadelphia: University of Pennsylvania Press, 1983.

———. "The Therapeutic Revolution: Medicine, Meaning, and Social Change in Nineteenth-Century America." In *The Therapeutic Revolution: Essays in the Social History of Medicine,* edited by Morris J. Vogel and Charles E. Rosenberg, 3–25. Philadelphia: University of Pennsylvania Press, 1979.

Rosenberg, Charles E., and Janet Golden, eds. *Framing Disease: Studies in Cultural History.* New Brunswick, NJ: Rutgers University Press, 1992.

Rothstein, William G. *American Physicians in the Nineteenth Century: From Sects to Science.* Baltimore: Johns Hopkins University Press, 1972.

———. "The Botanical Movements and Orthodox Medicine." In *Other Healers: Unorthodox*

Medicine in America, ed. Norman Gevitz, 29–51. Baltimore: Johns Hopkins University Press, 1988.

Rotundo, E. Anthony. *Transformations in Masculinity from the Revolution to the Modern Era.* New York: Basic Books, 1993.

Sandeen, Ernest R. *The Roots of Fundamentalism: British and American Millenarianism, 1800–1930.* Chicago: University of Chicago Press, 1970.

Satter, Beryl. *Each Mind a Kingdom: American Women, Sexual Purity, and the New Thought Movement, 1875–1920.* Berkeley: University of California Press, 1999.

Sawin, J. S. "Alliance History—Simpson: The Man and the Movement." Unpublished research paper, deposited at Christian and Missionary Alliance National Archives, Colorado Springs, CO.

Sawin, John, comp. "The Life and Times of A. B. Simpson." Transcribed by Carol Petkau. Unpublished research file, deposited at Christian and Missionary Alliance National Archives, Colorado Springs, CO.

Scarry, Elaine. *The Body in Pain: The Making and Unmaking of the World.* New York: Oxford University Press, 1985.

Schmidt, Jean Miller. *Souls or the Social Order: The Two-Party System in American Protestantism.* Brooklyn, NY: Carlson Publishing, 1991.

Schmidt, Leigh Eric. *Holy Fairs: Scottish Communion and American Revivals in the Early Modern Period.* Princeton, NJ: Princeton University Press, 1989.

Schoepflin, Rennie B. *Christian Science on Trial: Religious Healing in America.* Baltimore: Johns Hopkins University Press, 2003.

Sherrod, S. Marc. "That Great and Awful Change: Death and Protestant Practical Theology in the American Northeast, 1700–1900." Ph.D. diss., Harvard Divinity School, 2004.

Shorter, Edward. *Bedside Manners: The Troubled History of Doctors and Patients.* New York: Simon and Schuster, 1985.

———. *From Paralysis to Fatigue: A History of Psychosomatic Illness in the Modern Era.* New York: Free Press, 1992.

———. *A History of Women's Bodies.* New York: Basic Books, 1982.

Shryrock, Richard Harrison. *Medicine and Society in America, 1660–1860.* Ithaca, NY: Cornell University Press, 1972.

Sicherman, Barbara. "The Uses of a Diagnosis: Doctors, Patients, and Neurasthenia." *Journal of the History of Medicine and Allied Sciences* 32 (1977): 33–54.

Sklar, Kathryn Kish. *Catherine Beecher: A Study in American Domesticity.* New Haven, CT: Yale University Press, 1973.

Smith, Timothy L. *Revivalism and Social Reform in Mid-Nineteenth-Century America.* New York: Abington Press, 1957.

Smith-Rosenberg, Caroll. *Disorderly Conduct: Visions of Gender in Victorian America.* New York: Alfred A. Knopf, 1985.

———. *Religion and the Rise of the American City: The New York City Mission Movement, 1812–1870.* Ithaca, NY: Cornell University Press, 1971.

Smith-Rosenberg, Caroll, and Charles Rosenberg. "The Female Animal: Medical and Biological Views of Woman and Her Role in Nineteenth-Century America." *Journal of American History* 60:2 (September 1973): 332–56.

Sokolow, Jayme A. *Eros and Modernization: Sylvester Graham, Health Reform, and the Origins of Victorian Sexuality in America.* Rutherford, NJ: Fairleigh Dickinson University Press, 1983.

Stage, Sarah. *Female Complaints: Lydia Pinkham and the Business of Women's Medicine.* New York: W.W. Norton, 1979.

Starr, Paul. *The Social Transformation of American Medicine.* New York: Basic Books, 1982.

Stein, Stephen J. *Communities of Dissent: A History of Alternative Religions in America.* New York: Oxford University Press, 2003.

Stock, Jennifer. "George S. Montgomery: Businessman for the Gospel." *Assemblies of God Heritage* 9 (Spring 1989): 4–5, 17–18; and 9 (Summer 1989): 12–14, 20.

Storms, Jeannette. "A Theology of Healing Based on the Writings of Carrie Judd Montgomery." Unpublished Research Paper, Fuller Theological Seminary, 1996.

Sweet, Leonard I. *Health and Medicine in the Evangelical Tradition.* Valley Forge, PA: Trinity Press International, 1994.

Tambiah, Stanley J. *A Performative Approach to Ritual.* London: British Academy, 1981.

Taves, Ann. *Fits, Trances, and Visions: Experiencing Religion and Explaining Experience from Wesley to James.* Princeton, NJ: Princeton University Press, 1999.

Theriot, Nancy M. *Mothers and Daughters in Nineteenth-Century America: The Biosocial Construction of Femininity.* Rev. ed. Lexington: University Press of Kentucky, 1996.

Thomas, Robert D. *"With Bleeding Footsteps": Mary Baker Eddy's Path to Religious Leadership.* New York: Knopf, 1994.

Tompkins, Jane. *Sensational Designs: The Cultural Work of American Fiction, 1790–1860.* New York: Oxford University Press, 1985.

Tozer, A. W. *Wingspread: Albert B. Simpson—A Study in Spiritual Attitudes.* Harrisburg, PA: Christian Publications Incorporated, 1943.

Turner, James. *Reckoning with the Beast: Animals, Pain and Humanity in the Victorian Mind.* Baltimore: Johns Hopkins University Press, 1980.

———. *Without God, Without Creed: The Origins of Unbelief in America.* Baltimore: Johns Hopkins University Press, 1985.

Vance, Norman. *Sinews of the Spirit: the Ideal of Christian Manliness in Victorian Literature and Religious Thought.* New York: Cambridge University Press, 1985.

Vauchez, Andre. *Sainthood in the Later Middle Ages.* New York: Cambridge University Press, 1997.

Verbrugge, Martha H. *Able-Bodied Womanhood: Personal Health and Social Change in Nineteenth-Century Boston.* New York: Oxford University Press, 1988.

Vicinus, Martha. *Suffer and Be Still: Women in the Victorian Age.* Bloomington: University of Indiana Press, 1972.

Vogel, Morris J., and Charles E. Rosenberg, eds. *The Therapeutic Revolution: Essays in the Social History of Medicine.* Philadelphia: University of Pennsylvania Press, 1979.

Wacker, Grant. *Heaven Below: Early Pentecostals and American Culture.* Cambridge, MA: Harvard University Press, 2001.

———. "The Holy Spirit and the Spirit of the Age in American Protestantism, 1880–1910." *Journal of American History* 72:1 (June 1985): 45–62.

————. "Marching to Zion: Religion in a Modern Utopian Community." *Church History* 54 (December 1985): 496–511.

————. "Travail of a Broken Family: Evangelical Responses to Pentecostalism in America, 1906–1916." *Journal of Ecclesiastical History* 47 (July 1996): 505–28.

Waldvogel, Edith Lydia. "'The Overcoming Life': A Study in the Reformed Evangelical Origins of Pentecostalism." Ph.D. dissertation, Harvard University, 1977.

Walters, Ronald G. *American Reformers, 1815–1860*. New York: Hill and Wang, 1978.

Warner, John Harley. *The Therapeutic Perspective: Medical Practice, Knowledge, and Identity in America, 1820–1855*. Cambridge, MA: Harvard University Press, 1986.

Warner, Wayne E. "Home of Peace Celebrates Centennial." *Assemblies of God Heritage* 13 (Fall 1993): 181–89.

————. *The Woman Evangelist: The Life and Times of Charismatic Evangelist Maria B. Woodworth-Etter*. Metuchen, NJ: Scarecrow Press, 1986.

Watt, Tessa. *Cheap Print and Popular Piety, 1550–1640*. New York: Cambridge University Press, 1991.

Weber, Timothy P. *Living in the Shadow of the Second Coming: American Premillennialism, 1875–1982*. Chicago: University of Chicago Press, 1987.

Welter, Barbara. "The Cult of True Womanhood, 1820–60." *American Quarterly* 18 (Summer 1966): 151–74.

White, Helen. *Tudor Books of Saints and Martyrs*. Madison: University of Wisconsin Press, 1963.

Whorton, James. *Crusaders for Fitness: The History of American Health Reformers*. Princeton, NJ: Princeton University Press, 1982.

————. "Patient, Heal Thyself: Popular Health Reform Movements as Unorthodox Medicine." In *Other Healers: Unorthodox Medicine in America*, edited by Norman Gevitz, 52–81. Baltimore: Johns Hopkins University Press, 1988.

Wilson, Ernest G. "The Christian & Missionary Alliance: Developments and Modifications of Its Original Objectives." Ph.D. diss., New York University, 1984.

Winter, Alison. *Mesmerized: Powers of Mind in Victorian Britain*. Chicago: University of Chicago Press, 1998.

Wood, Ann Douglas. "'The Fashionable Diseases': Women's Complaints and their Treatment in Nineteenth-Century America." *Journal of Interdisciplinary History* 4 (Summer 1973): 25–52.

Wrobel, Arthur, ed. *Pseudo-Science and Society in Nineteenth-Century America*. Lexington: University of Kentucky Press, 1987.